PRIVATE LAW IN THE EXTERNAL RELATIONS OF THE EU

Private Law in the External Relations of the EU

Edited by
MARISE CREMONA
HANS-W. MICKLITZ

OXFORD
UNIVERSITY PRESS

OXFORD
UNIVERSITY PRESS

Great Clarendon Street, Oxford, OX2 6DP,
United Kingdom

Oxford University Press is a department of the University of Oxford. It furthers the University's objective of excellence in research, scholarship, and education by publishing worldwide. Oxford is a registered trade mark of Oxford University Press in the UK and in certain other countries

First Edition Published in 2016

Impression: 1

Published in the United States of America by Oxford University Press
198 Madison Avenue, New York, NY 10016, United States of America

British Library Cataloguing in Publication Data
Data available

Library of Congress Control Number: 2015959804

ISBN 978–0–19–874456–6

Printed and bound by
CPI Group (UK) Ltd, Croydon, CR0 4YY

Contents

PART II. EXTENDING EU LAW BEYOND THE BOUNDARIES OF THE INTERNAL MARKET

Contents

Table of Cases–Alphabetical List

EUROPEAN COURT OF JUSTICE (ECJ)/COURT OF JUSTICE OF THE EUROPEAN UNION (CJEU)

EUROPEAN FREE TRADE ASSOCIATION (EFTA)

THE GENERAL COURT OF THE EUROPEAN UNION ('THE GENERAL COURT')

UNITED STATES (US)

Table of Cases (European)–Chronological List

Table of Instruments

INSTRUMENTS AND ACTS OF LEGISLATION OR REGULATION

Directives (chronological order)

Legislative Proposals

Decisions

Table of Instruments (Other)

MULTILATERAL TREATIES AND INTERNATIONAL AGREEMENTS

REGIONAL INSTRUMENTS

European Union

List of Abbreviations

AB	Appellate Body
ACER	Agency for the Cooperation of Energy Regulators
ADR	Alternative Dispute Resolution
AETR	Accord Européen sur les Transports Routiers
AFSJ	Area of Freedom, Security and Justice
AIFM	Directive on Alternative Investment Funds Managers
AMCC	Affiliate Members Consultative Committee
APG	Asia/Pacific Group on Money Laundering
ARC	Accounting Regulatory Committee
BCBS	Basel Committee on Banking Supervision
BCS	Banking Supervision Committee
BIS	Bank for International Settlements
BRRD	Bank Recovery and Resolution Directive
CCP	Common Commercial Policy
CEER	Council of European Energy Regulators
CEIOPS	Committee of European Insurance and Occupational Pension Supervisors
CEN	European Committee for Standardization
CENELEC	European Committee for Electrotechnical Standardization
CESL	Common European Sales Law
CESR	Committee of European Securities Regulators
CETA	*Comprehensive Economic and Trade Agreement*
CGFS	Committee on the Global Financial System
CHMP	Committee for Medicinal Products for Human Use
CIS	Collective Investment Scheme
CJEU	Court of Justice of the European Union
CMDh	Coordination Group for Mutual Recognition and Decentralised Procedure–Human
CMR	Convention on the Contract for the International Carriage of Goods by Road
CPMP	Committee for Proprietary Medicinal Products
CPSS	Committee on Payment and Settlement Systems
CRA	Credit Rating Agency
CSR	corporate social responsibility
DCFTA	Deep and Comprehensive Free Trade Agreement
DSB	Dispute Settlement Body
DSO	Distribution System Operator
EBA	European Banking Authority
EC	European Community
ECB	European Central Bank

ECHR	European Convention on Human Rights
ECRB	Energy Community Regulatory Board
EEA	European Economic Area
EEC	European Economic Community
EFPIA	European Federation of Pharmaceutical Industries and Associations
EFTA	European Free Trade Association
EMA	European Medicines Agency
EnCT	Energy Community Treaty
ENI	European Neighbourhood Instrument
ENP	European Neighbourhood Policy
ENPI	European Neighbourhood and Partnership Instrument
ENTSOs	European Network of Transmission Operators
ERGEG	European Regulators' Group for Electricity and Gas
ERRA	Energy Regulators Regional Association
ESMA	European Securities and Markets Authority
ESRB	European Systemic Risk Board
EU	European Union
EWE	Early Warning Exercises
EWG	expert working group
FDA	Food and Drug Administration
FSAP	Financial Sector Assessment Program
FSB	Financial Stability Board
FSI	Financial Stability Institute
FSR	Florence School of Regulation
FYROM	former Yugoslav Republic of Macedonia
G20	Group of 20
GAAP	generally accepted accounting principles
GAFISUD	Financial Action Task Force on Money Laundering in South America
GATS	General Agreement on Trade in Services
GATT	General Agreement on Tariffs and Trade
GCP	Good Clinical Practice
GDDS	General Data Dissemination System
GDP	gross domestic product
GEDIP	European Group for Private International Law
GMO	genetically modified organisms
GMP	Good Manufacturing Practice
G-SIBs	globally systemically important banks
G-SIFI	globally systemically important financial institution
HCCH	Hague Conference on private international law
IAASB	International Auditing and Assurance Standards Board
IADI	International Association of Deposit Insurers
IAIS	International Association of Insurance Supervisors
IAS	International Accounting Standards
IASB	International Accounting Standards Board
IASCF	International Accounting Standards Committee Foundation

ICDRA	International Conference of Drug Regulatory Authorities
ICER	International Confederation of Energy Regulators
ICH	International Conference on Harmonization of Technical Requirements for Registration of Pharmaceuticals for Human Use
ICR	Insolvency and Creditor Rights
IEC	International Electrotechnical Commission
IEM	Internal Energy Market
IFAC	International Federation of Accountants
IFPMA	International Federation of Pharmaceutical Manufacturers and Associations
IFRS	International Financial Reporting Standards
ILO	International Labour Organization
IMF	International Monetary Fund
IO	international organization
IOSCO	International Organization of Securities Commissions
IRB	institutional review board
ISA	International Standards on Auditing
ISD	Investment Services Directive
ISO	Independent System Operator
ISO	International Organization for Standardization
ISPS Code	International Ship and Port Facility Security Code
ITO	Independent Transmission Operator
JFSA	Financial Services Agency of Japan
JPMA	Japan Pharmaceutical Manufacturers Association
KOREU	EU–South Korea Free Trade Agreement
LCR	Liquidity Coverage Ratio
MAA	marketing authorization application
MFP	Monetary and Financial Policy
MiFID	Markets in Financial Instruments Directive
MONEYVAL	Council of Europe Committee of Experts on the Evaluation of Anti-Money Laundering Measures and the Financing of Terrorism
MoU	Memorandum of Understanding
MUTRAP	Multilateral Trade Assistance Project
NGO	non-governmental organization
NRA	National Regulatory Authority
NTB	Non-tariff barrier
ODR	Online Dispute Resolution
OECD	Organisation for Economic Co-operation and Development
OIV	International Organisation of Vine and Wine
OSCE	Organization for Security and Co-operation in Europe
OTC	over-the-counter
OTCWG	OTC Working Group
PhMRA	Pharmaceutical Research and Manufacturers of America

ROSCs	Reports on the Observance of Standards and Codes
ROW	Rest of the World
SAA	Stabilization and Association Agreement
SDDS	Special Data Dissemination Standard
SEC	Securities Exchange Commission
SIFI	systemically important financial institution
SMEs	small and medium-sized enterprises
SOLAS Convention	International Convention for the Safety of Life at Sea
SPCT	statistical principles for clinical trials
SPS	Sanitary and Phytosanitary Agreement
SROCC	SRO Consultative Committee
SRS	self-regulatory organizations
SSM	Single Supervisory Mechanism
TBT	Agreement on Technical Barriers to Trade
TEC	Treaty Establishing the European Community
TEU	Treaty on European Union
TFEU	Treaty on the Functioning of the European Union
TSO	Transmission System Operator
TTIP	Transatlantic Trade and Investment Partnership
UN	United Nations
UNCITRAL	United Nations Commission on International Trade Law
UNCLOS	United Nations Convention on the Law of the Sea
UNODC	United Nations Office on Drugs and Crime
WIPO	World Intellectual Property Organisation
WTO	World Trade Organization

List of Contributors

Marise Cremona is Professor of European Law at the European University Institute.

Mateja Durovic is Assistant Professor at City University of Hong Kong.

Stephanie Francq is Professor of European Law and of Private International Law at the University of Louvain.

Stefan Grundmann is Professor of Transnational Private Law at the European University Institute.

Niilo Jääskinen is Judge of the Supreme Administrative Court in Finland and Visiting Professor of European Law and General Theory of Law at the University of Helsinki.

Antonio Marcacci works in the Compliance Function of a leading European financial firm. He was awarded with a PhD in Law by the European University Institute with a dissertation in Law of Banking and Financial Markets.

Anna Marhold is Assistant Professor at Tilburg Law School (TILEC Law and Economics Center).

Hans-W Micklitz is Professor of Economic Law at the European University Institute.

Jed Odermatt is Max Weber Fellow at the European University Institute, Italy.

Etienne Pataut is Professor of Private Law at the Université Paris I Panthéon Sorbonne.

Marco Rizzi is Lecturer in Law at the University of Seychelles.

Jules Stuyck is Professor of European Law and Consumer Law at the Catholic University of Leuven.

Christiaan Timmermans is the Pieter Sanders Professor at the Erasmus University Rotterdam.

Angela Ward is Visiting Professor at Birkbeck College, University of London, and Visiting Scholar at the Max Planck Institute for Comparative and International Private Law, Hamburg.

Jan Wouters is Professor of International Law and the Law of International Organizations and Director of the Leuven Centre for Global Governance Studies at the Catholic University of Leuven.

Introduction

Marise Cremona and Hans-W. Micklitz

1. The Purpose of the Book: Bringing Two Fields Together

This book is both an exploration and an invitation. It is intended to initiate an exploration of the interaction between European Union (EU) external relations law and private law, and a conversation between those working in these two fields. When we embarked on this project we had an intuition that the two fields are becoming increasingly interconnected and that this has important implications which are not always fully realized by either academics or practitioners. The experience of putting together this book has convinced us that the subject is indeed a significant one that needs more attention. We hope that the book establishes some of the themes and parameters for discussion, and provides some insightful sectoral examples as illustrations of those themes.

What does EU external relations have to do with private law? In what ways might European private law be a tool to achieve EU external policy objectives, especially in regulatory fields? In what ways might the rapidly developing EU external competence over the procedural dimensions of private law, including private international law, impact substantive law, both externally and internally? These are the key questions that we explore in this book. This short introduction highlights our understanding of the topic; our ideas are developed more fully in the following two chapters, which are intended to serve as a longer introduction to the book as a whole.

External relations and private law are usually seen as two separate fields, unconnected to each other. The mutual deficit in perspective is the following: private law appears to be essentially bound to the nation state, by which we mean that private law is generally regarded and discussed in the context of a private legal order forming part of the nation state. This is what we call traditional private law. When it comes to the external dimension, private *international* law is the means to cope with differences between traditional national private legal orders. From such a perspective it does not matter in principle whether the cross-border dimension at stake operates within the EU or beyond; private international law operates in both cases. EU external relations law, on the other hand, tends to focus on the competence of the EU to act within the realm of *public* international law, and within the various fields of law that come under an explicitly external umbrella, such as trade, development aid, and foreign policy. Traditional private law is barely visible in this context.

However, this picture changes dramatically if private law is understood as *regulatory private law*, the space where regulatory law intersects with private economic activity. This understanding of private law includes the directives and regulations the EU has adopted horizontally with regard to particular groups of citizens such as workers, consumers, and women, or vertically with regard to particular sectors such as telecommunications, postal services, energy, transport, financial services, or product safety.[1] Here the link between the European internal market and the global market—and thereby international law—is much more prominent. Again, we should differentiate between two sets of EU rules. First, those which have a direct link to the external world, such as international transport (e.g. the Open Skies Agreement between the US and the EU or the air passenger rights regulations). Second, those rules where the role of the EU as a regulator at the international level is less obvious. Regulated markets such as telecommunications, postal services, energy, transport, financial services, and product regulation (pharmaceuticals, chemicals, foodstuffs) may serve as prominent examples. Although less visible than, say, traditional trade policy, the European Commission is in fact heavily involved in rule-making via international organizations such as the Codex Alimentarius in the field of food safety, or IOSCO in the field of financial services, mainly with the purpose of opening up markets for European business and the consumer while maintaining or raising the standards of protection.

Within the law on external relations, an increased focus on private law has resulted first from the aim to establish in the EU, as one dimension of the Area of Freedom, Security and Justice, a 'common judicial area based on the principle of mutual recognition of judicial decisions'.[2] A 'common area' implies both boundaries to that area and its relations with other legal regimes and the external legal world. Indeed, in the field of private international law, the EU increasingly engages in treaty-making both multilaterally and bilaterally, and is developing an international identity separate from (but not always replacing) that of its Member States.[3] One obvious consequence is the impact that EU regulations in the field of international private law have on the outside world, an outside world regulated by treaties to which the Member States, but hitherto not the EU itself, are party. An increasing number of conflicts of jurisdiction, or over applicable law, occur in litigation between parties in the EU and its non-EU partners, quite often resulting from differences in standards of protection between EU law and international instruments.[4] In a parallel development, EU external competence in fields of direct

[1] See for more details Micklitz, 'The Visible Hand of European Private Law', 28 *Yearbook of European Law* (2009) 3.

[2] Preamble to Council Decision 2009/397/EC of 26 February 2009 on the signing on behalf of the European Community of the Convention on Choice of Court Agreements, OJ 2009 L 133/1.

[3] See e.g. Council Decision 2006/719/EC on the accession of the Community to the Hague Conference on Private International Law, OJ 2006 L 297/1; Council Decision 2009/397/EC on the signing on behalf of the European Community of the Convention on Choice of Court Agreements, OJ 2009 L 133/1.

[4] For example, case C-308/06, *Intertanko*, [2008] ECR I-4057; Case C-301/08, *Bogiatzi v. Deutscher Luftpool and Others*, [2009] ECR I-10185; Case C-533/08, *TNT Express Nederland BV v. AXA Versicherung AG*, [2010] ECR I-4107.

relevance to regulatory private law, in particular services and investment, has been put on a firmer footing by Article 207 TFEU (Common Commercial Policy). The implied powers doctrine has also enabled the EU to enter into external relations in areas such as transport and energy. Here, EU competence extends not only to market access rules but also to post-establishment regulation, and the exercise of that competence externally as well as internally may penetrate deeply into private law and the regulation of private enterprise. Against this background, in what ways is the legal position of private parties affected by EU external relations?

2. Private Law and EU External Competence

By a focus on competence we mean first and foremost the analysis of the overlapping scope of international law, EU law, and private law.

In private law matters, we have to distinguish clearly between traditional private law and regulatory private law. In traditional private international law, the EU's external powers are implied from its treaty-based internal competence. As the *Lugano* opinion of the European Court of Justice (CJEU) clearly demonstrated, the Court held that the EU possessed exclusive external competence in the field of the Brussels Regulation.[5] Ten years later, this exclusive competence has been held to cover the Hague Convention of 1980 on the civil aspects of international child abduction, based on the close connection between that Convention and the EU's Regulation 2201/2003 on jurisdiction and recognition and enforcement of judgments in matrimonial matters.[6] In regulatory private law, competence is more fragmented between the more general competences based on the common commercial policy (Article 207 TFEU) or internal market (Article 114 TFEU), and the specific sectoral competences in the fields of transport, energy, or telecommunications. Together they enable the EU to adopt external regulatory measures in order to further the objectives of the internal market. The practical effects of the extension of the common commercial policy competence to services and investment are still being worked out. How does this (exclusive) competence relate to the (shared) competence of the EU over regulation of services via Article 114 TFEU, capital movements under Article 63 TFEU, and specific sectoral competences such as energy?[7] In its judgment on the Convention on conditional access services, the CJEU took the significant step of finding that an international agreement intended to extend the internal market regulatory *acquis* to third countries fell within the scope of the common commercial policy.[8] On this basis the EU will be able to engage

[5] Opinion 1/03, [2006] ECR I-1145. [6] Opinion 1/13, of 14 October 2014.

[7] Under Art. 207(5) TFEU, external agreements in the field of transport are governed by the transport provisions of the Treaty, but the relationship with other services sectors is not made clear. On the scope of the common commercial policy in matters of intellectual property, see Case C-414/11, *Daiichi Sankyo Co. Ltd and Sanofi-Aventis Deutschland GmbH v. DEMO Anonymos Viomichaniki kai Emporiki Etairia Farmakon*, judgment of 18 July 2013.

[8] Case C-137/12, *Commission v. Council*, judgment of 22 October 2013.

in international agreements and to take a more powerful stand in the making of international rules on services. Enlarging the exercise of external competence in regulatory private law would shape a European identity in core areas of private law.

This discussion of the basis for competence leads us to consider two further questions. The first is the interrelationship between international law in the field of regulatory private law and (traditional) international private law, hitherto largely the province of Member State activity, and the increasing body of the EU *acquis* in the field, both internal and external. We have here a complex set of relationships which have developed over time and which interact in different ways: between national and EU private law and EU external activity, and between EU law and the international regulatory and private international law regimes to which the Member States are party. The second is to ask how specific is private law when we examine the law of EU external relations? To what extent does it possess specificities, or has it given rise to different tools or instruments in managing the relationship between internal and external regulation, between Member State and EU competence? The phenomenon which we are calling 'connection clauses' links these two questions: these are the clauses which regulate the relationship with existing (and possibly also future) treaties concluded by Member States on subjects coming within the scope of existing EU legislation; they are used noticeably in the context of private law. These clauses may incorporate into Union law, in whole or in part, an international treaty or convention to which the EU is not a party; they may link the instrument to EU law via an authorization of the Member States to participate, or they may regulate the relationship between existing Member State treaties and the EU *acquis*, including through so-called disconnection clauses. The first two chapters which form Part I will introduce these questions and they are then addressed in more specific contexts in Parts II and III.

3. Extending Traditional Private Law Beyond the Boundaries of the Internal Market

In Part II of the book, we explore the ways in which the EU is extending its own approach to traditional private law beyond the boundaries of the internal market. We start with a chapter in which Timmermans addresses the question of the specificity of private law in EU external relations and then present three chapters by Francq, Pataut, and Jääskinen and Ward on private international law, jurisdiction, applicable law, and enforcement of judgments, followed by Grundmann on contract and company law.

In recent years, with the declared objective of developing a common judicial space, the EU has adopted regulations on jurisdiction, on the applicable law in contract and tort, on family law, and on cross-border enforcement. These regulations focus on the inner world of the EU, free movement of judgments in the Area of Freedom, Security and Justice, the European legal order, and its constitutional charter. The bold opinion of the CJEU in *Lugano* has not in practice led to a centralization of external powers in the hands of the EU, perhaps wisely so. However, these procedural rules affect the relationship between the EU citizen and EU-based companies, and the outside world. This is most obvious and most advanced in steadily growing litigation over jurisdiction and applicable law. However, we can also see some of the same tensions arising as the growing EU *acquis* in family law, contract law, and company law carries external as well as internal market implications.

The fundamental premise of the EU regulations, in particular their basis in a high level of mutual trust between the Member States, is in tension with the basis of international private law which in principle does not allow for a distinction between Member States and non-Member States. The mere fact that the EU has established its own 'European' international private law rules, which determine the place of jurisdiction and the applicable law, already demonstrates the tension between a 'European' approach and an international approach as exemplified by the Hague Conference. In theory, procedure (the issue of jurisdiction: the Brussels Convention and Regulations) and substance (the issue of the applicable law: Rome I and II) should be kept separate. The hypothesis which has guided our analysis, however, is that in practice, in the case law of the CJEU, we can recognize an ever stronger interplay between procedure and substance, and a tendency to use jurisdiction as a means to 'defend' European substantive standards against different—and sometimes lower—international standards.

Company law is different. Contract and company law—market transactions and the firm—have considerably increased their global dimension over recent years. This raises the question of a global perspective also for European private law. The question asked is twofold: (i) to what extent does EU private law—in its two paradigmatic fields of contract and company law—respond to sets of problems from a global perspective? And (ii) in what respects could or should a more global reach be expected or desired? There is no equivalent of Rome I and II in company law. To some extent, the fundamental freedoms and in particular the case law of the ECJ serve as a substitute for the absence of political agreement over whether the law of the country where the company is located should remain applicable in cases where the company transfers its seat. It is only in the interplay between the Brussels and Rome Regulations and the substance of EU company law that we can discern the reach of the external dimension.

4. The Making of International Private Regulation and the Role of the EU

In Part III, our focus shifts to the ways in which the EU is helping to shape regulatory private law at the international level. What is at stake here has been nicely termed the 'Brussels effect',[9] by which is meant the tendency of the EU to influence non-member countries and legal orders through unilateral regulatory action

[9] Bradford, 'The Brussels Effect', 107 *Northwestern University Law Review* (2012) 1.

as well as participation in bilateral, regional, and multilateral agreements and fora. In environmental regulation, product safety, and human rights, the EU has already adopted an active international stance. The EU's objective is to contribute to a goal which has now been given shape in the Treaty, an international system based on good global governance.[10] A decisive step forward is the growing use of European private law as a tool to build a positive European identity, an identity where European private law enshrines values that are often under-represented in an international environment. The promotion by the EU of its approach to consumer protection in its neighbourhood and beyond, mainly through international agreements, is an example of this tendency, discussed here by Stuyck and Durovic. This section of the book focuses on the field of regulatory private law, where the role of the EU is less visible and much less debated.

This focus of our research is more empirical and case based. The contributions shed light not only on the legal question of whether the EU has competence and how it uses it but also on what happens in the practice of international law-making. The particular type of private regulation which is elaborated at the international level may escape a clear distinction between law and non-law but nevertheless plays an ever increasing role in the different sectoral markets for, inter alia, energy (Marhold), financial services (Wouters and Odermatt, and Marcacci), healthcare (Rizzi), and food safety. It goes without saying that these chapters represent examples and illustrations of the phenomenon we are exploring, and that they are designed to demonstrate some of the salient features of this domain of EU external relations law rather than to produce an exhaustive survey.

Here our task has been to identify the areas within regulatory private law where the EU plays a role, and then to draw attention to the more conceptual question of the use of European private law to achieve the EU's good governance objectives in its external relations, some hard legal issues on the handling of conflicts between lower standards in international conventions and higher standards in EU law, and, last but not least, the degree to which a genuine European (regulatory) identity takes shape in sectoral fields such as telecommunications, pharmaceuticals, financial services, and financial regulation.

The research leading to these results has received funding from the European Research Council under the European Union's Seventh Framework Programme (FP/2007–2013)/ERC Grant Agreement n. [269722].

[10] Art. 21(2)(h) TEU.

PART I

PRIVATE LAW AND EU EXTERNAL COMPETENCE

1

The Internal versus the External Dimension of European Private Law

A Conceptual Design and a Research Agenda

Hans-W. Micklitz

1. Clarifications

The concept of the external dimension of European private law is built on a number of premises: the need to distinguish between 'traditional' and 'regulatory' private law; the need to draw a line between national and European private law; and, last but not least, the need to keep the internal dimension of European Union (EU) private law distinct from its external dimension. This should be clarified.

A. Traditional and Regulatory Private Law

I have put much effort in analysing and explaining the rise of European *regulatory* private law over the years.[1] This does not have to be repeated here. In essence, the point is that European private law is neither built on the premise of freedom of contract, on private autonomy, on *autonomie de la volonté*, nor on tort, on *unerlaubte Handlung* (wrongful acts), or *responsabilité d'autrui*.[2] It is argued that freedom of contract and maybe even tort is built into the European Economic Constitution and can be found in the case law of the Court of Justice of the European Union (CJEU) on the four market freedoms.[3] However, this is

[1] Micklitz, 'The Visible Hand of European Private Law', 28 *Yearbook of European Law* (2009) 3–60; in Italian in: G. Alpa and R. Mazzei (eds), *Seminari del Consiglio Nazionale Forense: Collana 'Studi storici e guiridici'* (2010), at 125–192; in Finnish: *Lakimies* (2010) 330–356; in Japanese: 12 *Hokkaido Journal of New Global Law and Policy* (2011); and in French: 'La main visible du droit privé réglementaire Européen', 28 *Revue Internationale de Droit Economique* (2014) 5–57.

[2] Much could be said on the origins of these different terms. See my modest account: 'On the Intellectual History of Freedom of Contract and Regulation', to be published in 33 *Penn State International Law Review* (2015), EUI Working Paper LAW 2015/09.

[3] This is particularly true for the representatives of the 'ordo-liberal' school, a German-based undertaking to lay down the structure for a market economy after the Second World War; Gerber, 'Constitutionalizing the Economy: German Neoliberalism, Competition Law and the "New" Europe', 42 *American Journal of Comparative Law* (1994) 25. After the establishment of the European

a highly contested claim, as there is no agreement about the foundations and the outlook of the European Economic Constitution or about its content.[4] The adoption of the Charter of Fundamental Rights has partly remedied this uncertainty in that the Charter explicitly recognizes economic liberties. At the very least, since 2000, freedom of contract enjoys constitutional status at the EU level through Article 16.

What is missing at the EU level, is, in continental language, a European civil code or, in common law language, a European law on contract and tort. Pushed into action by the European Parliament, the European Commission launched a communication on European contract law in 2001,[5] which was meant to initiate a political debate about the need and feasibility of a European civil code. The European Commission requested the Study Group and the Acquis Group to elaborate a 'Common Frame of Reference'.[6] The model presented in 2008/2009, the so-called Academic Draft Common Frame of Reference, very much looks like a fully fledged European civil code. In 2011, Commissioner Reding launched a political debate through the publication of a draft proposal on a 'Common European Sales Law'.[7] In November 2014, the newly appointed European Commission officially withdrew the proposal. For the time being, the ambitious project of creating an equivalent to the grand codifications in continental Europe and the common law on contract and tort at the EU level seems 'dead'.[8]

Therefore, trans-border conflicts within the EU have to be solved through private international law means, a field of law which is designed to solve conflicts between different national private legal orders in the tradition of Fritz Carl von Savigny.[9] Here, Europeanization has been successfully achieved through the Brussels Convention (1968) and the Rome Convention (1980), three respectively four decades later transformed into the Brussels Regulations I and II *bis* on jurisdiction in private, commercial, and family law, and through the two Rome Regulations on contract (Rome I) and tort (Rome II). It is no longer national law that defines its

Economic Community, the second generation of ordo-liberals transferred the concept from the German context to the European Union; Mestmäcker, 'Auf dem Wege zu einer Ordnungspolitik für Europa', in E.-J. Mestmäcker, H. Möller, and H. P. Schwartz (eds), *Eine Ordnungspolitik für Europa—Festschrift für Hans v.d. Groeben* (1987) 9.

[4] M. Maduro, *We the Court—The European Court of Justice and the European Economic Constitution* (1998); review by Reich, 'Europe's Economic Constitution or: A New Look at Keck', 19 *Oxford Journal of Legal Studies* (1999) 337; K. Tuori and S. Sankari (eds), *The Many Constitutions of Europe* (2010).

[5] COM (2001) 398 final, available at <http://eur-lex.europa.eu/legal-content/EN/TXT/PDF/?uri=CELEX:52001DC0398&from=EN> (last accessed 5 June 2015).

[6] Research Group on the Existing EU Private Law (Acquis Group), *Principles of the Existing EU Contract Law (Acquis Principles): Contract I* (2007); Ch. v. Bar *et al.* (eds), *Principles, Definitions and Model Rules of European Private Law, Draft Common Frame of Reference (DCFR)* (Online edition, 2009).

[7] COM (2011) 635 final, available at <http://eur-lex.europa.eu/LexUriServ/LexUriServ.do?uri=COM:2011:0635:FIN:en:PDF>.

[8] In Communication (2015) 192 final, the Commission announces under 2.1 a proposal for a regulation on Internet sales.

[9] Muir Watt, 'Integration and Diversity: The Conflict of Laws as a Regulatory Tool', in F. Cafaggi (ed.), *The Institutional Framework of European Private Law* (2006) 191.

applicability, it is now European law. The EU managed to harmonize national private international law and replace it (more or less fully) by European private international law. The CJEU has jurisdiction to shape an autonomous body of European private international law.

Regulatory private law is different. Roughly speaking, we may distinguish between two waves of regulatory private law. The first goes hand in hand with the rise of the 'social', which started in the late nineteenth century and reached its peak with the welfare state of the Second World War.[10] Social regulation in private law is meant to restrict freedom of contract, private autonomy, and *autonomie de la volonté* to the benefit of workers in employment contracts, to the benefit of tenants in tenancy contracts, and, last but not least, to the benefit of consumers in contracts with their suppliers. The second wave of regulation is linked to the liberalization and privatization of public services in the last three decades of the twentieth century. This process started in the United States of America (US) in telecommunication and postal services, and then reached energy and transport. It has not yet come to a halt as healthcare and education—traditionally fields of public services—are coming under ever greater pressure.[11] The second wave of regulation enlarged the space for freedom of contract and at the same time set boundaries to it.[12]

Both waves of regulation are much older than the EU. However, gradually but steadily, the EU has first taken over social private regulation and later the liberalization and privatization of former public services, not to forget financial services. The decline of the welfare state model in the Member States and the transfer of regulatory competences to the EU are parallel developments. The shift from the national to the European level had its down sides. The 'social' was weakened. Matters of social justice via regulation have been substituted through a new model of European justice, called access justice. With the support and backing of the Member States, the EU became by far the most important regulator within the original domain of the 'social' and within regulated markets.

In these two domains, the visible hand of European private law has become ever more obvious. Since the 1970s, the EU has become involved in the domain of labour and employment, and in the 1980s became embedded even more successfully in the field of consumer law. The EU is not only regulating the new markets of telecoms, postal services, energy, transport, and, increasingly, financial services, but it is also indirectly and directly interfering with private law relations that govern other sectors: between business and business, between business and customers, but not between customers/consumers themselves. The domain of services covers

[10] Kennedy, 'Three Globalizations of Law and Legal Thought: 1850–2000', in D. Trubek and A. Santos (eds), *The New Law and Economic Development: A Critical Appraisal* (2006).

[11] M. Cremona (ed.), *Market Integration and Public Services in the European Union* (2011).

[12] N. Reich, *General Principles of EU Civil Law* (2013); Comparato and Micklitz, 'Regulated Autonomy between Market Freedoms and Fundamental Rights in the Case Law of the CJEU', in U. Bernitz, X. Groussot, and F. Schulyok (eds), *General Principles of EU Law and European Private Law* (2013) 121.

70 per cent of the gross income of the EU.[13] In this new emerging field, the EU succeeded in framing and shaping private law relations.

The rise of regulatory private law at the EU level is astonishing and deserves a short, though necessarily incomplete, explanation. What matters in our context are two phenomena: the rules on service contracts, enshrined in continental codifications which provide only rudimentary guidance. They are based on the distinction between *obligation de moyen* and *obligation de résultat*, dating back to the French Code Civil from 1804. The manufacturer of a 'work' is liable for the result and is only paid for the result. This might have worked in the pre-industrial age, when most products were manufactured by hand. Another type of manufacturer is the supplier of a work who is paid for the time he spends. The prototype has become the worker in Fordism. Today, we may observe a trend where the *obligation de résultat* is increasingly replaced by an *obligation de moyen*. There was a conceptual gap resulting from the rise of the service society,[14] which was gradually filled by regulatory private law, with the European Commission in the driver's seat. None of the EU Member States has undertaken serious efforts to reform the law on contract for services and to investigate the feasibility of a coherent and systematic body of rules that embodies the new domain of liberalized public services or, more precisely, of regulated markets.[15] The Study and the Acquis Groups could have opted for the elaboration of service contracts, but the attempts remained half-hearted, mainly because key economic domains were excluded from the scope of the analysis.[16] The most important type of contracts—service contracts outside the traditional domains already known for the last 200 years—escaped the political and academic attention of politicians and scholars in Europe. This, however, forms the core of European regulatory private law.

B. The Internal and the External Dimension

At first glance, the distinction is easy and self-explanatory. The internal dimension refers to the scope of EU law, which is restricted to the number of Member States which have joined the EU. In that sense, the internal dimension has much in common with the 'territory' of the EU. Just like nation states, the EU defines the reach of its law through its 'territory'. The external dimension is, then, outward looking: the attempt to analyse and define the reach and effect of European private law beyond EU territory.

[13] Services contributed 73.5 per cent of the EU-28's total gross value added in 2013: Eurostat, Data from May 2014, available at <http://ec.europa.eu/eurostat/statistics-explained/index.php/National_accounts_and_GDP>.

[14] R. Rosecrance, *The Rise of the Trading State, Commerce and Conquest in the Modern Welt* (1986).

[15] For a doctrinal account which does not go into the different areas of regulated markets, see: R. Zimmermann (ed.), *Service Contracts* (2010).

[16] Such as financial services, telecommunications, and energy; Study Group on a European Civil Code (ed.), *Service Contracts* (2007).

As the title indicates, this book seeks to explore the new, unchartered territory of European private law beyond EU borders. There is a need to analyse and understand the inward-looking character of European private law. However, the two areas, European private international law and European regulatory private law, follow different patterns.

Traditional law. Private international law is international in the sense that all national legal systems are treated alike. The ideology and the theory behind private international law is that no country—or more precisely, no nation state—should draw a distinction between categories of countries. The rules which design the reach of the jurisdiction and the applicable law should be the same, whether in a rich or a poor country, a developed or less developed country, a democracy or an authoritarian regime. The perfect world would be one where all national private international law rules follow the same pattern. This is what stands behind the 'Hague Academy' and what shapes its mandate.[17] 'Europeanizing' private international law rules necessarily entails difficult distinctions between the 'inside' and the 'outside', specifically of the EU. One possible solution to remain within the ideology of the 'international' in private international law would be to adopt a European private international law which is universally applicable. This would imply that the same rules apply to trans-border conflicts between Member States, and trans-border conflicts between Member States and non-Member States.

There are, however, two challenges to overcome. The first is whether and to what extent the EU body of private international law regulations follows this path systematically and coherently. Each and every exemption or reservation questions the universality of the approach and paves the way for ranking and classifying the legal orders of non-EU countries. Seen through the lens of the EU, one might define the border between the internal and external dimension with the candidate countries who applied to the EU and who are tied to the EU via a whole set of bilateral contracts which are intended to prepare them for full membership, but which are not yet proper Member States. Then there are countries belonging to the European Economic Area (EEA), still closely connected to the EU via joint administrative authorities and a mirror image of the CJEU, the European Free Trade Association (EFTA) Court. Here is not the place to provide a complete picture of this issue; what matters is noting that the broader one draws the circle, the weaker the influence of the EU law will be. This corresponds, however, with a growing feeling of alienation by those beyond the inner sanctum. One might assume that these reservations would reappear in the judicial practice of national and European courts.[18]

The second difficulty is less an obstacle than a consequence. Private international law rules are claimed to be 'neutral' as they do not contain or promote

[17] It suffices to consult the different series of publications, available at <https://www.hagueacademy.nl/publications/>.

[18] Some of the research on 'Europeanization' might be relevant but it is mainly directed at candidate states. This book does not focus on neighbouring/candidate states, except perhaps A. Marhold (Chapter 11) and, to some extent, J. Stuyck and M. Durovic (Chapter 10). It is helpful to distinguish these cases from the 'purer' international legal regimes.

a value judgment on the differences between legal orders. However, well-known contradictions exist.[19] All courts around the world tend to extend their jurisdiction beyond national territories—in terms of competences for the courts and in terms of the applicable law. In theory, the decision on jurisdiction and the decision on the applicable law are distinct. However, in practice they are more often than not closely interlinked. Once the court has established jurisdiction, the applicable law might very well be the national law.

In confirming European jurisdiction and the applicability of (harmonized) EU law, the EU courts and the Member State courts 'impose' on non-EU countries European procedural and substantive legal standards. It suffices to recall the dense body of mandatory rules within secondary EU law: in insurance law, in employment law, and consumer law. The consequence—perhaps not the intent—of any affirmative decision on European jurisdiction and on the applicability of (harmonized) EU law in trans-European litigation is far-reaching. The laws and regulations of the non-EU Member States are implicitly or explicitly measured against 'European legal standards'. It remains to be seen what the impact of the external dimension of Europeanized private international law rules looks like, whether there are ideological ruptures and, even more importantly, whether it is possible to identify common patterns in the different degrees of alienation.

Regulatory private law. The external dimension of European regulatory private law is even more opaque. It is necessary to go through all the bits and pieces of European social regulation and European rules on regulated markets in order to find out whether and to what extent the respective European directives and European regulations contain provisions on the external dimension at all, and, if this is the case, what they look like. The field of law which provides the best available knowledge thus far is consumer contract law.[20] The different consumer law directives contain rules on the external reach of mandatory standards. The Rome I Regulation has streamlined the different wordings and laid down common standards for consumer contract law.[21]

The picture is much less clear with regard to employment contracts, insurance contracts, financial services, company law, and rules on regulated markets, telecommunications, postal services, energy, and transport. Where there is research, it focuses on the internal dimension of the respective field of law. The external dimension of the different fields is analysed through the lens of the Europeanized private international law rules: the Brussels and the Rome Regulations. Such an approach is self-explanatory with regard to insurance and employment contracts that are explicitly regulated by the Brussels and Rome Regulations. When it comes to services in regulated markets, a full analysis would have to include explicit and implicit references in the regulations and directives on regulated markets. The

[19] See Chapter 4 on the two difficulties.

[20] This is due to the fact that the Rome Convention from 1980 had to be transposed into national law. There are numerous contributions in books and commentaries (in the German tradition) on what is called today the Brussels Regulation as well as the Rome I and Rome II Regulations.

[21] Reich in H.-W. Micklitz *et al.*, *Understanding European Consumer Law* (2nd edn, 2014).

mental barrier for such an exercise might be the deeply ingrained distinction between private law (the Brussels and Rome Regulations) and public law (the EU rules on regulated markets). The result is that most of the analysis undertaken so far falls short of the proclaimed holistic approach.

Similar to the Academic Draft Common Frame of References and the political project on a Common European Sales Law, scholarly research is focused on horizontal perspectives: on the scope and reach of Brussels I and II *bis*, on Rome I, and Rome II. It does not wade into the messy waters of European regulatory private law that provides rules on the external dimension of private law. The different contributions in this book shed light on financial services, on company law, on pharmaceutical law, and energy law. However, the book does not seek to provide a full analysis of the external reach of all the different fields and to compare them with the Brussels and Rome Regulations in order to identify gaps and contradictions.

2. Four Observations on the External European Private Law

Research on external European private law is still in its infancy; that is why it seems premature to strive towards overambitious objectives. In taking into account the different contributions in the book, it is possible to group the debate around four major observations which seem to hold external European private law and which indicate a shift from: (1) legal rules to legal practice; (2) formal law making to European governance; (3) substantive law to procedural law; and (4) private law to trade law. It will have to be demonstrated that these shifts by and large correspond to the distinction between traditional private law and regulatory private law.

The four observations are united by a common characteristic: the tensions and contradictions between each of the two poles, which also hold them together. That is why it seems more appropriate not to simply join the two using a simple 'and' but via a rather more antagonistic 'versus'. Of course, these observations are tentative and meant to trigger debate rather than to provide pat answers. Observations are based on practice, on impressions and assumptions. One possibility would be to reject the observations as ill-founded and to return to a clear distinction between private law and public law, delegating the recent development in regulated markets to public law. Similar considerations have long been voiced by those who regard 'mandatory' rules as regulation, to be kept separate from 'contract'.[22] However, only by testing the observations and assumptions will it be possible to push the debate further into unchartered waters, beyond the boundaries of a traditional understanding of private law which has found its own comfort zone. Each of the four observations start with a set of guiding hypotheses which condense the

[22] For a theoretical discussion of the distinction between contract and regulation, see Brownsword, 'Contract, Consent, and Civil Society: Private Governance and Public Imposition', in P. Odell and C. Willett (eds), *Civil Society* (2008) 5. For a different opinion, see: H. Collins, *Regulating Contracts* (1999).

implicit preconceptions, though these observations are based on research on regulatory private law that has been undertaken over the last 20 years.

A. Legal Rules versus Legal Practice

First, there are too many rules and not enough law in external European private law. Second, where there is law, we have no or limited practice. Third, where we have legal practice, it is about procedure and not about substance. Fourth, where we have extensive practice, we do not have enough law. Again, the distinction and differences between traditional private law and regulatory private law might help us to understand what is meant by these claims.

Traditional private law rules are very well developed. The two Brussels Regulations on jurisdiction and enforcement as well as the two Rome Regulations on the applicable law of contract and tort together form an impressive body of highly sophisticated legal rules. There is legal scholarship analysing and commenting on the regulations in great detail. However, there is an obvious contradiction. The two Brussels Regulations, in particular Regulation 44/2001, 'recast' (this is the official language) through Regulation 2015/2012, are of high practical relevance. Since the adoption of the Brussels Convention in 1968 an endless flow of references has been reaching the Court in Luxemburg and has led to a dense set of rules, in particular on consumer law, surrounding the concepts of the consumer and of the contract, both highly influential in that the CJEU does not draw a distinction between the Brussels regulation and the different consumer contract law directives.[23]

This finding stands in stark contrast to the still rather limited practical importance of the two Rome Regulations.[24] One might argue that the Regulations' predecessor, the Rome Convention, did not grant the CJEU jurisdiction, and that

[23] The CJEU is not drawing a distinction in the notion of the consumer under the Brussels Regulation/Convention, which provides for a fully harmonized set of rules on jurisdiction and the consumer contract law directives, which are mostly laying down minimum standards in a rather narrow context. On the trend towards a genuine and autonomous concept of contract, see Micklitz, 'Der Vertragsbegriff in den Übereinkommen von Brüssel und Rom', in R. Schulze, H. Schulte-Nölke, and L. Bernardeau (eds), *Europäisches Vertragsrecht im Gemeinschaftsrecht* (2002) 39.

[24] All in all, 20 cases so far and not all yet decided. Six cases under the Rome Convention: Case C-305/13, *Haeger & Schmidt*, judgment of 23 October 2014; Case C-184/12, *Unamar*, judgment of 17 October 2013; Case C-64/12, *Schlecker*, judgment of 12 September 2013; Case C-384/10, *Voogsgeerd*, [2011] ECR I-13275; Case C-29/10, *Koelzsch*, [2011] ECR I-1595; and Case C-133/08, *Intercontainer*, [2009] ECR I-9687. Six cases under the Rome I Regulation: Case C-483/14, *KA Finanz AG*, not yet decided; Case C-557/13, *Lutz*, judgment of 16 April 2015, not yet published; Case C-396/13, *Sähköalojen*, judgment 12 February 2015, not yet published; Case C-508/12, *Vaepenik*, judgment of 5 December 2013; Case C-190/11, *Mühlleitner*, judgment of 6 September 2012; Case C-585/08, *Pammer*, [2010] ECR I-12527. Eight cases under the Rome II Regulation: Case C-240/14, *Prüller*, judgment of 9 September 2015; C-475/14, *AAS Gjensidige Baltic*, not yet decided; Case C-359/14, *ERGO Insurance*, not yet decided; Case C-350/14, *Florin Lazar*, not yet decided; Case C-45/13, *Kainz*, judgment of 16 January 2014; Case Case C-22/12, *Haasová*, judgment of 24 October 2013; Case C-412/10, *Deo Antoine*, [2011] ECR I-11603; Case C-173/11, *Football Dataco*, judgment of 18 October 2012.

the Rome Regulations gained importance once the Member States were ready to accept the interpretative authority of the CJEU. However, with the exception of family law, private international law rules in the field of contract and tort have always played a rather limited role.

There are many open questions. Most of them are related to empirics. To what extent do the references that reach the CJEU have an external dimension? In addition, if they do, is the CJEU using the same methodology, the same arguments, and the same mode of interpretation as in internal EU cases? To my knowledge, no systematic and comprehensive analysis of the case law of the CJEU has been undertaken to shed light on possible differences between the internal and the external.[25] The spectacular cases decided by the CJEU that have a strong external dimension, such as *Ingmar*[26] on the external reach of mandatory rules in the Directive 86/653/EEC on commercial agents, or *West Tankers*,[27] *TNT*,[28] and *Gazprom*,[29] are well-known, but what kind of arguments can be drawn from the few cases that have received public attention?

There is more. What are the reasons for the differences between the role and importance of the Brussels and the Rome Regulations? An obvious explanation would be that businesses, in particular big businesses, prefer arbitration to litigation in (European) courts. If they opt for a particular court, they choose New York, London, or Switzerland as the place of jurisdiction.[30] Businesses do not engage in a sophisticated distinction between the internal and the external dimension of EU law. It simply does not matter whether two companies located in the EU, or two companies, one located in the EU, the other outside, are litigating. The result is the same. Businesses will opt for arbitration. These findings do not apply to consumer law. The rise of online sales has increased the number of cross-border transactions within and beyond the EU considerably. In theory, the carefully designed set of EU private international law rules should and could apply. They aim at protecting the consumer, granting him the right to litigate at his domicile (in the EU) and to rely on his (Europeanized) national consumer protection laws.[31] In reality, there is little litigation before courts, independent from the internal or the external dimension. Consumers shy away from going to court. Litigation is too costly and private international law rules are too complicated. The EU is promoting out-of-court

[25] I would like to thank Angela Ward, Réferendaire at the Court of Justice for the European Union, for this inspiring information.

[26] Case C-381/98, *Ingmar*, [2000] ECR I-9305.

[27] Case C-185/07, *Allianz SpA and Generali Assicurazioni Generali SpA v. West Tankers Inc.*, [2009] ECR I-663.

[28] Case C-533/08 *TNT Express Nederland BV v. AXA Versicherung AG*, [2010] ECR I-4107, with opinion by AG Kokott.

[29] Case C-536/13, *Gazprom OAO Lietuvos Respublika*, judgment of 13 May 2015, not yet published, which could be read so as to limit both *West Tankers* and *TNT*.

[30] S. Vogenauer and S. Weatherill (eds), *Harmonisation of European Contract Law* (2006); Calliess, 'Der Richter im Zivilprozess—Sind ZPO und GVG noch zeitgemäß', *Gutachten A zum 70. Deutschen Juristentag* (2014).

[31] Admittedly, this is a rather crude version of an extremely complex set of rules. On top of this, there is a great deal of pressure from business to cut down the privileges.

settlement for trans-border conflicts *within* the EU. The design of the Online Dispute Resolution (ODR) Regulation and the Alternative Dispute Resolution (ADR) Directive is not laid out to integrate trans-EU consumer litigation. It is quite simply too heavily dominated by the European Commission, which will run the ODR platform.[32] The complex EU model leaves room for access to court as a means of last resort. From a transnational perspective, the EU platform will have to compete with business models for conflict resolution, such as those provided by eBay worldwide, or Alibaba in China.[33] The United Nations Commission on International Trade Law (UNCITRAL) initiative, which promotes a rather simple arbitration model for low-cost consumer conflicts, seems to be quite promising.[34]

If this is correct, however, why have the Brussels Convention and, more recently, the Brussels Regulation gained such importance? Provided it is reasonable to assume that big businesses do not go to court, then small and medium-sized enterprises (SMEs) should be identified as possible litigants. Again, we lack knowledge about what happened before the advent of the CJEU between 1968 and 2015. All we know is that there are a number of consumer law cases which have been decided on the lieu of jurisdiction. Many of the references are related to dubious marketing practices where SMEs play around with jurisdiction in business transactions near the borders between two EU countries in order to escape the tighter grip of national consumer protection legislation in the consumer's domicile or even to render enforcement through courts more difficult for consumers.[35]

Regulatory private law outside the reach and scope of the four regulations differs as well. There is no coherence and there is no recognizable system. The law is erratic, piecemeal, opaque, and incomplete. This is the dominant (continental) view, at least, in legal scholarship, which proclaims private law to be coherent and consistent, transparent, and systematic. The EU rules on regulated markets might serve as a blueprint.[36] They do not focus on private law, or more particularly on

[32] For a more comprehensive discussion see: Eidenmüller and Engel, 'Against False Settlement: Designing Efficient Consumer Rights Enforcement Systems in Europe', 29 *Ohio State Journal on Dispute Resolution* (2014) 261; Rühl, 'Die Richtlinie über alternative Streitbeilegung: Han dlungsperspektiven und Handlungsoptionen', 127 *Zeitschrift für Zivilprozess* (2014) 61; Caponi, 'Just Settlement of Just About Settlement? Mediated Agreements: A Comparative Overview of the Basics', 79 *Rabels Zeitschrift für Ausländisches und Internationales Privatrecht* (2015) 117.

[33] See R. Metz *et al.* (eds), *E-Commerce in China and Germany—A Sino-German Comparative Analysis* (2012), with many facts on how the e-commerce and the conflict resolution is organized.

[34] Information available at <http://www.uncitral.org/uncitral/publications/online_resources_ODR.html>.

[35] The various judgments on sweepstakes (sales promotion strategies where the consumers are approached by sending a letter informing them that they have won a prize); for a discussion see H.-W. Micklitz, J. Stuyck, and E. Terryn (eds), *Cases, Materials and Text on Consumer Law* (2010) 546.

[36] Here I rely on extensive empirical research within the ERC project on European regulatory private law; see H.-W. Micklitz and Y. Svetiev, 'A Self-Sufficient European Private Law—A Viable Concept?', EUI Working Paper LAW 2012/31 (ERC-ERPL 01/2012); H.-W. Micklitz, Y. Svetiev, and G. Comparato (eds), 'European Regulatory Private Law—The Paradigm Tested', EUI Working Paper LAW 2014/04 (ERC-ERPL-09). With regard to financial services, see the editorial: Micklitz, 'The Public and the Private—European Regulatory Private Law and Financial Services', 10 *European Review of Contract Law* (2014) 473. Ottow and Svetiev, 'Financial Supervision in the Interstices Between Private and Public Law', 10 *European Review of Contract Law* (2014) 496; Marjosola, 'What Role for Courts in Protecting Investors in Europe—A View from Finland', 10 *European Review of*

contracts for services. They regulate the legal environment in which the contract is embedded. Characteristic of regulated markets is the variety of rule makers—the EU, the Member States implementing the rules, the sector-related agencies which are adopting rules and recommendations, and the variety of rules, European, national, binding, non-binding, soft and hard, which surround the contract for services. This is only on the law-making side. On the enforcement side, the EU rules on regulated markets provide for out-of-court settlement procedures to be applied between businesses and between businesses and consumers. They involve the regulatory agencies surveying and monitoring contractual practice, thereby blurring the line between law making and law enforcement. Litigation before courts, national and European, is the exception to the rule.

All this is considering the internal dimension only and it is already complex enough, in particular, if one assumes that each regulated market and each domain of regulatory private law is following its own rationality.[37] Whilst it seems possible and manageable to pierce the veil of ignorance in the internal market, the degree of complexity still increases considerably when it comes to the external dimension of European regulatory private law. At first glance, European regulations and directives adopted under the procedural (democratic) requirements set out in the EU Treaty suggest that the rules originate in Europe. This means that the European Commission, the European Parliament, and the Council are those who stand behind the substance laid down in secondary Union law. This, however, is only half the truth. The relevant EU rules on regulated markets are not free-standing; they are connected and affected by international rules of supranational and international bodies as well as national rules from outside the EU, in particular those of the US. The interaction between the EU and the rest of the world in standard setting may take various forms, which will be discussed later on.

At the level of enforcement beyond the EU, we must distinguish between the enforcement of private law rules via regulatory agencies across the EU borders, the enforcement of private law rules via out-of-court mechanisms, and, last but not least, litigation before courts. There are questions about questions. The regulatory agencies and the networks in which they are embedded are designed for the internal market, for the inner world of the EU. The same is true with regard to the ADR bodies, which are established within the relevant sectors, highly promoted by the EU. The status of non-EU regulatory agencies is not subject to systematic analysis. There are strong differences between the regulated markets. The most advanced model was established through the banking union.[38] The out-of-court

Contract Law (2014) 545; Della Negra, 'The Private Enforcement of the MiFID Conduct of Business Rules: An Overview of the Italian and Spanish Experiences', 10 *European Review of Contract Law* (2014) 571.

[37] As analysed and promoted by Fischer-Lescano and Teubner, 'Regime Collisions: The Vain Search for Legal Unity in the Fragmentation of Global Law', 25 *Michigan Journal for International Law* (2004) 999.

[38] Compare the rules on energy (see A. Marhold, Chapter 11, this volume) with the ones on the banking and financial services (J. Wouters and J. Odermatt, Chapter 8, this volume). Art. 55 of Directive 2013/36 in combination with Art. 33 of Regulation 1093/2010 empowers EBA to conclude

mechanisms are not accessible to consumers or businesses from non-EU countries. Article 2(1) requires both parties to have residence in the EU. However, what we do not know is whether and to what extent *in practice* non-EU regulatory agencies are involved in enforcement issues (surveillance of contractual practices), and what happens if non-EU litigants ask for access to the ADR bodies.

The first observation culminates in important questions: why is legal practice so important for understanding the external reach of European private law? What do all the rules, the Treaty, the competences in the Treaty, the directives and regulations, the few court decisions, and all the publicly available knowledge tell us about the 'law', if we accept that knowledge of law making and law enforcement, that rules and practice, are all required to understand what the 'law' is? Without intensive empirical studies of out-of-court settlement bodies, without investigating reports of regulatory agencies, and—even further—without talking to those who are in charge of enforcement, there is little chance to obtain a realistic picture. K.-H. Ladeur's forthcoming work analyses the key role of 'legal practice'. He questions the 'imperialism of legal theory' against legal practice. The key to understanding legal practice is claimed to be the 'textuality of the law'.[39]

B. Experimentalist Governance versus Formal Regulation

First, European regulatory private law is much more appropriate for experimentalism than traditional private law. Second, the limits of EU competences are compensated for by innovative competence creeping through the kinds of experimentalism. Third, regulatory private law in external relations provides a much better testing ground than regulatory private law in and for the internal market. This is, last but not least, the consequence of the less rigid democratic oversight in external relations. All in all, it can be said that the EU is an ideal laboratory for regulatory innovation.[40]

The groundbreaking article by Charles Sabel and Jonathan Zeitlin[41] on experimentalist governance focused on administrations and administrative law, in the

non-binding cooperation agreements with the supervisory authorities of third countries; Art. 8 of the SSM Regulation 1024/2013, which establishes the Banking Union, allows the ECB to enter into non-binding administrative arrangements with supervisory authorities, international organizations, and the administrations of third countries 'subject to appropriate co-ordination with EBA'.

[39] I would like to thank K.-H. Ladeur for letting me know about his forthcoming book, a theory on legal practice, based on post-structuralists such as Agamben, Derrida, Nancy, and Menke.

[40] On the EU model in the light of the debate around its philosophical foundations, see: Micklitz, 'The European Union Project', in J. Dickson and P. Eleftheriadis (eds), *The Philosophical Foundations of European Union Law* (2013) 1.

[41] Sabel and Zeitlin, 'Learning from Difference: The New Architecture of Experimentalist Governance in the EU', 14 *European Law Journal* (2008) 271; C. Sabel and J. Zeitlin (eds), *Experimentalist Governance in the European Union: Towards a New Architecture* (2010); Sabel and Simon, 'Epilogue: Accountability Without Sovereignty', in G. de Búrca and J. Scott (eds), *Law and New Governance in the US and the EU* (2006), at 395; recently Svetiev, 'Settling or Learning: Commitment Decision as a Competition Enforcement Paradigm', 33 *Yearbook of European Law* (2014) 466.

European context, linked to the multi-level governance structure of the EU, in the transnational context, renamed as global administrative law.[42] However, the model and the thinking behind it are gaining ever stronger legal ground in contract law through contract governance, and in constitutional law through the kind of democratic experimentalism.[43] This is not the place to engage in a discussion about whether it is feasible to set a legal frame for experimentalism or, quite to the contrary, whether experimentalism in whatever field of the law is undermining to the integrity of the law itself.[44] The purpose here is different. The intention of the analysis is to show how experimentalism has already become 'reality' in the external dimension of European regulatory private law.

In line with Möslein and Riesenhuber,[45] I will distinguish between four forms of governance: the structural level, the procedural level, the content level, and the instrumental level. The structural side of governance invokes the distinction between the public and the private, the global and the regional or the national. The procedural level deals with inclusion and participation. The content level has to deal with autonomy and regulation, and the instrumental level with contracts as a means to implement codes, technical standards, and/or public values.

Regulatory private law requires technical standards.[46] They are vital for access to markets. Technical standards have multiple functions. They have a genuine technical component (unifying sizes and measuring systems), but they may go beyond this and lay down requirements on the quality of the products, or, even further, enshrine social values on health and safety, on environmental protection, on human rights, or on complaint procedures. The line between product standards and services, between technical and behavioural requirements, between standards and codes of practice, is becoming blurred.[47] Technical standards are everywhere to be found: in contracts on foodstuff, on pharmaceuticals, on financial services, on energy, on telecom, and on transport. They shape the quality of the product, the safety of the consumer in using it, and the environment in which it is being used.

[42] Kingsbury, Krisch, and Stewart, 'The Emergence of Global Administrative Law', 68 *Law and Contemporary Problems* (2005) 15; and K.-H. Ladeur, 'The Emergence of Global Administrative Law and the Evolution of General Administrative Law', Osgoode CLPE Research Paper 16/2011.

[43] Joerges, 'What is Left of the European Economic Constitution? A Melancholic Eulogy', 30 *European Law Review* (2005) 461, at 483–484. Advocating the constitutionalization of governance: M. Dawson, *New Governance and the Transformation of European Law: Coordinating EU Social Law and Policy* (2011); E. Korkea-aho, *Adjudicating New Governance, Deliberative Democracy in the European Union* (2015); M. Dawson, C. Joerges, and H. Enderlein (eds), *The Transformation of the European Union: Challenges of Functionality, Design and Legitimacy* (2015).

[44] The term has been coined by R. Dworkin, *Law's Empire* (1986); see Joerges, 'The European Economic Constitution and its Transformation through the Financial Crisis', forthcoming in D. Patterson and A. Södersten (eds), *A Companion to European Union Law and International Law* (2015); along the same lines: Renner, 'Death by Complexity—The Financial Crisis and the Crisis of Law in the Modern World' in P. Kjaer (ed.), *The Financial Crisis in Constitutional Perspective* (2011) 93.

[45] Möslein and Riesenhuber, 'Contract Governance—A Draft Research Agenda', 5 *European Review of Contract Law* (2009) 248.

[46] This statement deserves a much deeper explanation. I will leave this for another occasion.

[47] On the conceptual issues of self-regulation: F. Cafaggi (ed.), *Reframing Self-Regulation in European Private Law* (2006).

Non-compliance with standards may lead to warranty claims and, provided they define the level of safety, trigger liability. Provided they define the level of safety, non-compliance triggers liability. They serve as the blueprint for analysing the different levels of governance and act as a gateway to the integration of international standards into EU rules.

The most obvious experimentalism takes place at the *institutional* level. Technical standards are elaborated by standardization bodies. They vary in the degree to which they enjoy an institutional status within the system of international organizations. They may be formally recognized or they may exist as informal bodies; they may have a firm structure of membership or may not; they may have clear rules on who is allowed to participate and who may not; they may have formalized decision procedures or may not. The variety of institutions is hard to overlook and, once identified, the institutional setting has to be placed and analysed in the particular context in which it operates. The EU cavorts like a fish in the water, despite the rather tight competence structure, which still relies on enumerated powers. This is not to say that there is no link between formal competences entrusted to the EU and its institutional role in the transnational environment. The EU is certainly stronger where it has a clear and defined competence. However, competence is not a necessary requirement for the EU to be involved, to be heard and to influence standardization. Here the door is open towards governance in external relations.

At the international level, the most well-known standard bodies are the International Organization for Standardization (ISO) and the International Electrotechnical Commission (IEC), as well as Codex Alimentarius in food safety. In financial services, the International Organization of Securities Commissions (IOSCO) is less well known. The EU is making great use of the work done by private parties and established international organizations in standardizing products and services, though to a different degree and in different roles and functions. The EU is strongest in the traditional field of standardization meant to reduce non-barriers to trade. Here, it enjoys exclusive competence. The key institutions in Europe are the European Committee for Standardization (CEN) and the European Committee for Electrotechnical Standardization (CENELEC). The relationship between the EU and the standards bodies is laid down in a memorandum of understanding. There are institutional links between CEN/CENELEC and ISO/IEC.[48] The EU may influence the setting of technical standards, either directly via CEN/CENELEC as a societal player benefitting from its weight in a regional economy of 500 million people or, more directly, via the EU institutions, provided the European Commission has mandated CEN/CENELEC to elaborate a particular standard for the Internal Market. Again, this is a variation of the proclaimed *Brussels effect*.[49]

[48] CENELEC Guide 13—CENELEC Agreement on Common Planning of New Work and Parallel Voting, edition 1, 2001-01; ISO/CEN Agreement on Technical Co-operation between ISO and CEN Vienna Agreement, version 3.3. 2001-09-20.

[49] Bradford, 'The Brussels Effect', 107 *Northwestern University Law Review* (2012) 1.

The EU is weakest in the field of setting standards in the banking and financial services. Here, the technical standards are elaborated within the Basel Committee and IOSCO, where the EU has observer status only, and has limited opportunity to influence things formally at concrete, working level. However, both operate on the basis of consensus and it seems that the particularities of the decision-making process allow for the institutions representing the EU in these two committees to have a say in the outcome.[50] In IOSCO, the EU works more like a catalyst in the elaboration of standards which are integrated into the Markets in Financial Instruments Directive (MiFID) I and MiFID II.[51] The political decision of the EU Member States to establish the Banking Union has brought the European Central Bank (ECB) into the frame as it must cooperate with the European Banking Authority (EBA) in banking regulation. Currently, the impact of the EU via the EBA and ECB on the Basel Committee is hard to foresee, but the overall expectations seem to be that the EU's influence is increasing. The problem remains that non-European members claim that Europe is over-represented already in the Basel Committee.[52]

The *procedural* level is closely connected to the institutional level and the degree to which the institution in place is settled and established. Participation is first and foremost linked to economic power and political importance. That is why the EU is given a place at the table in bodies like the Basel Committee and IOSCO. Politics (represented by parliaments in democracies) does not seem to matter so much, which is justified with reference to the mere technical character of the rules. This is a rather weak argument in light of the thin line between technical standards (for the executive) and standards with a societal impact (for parliaments) or, in the Banking Union, the difference between regulatory (European Parliament) and implementing standards (European Commission).[53] The growing public awareness of standardization is directed at the legitimacy of the standard-making bodies, which in turn raises questions about participation, not only of the most powerful countries or the most powerful companies, but of civil society itself. In theory, the rather flexible institutional setting leaves room for experimentalism in standard setting. In practice, there are only a few notable examples where standard-setting bodies have opened their doors to non-governmental organizations representing civil society.[54] More prominent among this kind of experimentation might be the

[50] Statement of Andrea Enria, Chairman of the European Banking Authority at the State of the Union (7 May 2015) within the panel on 'Banking Supervision—Global Challenges and Opportunities for the EU after the Banking Union'.

[51] See A. Marcacci, 'Protecting Investors in Financial Times: The Design and Functioning of the Legal Protection of Retail Investors' (PhD EUI, 2013) and Chapter 9, this book.

[52] For details on the Basel committee see J. Wouters and J. Odermatt, Chapter 8, this book.

[53] The Art. 290 TFEU procedure applies to binding regulatory standards, the Art. 291 TFEU procedure to binding implementing standards.

[54] Providing information in some areas: O. Dilling, M. Herberg, and G. Winter (eds), 'Transnational Administrative Rule Making, Performance, Legal Effects and Legitimacy' (2011); more theoretically: C. Bratschi, Transnational Law beyond Bi-Polarity: The FSB Key Attributes of Effective Resolution Regimes for Financial Institutions in National, European and Transnational Law (PhD EUI, 2015).

cooperation between institutions representing broad policy fields, for example the involvement of the ISO and the International Labour Organization (ILO) in the elaboration of ISO 26000.[55]

The *content* level represents the proof of the pudding. How are technical standards and private law interlinked in handling conflicts with non-EU litigants? Are these not two separate worlds, living apart from each other, challenging the rhetoric of regulatory private law? There is a need to distinguish between the role and function of standards in regulatory private law and in traditional private law. In the former, there might well exist an impact of international standards on European private law-making in regulated markets. This will be done in the context of the third observation, the shift from substance to procedure. Traditional private law is summoned when issues arise that cannot be contained and solved within the regulated markets. In contract and tort, regulatory private law and traditional private law are coming together. In trans-border litigation, there is room for the European regulations on private international law *within* the EU and *outside* the EU.

The bridge between technical standards and private law is contractual and tortious remedies.[56] The ideology of traditional contract is that the two parties individually agree on rights and duties, they agree on the price and on the quality. This is only half the truth. Since the beginning of the industrial age, in the services society and now in the information society, goods and services are largely standardized. The quality of a product or service is predefined via standards bodies outside and beyond the individual contractual agreement. When it comes to defining whether or not there has been non-compliance, the yardstick is more often than not the technical standard, to which the parties implicitly or explicitly refer. This might be a national, a regional, or ever more often, an international one. Contract doctrine is struggling hard with the economic reality of standardized quality, notwithstanding the level of origin.[57] Similar phenomena can be observed in tort liability. Here, technical standards, provided they exist, may serve as benchmarks against which the potential liability of the wrongdoer is measured. Compliance with a technical standard presumes that the potential infringer has done what needs to be done to ensure a reasonable level of safety. In practice, it is then for the victim to show that the

[55] R. Schmidt, 'Public-Private Cooperation in Transnational Regulation' (PhD EUI, 2015).

[56] The CJEU is about to develop a new type of remedy which is related to the procedural character of regulatory private law. Januek, Feryn, and Invitel are outstanding examples of these tendencies, see Kas, 'A Socio-Legal Study on the Operation of Hybrid Collective Remedies in the Area of European Social Regulation', in H.-W. Micklitz, Y. Svetiev, and G. Comparato (eds), 'European Regulatory Private Law—The Paradigm Tested', EUI Working Paper LAW 2014/04 (ERC-ERPL-09), at 19. However, these remedies have no external reach so far. That is why it might be premature to discuss them in the current context.

[57] It might be sufficient to recall the debate during the adoption of the Consumer Sales Directive 99/44 or during the elaboration of the respective rules in the Draft Common Frame of Reference. The dominating perspective in scholarship is that parties have to agree individually. The differences between the two types of agreements, individually or standardized, are not thought through; see for an early account: Knieper, 'Eigentum und Vertrag' as well as 'Sachmängelgewährleistung und Verbraucherschutz', both in R. Knieper, *Zwang, Vernunft, Freiheit: Studien zur juristischen Konstruktion der Gesellschaft* (1981), at 54 resp. 144.

standard in question was insufficient to guarantee the necessary level of personal integrity. The current litigation around PIP, the bankrupt French producer of defective breast implants, encapsulates in a nutshell the interplay between technical standards (the breast implant as a medical device), and the opportunities and limits of transnational litigation within and beyond the EU.[58]

The *instrumental* level of governance can be demonstrated by the interplay between contracts, technical standards/codes of conduct, and corporate governance. Once they overstep the technical and enter into the social sphere, technical standards may easily turn into codes of practices, or more generally codes that enshrine rules and obligations to be observed by those who subscribe to them. There are two ways to integrate these codes/standards into a governance structure: via contract governance (a prominent example comprises (transnational) supply chains)[59] or via corporate governance (via corporate social responsibility (CSR)).[60] Contract governance in supply chains exists thus far mainly on company level and has not yet reached a level of generalization. To my knowledge, there is no code on contract governance providing guidance for companies on how to use social standards (human rights standards) in supply chains.

Corporate governance is a well-established business strategy, which combines profit seeking with good conduct through institutional self-regulation. Companies started to impose codes of good conduct on themselves, which they announced to the outside world as part of their business strategies. The EU, the Organisation of Economic Co-operation and Development (OECD), and the United Nations (UN) viewed CSR as a prominent field of political action, not least due to the failure of the international community of states to come to some form of an agreement for an international convention on CSR. The legal and jurisprudential discussion concentrates on the regulatory nature of CSR[61] and on its enforceability.[62] Much less attention has been given to the efforts of companies which try to enforce CSR standards through contracts. Here, CSR and contract governance[63] combine

[58] See the different contributions in the Special Issue of the *Revue Internationale de Droit Economique* 1/201 'L'indemnisation des victims de produits de santé défectueux en Europe—L'affaire PIP'.

[59] Cafaggi, 'The Regulatory Functions of Transnational Commercial Contracts: New Architectures', 36 *Fordham International Law Journal* (2003) 1558.

[60] A. Beckers, *Enforcing Corporate Social Responsibility Codes: On Global Self-Regulation and National Private Law* (2015).

[61] Porter and Kramer, 'Strategy and Society: The Link between Competitive Advantage and CSR', *Harvard Business Review* (2006) 78. A good overview can be found in: Caroll and Shabana, 'The Business Case for Corporate Social Responsibility: A Review of Concepts, Research and Practice', 12 *International Journal of Management Reviews* (2010) 85. For a path-breaking view, see: M. Herberg, *Globalisierung und Private Selbstregulierung. Umweltschutz in Multinationalen Unternehmen* (2007); Herberg, 'Global Legal Pluralism and Interlegality: Environmental Self-Regulation in Multinational Enterprises as Global Law-Making', in O. Dilling, M. Herberg, and G. Winter (eds), *Responsible Business—Self-Governance and Law in Transnational Economic Transactions* (2008) 17.

[62] A. Beckers, *Enforcing Corporate Codes, On Global Self-Regulation and National Private Law* (2015).

[63] S. Grundmann, F. Möslein, and S. Riesenhuber (eds), *Contract Governance—Dimensions in Law and Interdisciplinary Research* (2015).

an increasingly important field or regulatory private law, far beyond the internal dimension of EU private law.

1. *Substance versus Procedure*

First, in the supranational context, the clear-cut distinction between substance and procedure is vanishing. This is true with regard to law making as well as with regard to law enforcement. Second, with the increasing relevance of the international dimension, there is on overall shift away from substance to procedure. Third, the development of regulatory private law is characterized by an ever-stronger fragmentation of sectors which are only loosely interconnected. Fourth, the biggest challenge is to develop cross-sectoral procedural requirements that may overcome a deficit of legitimacy.

There is an explanation needed of the meaning and use of procedure in traditional and regulatory private law. Procedure is meant to cover the rights and remedies structuring the enforceability of contractual rights or of rights protecting property and personal integrity. In the transnational context, the distinction reappears as one drawing a line between jurisdiction and applicable law. Regulatory private law is different. Here, law-making and law enforcement often go hand in hand. This has to do with the phenomenon that the laws adopted via parliaments set out a broad frame only, which then has to be given shape by the executive. The delegation of power from the legislature to the executive is the key to understanding why the line between law-making via the executive and law enforcement via the executive becomes blurred.[64] Enforcement of rights granted under regulatory private law takes two forms: horizontally, in the relationship between the parties, and vertically, between the parties and the executive agencies. The duplication or even multiplication of enforcers (courts, ADR bodies, arbitration, but also administrative agencies) is even more complex in the external dimension of European regulatory private law.

There is a paradox. In traditional private law, we may observe the overall tendency to use *internal* procedural rules to 'impose' *internal* substantive standards on the *outside* world. In regulatory private law, we may observe both the export of internal procedural rules to the rest of the world and the import of procedural rules into the EU. The most striking example in traditional private law is the Brussels I Regulation. The decision on whether a conflict between two parties comes under the scope of application is a purely procedural one in private law doctrine, clearly disconnected from the decision over the applicable law. In practice, however, there is ample evidence that the CJEU is using the procedural requirements of the Brussels I Regulation to submit international conventions and international rules more broadly speaking to a compatibility test.[65] The most striking example

[64] Taggart, 'From "Parliamentary Powers" to Privatization: The Chequered History of Delegated Legislation in the Twentieth Century', 55 *University of Toronto Law Journal* (2005) 575.

[65] See N. Jääskinen and A. Ward, Chapter 6, this volume.

is the *Kadi* judgment.[66] Usually, it is analysed from a constitutional human rights perspective. However, it should not be forgotten that the legal action of Mr Kadi was directed against the claimed illegal seizure of his assets. The CJEU 'defended' higher European human rights standards against lower external international human rights standards. The same type of thinking—though without a reference to *Kadi*—may be found in *West Tankers, TNT*, and *Gazprom*.[67] Whether they are international conventions in commercial law or international security regulation, what happens is a variation of what Bradford calls the 'Brussels effect', which generally describes the actions of legislatures and standard-setting bodies rather than courts.

The EU is shielding its higher standards. As a result, the rest of the world is faced with the problem of whether to adapt its own rules to those of the EU, to create a conflict, or to seek a compromise. This means the tool to extend EU standards beyond the EU territory—and this is the 'trick'—is the Brussels Regulation, not the Rome Regulation. By means of the former, the EU avoids sensitive discussions about how to amend international conventions, in particular about how to bring together the 'higher' EU level with the 'lower' international level. 'Lower' and 'higher' are difficult categories in themselves and they are even more complicated when pondered in an international environment. Provided they are kept legally separate, they suggest that there is a substantial difference between the inside and the outside of EU law. There is, however, a common characteristic most of the EU cases share. The EU rules provide for substantive law rules which reach beyond the less developed and often much older international conventions. It might suffice it here to recall the differences between the Montreal Convention and the EU Regulation on passenger rights.[68] All in all, the EU rules are 'more protective', be it to the benefit of EU travellers or of EU businesses. There seems to be a 'status' element enshrined in the judgments referring to the Brussels Regulation. This means the 'better' protection is not granted per se but is linked to the particular position of the EU consumer or business party in the business relationship with a non-EU party.

In external European regulatory private law, the situation looks different. Here, no coherent approach and no coherent body of EU rules exist. Whether and to what extent EU law provides for rules regulating the external dimension differs widely and needs a sector-related analysis. The contributions in this book provide insights on pharmaceuticals, energy, consumer protection, banking and financial services. As explained, the interplay between substance and procedure is very much related to the EU's position of power. What remains to be explained is the suggested move from substance to procedure.

Taking technical standards as a blueprint, there is a clear relationship between substance/procedure and the degree of internationalization. In supranational and

[66] Joined Cases C-402/05 P and C-415/05 P, *Yassin Abdullah Kadi and Al Barakaat International Foundation*, [2008] ECR I-6351.

[67] See references *supra* notes 28–30.

[68] Case C-344/04, *R v. Department of Transport ex parte IATA*, [2006] ECR I-403.

international fora, conflicts over substance are hidden in procedural compromises. A prominent example is the IOSCO. The broad guidance and direction enshrined in IOSCO rules is given concrete form in MiFID I and MiFID II.[69] The international level sets politically acceptable *procedural* standards; the *substance* is left to the states and the regions (EU). Coordination or even integration between the EU version of IOSCO and the US version of IOSCO bounces back to IOSCO or any other forum in which knowledge and information is exchanged beyond all national and supranational boundaries in a largely democratically uncontrolled safe harbour. Beck branded the phenomenon 'Weltinnenpolitik' (the world's internal policy): state representatives, international organizations, private standard bodies, NGOs from all over the world collaborate to shape 'standards', which then have to be reintegrated into national legal systems.[70]

When it comes to enforcement of these largely sectorial rules, the fine distinction between law-making and law application, between standard-making and standard application, becomes blurred. *Internally*, the European Commission, the European agencies (in regulated markets), and, more recently, the ECB (in banking) are mandated to ensure uniform compliance with the European standards (which might in fact be international standards). It is exactly through this mechanism that the borderline between law-making and law enforcement is disappearing. Provided the 'guidance' takes place at the EU level, the Member State authorities are turned into agents who execute what has been decided and agreed upon in the networks that tie the European agencies together with the rest of the world.[71] *Externally*, the EU is not speaking with one voice. This would require an exclusive competence of the EU, although one may find evidence of unanimity in fields of shared competences.[72] When it comes to the enforcement of the EU rules beyond its territory, coordination is needed between the national enforcement authorities, the European agencies, and the European Commission. Coordination points to procedure, not to substance. If there is substance, the benchmark will be what has been agreed upon *internally*. Interestingly enough, in regulated markets—the core area of European regulatory private law—there is very little case law of the CJEU. This means, contrary to traditional private law, that there is 'only' and 'mainly' sector-related administrative practice. To put it bluntly, in order to understand the role and function of the EU in the external dimension of health and safety standards (Codex Alimentarius) and financial services (IOSCO), extensive empirical research is needed in order to get at least an idea of what is actually happening in the different sectors, whether the EU standards are applied, by what procedure, and by whom. All that remains is the theoretically well-founded assumption that there is a shift from substance to procedure in private law rule-making and in private law rule application.

[69] See Chapter 9, this volume.

[70] U. Beck, *Risikogesellschaft: Auf dem Weg in eine andere Moderne* (1986); English title: *Risk Society*.

[71] In our project we have ample empirical evidence at least for the energy and the telecoms sector as well as for financial services; information available at <https://blogs.eui.eu/erc-erpl/>.

[72] See Chapter 2 in this volume, referring to the PFOS case on environmental standards.

There is an additional layer to be found for procedural law in the transnational environment. Traditional private law, enshrined in the grand codifications or in the common law on contracts and tort,[73] provides for a coherent body of rules. This is also true for the common law. In theory, we may know and we may study what the law looks like, what its state of affairs might be, and what kind of role the judiciary is playing. Regulatory private law, even more so in its external dimension, is first and foremost fragmented, broken down into sectors, each of them determined and governed by a particular community of lawyers, economists, politicians, and sometimes even non-governmental organizations (NGOs).[74] This community cuts across national and transnational boundaries and may easily reach global level. With effort, it is possible to study the different sectors and to identify the law and how it is operating in practice. However, there is often little, if any, interaction between the different sectors. From a bird's-eye perspective, there are obvious similarities in the regulatory design of a given contract drafted for one sector as compared with another (e.g. telecommunications and energy). These similarities invite scholars to think about a more coherent approach to service contracts. What seems to be more realistic in an external legal environment is to promote coordination mechanisms across sectors. If there was willingness to embark on such an exercise, we would again be looking at the procedural side, technically within experimentalist governance.[75]

2. *Private Law versus Trade Law*

Private lawyers will insist on the differences between these two domains. They may at best understand trade law as framing the international economic constitution,[76] as embedding private law (the 'private law society' (*Privatrechtsgesellschaft*) in the ordo-liberal sense). The discussion is most advanced at the EU level, where the relationship between the market freedoms and private law has attracted scholarly attention. However, in the elaboration of the Draft Common Frame of Reference and later the Common European Sales Law, this dimension has been ignored. In trade law, in particular in its international dimension, private law relations are entirely off the radar. If taken into account at all, private law is regarded as a

[73] Setting aside the famous saying from Lord Goff who, when asked to speak about the state of the common law, replied: 'there is no such thing as "the" common law'; 'The Future of the Common Law', 46 *International and Comparative Law Quarterly* (1997) 745.

[74] The famous findings of Bernstein, 'Private commercial law in the cotton industry: Creating Cooperation through Rules, Norms and Institutions', 99 *Michigan Law Review* (2001) 1724 can easily be generalized; with regard to the community of standards bodies see: Van Gestel and Micklitz, 'European Integration through Standardisation: How Judicial Review is Breaking down the Club House of Private Standardisation Bodies', 50 *Common Market Law Review* (2013) 145.

[75] Private law or private regulation where the EU is involved constitutes no more than one facet of the overall debate on the EU and on private law making and enforcement beyond the state, its nature, and its legitimacy. Here we are in the middle of the debate on transnational law, its theoretical, conceptual, and philosophical foundations.

[76] See the writings of U. Petersmann, *International Economic Law in the 21st Century: Constitutional Pluralism and Multilevel Governance of Interdependent Public Goods* (2012).

tricky field which might interfere with the broad policy objectives of international organizations promoting free trade. Any undertaking seeking to link the two areas and to find a common language is not an easy task. The assumptions underlying this comprise: first, behind trade law conflicts there is more often than not litigation between two private parties; second, in traditional private law, the interconnection between the two is operated through constitutionalization of private law; and third, in regulatory private law, the interconnection is condensed in private regulation which interferes with trade relations.

Gareth Davies opens his contribution in *The Involvement of EU Law in Private Law Relationships* with the following observation:

> If a party wishes to enter the market of a certain Member State, that is another way of saying the he or she wishes to conclude contracts with persons within that market. Sale and purchase of goods, services, labour or capital assets take place via contracts. Any restriction on free movement—understood to mean cross border economic activity—is therefore a restriction on the formation of contracts between domestic and foreign actors.[77]

He has the internal market in mind: the four economic freedoms in the Treaty, and how the CJEU used these four freedoms to shape and influence our understanding of private law. A similar statement could easily be made with regard to the EU Common Commercial Policy (CCP) and the General Agreement on Tariffs and Trade (GATT)/World Trade Organization (WTO) rules. Behind most of the cases pending before the CJEU, internally (internal market) and externally (CCP), as well as before the Dispute Settlement Body and the Appellate Body (AB), there is a contract. There are parties to a contract who are barred from access to the internal market, to the global market, equated here with the market composed of the members of GATT/WTO. Regulations might prevent parties from fulfilling their contractual obligations, thereby affecting the validity of the contract and its enforceability. The party who is denied access might invoke remedies, to terminate the contract, to be relieved from payment and delivery, or to claim compensation.

The EU and the GATT share the view that private law conflicts about access must be given a twist towards statutory barriers in order to bring the case before the CJEU and DSB/AB. A well-known example—though again not analysed from the private law perspective—is the conflict about the 'dollar bananas', which involved national courts, constitutional courts, the CJEU, and the GATT/WTO.[78] Before the CJEU, private parties can use the preliminary reference procedure, but this does mean that they no longer have to overcome the existing hurdle of the lack of horizontal direct effect of primary EU law. A barrier to trade enshrined in statutory regulation is needed. Within GATT/WTO, private parties have no right to access DSB/AB; they need to convince their home states to act on their behalf. The decisions taken by these bodies will usually not reveal the private law dimension

[77] Davies 'Freedom of Contract and the Horizontal Effect of Free Movement Law', in S. Weatherill and D. Leczykiewicz (eds), *The Involvement of EU Law in Private Law Relationships* (2013) 53.

[78] For a short summary of a complicated story: A. Shah, 'The Banana Trade War', Global Issues (2010), available at <http://www.globalissues.org/article/63/the-banana-trade-war>.

behind the case. They are discussed as trade law problems dealing with the tension of market freedom versus the legitimacy of national or regional regulation narrowing or limiting trade. The private law dimension is lost and can only be excavated by looking into the facts of the case and reconstructing the ups (the litigation from the national to the supranational) and the downs (how the decision by the CJEU and or DSB/AB is re-translated into the national legal system). Some research has been done on the impact of primary EU law on private law,[79] though most of the research is outdated. I am not aware of any research undertaken to investigate systematically the relationship between international trade law (GATT/WTO) and private law/contract law.

If we look into the relationship between regulatory private law and trade law, standards, again, play a key role: standards on quality of products and services, standards on health and safety, standards creeping into on all sorts of sectorial services, telecoms, energy, and financial services, and, last but not least, behavioural standards. There are two ways to look at the role and function of standards which interconnect private law and trade law. Considering traditional private law, standards might play a role in the enforcement of contracts and in the benchmark that triggers liability. From a regulatory private law perspective, the question is whether and to what extent the rules on regulated markets (to remain with that example) comply with the EU CCP, the WTO Agreements on Technical Barriers to Trade (TBS) and Sanitary and Phytosanitary Measures (SPS) and sectoral agreements inside or outside the GATT/WTO, or whether they can be justified via public policy concerns.[80] Recall the so-called hormone conflict or the genetically modified organisms (GMO) conflict between the US and the EU.[81] Bringing both areas of law together, one should hasten to add, does not mean separating the two from each other, that is to let the local private law dimension be decided internationally via arbitration, and the public law dimension before European courts and the DSB/AB. Instead, a holistic perspective is indispensable, one which combines the origin of the conflict (the contract) with the decision on the compatibility of trade restrictions with the market freedoms of supranational and transnational fora, upwards from the conflict to the international fora and downwards again to the decision taken by national courts or by international arbitration bodies.

[79] E. Steindorff, *EG-Vertrag und Privatrecht* (1996);C. Schmidt, *Die Instrumentalisierung des Privatrechts durch die Europäische Union* (2010); S. Grundmann, *Europäisches Schuldvertragsrecht* (1999); A. Hartkamp, *European Law and National Private Law* (2012). Carla Sieburgh and I have a project underway which is trying to shed light on six different areas of EU law.

[80] In Case C-122/95, *Federal Republic of Germany v. Council of the European Union*, [1998] ECR I-973, the Court makes a distinction between discrimination between EU traders (not allowed) and discrimination between traders which simply reflects the discrimination between EU and non-EU countries (allowed), at para 56: 'there is no general principle of Community law obliging the Community, in its external relations, to accord third countries equal treatment in all respects'.

[81] There is abundant literature on the topic, A. Bletschacher, '"Continued Suspension of Concessions"; "EC-Biotech" and the Proceduralisation of SPS Issues' (PhD University of Bamberg, 2015); M. Weimar, *Constitutionalising EU Administrative Risk Governance—A Case Study of GMO Authorisations* (forthcoming 2015).

2

A Triple Braid

Interactions between International Law, EU Law, and Private Law

Marise Cremona

1. An Evolution in Competence and in Practice

This chapter sets out to provide a context for the following chapters by tracing the interlocking relations which are at the heart of this book: between the EU, its Member States, and international legal regimes; between EU private law (both traditional and regulatory), the international treaties of the Member States, and the EU's external treaty law. These different legal sources each have their own dynamic and have evolved over time. Here we are interested in the way that they interact with each other to create the dynamic which this book seeks to explore: the increasing role of the EU in the international dimension of private law—including international regulatory private law—and the corresponding impact this has on 'domestic' (national and EU) private law. The approach of this chapter is conceptual rather than substantive: we will explore the interactions between these legal sources from two different perspectives. The first demonstrates the evolution of practice and law over time so as to gain an understanding of the genesis of the rather complex picture we now see. The second addresses the legal principles handling the relationships and conflict situations which have emerged in practice. This will give an idea of the legal tools available to handle the more specific procedural and substantive issues which will be explored in subsequent chapters.

In this first section, we will adopt a bird's-eye view of the way that the relationships between private law, international law, the Member States, and the EU have developed over time. We can trace three evolutionary stages, each representing a different axis in the relations between the EU and its Member States, between private law and EU external relations law, and between EU law and international law. These three stages have succeeded but not replaced each other, and are each part of the current multi-level structure.

In the first stage, the axis *Member States–private law–international law* is to the fore. Historically, the international fora for the development of traditional private international law have been the Hague Conference on private international law (founded in 1893) and the Council of Europe (founded in 1949), not the EU. These are classic intergovernmental organizations working through international conventions. The EU Member States have over the years been active in these organizations and have helped to create a substantial body of international treaty law in the field of private law (private international law). To these fora we may add other international bodies which have structured the development of international regulatory private law, including, for example, the World Intellectual Property Organisation (WIPO) and the Bretton Woods system.

The EU enters the picture during this phase, but not as an international actor or even as legislator. We see the emergence within the EU framework of the Brussels Convention on Jurisdiction and Enforcement of Judgments in Civil and Commercial Matters, an intra-EU Convention concluded between the six (at the time) European Economic Community (EEC) Member States as early as 1968.[1] This was an international law instrument, but with strong links to the EU: the parties define themselves as the 'High Contracting Parties to the Treaty establishing the European Economic Community', there is a reference to Article 220 EEC in the Convention preamble, and the Court of Justice was granted jurisdiction to interpret the Convention by a 1971 Protocol.[2] The Brussels Convention itself expanded with the enlargement of the Community, but in addition the regime it established developed an external dimension with the extension of the Brussels regime to some third countries (members of the European Free Trade Association (EFTA)) through the Lugano Convention in 1988.[3]

Here then we see the Member States' engagement with private law through classic international legal instruments. The EU is rather in the background, as the context within which some States come together to develop regional arrangements but still within the framework of international law. Nevertheless its presence is felt, notably in the emergence of a specific private international law regime for EU Member States, thereby creating a distinction between EU and non-EU States.

In the second stage, the focus is on the dimension *EU–private law–EU law*. Here the EU moves more clearly into the picture, enacting private law instruments at an internal level and bringing private law firmly within the scope of EU legislative and regulatory activity. These developments include the adoption of consumer protection directives from the 1980s onwards,[4] the transformation of the Brussels

[1] 1968 Brussels Convention on jurisdiction and the enforcement of judgments in civil and commercial matters, OJ 1972 L 299/32. The use of such international conventions between the Member States in fields which were not (then) envisaged as falling within the scope of EEC activity, was foreseen in Art. 220 EEC.

[2] On the debate concerning the status in EU law of these Art. 220 EEC/Art. 293 EC conventions, see R. Schütze, *Foreign Affairs and the EU Constitution* (2014), at 146–150.

[3] Lugano Convention on jurisdiction and the enforcement of judgments in civil and commercial matters, concluded between the EU Member States and the then EFTA States Austria, Finland, Iceland, Norway, Sweden, and Switzerland, OJ 1988 L 319/9.

[4] For example, Council Directive 85/374/EEC on liability for defective products, OJ 1985 L 210/29; Council Directive 93/13/EEC on unfair terms in consumer contracts, OJ 1993 L 95/29; Directive 99/44/EC on consumer sales, OJ 1999 L 171/12; Directive 2011/83/EU on consumer rights, OJ 2011 L 304/64.

Convention into a regulation in 2001,[5] the adoption of the Rome I and Rome II Regulations[6] as well as other regulations on private international law,[7] and the use of the EU's regulatory competence in relation to services and establishment.[8] In a number of instances, the EU's internal legislation recognizes the relevance of, and makes express reference to, existing international regimes developed by the Member States, either to defer to an international instrument or, conversely, to give precedence to the internal EU regime. Article 71(1) of the Brussels I Regulation, for example, provides: '[t]his Regulation shall not affect any conventions to which the Member States are parties and which in relation to particular matters, govern jurisdiction or the recognition or enforcement of judgments.' The rationale for this, as explained in the Preamble, was 'respect for international commitments entered into by the Member States'.[9] Regulation 2201/2003, which has a close relationship with the 1980 Hague Convention on the civil aspects of international child abduction,[10] provides that in relations between Member States, the Regulation shall take precedence over (inter alia) the Hague Convention; however, in matters not governed by the Regulation, the Hague Convention will continue to apply between the Member States.[11] According to AG Jääskinen, for certain issues '[t]he legislature has therefore chosen to refer to the provisions of an existing instrument of public international law rather than adopt provisions of European Union law concerning the same matters.'[12] In other cases, an international instrument may itself make provision for the application of EU internal law as between the Member States of the EU in matters falling within its scope.[13]

The international relations system of the EU has thus inherited a network of pre-existing treaty relationships entered into by the Member States. It has in some cases incorporated these into the EU system; it has built on them and found ways to take them into account. In this sense it is open to the international law obligations of its Member States, precisely because they are not only 'States' but '*Member* States'. This openness, however, is not entirely open-ended nor is it unconditional.

[5] Regulation 44/2001, known as the Brussels I Regulation, OJ 2001 L 12/1.

[6] Regulation 593/2008/EC on the law applicable to contractual obligations (Rome I) OJ 2008 L 177/6; Regulation 864/2007/EC on the law applicable to non-contractual obligations (Rome II) OJ 2007 L 199/40.

[7] For example, Council Regulation 4/2009/EC on jurisdiction, applicable law, recognition and enforcement of decisions, and cooperation in matters relating to maintenance obligations, OJ 2009 L 7/1.

[8] For example, in the setting of minimum prudential standards for credit institutions.

[9] Art. 71 and the preambular statement are both retained in the replacement Regulation 1215/ 2012, OJ 2012 L 351/1.

[10] Council Regulation 2201/2003/EC concerning jurisdiction and the recognition and enforcement of judgments in matrimonial matters, OJ 2003 L 338/1. According to the CJEU, the 1980 Convention and Regulation 2201/2003 form 'a unitary body of rules which applies to the procedures for returning children who have been wrongfully removed within the EU,' Opinion 1/13 of 14 October 2014, not yet published, para. 78; see further *infra*.

[11] Council Regulation 2201/2003/EC, *supra* note 10, Arts 60 and 62.

[12] View of Advocate General Jääskinen in Case C-400/10 PPU, *J. McB.v. L. E*, [2010] ECR I-8965, para. 40.

[13] See e.g. the Convention on Choice of Court Agreements 2005, Art. 26(6). On such clauses, see further *infra*.

The EU (and its Court) has itself derived a series of mechanisms and conditions which may be applied to these Member State treaty commitments, and it has established the framework for their recognition by, and sometimes entry into, the EU legal system. These mechanisms, articulating the relationship between the international obligations of Member States and EU law, will be explored further in the following sections of this chapter.

Then, in a third stage, and alongside the internal legislative activity of the EU, we see the emergence of the axis *EU–external relations–international law*. The EU moves into the international arena, concluding international agreements itself on the basis of different sources of competence, both express and implied. Initial steps in developing a strategy on the external dimension of the Area of Freedom, Security and Justice were taken in the follow-up to the 2004 Hague Programme.[14] In 2005, the Council adopted a strategy paper on the global dimension of Justice and Home Affairs,[15] and this was followed by strategies specifically on civil justice cooperation.[16] These documents do not contain detailed programmes of action but they indicate the EU's priorities. They emphasize: (i) the link between external action and the exercise of competence internally: cooperation with third countries in the field of judicial cooperation in civil matters 'should focus on the areas covered by EC legislation';[17] (ii) the importance of international negotiations at multilateral level, especially in the context of the Hague Conference on Private International Law; (iii) that bilateral cooperation should prioritize the candidate and potential candidate states, the Lugano states,[18] and other neighbourhood states.

According to Article 216(1) TFEU, the EU has the competence to conclude international agreements 'where the Treaties so provide or where the conclusion of an agreement is necessary in order to achieve, within the framework of the Union's policies, one of the objectives referred to in the Treaties, or is provided for in a legally binding Union act or is likely to affect common rules or alter their scope'. Let us briefly examine these possibilities for founding external competence in turn.

The Treaty provision on judicial cooperation in civil matters, Article 81 TFEU, does not expressly refer to external action. Nevertheless, other express external competences may provide the basis for external action in the field of private law. These include, first, the competence to conclude association agreements and other types of cooperation, partnership, and development agreements.[19] Increasingly, such agreements include clauses on the provision of services, on consumer protection, and on judicial cooperation on civil matters.[20]

[14] *The Hague Programme: Strengthening Freedom, Security and Justice in the European Union*, Doc. 16054/04 JAI 559.

[15] *A Strategy for the External Dimension of JHA: Global Freedom, Security and Justice*, Doc. 5003/1/06 REV 1 JAI 1 RELEX 1.

[16] Aspects of judicial cooperation in civil matters in the framework of the *Strategy for the External Dimension of JHA: Global Freedom, Security and Justice*, 11 April 2006, Doc. 8140/06 JUSTCIV 93, RELEX 228, JAI 177. *External Relations Strategy in the Field of Judicial Cooperation in Civil Matters*, 7 May 2008, Doc. 9045/08, JUSTCIV 90, RELEX 275, JAI 217.

[17] Aspects of judicial cooperation in civil matters, *supra* note 16, para. 6.

[18] That is, Iceland, Norway, Switzerland.

[19] Arts 209, 212, and 217 TFEU.

[20] For example, the Association Agreement with Ukraine, which provides in Art. 24(2): 'The Parties agree to facilitate further EU–Ukraine judicial cooperation in civil matters on the basis of

Second, the EU's competence over the common commercial policy covers measures and agreements relating to trade in services (Article 207 TFEU), by which is meant measures which are 'essentially intended to promote, facilitate or govern trade and [have] direct and immediate effects on trade', and which relate to 'trade with non-member countries, not to trade in the internal market'.[21] In case C-137/12 *Commission v. Council*, the Court found that an international agreement that was intended to extend to non-EU states the regime established in Directive 98/84/EC for the protection of conditional access broadcasting rights, fell within the common commercial policy.[22] The common commercial policy may therefore be used as a basis for external action which is concerned with the regulatory aspects of trade in services with third countries. Furthermore, since the coming into force of the Lisbon Treaty, the common commercial policy also includes foreign direct investment, covering not only market access issues but also measures concerning post-establishment treatment of investment and thus significant regulatory aspects of international trade.[23]

According to Article 216(1) TFEU, the EU's treaty-making power may be derived not only from an express provision in the Treaties themselves, but also from a provision in a 'legally binding Union act'. As an example of such a provision we may take Directive 2013/36/EU on the prudential supervision of credit institutions, which contains a title on relations with third countries, including provision for the conclusion of international agreements on market access, and cooperation with the supervisory authorities of third countries.[24]

Article 216(1) TFEU goes on to specify a treaty-making power in cases 'where the conclusion of an agreement is necessary in order to achieve, within the framework of the Union's policies, one of the objectives referred to in the Treaties'. An example might be the accession of the European Community (EC) (as it then was) to the Hague Conference on private international law (HCCH). This was based on Article 61(c) EC, which enabled the Council to adopt 'measures in the field of judicial cooperation in civil matters', but which did not refer explicitly to external action. According to the preamble of the Decision on accession:

the applicable multilateral legal instruments, especially the Conventions of the Hague Conference on Private International Law in the field of international Legal Cooperation and Litigation as well as the Protection of Children.' The agreement also contains a chapter on cooperation in relation to consumer protection.

[21] Case C-137/12 *Commission v. Council*, judgment of 22 October 2013, not yet published, paras 56–57.

[22] Case C-137/12 *Commission v. Council*, *supra* note 21, paras 64–65.

[23] On the scope of the EU's competence over foreign direct investment, see Karl, 'The Competence for Foreign Direct Investment—New Powers for the EU', 5 *Journal of World Investment and Trade* (2004) 413; Leczykiewicz, 'Common Commercial Policy: The Expanding Competence of the European Union in the Area of International Trade', 6 *German Law Journal* (2005) 1673; Dimopoulos, 'The Common Commercial Policy After Lisbon: Establishing Parallelism Between Internal and External Economic Policy', 4 *Croatian Yearbook of European Law and Policy* (2008) 102.

[24] Directive 2013/36/EU on access to the activity of credit institutions and the prudential supervision of credit institutions and investment firms, OJ 2013 L 176/338, Arts 47–48.

Since the entry into force of the Treaty of Amsterdam, the Community has competence to adopt measures in the field of judicial cooperation in civil matters having cross-border implications insofar as necessary for the proper functioning of the internal market. The Community has exerted this competence by adopting a number of instruments, many of which coincide, partially or fully, with the areas of work of the HCCH. It is essential that the Community be granted a status that corresponds to its new role as a major international player in the field of civil judicial cooperation and that it be able to exercise its external competence by participating as a full member in the negotiations of conventions by the HCCH in areas of its competence.[25]

Here we see the need for the Community to be an 'international player', linked to its exercise of 'internal' competence in the field of civil judicial cooperation. We remember the strategic decision that the EU should focus its external action on areas covered by EU legislation.[26]

This link to internal legislation is also made by Article 216(1) TFEU when it refers to the EU's power to conclude an agreement which 'is likely to affect common rules or alter their scope'. Indeed, in such cases, following Article 3(2) TFEU, the EU's external power may even be exclusive.[27] Notwithstanding the very similar wording between Article 216(1) and Article 3(2) TFEU, the approach of the Court to the two questions (the existence of competence and its possible exclusive character) is rather different. We may illustrate this by looking at the Court's Opinion on the EU's competence in relation to the 1980 Hague Convention on civil aspects of international child abduction. As regards the existence of EU competence, the Court's reasoning takes the form of a simple assertion, based on the identification of an internal power, and the fact that that power has been exercised:

[T]he 1980 Hague Convention concerns civil cooperation where children are moved across borders. The Convention thus falls within the area of family law with cross-border implications in which the EU has internal competence under Article 81(3) TFEU. Moreover, the EU has exercised that competence by adopting Regulation No 2201/2003. In those circumstances, the EU has external competence in the area which forms the subject-matter of the Convention.[28]

However, when it comes to the question of whether the EU's external competence is exclusive, the Court embarks on a detailed examination of both the Regulation and the Convention in order to determine whether the latter may 'affect' or 'alter the scope' of the common rules established in the Regulation.[29]

Thus, in addition to competence based on express external policy competences, we may say that when the Union exercises its internal regulatory competence over the provision of services, or adopts legislation in the field of private international

[25] Council Decision 2006/719/EC on the accession of the Community to the Hague Conference on Private International Law OJ, 2006 L 297/1. The European Community became a full member of the Hague Conference on 3 April 2007.

[26] See *supra* note 17.

[27] According to Art. 3(2) TFEU, the EU shall have exclusive competence for the conclusion of an international agreement 'in so far as its conclusion may affect common rules or alter their scope'.

[28] Opinion 1/13, *supra* note 10, para. 68. See also Opinion 1/03, [2006] ECR I-1145, para. 134.

[29] See further *infra*.

law, this may provide a basis (not necessarily exclusive) for external action.[30] An increasing use of these powers, both internal and external, in fields hitherto dominated by Member States' private law raises questions over the relationship between the sources of law produced during each of these three stages: the Member States' international obligations, the EU's internal law, and the EU's own international action. It is the principles governing these relationships to which we will now turn.

2. The Interaction between Legal Norms

We now move to consider the interaction between these three sources of private law regulation: internal EU law, and the international obligations of the Member States and of the EU. The aim is not to be comprehensive but instead to suggest where some of the points of conflict may lie and what mechanisms have been developed to address them, so as to provide a context for the chapters that follow.

A. EU Internal Law and EU International Obligations

As already mentioned, the EU is now active both internally and externally in matters concerning international and regulatory private law. What are the principles which govern the relationship between the instruments that result from this internal and external action? This is the issue that we will briefly address in this section.

International agreements that are concluded by the Union bind both the Union's institutions and its Member States (Article 216(2) TFEU). We will touch on the consequences for the Member States in the next section of this chapter. Here we will examine what this means for the EU. We should first note that although Article 216(2) TFEU may be said to be an expression of *pacta sunt servanda*, the binding nature of international agreements to which the EU is a party flows from international law itself and not from Article 216(2). This provision establishes the effects of such agreements within EU constitutional law.

According to a now-hallowed expression of the Court of Justice, such agreements form an integral part of Union law.[31] The act of conclusion (now always a decision of the Council under Article 218(6) TFEU, subject to varying degrees of involvement of the European Parliament) itself incorporates the agreement into Union law. As such, the agreement may be the subject of preliminary ruling requests from national courts and interpreted by the Court of Justice. The decision concluding the agreement is subject to the possibility of judicial review and even annulment, although this will not affect the binding quality of the agreement in international law.[32] Such judicial review may be based on breach of a procedural

[30] For example, see Council Decision 2014/887/EU on the approval, on behalf of the European Union, of the Hague Convention of 30 June 2005 on Choice of Court Agreements, OJ 2014 L 353/5.

[31] Case 181/73, *R & V Haegeman v. Belgian State*, [1974] ECR 449.

[32] For examples of cases where a decision concluding an international agreement has been annulled, see case C-327/91, *France v. Commission*, [1994] ECR I-3641; Case C-122/95, *Germany v. Council*,

requirement in concluding the agreement, on incorrect legal basis, or lack of competence. The Court may also review the compatibility of the substantive provisions of the international agreement with primary EU law (the Treaties, the Charter, and general principles of law including fundamental rights), and this possibility makes it clear that as far as the Union legal order is concerned, international agreements do not prevail over primary law.[33]

In contrast, an agreement concluded by the Union takes priority over EU secondary law. As the Court put it in *Intertanko*:

> It is clear from Article 300(7) EC [now Article 216(2) TFEU] that the Community institutions are bound by agreements concluded by the Community and, consequently, that those agreements have primacy over secondary Community legislation…It follows that the validity of a measure of secondary Community legislation may be affected by the fact that it is incompatible with such rules of international law.[34]

As the Court went on to say in the same case, however, the effect on the validity of secondary legislation is subject to two conditions. The first is that the Union is bound by the international agreement; this is clear in cases where the Union itself is a party to the agreement, and has been extended to cases of functional succession.[35] However, if the Union is *not* bound by the agreement, unless it can be argued that the agreement represents a codification of customary international law, it cannot affect the validity of EU secondary legislation.[36] The second condition is more difficult, both to justify and to satisfy:

> [T]he Court can examine the validity of Community legislation in the light of an international treaty only where the nature and the broad logic of the latter do not preclude this and, in addition, the treaty's provisions appear, as regards their content, to be unconditional and sufficiently precise.[37]

In *Intertanko* the Court found that the United Nations Convention on the Law of the Sea (UNCLOS) did not meet the 'nature and broad logic' condition on the grounds that 'UNCLOS does not establish rules intended to apply directly and immediately to individuals and to confer upon them rights or freedoms capable of being relied upon against states, irrespective of the attitude of the ship's flag

[1998] ECR I-973; Joined Cases C-317/04 and C-318/04, *European Parliament v. Council*, [2006] ECR I-4721; Case C-28/12, *Commission v. Council*, judgment of 28 April 2015.

[33] Joined Cases C-402/05 P and C-415/05 P, *Yassin Abdullah Kadi and Al Barakaat International Foundation v. Council and Commission*, [2008] ECR I-6351, para. 308. See also Case C-122/95, *Germany v. Council*, [1998] ECR I-973, para. 82. In order to forestall the difficulties caused where an agreement already concluded is found to be incompatible with EU primary law, the Treaty in Art. 218(11) TFEU establishes a system of prior control by the Court of Justice, on request from a Member State, the European Parliament, the Council, or the Commission.

[34] Case C-308/06, *Intertanko*, [2008] ECR I-4057, paras 42–43.

[35] See further *infra*.

[36] Case C-308/06, *Intertanko, supra* note 34, paras 46–50. Such an agreement may, however, have effects in different ways: see the discussion on Member State agreements in section 3 *infra*.

[37] Case C-308/06, *Intertanko, supra* note 34, para. 45. See also Case C-344/04, *R v. Department of Transport ex parte IATA and ELFAA*, [2006] ECR I-403, para. 39; Case C-366/10, *The Air Transport Association of America and Others*, [2011] ECR I-13755, paras 53–55.

state'.[38] This wording suggests that the Court is essentially applying a 'direct effect' test.[39] Such a test, based on the creation of individual rights, may seem justified where the challenge to the validity of EU secondary legislation comes via a preliminary reference from a national court and is thus being maintained by a private party to national court proceedings, as was the case in *Intertanko* itself and also in the *Air Transport Association of America* case. It is less obviously appropriate in the case of a direct action based on Article 263 TFEU brought by a Member State or a Union institution challenging the validity of secondary legislation for non-conformity with an international agreement binding the Union.[40]

Where the conditions for judicial review are not satisfied, the Court will nevertheless recognize the legal effect of international agreements binding the Union through an obligation of conforming interpretation:

> [T]he primacy of international agreements concluded by the Community over provisions of secondary Community legislation means that such provisions must, so far as is possible, be interpreted in a manner that is consistent with those agreements.[41]

Such questions may be raised in the context of regulatory private law, in particular where the Union, through its internal legislation, has chosen to impose stricter regulatory obligations than an existing international agreement (especially in cases where the international standards establish limits to liability), as private parties or industry associations seek to challenge the compatibility of the internal EU regulation with the international standards.

In *R v. Department of Transport ex parte IATA*,[42] for example, the International Air Transport Association and European Low Fares Airline Association challenged the validity of Regulation 261/2004/EC which establishes rules on compensation for air passengers in cases of denied boarding or long delays to flights. They argued, inter alia, that the Regulation was incompatible with the Montreal Convention, to which the EU is a party and which imposes limits on the liability of airlines in the case of actions for damages. Having first found that the relevant articles of the Montreal Convention meet the conditions mentioned above and therefore 'are among the rules in the light of which the Court reviews the legality of acts of the Community institutions',[43] the Court then interpreted the Convention and the Regulation in such a way as to ensure that there was no conflict between them. It found that the two instruments deal respectively with two different types of damage caused by flight delays. The Convention deals with (and limits) compensation

[38] Case C-308/06, *Intertanko, supra* note 34, para. 64.

[39] In a discussion of the same issue in Case C-366/10, *Air Transport Association of America, supra* note 37, at para. 55 the Court cites a summary of the criteria for the direct effect of an international agreement given in Case C-240/09 *Lesoochranárske zoskupenie*, [2011] ECR I-1255, para. 44.

[40] See Case C-377/98, *Netherlands v. Council*, [2001] ECR I-7079, paras 53–54. The WTO Agreements, whatever the source of the challenge, have been resolutely declared many times as 'not in principle, having regard to their nature and structure, among the rules in the light of which the Court is to review the lawfulness of measures adopted by the Community institutions'. Ibid., para. 52.

[41] Case C-61/94, *Commission v. Germany*, [1996] ECR I-3989, para. 52.

[42] Case C-344/04, *IATA and ELFAA, supra* note 37.

[43] Ibid., para. 39.

for 'individual damage, inherent in the reason for travelling, redress for which requires a case-by-case assessment of the extent of the damage caused and can consequently only be the subject of compensation granted subsequently on an individual basis'.[44] The Regulation, on the other hand, deals with damage from delay 'that is almost identical for every passenger, redress for which may take the form of standardized and immediate assistance or care for everybody concerned, through the provision, for example, of refreshments, meals and accommodation'.[45] The Court found nothing in the Convention suggesting that compensation for damage of the second kind should be limited or excluded: '[t]he system prescribed in Article 6 [of the Regulation] simply operates at an earlier stage than the system which results from the Montreal Convention.'[46] Thus the two regulatory systems complemented each other rather than being in conflict.[47]

In *Air Transport Association of America*, the Court was faced with a challenge to the EU's Directive 2008/101/EC which amends the EU's greenhouse gas emission trading scheme to include aviation.[48] It held that it could not review the legality of the Directive on the basis of either the Chicago Convention (which is not binding on the EU) or the Kyoto Protocol (although binding on the EU, the provision relating to aircraft emissions cannot in the view of the Court 'be considered to be unconditional and sufficiently precise so as to confer on individuals the right to rely on it in legal proceedings in order to contest the validity of Directive 2008/101').[49] Review on the basis of the 'Open Skies' agreement between the EU and the US, on the other hand, was possible, the Court then concluding that the emissions trading scheme was non-discriminatory and did not have the effect of imposing taxes, duties, or charges prohibited by the agreement. Again, therefore, the Court interpreted EU legislation so that it did not conflict with the regulatory regime established by an international agreement.

B. EU International Agreements and Member State International Action

As already mentioned, under Article 216(2) TFEU international agreements concluded by the Union are binding on the Member States as a matter of EU law. Compliance with such agreements thus becomes a matter of EU legal obligation and subject to the possibility of enforcement actions brought by the Commission,[50] as well as preliminary references designed to ascertain whether a provision of a Union agreement is directly effective and may be relied on by individuals against

[44] Ibid., para. 43. [45] Ibid., para. 43. [46] Ibid., para. 46.

[47] For a similar style of reasoning in a case where the EU was not a party to the international Convention in question, and where the question was whether internal EU legislation had replaced the Convention as far as the Member States are concerned, see Case C-301/08, *Bogiatzi v. Deutscher Luftpool and Others*, [2009] ECR I-10185, discussed *infra* at note 78.

[48] Case C-366/10, *Air Transport Association of America, supra* note 37; Directive 2008/101/EC OJ 2009 L 8/3.

[49] Case C-366/10, *Air Transport Association of America, supra* note 37, para. 77.

[50] Case C-61/94, *Commission v. Germany, supra* note 41.

Member State authorities.[51] Where the agreement is mixed (i.e. the Union and Member States are parties alongside each other), this may require analysis of the degree to which the agreement falls within the scope of Union law.[52]

The conclusion of international agreements by the Union, like the enactment of internal legislation, also affects the external competence of the Member States. Article 3(2) TFEU establishes that the Union's competence to conclude an international agreement will be exclusive 'insofar as its conclusion may affect common rules or alter their scope', and such 'common rules' may be established by way of an international agreement as well as through internal legislation,[53] or indeed by a combination of the two.[54] As the Union *acquis* (both internal and external) expands we should therefore expect to see a gradual diminution of the international role of the Member States, and to some degree this process is indeed visible.[55] However, this picture should be nuanced; in practice we find that the Member States have a continuing presence internationally in the private law sphere. This results from several factors, including: the continuing presence—and importance—of mixed agreements;[56] cases in which the Member States are authorized to maintain in place or to conclude new international obligations notwithstanding exclusive EU competence;[57] and cases where the EU is not able to become a party to the agreement and the Member States must act on its behalf.[58]

In all these cases the Member States continue to act, but their international action is subject to their obligations as EU Member States. This means that their

[51] Case C-265/03, *Simutenkov*, [2005] ECR I-2579; Case C-228/06, *Soysal*, [2009] ECR I-01031; Case C-240/09, *Lesoochranárske zoskupenie VLK v. Ministerstvo životného prostredia Slovenskej republiky*, [2011] ECR I-1255.

[52] Case C-13/00, *Commission v. Ireland*, [2002] ECR I-2943; Case C-239/03, *Commission v. France*, [2004] ECR I-9325; Case C-431/05, *Merck Genéricos v. Merck & Co. Inc. and Merck Sharp & Dohme L^{da}*, [2007] ECR I-7001. Note that as far as the TRIPS is concerned (the subject of the last-mentioned case), the entire agreement has now been held to fall within the scope of Union law as a result of the extension of the EU's common commercial policy by the Lisbon Treaty: Case C-414/11, *Daiichi Sankyo*, judgment 18 July 2013.

[53] Opinion 1/03, *supra* note 28.

[54] For an example of the latter, see Opinion 1/13 discussed *supra* at note 98.

[55] See for example Case C-114/12, *Commission v. Council*, judgment of 4 September 2014, not yet published; Case C-399/12, *Germany v. Council*, judgment of 7 October 2014, not yet published (discussed *infra* at note 94).

[56] For example, the Kyoto Protocol to the United Nations Framework Convention on Climate Change, concluded for the Union by Decision 2002/358/EC, OJ 2002 L 130/1.

[57] Regulation 662/2009/EC on the negotiation and conclusion of agreements between Member States and third countries on the law applicable to contractual and non-contractual obligations, OJ 2009 L 200/25; Regulation 664/2009/EC on the negotiation and conclusion of agreements between Member States and third countries concerning jurisdiction, recognition, and enforcement of judgments and decisions in matrimonial matters, OJ 2009 L 200/46; Regulation 1219/2012/EU establishing transitional arrangements for bilateral investment agreements between Member States and third countries, OJ 2012 L 351/40.

[58] For example, Council Decision 2004/246/EC authorizing the Member States to sign, ratify or accede to, in the interest of the European Community, the Protocol of 2003 to the International Convention on the Establishment of an International Fund for Compensation for Oil Pollution Damage of 1992, OJ 2004 L 78/22, discussed in Case C-188/07, *Commune de Mesquer v. Total*, *infra* note 100. See also the 1980 Hague Convention on Civil Aspects of International Child Abduction, discussed in Opinion 1/13, *infra* note 98.

domestic law, enacted to implement an international agreement, must comply with EU law and that when participating in the institutional structures responsible for the ongoing management of such agreements, they participate *as Member States* and need to consider their obligation to further the interests and objectives of the Union.[59] As we shall see in the next section of this chapter, their international agreements may interact closely with EU law.

C. Member States' International Obligations and Internal EU Law

1. Member State Treaties which Become Binding on the EU

Perhaps the best-known but least common phenomenon is what is often called functional succession: cases where it has been held that the EU has 'taken over' the obligations of the Member States under a treaty, and the EU thus becomes bound (as a matter of EU law) by the treaty, albeit not formally a contracting party. The most well-known example was the General Agreement on Tariffs and Trade (GATT),[60] and although there are others,[61] in most cases where the argument has been tried it has not succeeded.[62] The conditions appear to be (i) that all Member States are party to the treaty; (ii) that it covers a field where the EU has acquired (probably exclusive) competence (a 'full transfer of powers' the Court of Justice called it in *Intertanko*);[63] and (iii) that the EU has assumed responsibility for implementing the obligations arising from the treaty in question and this role is accepted by both Member States and third state treaty partners. The logic is that with the assumption and exercise of competence in the field covered by the Member State treaty comes the assumption of an obligation to implement those existing international obligations of the Member States. In such cases the international law obligation to implement the treaty remains with the Member States; however, the EU is regarded as also bound *as a matter of EU law* and as a corollary there is *an EU obligation* (as well as an international law obligation) on the Member States to comply with the treaty.[64]

[59] See Case C-246/07, *Commission v. Sweden*, [2010] ECR I-3317 for a case involving shared competence; and Case C-45/07, *Commission v. Greece*, [2009] I-701 and Case C-399/12, *Germany v. Council*, judgment of 7 October 2014, not yet published, for cases where the Court held that competence was exclusive.

[60] Cases 22–24/72, *International Fruit Company*, [1972] ECR 1219.

[61] For example, the 1950 Convention on customs nomenclature: Case 38/75, *Nederlandse Spoorwegen*, [1975] ECR 1439.

[62] For example, Case C-308/06, *Intertanko, supra* note 34 on Marpol; Case C-301/08, *Bogiatzi v. Deutscher Luftpool and Others, supra* note 47, on the Warsaw Convention; Case C-366/10, *Air Transport Association of America, supra* note 37, paras 57–71 on the Chicago Convention.

[63] Case C-308/06 *Intertanko, supra* note 34, para. 49.

[64] On the EU law obligation on Member States to comply with treaties which are binding on the EU, see Case C-61/94, *Commission v. Germany, supra* note 41.

2. Treaties not Directly Binding the EU

Where, as is more normally the case, a Member State treaty is not binding on the EU through the doctrine of functional succession, it is in itself worth remarking that the EU legal system takes notice of such treaties at all. In fact it has developed different modes of interaction with such treaties, ranging from separation and avoidance to conditional application or domestication. The result is a degree of apparent porousness of the EU legal order to these sources of international law that are not formally binding on the EU, but in all these interactions we see the EU legal system (often via the Court of Justice) seeking to preserve its own integrity, and achieving this in different ways.

Obligations towards third states arising under agreements concluded by a Member State before accession to the EU are to some extent protected by Article 351 TFEU.[65] This provision acts as a justification for the Member State, allowing it to set aside an EU law obligation where necessary to fulfil an obligation under a prior treaty with a third state. However, its scope of operation is limited: the Member State treaty does not in any sense become binding on the EU,[66] nor is the Member State entitled to act in breach of EU law so as to assert its rights under the prior treaty,[67] nor does Article 351 apply to Member States' *inter se* obligations under prior agreements.[68] In addition, under the *Kadi* case law, Article 351 does not justify the setting aside of the fundamental principles of EU law.[69] In any case, such setting aside of EU law obligations is only temporary: the Member States are under an obligation to remove any incompatibilities (and thus restore the primacy of EU law), including by denunciation of the agreement if necessary,[70] and this obligation may arise where the incompatibility is not actual but potential.[71]

An international agreement between Member States may apply unless and until its provisions are superseded by EU law. If there is a conflict, the Member States will be bound by the primacy of EU law. In case 10/61 *Commission v. Italy*, the Court held that '[i]n matters governed by the EEC Treaty, that Treaty takes precedence over agreements concluded between Member States before its entry into force, including agreements made within the framework of GATT.'[72] In *Van Gend en Loos* the Court applied the same principle to a *later* international agreement.[73]

[65] Art. 351 TFEU applies to treaties between a Member State and a third state concluded before the entry into force of the Treaty of Rome (1 January 1958), or before the date of accession of the Member State in question.

[66] Case C-366/10, *Air Transport Association of America, supra* note 37, para. 61.

[67] Case C-170/98, *Commission v. Belgium*, [1999] ECR I-5493; Case C-62/98, *Commission v. Portugal*, [2000] ECR I-5171; Case C-84/98, *Commission v. Portugal*, [2000] ECR I-5215.

[68] Case C-301/08, *Bogiatzi v. Deutscher Luftpool and Others, supra* note 47, paras 18–19.

[69] Joined Cases C-402/05 P and C-415/05 P, *Kadi and Al Barakaat, supra* note 33, para. 304.

[70] Art. 351(2) TFEU.

[71] Case C-205/06, *Commission v. Austria* (BITS), [2009] ECR I-1301; Case C-249/06, *Commission v. Sweden* (BITS), [2009] ECR I-1335; Case C-118/07, *Commission v. Finland* (BITS), [2009] ECR I-10889.

[72] Case 10/61, *Commission v. Italy Republic*, [1962] ECR 1 (English Special Edition).

[73] Case 26/62, *NV Algemene Transport- en Expeditie Onderneming van Gend & Loos v. Netherlands Inland Revenue Administration*, [1963] ECR 1 (English Special Edition).

The primacy of EU law with respect to the Member States' international commitments towards third countries was initially more uncertain,[74] but it is now established as a matter of EU law.[75] In one of the best-known examples, the Court of Justice found that several Member States had infringed EU rules on rights of establishment and non-discrimination between EU nationals by concluding non-compliant bilateral 'Open Skies' agreements.[76] This application of primacy, it should be stressed, does not depend on a finding of exclusive competence or pre-emption. The Member States are operating in fields in which they retain competence, such as double tax treaties. They are nevertheless required to ensure that in so doing they comply with EU law, including the principle of non-discrimination. That being the case, it will sometimes be necessary to determine the extent to which EU law coincides with, or overlaps, the provisions of a treaty concluded by the Member States. In *Bogiatzi*, for example, the Court was asked whether Article 29 of the Warsaw Convention, which establishes the limitation period for bringing claims against an air carrier, continues to apply to air travel between EU Member States, in the light of Regulation 2027/97 on air carrier liability. All the Member States are party to the Warsaw Convention but the EU is not a party. The Court started by finding that Article 307 EC (now Article 351 TFEU) did not apply in this case, since the rights of third states were not involved.[77] It then held that the doctrine of functional succession does not apply to the Warsaw Convention since, although the EU had adopted several pieces of relevant legislation, 'the Community has not assumed all the powers previously exercised by the Member States in the field to which the Warsaw Convention applies'.[78] Then the Court turned to the interpretation of Regulation 2027/97, which was designed to improve the protection of air passengers, in particular by raising the limits of liability set by the Convention. However, according to the Court, the Regulation did not entirely displace the Convention between the Member States, but did so only insofar as it laid down rules which were specifically intended to replace the Convention system; elsewhere the two were intended to operate as 'complementary and equivalent to each other'.[79] Since the Regulation did not deal with limitation periods, the Convention rules could apply.

In *West Tankers*, the scope of an EU Regulation and its impact on an international private law regime were also at issue.[80] The case involved the compatibility with Regulation 44/2001 (Brussels I) of an anti-suit injunction, intended to

[74] Schütze, 'Dual Federalism Constitutionalized: The Emergence of Exclusive Competences in the EC Legal Order', 32 *European Law Review* (2007) 3.

[75] See e.g. Case C-307/97, *Saint-Gobain ZN*, [1999] ECR I-6161 on double tax treaties; Case C-55/00, *Gottardo v. INPS*, [2002] ECR I-413, holding that a bilateral social security convention concluded by a Member State with a third country must be implemented in such a way as to comply with the principle of non-discrimination.

[76] Case C-476/98, *Commission v. Germany*, [2002] ECR I-9855, para. 149.

[77] See *supra* note 68.

[78] Case C-301/08, *Bogiatzi*, *supra* note 47, para. 32.

[79] Ibid., para. 43.

[80] Case C-185/07, *Allianz SpA and Generali Assicurazioni Generali SpA v. West Tankers Inc.*, [2009] ECR I-663.

enforce an arbitration agreement between the parties to a contract. The referring court (the House of Lords) suggested to the Court of Justice that 'since all arbitration matters fall outside the scope of Regulation No 44/2001, an injunction addressed to Allianz and Generali restraining them from having recourse to proceedings other than arbitration and from continuing proceedings before the Tribunale di Siracusa cannot infringe the regulation'.[81] The Court of Justice took a different approach. The Regulation's rules on jurisdiction do not apply to arbitration, but Member States must take account of the Regulation's objectives in applying their law on arbitration, including the possibility of an anti-suit injunction. More particularly, it is the court first seized (here the Tribunale di Siracusa) which should rule on its jurisdiction to hear the dispute, including the validity or applicability of an arbitration agreement, and this power must not be jeopardized by an anti-suit injunction granted by another court.[82] The Court noted that this approach was 'supported by' Article II(3) of the New York Convention on the Recognition and Enforcement of Foreign Arbitral Awards (to which the EU is not a party). The case is interesting here both for the emphasis placed on mutual trust between the Member States' legal systems as a basis for the internal EU regime, and as an example of the effects that EU law may have even on aspects of private law that seem at first sight to be outside its scope.[83]

These are the general principles. EU law keeps these Member State treaty commitments at arms' length; they may be permitted to continue but under conditions of compatibility, and any adverse effect on the Member States' EU law obligations is kept under strict control. This, however, is not the whole story. It may be the case that either the international agreement or EU law itself contains a provision which seeks to govern the relationship between them, through either 'disconnection' or 'connection' clauses.

3. Disconnection Clauses

One way of giving expression to the primacy of EU law for the Member States in their *inter se* relations is a so-called disconnection clause. In some cases, especially within the framework of the Council of Europe and where a multilateral convention covers a field already subject to EU law, it may include a clause whereby *as between the EU Member State parties* it is EU law rather than the convention that will apply. The Council of Europe Convention which was at issue in case C-137/12 *Commission v. Council*[84] contains such a clause:

> In their mutual relations, Parties which are members of the European Community shall apply Community rules and shall not therefore apply the rules arising from this

[81] Case C-185/07, *West Tankers, supra* note 80, para. 16. [82] Ibid., paras 29–30.

[83] Nevertheless, one should not see *West Tankers* as implying a general disregard for the exclusion of arbitration from Regulation 44/2001. In Case C-536/13, *Gazprom*, judgment of 13 May 2015, not yet published, paras 33–41, the Court distinguished *West Tankers*, holding that Regulation 44/2001 did not prevent the enforcement of an arbitral award by a national court, since in this case there would be no 'interference of a court of one Member State in the jurisdiction of the court of another Member State', nor would it put in question the mutual trust between Member State courts on which the Regulation is based.

[84] *Supra* note 21.

Convention except in so far as there is no Community rule governing the particular subject concerned.[85]

The effect is to regard intra-Member State relations as in some sense 'domestic' despite the fact that the Member States are participating in an international instrument. Indeed in case C-137/12 *Commission v. Council*, the presence of the disconnection clause was referred to by the Court to support its argument that the Convention itself was concerned with external, and not intra-EU, trade.[86] A standard Declaration on such clauses by the EU and its Member States seeks to assure the other Contracting Parties that the clause is not intended to affect their obligations towards non-EU parties: 'This clause is not aimed at reducing the rights or increasing the obligations of a non-European Union Party vis-à-vis the European Community/European Union and its Member States, inasmuch as the latter are also parties to this Convention.'[87]

Legally speaking, the disconnection clause has the following effects. First, it inserts into the international agreement itself recognition of the principle of primacy of EU law for the Member States; it thus removes the risk of a Member State facing a conflict between its international and its EU law obligations. Second, it operates automatically to ensure that EU law and not the international law rule will apply; this does not depend on the identification of a conflict between the two but is simply an automatic choice of law rule. The effect of the disconnection clause is thus to improve certainty and transparency; however, this is at the expense of the uniformity of application of the convention-based regime and will thus not be suited to all cases; as already mentioned, it tends to be used where the Convention regime closely matches the internal EU regime.

We have included disconnection clauses here in the context of Member State agreements. They may also be used in mixed agreements, to which the EU is party as well as the Member States.[88] In such cases, of course, the EU will be under an obligation to ensure that its own legal system complies with the convention; the disconnection clause will then preserve the application of EU law between the Member States, ensuring that insofar as there are EU rules in place, the convention provisions are applied in intra-Member State relations in a 'domesticated' or internalized form, via EU law, and not directly.

[85] European Convention on the Legal Protection of Services based on, or consisting of, Conditional Access, CETS No 178, 2001, Art. 11(4).

[86] Case C-137/12, *Commission v. Council, supra* note 21, para. 67: 'Article 11(4) of the Convention confirms that, since the approximation of the legislation of Member States in the field concerned has already been largely achieved by Directive 98/84, the primary objective of the Convention is not to improve the functioning of the internal market, but to extend legal protection of the relevant services beyond the territory of the European Union and thereby to promote international trade in those services.'

[87] Council of Europe Convention on Laundering, Search, Seizure and Confiscation of the Proceeds from Crime and on the Financing of Terrorism, CETS No. 198, 2005, declaration attached to Art. 52(4).

[88] CETS No. 198, *supra* note 87, is an example.

4. Connection Clauses

In other cases, and in an opposite direction, EU legislation may make an explicit *renvoi*, or 'connection' to an international convention.[89] There are instances where Member State treaties are effectively incorporated into EU law via reference in secondary legislation. For example, in the case of the Accord Européen sur les Transports Routiers (AETR), despite the Court's famous ruling on implied external competence, it was accepted that the Member States should conclude the agreement 'in the interest and on behalf of' the EU. This was followed by Regulation 2829/77 which was titled 'on the bringing into force' of the AETR and provided that the AETR would apply directly to the relevant types of international road transport operations:

> The European Agreement concerning the work of crews of vehicles engaged in international road transport (AETR) shall apply to international road transport operations to and/or from third countries which are contracting parties to that Agreement, or in transit through such countries.[90]

The same is true of the 2006 Regulation currently in force.[91] Incorporation of this kind will entail obligations for the Member States under EU law on the basis of the EU secondary legislation, as well as the Court's ability to interpret the international treaty. In *Commission v. Greece*, the Court asserted the exclusive competence of the Community to take initiatives designed to ensure compliance with international rules on maritime safety which had been incorporated into a Community Regulation.[92] In another example, the International Organisation of Vine and Wine (OIV), to which a majority of Member States but not the EU belong, issues recommendations on oenological practices which are used as an explicit reference point in the relevant EU legislation. Thus, for instance, when authorizing oenological practices, the Commission is to 'base itself on the oenological practices recommended and published' by the OIV.[93] As a result of this 'incorporation' of the OIV recommendations into the EU legislation, the Court of Justice held that they 'are capable of decisively influencing the content of the legislation adopted by the EU legislature in the area of the common organisation of the wine markets',[94] and that therefore the procedure for the adoption of an EU position in the OIV decision-making procedures should be governed by Article 218(9) TFEU:

> [S]uch recommendations, in particular by reason of their incorporation into EU law... have legal effects in that area for the purposes of Article 218(9) TFEU and...the European

[89] 'Connection clauses' is a term used by Timmermans in Chapter 3 of this volume.

[90] Regulation 2829/77/EEC, OJ 1977 L 334/11, Art. 1.

[91] Regulation 561/2006/EC on the harmonisation of certain social legislation relating to road transport, OJ 2006 L 102/1.

[92] Case C-45/07, *Commission v. Greece*, [2009] ECR I-701. Regulation 725/2004/EC on enhancing ship and port facility security, OJ 2004 L 129/6, is intended to provide a basis for the harmonized implementation and monitoring of Chapter XI-2 of the International Convention for the Safety of Life at Sea (the SOLAS Convention) and the International Ship and Port Facility Security Code (the ISPS Code).

[93] Council Regulation 1234/2007/EC establishing a common organization of agricultural markets and on specific provisions for certain agricultural products (Single CMO Regulation), OJ 2007 L 299/1, Art. 120f.

[94] Case C-399/12, *Germany v. Council*, judgment of 7 October 2014, para. 63.

Union, while not a party to the OIV Agreement, is entitled to establish a position to be adopted on its behalf with regard to those recommendations, in view of their direct impact on the European Union's acquis in that area.[95]

These cases are rather special and this type of incorporation by reference tends to be used where the subject matter of the treaty falls within exclusive EU competence, and the Member States are parties 'on behalf of' the EU, but a *renvoi* to an international treaty may be used in other contexts and take other forms.

A legislative provision may define its scope of application by reference to the treaty. For example, Directive 2005/35 on ship-source pollution makes reference to Marpol, the International Convention for the Prevention of Pollution from Ships, in determining the definitions of 'polluting substances' and 'discharge' for the purposes of the Directive.[96]

It may establish the procedures under which the provisions of an international treaty—binding on the Member States but not on the EU—will be implemented in the Union. For example, Article 11 of Regulation 2201/2003 on jurisdiction and the recognition and enforcement of judgments in matrimonial matters makes reference to, and is designed to operate in conjunction with, procedures for the return of children established under the 1980 Hague Convention on Civil Aspects of International Child Abduction.[97] As the Court expressed it in Opinion 1/13, the Regulation 'complements and clarifies' certain rules in the Convention; its provisions,

> either (i) are based on the rules of the 1980 Hague Convention or (ii) establish the consequences that are to follow when those rules are applied. Those two categories of provisions thus form a unitary body of rules which applies to the procedures for returning children who have been wrongfully removed within the EU.[98]

Moreover, Article 60 of the Regulation provides that the Regulation is to take precedence over the Convention in so far as the matters governed by the two instruments overlap. This 'overlap and the close connection' between the Regulation and the Convention led the Court to conclude that the EU's competence in the matters covered by the Convention is exclusive within the meaning of Article 3(2) TFEU. Thus, the connection between an international treaty and EU legislation, created by the EU legislation itself, may have the effect of creating an exclusive competence for the EU even in a case where the EU itself is not a party to the international instrument.[99]

[95] Ibid., para. 64. [96] Directive 2005/35, OJ 2005 L 255/11.

[97] Regulation 2201/2003/EC, *supra* note 10.

[98] Opinion 1/13, *supra* note 10, paras 77–78.

[99] In this particular case, the dispute was over the competence to accept third State accessions to the Hague Convention. The Court took the view that this was a matter of exclusive competence since divergent Member State practice on the acceptance of accession by a third State would affect the uniform and consistent application of the regime established by the Regulation: Opinion 1/13, *supra* note 10, paras 89–90.

A legislative act may even provide that it is the international treaty rather than the EU legislation which should apply in certain circumstances. The significance of such a provision—and its absence—appears clearly in *Commune de Mesquier*.[100] Although Directive 2004/35 on liability for environmental damage provides that it shall not apply to damage falling within the scope of (inter alia) the International Convention on Civil Liability for Oil Pollution Damage,[101] Directive 75/442 on waste contains no such provision. As a result, the Court interpreted Directive 75/442 as applicable to accidental oil spillages causing pollution to the coastline of a Member State. Although the Member States may establish liability rules for oil spillage pursuant to their commitments under the Civil Liability Convention, they must ensure that the requirements of Directive 75/442 are also met and national courts are under an obligation to interpret national law (even national law intended to give effect to international treaty obligations) 'in the light of the wording and the purpose of the directive, in order to achieve the result pursued by the directive'.[102]

In this case, Directive 2004/35 expressly listed relevant international instruments in an Annex, but the reference may be more general. As already mentioned, Article 71(1) of the Brussels I Regulation provides: '[t]his Regulation shall not affect any conventions to which the Member States are parties and which in relation to particular matters, govern jurisdiction or the recognition or enforcement of judgments.'[103] As Advocate General Kokott has said, 'there is a degree of tension between that restriction of the field of application of Regulation No 44/2001 and the fundamental claim to applicability of European Union law and its precedence over national law, including conventions concluded by the Member States'.[104] This tension is highly visible in *TNT Express*,[105] in which the Court of Justice interpreted Article 71 in a case involving the Convention on the Contract for the International Carriage of Goods by Road, or CMR.[106] The Court held that despite its apparently clear wording, Article 71 must be interpreted so as to include an implied condition: the specialized conventions referred to apply only to the extent to which they do not undermine what the Court called the 'underlying

[100] Case C-188/07, *Commune de Mesquer v. Total*, [2008] ECR I-4501.

[101] Directive 2004/35/EC on environmental liability with regard to the prevention and remedying of environmental damage, OJ 2004 L 143/56. Art. 4(2) provides: 'This Directive shall not apply to environmental damage or to any imminent threat of such damage arising from an incident in respect of which liability or compensation falls within the scope of any of the International Conventions listed in Annex IV, including any future amendments thereof, which is in force in the Member State concerned.' These include the International Convention of 27 November 1992 on Civil Liability for Oil Pollution Damage and the International Convention of 27 November 1992 on the Establishment of an International Fund for Compensation for Oil Pollution Damage.

[102] Case C-188/07, *Commune de Mesquer v. Total, supra* note 100, para. 84.

[103] Regulation 1215/2012; see *supra* note 9.

[104] Case C-533/08, *TNT Express Nederland BV v. AXA Versicherung AG*, [2010] ECR I-4107, Opinion of AG Kokott, para. 35.

[105] Ibid.

[106] Convention on the Contract for the International Carriage of Goods by Road (CMR) 1956, 399 UNTS 189, which came into force in 1961. The Convention has 55 parties including all the Member States of the EU but the EU itself is not a party.

principles' of the Brussels Regulation, including the principles of mutual trust and free movement of judgments. The Court's interpretation of Article 71 is based on a teleology defined with reference to achieving the EU's internal objectives, ignoring the policy choices in favour of a broader international regime that the legislature might have had in mind. The case in question was 'internal' in the sense of involving the jurisdiction of courts in two Member States and this no doubt influenced the Court in its emphasis on mutual trust and in giving priority to the operation of the internal market. However, the judgment is not based on this reasoning and the effects of the judgment will have an impact on the international regime more generally, including in cases involving third countries.[107]

5. *Interpretation Issues*

Insofar as questions concerning Member State agreements arise before the Court of Justice, the ability of—and need for—the Court to interpret the agreement may arise, and where the EU is not a party to the agreement this is not a straightforward question.[108] As a general rule we may say that the Court does not have jurisdiction to interpret agreements to which the EU is not a party and which are not part of Union law,[109] but we need to consider a number of ways in which this picture may be refined.

Where the doctrine of functional succession applies, then, as we have seen, the agreement will be regarded as binding the EU within the framework of EU law, and it then becomes subject to the Court's interpretative jurisdiction.[110]

Where the agreement was entered into by the Member States on behalf of the Union, in particular where its subject matter falls within exclusive Union competence, then the Court of Justice will also have jurisdiction to interpret it. This was the case for the AETR agreement, the Court holding in *Libor Cipra* that 'the AETR Agreement forms part of Community law and that the Court has jurisdiction to interpret it'.[111]

Where an agreement is wholly or partly incorporated into Union legislation, then too the Court will have jurisdiction to interpret that legislation, and thus indirectly, the international agreement. The same may be true in cases of express reference. So, for example, in interpreting a term used in the First Trade Mark Directive the Court turned for guidance to the Paris Convention for the Protection of Industrial Property which is referred to in the Directive—although concluding that the Convention contained no guidance for defining the concept

[107] Note, for example, the possibility of *lis pendens* being applied by a court of a Member State in relation to proceedings before a court of a third State under Art. 33 of Regulation 1215/2012.

[108] Where the EU is a party to the agreement, then it is treated as a part of Union law and subject to the Court's normal interpretative jurisdiction, including under Art. 267 TFEU: Case 181/73, *Haegeman*, [1974] ECR 449.

[109] Case C-301/08, *Bogiatzi, supra* note 47, para. 24.

[110] Cases 22–24/72, *International Fruit Company*, [1972] ECR 1219.

[111] Case C-439/01, *Libor Cipra et Vlastimil Kvasnicka v. Bezirkshauptmannschaft Mistelbach*, [2003] ECR I-745.

in question.[112] As Advocate General Jääskinen put it, 'where a similar definition is used both in the 1980 Hague Convention [on civil aspects of international child abduction] and in Regulation No 2201/2003, the view can be taken that such a formulation has been "communitarised" and the Court can interpret it'.[113] Nevertheless, as the Advocate General also said, the Court will need to be aware of any differences between the internal EU legislation and the international agreement and its ultimate task is that of interpreting Union law.

The Court has declared itself prepared to '*take account of*' international commitments of the Member States in interpreting EU legislation where, although the functional succession conditions are not satisfied, all Member States are party to an international agreement and there is evidence that the relevant EU secondary legislation is intended to give it effect. For example, in *Intertanko*, with reference to Marpol, the Court said that although Marpol could not affect the validity of the Directive at issue (because it is not binding on the EU), it should be taken into account in interpreting the Directive. The Court based this on 'the customary principle of good faith, which forms part of general international law' and on the principle of sincere cooperation now expressed in Article 4(3) TEU.[114] So, although the EU is not bound by the treaty to which it is not a party, the EU legislation in question makes reference to the treaty and thus it forms part of the interpretative context for the Court.[115]

In contrast, in the *TNT Express* case, the Court simply stated that since functional succession did not apply it had no jurisdiction to interpret the convention at issue in the case.[116] This approach, while straightforward, may give rise to problems since the Court also held—as we have seen—that the rules in the convention may only apply provided that they 'ensure, under conditions at least as favourable as those provided for by the regulation, the free movement of judgments in civil and commercial matters and mutual trust in the administration of justice in the European Union'.[117] The courts of the Member States are therefore required to make this far from straightforward assessment of an international convention, and with no guidance as to its interpretation from the Court of Justice, their views are likely to differ. Advocate General Kokott adopted a more nuanced approach. Although also coming to the view that the Court could not interpret a convention which does not form part of the Union's legal system, and which cannot be said to have been 'incorporated by reference', she suggested that 'the Court of Justice must

[112] Case C-40/01, *Ansul*, [2003] ECR I-2439, paras 32–34. The preamble to Council Directive 89/104/EEC on the approximation of the laws of the Member States relating to trade marks, OJ 1989 L 40/1, states that 'all Member States of the Community are bound by the Paris Convention for the Protection of Industrial Property [and] it is necessary that the provisions of this Directive are entirely consistent with those of the Paris Convention'.

[113] Case C-400/10 PPU, *J. McB. V L. E., supra* note 12, view of Advocate General Jääskinen, para. 43.

[114] Case C-308/06, *Intertanko, supra* note 34, para. 52.

[115] In *Intertanko* itself, the Court, having made this general point, does not then go on to refer to Marpol when interpreting the Directive under challenge, presumably because it was interpreting an article of the Directive which did not refer to Marpol.

[116] Case C-533/08 *TNT Express, supra* note 104, paras 62–63.

[117] Ibid., para. 56.

have jurisdiction to *take cognisance of* the content of a convention on a particular matter to which Member States are parties when applying Article 71 of Regulation No 44/2001. For it would otherwise be unable to determine the field of application of the regulation and thus secure the uniform application of European Union law.'[118] As she argued, 'the rules contained in the convention form the legal and factual background to the specific interpretation of European Union law'.[119]

The *TNT Express* case illustrates, as do others discussed here, the difficulties caused where the EU *acquis* starts developing in a field hitherto dominated by international conventions to which the EU is not a party. No doubt many of the problems would, and perhaps will, be resolved by wider EU participation. However, in the interim, and as things stand, ways need to be found to enable EU law to live with existing and successful international regimes. The Court's approach to the connection clauses we have discussed can be revealing of its attitude to alternative legal regimes in which the Member States participate, and how they interact with EU law. What appears to be a connection or bridge between EU law and an international legal regime may turn out to operate in practice as a customs post or access control mechanism.

3. Conclusion

This chapter has introduced a number of themes. First, the gradual development of EU competence and activity in the field of international and regulatory private law, initially at an internal level but increasingly involving engagement in regional and international initiatives. Second, the ways in which the different sources of international and regulatory private law interact within the EU system: the relations between the international obligations of the EU, internal EU law, and the international treaties of the Member States. We traced the applicable principles of EU law, the place of international agreements within the Union's legal system, and the significant ways in which the Member States' international action is affected by their membership of the EU—the fact that they are acting *as EU Member States*.

Third, we looked in more detail at a phenomenon that is particularly relevant when considering the ways in which EU private law engages with international law. EU law has needed to find ways of handling the vast and still 'live' international treaty commitments of its Member States. In considering the implications of this phenomenon a distinction should be made between the two types of international private law with which this book is concerned: traditional private international law, and international regulatory private law. Private international law in the traditional sense is intended to establish rules (of jurisdiction, applicable law, and enforcement) which apply without distinction to all national legal systems. The EU, as is pointed out in Chapters 1 and 4, has been very successful in crafting

[118] Ibid., Opinion of AG Kokott, para. 76 (emphasis added).
[119] Ibid., Opinion of AG Kokott, para. 77.

a EU-wide system of international private law based on the traditional principles of universality and neutrality, but in so doing it has inevitably created distinctions between 'inside' and 'outside', between the system which applies between the Member States, with its high level of mutual trust and emphasis on 'free movement of judgments', and the private international law systems of non-EU Member States. It thus challenges one of the foundations of private international law. The EU's own international action, including its participation in the work of the Hague Conference, is one way of mitigating this effect but, as we have seen, in articulating the relationship between EU private international law and international regimes, the Court's priority has been to ensure the integrity and internal functionality of the EU system.

The dynamic at the heart of international regulatory private law is different and the challenges for the EU are different too. The EU is a regional regulatory system which may cooperate with, and participate in, other regulatory systems (national, regional, and international) of formal or less formal character. Norm conflicts may be avoided through mutual recognition or harmonization, or mitigated through regulatory cooperation. Legally speaking, the position is complicated by the fact that it is the Member States that participate in many international regulatory regimes, and by the fact that much international regulatory norm-setting operates within the framework of international organizations but outside formal international treaty-law. The EU, which both exports and imports norms in fields as various as food safety, dangerous substances, environmental protection, and banking and finance, has developed its own techniques of reference to or incorporation of external international regulatory sources, of participation in international regulation-setting, while seeking to preserve the autonomy of its own regulatory choice. In doing so it has been creative in devising different mechanisms for connecting and disconnecting the EU regime from other international regimes. It is hardly surprising that these connections and disconnections are made on the EU's own terms; that EU law itself decides on what basis, to what extent, and under which conditions it takes account of its Member States' treaty commitments. In this it is behaving like a domestic legal system, but the result is twofold. First, to the extent that EU law recognizes these Member State treaties, it domesticates them. By integrating them, it shapes them and subjects them to its own (internal) priorities. Therefore second, the EU finds it difficult simply to live side by side with alternative international regimes, or rather, it finds it difficult to live with its Member States being part of the EU and also part of alternative international systems without subjecting those systems to 'domestication'.

PART II

EXTENDING EU LAW BEYOND THE BOUNDARIES OF THE INTERNAL MARKET

3

The Specificity of Private Law in EU External Relations

The Area of Freedom, Security and Justice

Christiaan Timmermans

1. Some Preliminary Observations

This contribution will focus on the private law dimension of the Area of Freedom, Security and Justice (AFSJ); that is, judicial cooperation in civil matters including private international law.

In the workshop during which these chapters were discussed, the question was raised whether European private law might be a tool to achieve EU external policy objectives. *Prima facie* I do not see many possibilities for this. The main reason is that there does not exist a specific, autonomous external EU competence in the field of private law allowing the development of a fully fledged external policy in this field to achieve one or more particular external policy objectives.

Of course, to some extent existing external EU policies may, sometimes unexpectedly, touch upon private law issues, such as the common commercial policy (TRIPS), external environmental policy (liability issues),[1] and international action to combat terrorism (Article 215 TFEU, freezing of assets). Another obvious example where private law may directly serve external policy objectives concerns EU action within the framework of pre-accession strategies, association and neighbourhood policies with regard to third countries, fostering respect of the rule of law in those countries, including fundamental rights, access to justice, property rights protection, institution building, etc., and sometimes, but rarely, also judicial cooperation on civil matters.[2] These actions are indeed directly related to some of the general external policy objectives referred to in Articles 3(5) and 21(1) TEU.

[1] See, for instance, CJEU Case C-344/04, *IATA*, [2006] ECR I-403; Case C-188/07, *Commune de Mesquer*, [2008] ECR I-4501.

[2] See *The Stockholm Programme: An Open and Secure Europe Serving and Protecting Citizens*, OJ 2010 C 115/1 para. 7.5; Communication from the Commission to the European Parliament and the Council, *An Area of Freedom, Security and Justice Serving the Citizen*, COM (2009) 262 final, para. 3.5; Communication from the Commission, *A Strategy on the External Dimension of the Area of Freedom, Security and Justice*, COM (2005) 491 final.

However, most external actions in the field of private law (and they are rapidly increasing) and also in regulatory fields, are directly related to and dependent on *internal* EU policies, more particularly those related to the internal market and the AFSJ.[3] The relevant competences for such action are mostly competences based on the Accord Européen sur les Transports Routiers (AETR) approach, now codified and made explicit in Articles 3(2) and 216(1) TFEU.[4] Thus, the question earlier raised could perhaps be rephrased: in what ways might external EU action be a tool to achieve the objectives for which private law-related internal EU policies are being developed?

This is not merely a matter of phraseology. The absence of an explicit legal base for an external policy in the field of private law, apart from AETR and the necessity test of Opinion 1/76, now also codified in Articles 3(2) and 216(1) TFEU, seriously restricts the possibility for the EU to take effective external action in this field.

Let me give an example. In its Decision of 2006 on the accession of the Community to the Hague Conference on Private International Law, the Council considers in the preamble that it is essential that the Community be granted a status that corresponds to its new role as a major international player in the field of civil jurisdiction cooperation, and that it be able to exercise its external competence.[5] Also, later Council decisions approving Hague Conference Conventions[6] or authorizing Member States to ratify or accede to such Conventions[7] underline the valuable contribution made by these Conventions to establish an adequate regime on the international level. This approach is very much to be welcomed not least for reasons of subsidiarity: it is better, if possible and if the regime in question is adequate, to accede to a multinational convention than to elaborate autonomous EU legislation. However, the limited scope of existing external competences in these fields (unduly, one is inclined to say) restricts the Union's freedom of action to follow that approach. Indeed, in the absence of already existing EU legislation,

[3] See more particularly with regard to private international law Wilderspin and Rouchaud-Joët, 'La competence externe de la Communauté européenne en droit international privé', *Revue Critique de Droit International Privé* (2004) 1; see also J. Monar, *The External Dimension of the EU's Area of Freedom, Security and Justice, Progress, Potential and Limitations After the Treaty of Lisbon* (2012), at 1; S. Peers, *EU Justice and Home Affairs* (3rd edn, 2012) 127.

[4] See for instance Council Decision 2006/719/EC on the accession of the Community to the Hague Conference on Private International Law, para. 2 of the preamble and declaration of competence see paras 5 and 6; see also Opinion 1/03 on the *Lugano Convention* in which the Court's analysis with regard to the external competence is entirely *AETR* oriented, [2006] ECR I-1145.

[5] Para. 3 of the preamble of the Decision, *supra* note 4.

[6] See, for instance, Council Decision 2009/397/EC on the signing on behalf of the European Community of the Convention on Choice of Court Agreements, OJ 2009 L133/1, preamble para. 2; Council Decision of 9 June 2011 on the approval, on behalf of the European Union, of the Hague Convention of 23 November 2007 on the International Recovery of Child Support and Other Forms of Family Maintenance, OJ 2011 L 192/39, preamble para. 2; see also the Stockholm Programme, *supra* note 2, para. 3.5.1.

[7] See Council Decision 2008/431/EC authorizing certain Member States to ratify, or accede to, in the interest of the European Community, the 1996 Hague Convention on Jurisdiction, Applicable Law, Recognition, Enforcement and Cooperation in respect of Parental Responsibility and Measures for the Protection of Children, OJ 2008 L 151/36, preamble para. 2.

an AETR competence cannot be invoked. Moreover, in most of the cases relating to judicial cooperation on civil matters, it will hardly be possible to argue that accession is necessary to achieve the objectives of the internal competence.

The Union could of course unilaterally incorporate, wholly or partly, the substance of such a convention in EU law. That would normally trigger an AETR competence. This is exactly what happened with the 2007 Hague Convention on the International Recovery of Child Support and the 2007 Protocol on the law applicable to maintenance obligations, both of which were 'taken into account', but in fact largely taken over, by Regulation 4/2009,[8] which was adopted before the Council approved that Convention and Protocol.[9] The Union had been able to participate together with Member States in the negotiations on these instruments because to some extent there existed already an AETR competence based on Regulation 44/2001 applicable to these issues.[10] Indeed, without pre-existing EU legislation, the EU would not have been able in this case to assume its role as 'major international player', to quote again from the preamble of the Council Decision on accession to the Hague Conference.

2. Is There Anything Special About Private Law when Applying EU External Relations Law?

A first glance at the numerous instruments enacted by the EU regulating external relations in the AFSJ field of private law does not give that impression. On the contrary, the general picture is one of normal application of the principles and general rules of EU external relations law. That approach is in a way already predetermined by the general rules on the competence divide between EU and Member States laid down by the Treaty. Indeed, the AFSJ is explicitly mentioned in the list of shared competences (Article 4(2)(j) TFEU), but without prejudice to the emergence through the exercise of the internal competence of an exclusive external Union competence in the three situations mentioned by Article 3(2) TFEU. Decision-making practice, also preceding the Lisbon Treaty, largely confirms this by giving clear-cut examples of application of AETR principles,[11] largely

[8] Regulation 4/2009 (maintenance obligations), preamble para. 8. Regulations and directives referred to in the footnotes in abbreviated form are listed with full references in the table of instruments.

[9] See for the Council Decision approving the 2007 Convention, *supra* note 6. The 2007 Protocol was concluded by Council Decision 2009/941/EC of 30 November 2009, OJ 2009 L 331/17. See also Beaumont, 'International Family Law in Europe—The Maintenance Project, the Hague Conference and the EC: A Triumph of Reverse Subsidiarity', 73 *Rabels Zeitschrift für Ausländisches und Internationales Privatrecht* (2009) 509.

[10] Regulation 44/2001 (Brussels I). This regulation has been repealed and replaced by Regulation 1215/2012.

[11] See the Council Decision on accession to the Hague Conference already mentioned, *supra* note 4; see also Regulation 662/2009 (authorization procedure of Member States agreements with third countries on particular matters concerning the law applicable to contractual and non-contractual obligations), Regulation 664/2009 (authorization procedure of Member States agreements with third countries concerning matrimonial matters, matters of parental responsibility, and matters relating to maintenance obligations), Council Decision 2008/431 authorizing certain Member States to ratify, or

inspired one might presume by the *Lugano* Opinion of the European Court of Justice (CJEU).[12]

Is there nothing special to be mentioned for private law in this respect? That would be too simple. Let me mention at least two aspects where external relations in the field of private law might show some specificity.

A. The Phenomenon of Connection Clauses

If specificity exists, this might be that in some of the private law fields, particularly private international law, but also judicial cooperation on civil matters, there exists a myriad of bilateral and multilateral conventions between Member States, sometimes Member States only, sometimes also together with third countries. What ought to be done with these conventions? Should they be replaced by EU legislation as far as these conventions apply to relationships between Member States? Could they be maintained and, if so, under what conditions? If EU rules are being established, could Member States still be allowed, and if so, under what conditions, to enter into new conventional relationships with other Member States, whether or not together with third countries?

This is the subject of what I call connection clauses. By the phrase 'deconnection clauses', we understand clauses in new conventional relationships entered into by the EU, which intend to exclude the application of the convention rules between Member States.[13] By the term 'connection clauses', I mean clauses in existing EU legislation regulating the relationship with existing and possibly also future conventions concluded by Member States on subjects coming within the scope of that legislation. The frequent use of such connection clauses might be a specificity of EU legislation on private law matters, much more so than in the public law field. I say, 'might' because I have not carried out a full analysis in this regard.

These connection clauses could be categorized in three main groups which will be discussed in turn.

1. Group 1: Incorporation into EU Law

The first group is the most far-reaching. It concerns all such clauses establishing the most intimate connection by achieving a fully fledged incorporation into Union law, in whole or in part, of an international treaty or convention to which the EU is not a party. A most obvious example is given by the European Convention on Human Rights (ECHR) because of Article 52(3) EU Charter of

accede to, in the interest of the European Community, the 1996 Hague Convention on Jurisdiction, Applicable Law, Recognition, Enforcement and Cooperation in respect of Parental Responsibility and Measures for the Protection of Children, and authorizing certain Member States to make a declaration on the application of the relevant internal rules of Community law, OJ 2008 L151/36.

[12] *Supra* note 4.

[13] See Cremona, 'Disconnection Clauses in EU Law and Practice', in C. Hillion and P. Koutrakos (eds), *Mixed Agreements Revisited* (2010) 160.

Fundamental Rights, incorporating the protection granted by the ECHR as a minimum level with regard to Charter rights which correspond to Convention rights. This even entails incorporation into EU primary law, the Charter having been granted that status. Another example is the 1951 Geneva Convention and 1967 Protocol on Refugees as referred to in Article 78 TFEU. Union policy on asylum, subsidiary protection, etc. must be in accordance with that Convention and Protocol.[14]

In the field of private law in the regulations regarding private international law but also the instruments concerning judicial cooperation on civil matters, one finds clauses incorporating, mostly by way of an explicit reference, individual provisions of international, mostly multilateral treaties to which the Union is not a party.[15] Regulation 4/2009 on maintenance obligations, mentioned earlier, offers a special example by incorporating the substance of the 2007 Convention and Protocol on child support and maintenance obligations for the Member States bound by these instruments, and by doing so anticipating the subsequent accession by the EU to these instruments. Another special example may be found in Article 75(1) of Regulation 650/2012 on Succession[16] which obliges Member States who are parties to the 1961 Hague Convention on Conflict of Laws regarding Forms of Testaments to continue to apply the provisions of that Convention instead of Article 27 of the regulation.

The systematization of these connection clauses is also important to determine the status of the conventions thus connected in the EU legal order. When and under what conditions do they become part of the EU legal order? When does the Court of Justice of the European Union (CJEU) acquire jurisdiction to interpret these conventions?

In this first category of cases where international treaty rules are wholly or partly incorporated by way of reference in a Union instrument, they may be considered to form part of Union law and be subject to the jurisdiction of the Court.

2. *Group 2: Authorization of Member States to Conclude or Accede to Treaties*

A second and rather special category concerns those cases where Member States are authorized by Council decision to conclude, on behalf of the EU or in the interest of the EU, international treaties or conventions, or accede to those.[17] Of course, this category is not at all limited to private law. These decisions also establish a

[14] See Case C-31/09, *Bolbol*, [2010] ECR I-5539; Case C-364/11, *Abed El Karem El Kott*, judgment of 19 December 2012. However, Case C-481/13, *Qurbani*, judgment of 17 July 2014, seems to be more restrictive.

[15] For instance Regulation 1215/2012 (Brussels I), Art. 28 (4); Regulation 2201/2003 (matrimonial matters), Arts 11, 18(3).

[16] See annex.

[17] See Cremona, 'Member States as Trustees of the Union Interest: Participating in International Agreements on Behalf of the European Union', in A. Arnull *et al.* (eds), *A Constitutional Order of States: Essays in European Law in Honour of Alan Dashwood* (2011) 435.

connection between those treaties and conventions and the EU legal order. Just as in cases of incorporation, these instruments too may in principle be considered to form part of Union law and be subject to the jurisdiction of the Court. This can be found as well in those cases in which Member States have been authorized to conclude in the interest of the Union, at least if there exists an AETR rationale for such authorization.[18]

These cases are to be distinguished from authorizations to Member States to conclude new treaties after a draft instrument has first been submitted to the Commission and assessed by it as to its compatibility with Union law.[19] These treaties will normally not become part of Union law.

3. *Group 3: Clauses Regulating the Relationship between an EU Act and Treaties concluded by Member States*

A third and largest category groups all those clauses which specifically regulate the relationship between an EU instrument and existing or future treaties concluded by Member States:

(a) Existing treaties

The EU instruments on private international law and judicial cooperation on civil matters normally contain clauses allowing Member States to continue applying existing treaties. The wording of these clauses differs ('does not affect',[20] 'does not prejudice', or 'without prejudice to',[21] 'not precluded from maintaining'[22]), sometimes special conditions are imposed,[23] however most often they are not.

The question arises whether the Union legislator may claim full discretion in this regard, more particularly to allow the continuing application of existing treaties, the contents of which are not well reconcilable with the regime laid down by the Union instrument. This question becomes even more pressing with regard to a continuing application of an existing treaty on relationships between Member States. It is interesting to note that in some regulations the continuing application of an existing treaty is explicitly conditioned by a requirement of compatibility

[18] For instance Council Decision 2008/431/EC, *supra* note 11.

[19] See Regulations 662/2009 and 664/2009 (see annex).

[20] For instance Regulation 1348/2000 (Service judicial documents), Art. 21 (1), maintained in the recasting Regulation 1393/2007; Regulation 44/2001 (Brussels I), Arts 71(1) and 72, maintained in the recasting Regulation 1215/2012 the latter adding the new Art. 73; Regulation 4/2009 (Maintenance obligations) Art. 69(1); Regulation 1259/2010 (Divorce), Art. 19(1); Regulation 650/2012 (Succession), Art. 75(1).

[21] For instance Regulation 2201/2003 (Matrimonial matters), Art. 63; Regulation 864/2007 (Rome II), Art. 28(1); Regulation 593/2008 (Rome I), Art. 25.

[22] For instance Regulation 1348/2000 (Service judicial documents), Art. 20(2), maintained in the recasting Regulation 1393/2007; Regulation 1206/2001 (Taking of evidence), Art. 21(2); Regulation 4/2009 (Maintenance obligations), Art. 69(3); Regulation 650/2012 (Succession), Art. 75(3).

[23] For instance Regulation 1348/2000 (Service judicial documents), Art. 20 (1), maintained in the recasting Regulation 1393/2007; Regulation 1206/2001 (Taking of evidence), Art. 21(2); Regulation 650/2012 (Succession), Art. 75(3).

with the regulation in question.[24] One should also note in this context that the Court in the *TNT* case, regarding Article 71 of the Brussels I Regulation, has not been willing to accept unconditionally such a 'does not affect' clause, and submitted its application to severe limits. Indeed, the Court considered that the application of specialized conventions (which should not be affected by the regulation according to Article 71) cannot compromise the principles underlying the regulation. Thus, a specialized convention may be applied as *lex specialis*, but only and in so far as the principles of the regulation are being respected.[25]

For obvious reasons, the Union legislator, when enacting new legislation, should as far as possible avoid putting Member States in the impossible situation of only being able to respect Union law by violating their international law obligations. The Court also has shown willingness to avoid that dilemma by accepting that the EU rules in question should be interpreted 'taking account of' international law obligations binding the Member States.[26] However, this obligation seems to be less stringent than the obligation of consistent interpretation accepted by the case law with regard to international law rules, which are binding upon the Union.[27]

These connection clauses allowing Member States to respect obligations arising from conventions concluded with one or more third countries before the entering into force of the regulation[28] or at the time of its adoption[29] may benefit from Article 351 TFEU in so far as these clauses cover conventions concluded before the entering into force of the European Economic Community treaty or the date of accession. Indeed, some of these clauses explicitly refer to that Article.[30] However, they also cover conventions and agreements concluded subsequently. To that extent, these connection clauses could be regarded as an application by analogy of Article 351 TFEU. Whether such an application is in itself legally acceptable has, in my view, not yet been entirely clarified by the case law.[31]

Are these clauses legally problematic? Of course, giving priority to Member States' international obligations arising from earlier treaties concluded with third countries will affect the uniform application of the Union regime, but this does not necessarily mean it is illegal. Avoiding the need for Member States to violate their international law obligations in order to respect Union law is in itself a legitimate interest which is also accepted by the case law as we have just seen (*Intertanko*).[32]

[24] For instance Regulation 1348/2000 (Service judicial documents), Art. 20(2); Regulation 1206/2001 (Taking of evidence), Art. 21(2).

[25] Case C-533/08, *TNT*, [2010] ECR I-4107, paras 46–53.

[26] Case C-308/06, *Intertanko*, [2008] ECR I-4057, para. 52.

[27] Case C-61/94, *Commission v Germany*, [1996] ECR I-3989, para. 52.

[28] Regulation 1346/2000 (Insolvency), Art. 44(2); Regulation 1215/2012 (Brussels I), Art. 73(3).

[29] This drafting would seem preferable. Regulation 4/2009 (Maintenance obligations), Art. 69(1); Regulation 1259/2010 (Divorce), Art. 19(1); Regulation 650/2012 (Succession), Art. 75(1).

[30] Regulation 4/2009 (Maintenance obligations), Art. 69(1), Regulation 1259/2010 (Divorce), Art. 19(1).

[31] Advocate General Kokott seems to consider this 'conceivable' in Case C-188/07, *Commune de Mesquer*, [2008] ECR I-4501, para. 95. See also on the issue of analogous application of Art. 351 TFEU, P. Eeckhout, *EU External Relations Law* (2nd edn, 2011) 396.

[32] *Supra* note 26.

Honouring that interest may justify some inroads made into uniformity. Problems may arise with the principle of equality, possibly also with the obligation on the Union legislature to respect the objectives to be pursued as defined by the relevant legal basis when exercising its legislative competence. One might suppose that such problems would generally be more serious for internal market legislation than for AFSJ legislation. In any event, if these problems could be considered serious enough to risk endangering the legality of a blanket authorization for Member States to honour pre-existing agreements not covered by Article 351 TFEU, the Union legislature could consider limiting that authorization in time in order to allow Member States to withdraw from such agreements. Inspiration could be sought in Article 351(2) TFEU.

Many connection clauses allowing the continuing application of existing treaties make an exception with regard to the relationships between Member States who are parties to such treaties. With regard to these relationships, the Union regime should be respected. Under international law this should normally not be objectionable in the absence of any *pacta sunt servanda* problems with regard to third countries. There exist striking differences in the drafting of these clauses and their legal consequences, striking because the reasons for their variety are not always obvious. Some standardization might be desirable in this respect.

In some cases, including the Insolvency and the Brussels I Regulations, the application of existing treaty regimes with regard to relations between Member States is completely discarded in favour of the Union regime, the latter being stated to 'replace' or to 'supersede' the former.[33] However, more frequently and particularly also in more recent instruments, a rule of conflict is introduced stating that in relations between Member States, the Union regime 'prevails'[34] or 'takes precedence'[35] over existing treaty regimes. This drafting seems to imply that the latter may continue to be applied in relationships between Member States, the Union regime prevailing when a conflict arises.[36] In the Rome I and Rome II Regulations as well as the Divorce and Succession Regulations, such clauses only concern conventions concluded between Member States.

(b) New Member States treaties

I have found three EU instruments, adopted in 2000 and 2001 respectively, which generally allow Member States to conclude new treaties regarding issues regulated

[33] Regulation 1346/2000 (Insolvency), Art. 44(1); Regulation 44/2001 (Brussels I), Art. 69, maintained but slightly redrafted in Art. 69 of the recasting Regulation 1215/2012; Regulation 2201/2003 (Matrimonial matters), Art. 59(1).

[34] Regulation 1348/2000 (Service judicial documents), Art. 20 (1); Regulation 1206/2001 (Taking of evidence), Art. 21(1).

[35] Directive 2002/8 (Access to justice), Art. 20; Regulation 2201/2003 (Matrimonial matters), Art. 60; Regulation 864/2007 (Rome II), Art. 28(2); Regulation 593/2008 (Rome I), Art. 25(2); Regulation 1259/2010 (Divorce), Art. 19(2); Regulation 650/2012 (Succession), Art. 75(2).

[36] See also Regulation 2201/2003 (Matrimonial matters), Art. 62(2).

by these instruments on the condition that they provide for more favourable solutions and, apart from Regulation 1347/2000, are compatible with the Union instrument.[37] Such general, rather open-ended authorizations are of course not without risks, also with regard to ensuring respect for AETR principles. However, I have found no more recent examples.

On the contrary, for instance, Article 39(1) of the 2000 Regulation on matrimonial matters which allowed Member States to conclude new agreements has been deleted by the recasting of the regulation in 2003.[38] With regard to the Rome I and II Regulations, new Member State agreements are not excluded but these are made subject to an authorization procedure.[39] A draft agreement has to be submitted for authorization to the European Commission. Similar procedures were introduced with regard to the 2003 Regulation on matrimonial matters and the 2009 Regulation on maintenance obligations.[40] The introduction of these procedures is very much to be welcomed, not least because it diminishes the risk of discovering problems of compatibility with Union law only after such agreements have been concluded. Indeed, the 2000 and 2001 Regulations which generally allowed the conclusion of new agreements already imposed an obligation on Member States to submit drafts of such agreements to the Commission. An explicit authorization by the Commission was not required, nevertheless this notification allowed the Commission to intervene where necessary.

Finally, it should be observed that the existing or new Member States treaties covered by this third category of connection clauses will normally not form part of Union law and therefore they will not be subject to the jurisdiction of the Court.[41]

Obviously, the regulatory situation resulting from the interplay between applicable Union instruments and the continuing application, wholly or partly, conditionally or unconditionally, of existing Member States treaties and even the conclusion of new treaties by Member States, may become fairly complex. For the non-specialist practitioner, getting to know the law as it stands might require difficult and time-consuming research. It is therefore to be welcomed that some of these regulations, particularly Rome I and II,[42] as well as the recast Brussels Regulation,[43] require Member States to notify to the Commission relevant existing treaties to which they are parties, lists of which will then be published in the Official Journal of the EU. This information is moreover being made accessible on the website of the European Judicial Network.[44]

[37] Regulation 1347/2000 (Matrimonial matters), Art. 39(1); Regulation 1348/2000 (Service judicial documents), Art. 20(2); Regulation 1206/2001 (Taking of evidence), Art. 21(2).

[38] Regulation 2201/2003. [39] Regulation 662/2009. [40] Regulation 664/2009.

[41] See in this regard Case C-533/08, *TNT*, [2010] ECR I-4107, paras 57–63.

[42] Regulation 864/2007 (Rome II), Art. 29; Regulation 593/2008 (Rome I), Art. 26.

[43] Regulation 1215/2012 (Brussels I), Art. 76.

[44] See Council Decision 2008/976/JHA of 16 December 2008 on the European Judicial Network, OJ 2008 L 348/130.

B. A Fundamental Rights Specificity?

A possible further specificity with regard to the external dimension of the AFSJ as far as private international law and judicial cooperation on civil matters is concerned, but certainly not limited to these areas, might be the importance of fundamental rights issues. The areas of law involved are by their very nature fundamental rights-sensitive. External action by the EU on these matters should also heed this sensitivity. Of course, the obligations imposed on the EU political authorities by the EU Charter on fundamental rights also apply, and without restriction, to external EU action (and so one should add to Member States external action falling within the scope of EU law). This is implicitly and rightly emphasized by the first Article of Title V TFEU concerning the AFSJ, according to which '[t]he Union shall constitute an area of freedom, security and justice with respect for fundamental rights'. The *Kadi* judgment of the CJEU illustrates the importance of fundamental rights protection as an unconditional, essential requirement of the EU legal order, which the EU legislator must also respect when implementing highest-ranking instruments of international law.[45]

It follows that when considering the incorporation of international treaties, wholly or partly, into EU law, or allowing Member States to continue to apply existing international treaties through the insertion of one or another connection clause in EU legislation, or when authorizing Member States to conclude such treaties, whether or not on behalf of or in the interest of the Union, the EU legislator must submit these instruments to scrutiny regarding fundamental rights. This would seem to be an obvious task for the Commission when preparing impact assessments for new initiatives.

A particular question to be raised in this context concerns the possible application of the principles of mutual recognition and mutual trust, said to be the core principles for the realization of the AFSJ,[46] when establishing EU treaty relationships with third countries or accepting existing treaty relationships entered into by Member States. Of course, this principle is of a different nature than fundamental rights. They are, nevertheless, related. The principles of mutual recognition and mutual trust are liberalization principles (e.g. free movement of judgments), the application of which may be restricted by the rule of law, including fundamental rights requirements. To find the right balance between the two is a delicate issue.[47]

A number of complex and important questions arise, such as:

- Is this principle of mutual recognition, which is considered to be the cornerstone of judicial cooperation within the EU, now also explicitly mentioned in

[45] Joined Cases C-402/05 P and C-415/05 P, *Kadi and Al Barakaat*, [2008] ECR I-6351.

[46] See Bay Larsen, 'Some Reflections on Mutual Recognition in the Area of Freedom, Security and Justice', in P. Cardonnel, A. Rosas, and N. Wahl (eds), *Constitutionalising the EU Judicial System Essays in Honour of Pernilla Lindh* (2012) 139.

[47] See, for instance, Case C-619/10, *Trade Agency*, judgment of 6 September 2012, not yet published; Joined Cases C-411/10 and C-493/10, *N.S. and M.E. and others*, [2011] ECR I-13905; Case C-491/10 PPU, *Zarraga*, [2010] ECR I-14247. See also Case C-617/10, *Akerberg Fransson*, judgment of 7 May 2013, para. 29.

the Lisbon treaty (Articles 67, 81, and 82 TFEU), a legal principle? I do not think so. It acts more as a guiding principle for the EU legislator and also for the EU Courts when interpreting the relevant texts.

- Could respect for this principle be imposed by the EU legislator without any accompanying harmonization and without any exception allowing for *ordre public* and fundamental rights protection?

It might be useful when considering these questions to take into account the long-standing case law on the application of the comparable concept of the country of origin principle in the context of the fundamental economic freedoms. The case law demonstrates that this principle is certainly not absolute and it allows for exceptions, in the absence of harmonization, to protect legitimate public interests, where necessary and proportionate.

These questions cannot be further explored here. Suffice it to say that the application of a principle of mutual recognition might certainly be accepted by the EU in treaty relationships with third countries (see the Lugano Convention), but the necessity of leaving sufficient room to manoeuvre in order to allow for exceptions, particularly in order to guarantee an adequate protection of fundamental rights, should be considered in each individual case. In that regard it is important to note that where the principle of mutual recognition in relationships between Member States could be considered as a kind of legal presumption with primary law status, that will certainly not be so with regard to third countries.

4

The External Dimension of Rome I and Rome II

Neutrality or Schizophrenia?

Stéphanie Francq

The Rome I and Rome II Regulations provide for a comprehensive set of rules on the conflict of laws in the field of contractual and non-contractual obligations.[1] With few exceptions concerning specific damages or contracts (in the fields of family matters, nuclear damage, damages and contracts linked to the internal functioning of a corporation etc.), the combined substantive scope of the two regulations is meant to cover any question concerning the applicable law to tort or contract arising in the EU.[2] Undoubtedly, these two regulations concern (also) external relations, yet an analysis of the external dimension of EU private international law in the field of obligations cannot be limited to these two regulations.

The treatment of external relations in European private international law (and in the field of obligations in particular) may take different forms and occur in different spheres of power. At least three different settings can be identified in this respect and these are highlighted in the various chapters of this book. First, from a private law perspective, external relations are addressed by the EU when the Commission takes part in international negotiations leading to treaties or model laws in private (international) law; for instance, at the Hague Conference on Private International Law. In this case, as mentioned elsewhere in the book, the EU takes the role formerly reserved to Member States in diplomatic relations. Second, EU law also deals with external relations in imposing its private

[1] Regulation 864/2007 of the European Parliament and the Council of 11 July 2007 on the law applicable to non-contractual obligations (Rome II), OJ 2007 L 199/40; Regulation 593/2008 of the European Parliament and the Council of 17 June 2008 on the law applicable to contractual obligations (Rome I), OJ 2008 L 177/6. Hereafter Rome I and Rome II.

[2] As such, the two Regulations accomplish the hopes formulated at an early stage of the negotiations that led in 1980 to the adoption of the Rome Convention on the law applicable to contracts. The first ambition at the time was to cover both contractual and non-contractual obligations: see the preliminary draft convention, *Revue Critique de Droit International Privé* (1973) 209, commented on by Foyer, *Journal du Droit International* (1976) 555.

law (substantive or procedural) to situations partially or totally found outside the EU. External relations are then addressed through the determination of the geographical (or spatial) scope of EU law; for instance, the scope of conflicts regulations such as Rome I and Rome II, or of other regulations or directives dealing with substantive private law issues. Third, European conflict rules may distinguish between 'European' and 'foreign' situations. Even when they do not, the absence of such distinction tells us something about the way in which the EU legislature conceives the external dimension of private international law.

In each situation, the treatment of external relations (as opposed to 'European' situations) may be more or less conceptualized or directly addressed. It may or may not also result from a specific internal substantive policy or from a specific diplomatic agenda (a foreign policy).

This chapter argues that in the field covered by the Rome I Regulation and the Rome II Regulation (i.e. conflict of laws in contractual and non-contractual obligations), there is a sharp contrast between the way in which external relations are dealt with in these two regulations, on the one hand, and in other instances of EU law, on the other hand. Rome I and Rome II were drafted almost entirely without any special concern for external situations as opposed to 'European' situations, the objectives of EU law on the international scene, or the specific relations among Member States in contrast to relations towards third states (see section 1 following). On the other hand, substantive secondary EU law in the field of obligations determines how far external situations are subject to EU law as a result of the respective substantive policy at stake, and sometimes clearly pursues a specific policy in regards to external relations (see section 2 following). This contrast creates tension between the two sets of secondary law (Rome I and Rome II on the one hand, substantive EU law on the other hand), which the EU legislature seems to ignore. The explanation for this apparently schizophrenic approach to external relations can be traced to several factors but, most importantly, it is indicative of the lack of consideration in regulations such as Rome I and Rome II for the distinct environment in which they were enacted (see section 3 following). In the long run, without neglecting the acquired wisdom of many years of private international law, the EU needs to reflect on what the consequences of the distinctive relations among Member States, based on trust, solidarity, and the pursuit of common substantive policies, are for regulations such as Rome I and Rome II.

1. Regulation Rome I and II: An External Dimension without Policy or the 'Swiss Policy'

Briefly stated, the way in which Rome I and Rome II treat external relations is by treating internal/European situations and foreign situations alike. This is true with regard to the scope of the regulations (see section A following) and with regard to the content of their conflict rules (see section B following). The absence of such a distinction might be wise in regard to the difficulties raised by taking the opposite position: trying to identify what is European and what is foreign and drafting specific conflict rules for different sets of situations might lead to significant technical difficulties and endless debate at the political level.[3] Still, the absence of a specific identification of what is 'European' and what is 'foreign' sometimes seems very odd and is indicative of the way we conceive (or fail to conceive) of the specific values and reach of the EU legal regime. Despite the absence of a distinction between European and foreign situations and despite the lack of effort to protect specific European values, Rome I and Rome II certainly have an external dimension: not only do they apply to situations beyond the EU, but a few specific provisions have been drafted relating to the tension between the internal and external dimension of EU law (see section C following). This external dimension, however, is rarely the expression of a specific substantive policy.

A. A Universal Scope

1. *No Limits Other Than Effectiveness*

The spatial reach of Rome I and Rome II is *a priori* unlimited. The application of these two regulations is not subject to, or dependent upon, any specific factual link to the EU. In the fields covered, the application of the regulations could have been made subject to some kind of minimal conditions establishing a connection between the situation and the EU; for instance, the establishment of one of the parties in the EU, the performance of a contract in the EU, the occurrence of the harm in the EU, or the location of the victim or the tortfeasor within the EU. However, such a condition was never seriously contemplated at any stage of the regulations' adoption process. As a result, the regulations are deemed universally applicable with regard to situations covered, meaning in practice that the regulations could apply even when all relevant aspects of a case occurred in a third state and the case only incidentally happens to be litigated in the EU, for instance, due to a choice of court clause.

The true limitation of the geographical application of Rome I and Rome II actually comes from the reach of their obligatory force and the content of the jurisdiction rules that allows a European judge to assume jurisdiction in a specific situation.

Rome I and Rome II, like any European regulation, are only binding on the public authorities of the Member States. The regulations' obligatory force is thus

[3] On internal versus external situations, see: Basedow, 'Materielle Rechtsangleichung und Kollisionsrecht', in A. Schnyder, H. Hess, and B. Rudisch (eds), *Internationales Verbraucherschutzrecht* (1995) 11–34, at 13–14, and 32 (showing how various categories of conflict rules operate in the EU with regard to different contexts, with specific rules addressing internal situations; in contrast to what will be explained later in this chapter, he denies that internal policies should be given an international reach); Bergé, 'La double internationalité interne et externe du droit communautaire et du droit international privé', *Travaux du Comité Français de Droit International Privé 2004–2006* (2008) 29; Fallon, 'Le domaine spatial d'un code européen de droit international privé. Emergence et modalités de règles de caractère universel', in M. Fallon, P. Lagarde, and S. Poillot-Peruzzetto (eds), *Quelle architecture pour un code européen de droit international privé?* (2011) 137 (showing the reasons for considering limitation of the territorial scope of European private international law but also the difficulties of identifying the proper limits).

limited in their geographical reach. In this respect, Rome I and Rome II present some particularities. In contrast to other EU regulations and directives, regulations enacted under the former Title IV of the EC Treaty (now Title V of Part 3 of the TFEU) are not binding for the United Kingdom, Ireland, and Denmark.[4] According to the terms of Protocols 21 and 22 concerning, respectively, the situation of the UK and Ireland, on the one hand, and of Denmark, on the other hand, regarding acts adopted in the area of civil justice, the UK and Ireland may choose, either at the beginning of the adoption process or after the adoption of the regulation, to take part in it. Denmark, in contrast, does not have such an option and, as a result of Protocol 22, is entirely left out of the adoption process. As stated by Recitals 44 and 45 of Rome I, Ireland chose to participate in Rome I from the start and the UK notified its intention to participate in the regulation after its adoption.[5] With regard to the Rome II Regulation, both the UK and Ireland chose to take part from the start of the adoption process.[6] Denmark could not take part in the regulations at all due to the formulation of Protocol 22, and so it would take a specific international convention that could be entered into between it and the EU to ensure that provisions of Rome I and Rome II would be implemented in that country.[7] This technique has been used in the field of jurisdiction to ensure that Danish courts could assert their jurisdiction on provisions similar to those of Brussels I, but thus far such a convention has not even been considered in the field of conflict of laws.[8] As an alternative solution, Denmark could also transpose the European conflict rules into its national legislation.

The second limit to the reach of Rome I and Rome II is, as already mentioned, set by jurisdiction rules. The Rome I and Rome II Regulations apply to any dispute raising a conflict of law issue in the field of contractual or non-contractual obligations submitted to the courts of a Member State. Of course, parties to a contract can rely on the provisions of Rome I in the absence of any litigation in order to anticipate the law applicable to the contract at hand, but they would have no reason to do so if a potential matter between them is more likely to be litigated in the US than in the EU. Depending on the location of the parties (as the Brussels I and Brussels I *bis* Regulations apply, in principle, only when the defendant is domiciled

[4] For an overview of the impact of variable geometry on external relations, see Martenczuk, 'Variable Geometry and the External Relations of the EU: the Experience of Justice and Home Affairs', in B. Martenczuk and S. Van Thiel (eds), *Justice, Liberty, Security, New Challenges for EU External Relations* (2008) 493.

[5] See Commission Decision 2009/26 of 22 December 2008, OJ 2009 L 10/22, accepting the participation of the UK to Regulation Rome I.

[6] Recital 39 of Rome II.

[7] See Recitals 40 of Rome II and 46 of Rome I.

[8] See, for instance, with regard to Brussels I, the agreement between the European Community and the Kingdom of Denmark on jurisdiction and recognition and enforcement of judgments in civil and commercial matters, OJ 2005 L 299/62, as approved by Council decision 2006/325 of 27 April 2006, OJ 2006 L 120/22. Interestingly, in the field of alimony governed by Regulation 4/2009, a similar process was followed, but the chapter on conflict of laws was left out of the agreement (see Agreement between the European Community and the Kingdom of Denmark on jurisdiction and the recognition and enforcement of judgments in civil and commercial matters, OJ 2009 L 149/80).

on the EU),[9] the international jurisdiction of EU Member States' courts can be determined by the Brussels I (or Brussels I *bis*) Regulation, or by national rules on international jurisdiction, or even by an international agreement.[10] Those rules on international jurisdiction (irrespective of their national, European, or international source) confer the true and effective limit to the geographical reach of the European conflict rules in the field of obligations.

2. *The EU Taking over the Role of Member States*

The analysis of the universal scope of the Rome I and Rome II Regulations evokes an analogy between the position of the EU and that of a state with regard to private international law.[11] As such, the universal scope of the Rome I Regulation does not in itself represent an innovation. Its predecessor, the Rome Convention, already prescribed a universal scope for the situations covered.[12] When the EU legislature transformed the 1980 Convention into a regulation, it therefore merely replicated a choice made earlier by the Member States regarding its scope. For Rome II, it seemed logical to follow the model of the Rome Convention on this matter.

Universal scope in an EU regulation nevertheless represents an important policy choice because two consequences are attached to a regulation with universal scope. First, the argument for an exclusive external competence of the EU based on implied powers deriving from the internal exercise of legislative capacity is much stronger for regulations bearing a universal scope than regulations limited to situations found only within the EU.[13] Second, as a result of the universal scope, for any matter falling within the substantive scope of the Convention (or regulation),

[9] Regulation 44/2001 of 22 December 2000 on jurisdiction and the recognition and enforcement of judgments in civil and commercial matters, OJ 2001 L 12/1, Art. 4(1); Regulation 1215/2012 of 12 December 2012 on jurisdiction and the recognition and enforcement of judgments in civil and commercial matters, OJ 2012 L 351/1, Art. 6(1).

[10] See, for instance, the Hague 2005 Convention on Choice of Court Agreements, signed by the EU, but not yet entered into force.

[11] The analogy also concerns the limits of this universal application. For instance, the effective limits of Rome I and II, as mentioned above, are due to the limits of their binding force and to the international jurisdiction rules in force in the EU. This is true as well for national conflict rules. The difficulties stemming from the 'multispeed Europe' with regard to the binding force of the two Regulations can be seen to be analagous with the problems faced by Member States at the time of the Rome Convention about its binding force's expansion with each accession of a new Member State.

[12] Rome Convention on the law applicable to contractual obligations of 19 June 1980, OJ 1980 L 266/1.

[13] In the *Lugano Opinion* (Opinion 1/03, [2006] ECR I-1145), the Court acknowledged the external competence of the EU in the field covered by the Brussels I Regulation even though the scope of that regulation was not universal and left room for the use of national jurisdiction rules where a defendant is domiciled outside the EU. Part of the argument of the Court in Opinion 1/03 consisted in extending the scope of the regulation to situations that were not conceived as falling under Brussels I up until then. This is the case for jurisdiction clauses designating the tribunal of a third state, about which the court apparently implies (i) that Brussels I applies, in particular Art. 23 thereof; and (ii) that they are invalid with regard to Art. 23 (para. 153, *in fine*). Art. 23, Brussels I contains a condition regarding the designation of Member State courts, which had been interpreted as a condition of applicability (meaning that the regulation does not apply if the jurisdiction clause designates courts of a third state) and not as a condition of validity (presumptive position of the Court in Opinion 1/03).

national conflict rules are rendered obsolete. Member States essentially have to abrogate or refrain from enacting conflict rules in the field of obligations (except for the few topics left outside the substantive scope of Rome I and Rome II).[14] Interestingly, by replicating, in Rome I and Rome II, the policy choice made earlier by Member States regarding the scope of the Rome Convention, the EU takes the place formerly occupied by the Member States not only with regard to relations with third states, but also within the internal legal system of Member States by replacing former domestic conflict rules.

On a more theoretical level, the universal scope of these two regulations leads to a reconsideration of the nature of the EU legal order. It is often argued that nation states, as they were establishing themselves and correspondingly enacting national codifications in the field of private law,[15] were devising solutions that could apply to any situation raising a private law issue, irrespective of the links that situation might have with the state. The potentially 'universal' application of national rules in private law is said to derive from the purely rational and abstract nature of these rules[16] (in contrast to a vision of private law as the result of a social experience, discussed further below), or from the fact that in order to avoid a denial of justice, a legal system needs to provide for an answer for any legal situation.[17] While the need for substantive private law with universal scope can be debated (see below), the argument is certainly valid for private international law: national rules of private international law are meant to guide the judge in treating any international matter before her. Thus, national codifications of conflict of laws rules, where they exist, are obviously 'universal' as their function is to provide the necessary guidance for international situations. Now, the EU legislature, in enacting universal regulations on conflicts of laws, takes over the role of the nation state to provide guidance for any international situation that could arise in the EU in order to avoid a denial of justice. Presenting the EU as the regulator of an entire field of private law has a strong symbolic connotation as a definitive assimilation of the EU's functions to those of a state, at least in a given field.[18]

For more detail see Francq, 'Les clauses d'élection de for après la refonte du règlement Bruxelles I', in E. Guinchard (ed.), *Le nouveau règlement Bruxelles I bis* (2014) 107.

[14] In Belgium, for instance, the Code on private international law has been adapted after the enactment of Rome II, to refer to the Regulation (*Loi du 30 décembre 2009 portant des dispositions diverses en matière de justice* (Law of 30 December 2009) [2010] Moniteur belge 1889). For contractual obligations, as from its entry into force in 2004, the Code simply referred to the Rome Convention (this reference implicitly also covers Rome I) even for matters placed outside its scope (Art. 98(1)). No conflict rules on contractual obligations have been inserted into the Code.

[15] On the link between the establishment of nation states and national codification, see: Micklitz and Patterson, 'From the Nation State to the Market: The Evolution of EU Private Law as Regulation of the Economy beyond the Boundaries of the Union', in B. Van Vooren, S. Blockmans, and J. Wouters (eds), *The EU's Role in Global Governance: The Legal Dimension* (2013) 59.

[16] Mayer, 'Le phénomène de la coordination des ordres juridiques étatiques en droit privé', 327 *Recueil des Cours de l'Academie de Droit International* (2007) 9, at 26–34, 138–140, 145–146.

[17] Fallon, 'L'application de l'article 3, alinéa 3, du Code civil par la jurisprudence belge du 19e siècl', in *Liber Memorialis François Laurent* (1989) 765.

[18] Such an understanding is, however, difficult to reconcile with the terms of the Tobacco ruling, Case C-376/98, *Tobacco* I, [2000] ECR I-8419.

The symbolic and the practical impact of the universal scope of these legal instruments stands among the reasons why the competence of the EU to enact such universal regulations was so fiercely debated. At its peak, the controversy pitted two groups of French academics against each other.[19] The controversy focused on the limits of the legal basis and the treatment of national mandatory rules, but the role of the EU in the field of private international law was also discussed. Some scholars strongly opposed the idea that the EU would assume much of the role of the Member States in the field of private international law (both internally and externally) and make all the policy choices that could accompany conflict rules concerning obligations (mainly where national mandatory rules exist).[20] More pragmatically, many authors discussed the reach of Article 65 EC in external situations. The question was whether a provision subjecting the approximation (or rather, the promotion of the 'compatibility') of conflict rules to the 'proper functioning' of the internal market allowed for the enactment of conflict rules applicable to situations with no or only a distant connection to the EU. Even if the question had been raised during the enactment process of Rome I and Rome II,[21] the negotiators had not seriously addressed it. The Green Paper and the Rome I Regulation Proposal do not even raise the possibility of limiting European conflict rules to situations presenting a close connection with the internal market,[22] and the issue is only briefly discussed in the Rome II Proposal.[23] Many scholars obviously spotted the problem but tended to consider that a single set of conflict rules was desirable.[24] The formulation of the

[19] Heuzé, 'Lettre ouverte—L'Union européenne, la démocratie et l'État de droit', *La Semaine Juridique Edition Générale* (2006), act. 586, 2213; Lagarde, Gaudemet-Tallon, and Kessedjian, 'Observations sur la lettre ouverte au président de la République intitulée "L'Union européenne, la démocratie et l'État de droit"', *La Semaine Juridique Edition Générale* (2007), act. 18, 13; Heuzé, 'L'honneur des professeurs de droit—Explications d'une lettre ouverte sur l'Union européenne, la démocratie et l'État de droit', *La Semaine Juridique Edition Générale* (2007), I-116, 17.

[20] See the signatories of the 'Open Letters' of V. Heuzé.

[21] R. Plender and M. Wilderspin refers to the critical opinion of Lord Wilberforce in the United Kingdom and of some officials of the Legal Service of the Council and of the British delegation negotiating Rome II; see R. Plender and M. Wilderspin, *The European Private International Law of Obligations* (2009), at Nos 4-016 and 17-009.

[22] Green Paper on the conversion of the Rome Convention of 1980 on the law applicable to contractual obligations into a Community instrument and its modernization, COM (2002) 654 final. The proposal for Rome I simply referred to the discussion that took place in the proposal for Rome II: Proposal for a Regulation of the European Parliament and the Council on the law applicable to contractual obligations (Rome I), COM (2005) 650 final, at 5 (discussing only the title of Art. 2).

[23] The Rome II Proposal addresses the issue (confounding it with the possibility for the conflict rules to designate the law of a third state, which is a different problem), and considers uniform conflict resolution rules for internal and external situations necessary in regard of the difficulty of distinguishing both situations, in order to offer a single set of rules for the national judge to handle, and in regard of close links with Regulation Brussels I and of the circulation of judgments among Member States (the latter point is unclear since judgements circulate among Member States without review of the law applied by the first court): Proposal for a Regulation of the European Parliament and the Council on the law applicable to non-contractual obligations (Rome II), COM (2003) 427 final, at 9–10 (explanation of Art. 3).

[24] For instance: Leible and Staudinger, 'Art. 65 of the EC Treaty in the EC system of Competences', 4 *European Legal Forum* (2000–2001) 225, at 230 (taking the position that a reference to the proper functioning of the internal market is less demanding than a reference to the mere functioning of the international market, and that a different set of conflict rules for external situations and for

legal basis after the Lisbon Treaty diminishes the importance of the reference to the internal market (Article 81 TFEU): measures aimed at promoting the compatibility of national conflict rules may be adopted '*particularly* when necessary for the proper functioning of the internal market'. However, since Article 81 TFEU is placed in a title dedicated to the creation of the Area of Freedom, Security and Justice (AFSJ), the question simply takes on another dimension: to what extent does the establishment of the AFSJ require conflict rules for situations with no connection to the EU?[25] Interestingly, the CJEU has, in a series of decisions, admitted that not every situation falling within the scope of a piece of secondary legislation must systematically match the prerequisites of its legal basis.[26] If this case law, originally concerning Article 95 EC, can be transposed to Article 81 TFEU, not all situations covered by Rome I and Rome II would need to present a direct link with the AFSJ.[27] If this line of case law is taken seriously then the EU enjoys a wide autonomy in determining the spatial scope of application of secondary law.[28] Grounding law in policies that establish the internal market or the AFSJ may thus imply authority to regulate situations at least partially situated in third states.[29] It is indeed for the EU legislature to assess the 'needs' of the internal market or of the ASFJ and their implications in geographic terms.[30] The wide margin of autonomy left to the EU in regard of the geographical scope of secondary legislation reinforces the parallel with the role of

international situations would lead to distortion of competition); R. Plender and M. Wilderspin, *The European Private International Law of Obligations* (2009), at para. 4-016 (considering that the formulation of Art. 65 EC certainly questions the possibility of a universal scope, but eventually accepting such a scope based on arguments presented by the Commission in Rome II Proposal).

[25] The most comprehensive analysis of the issue has been led by Fallon, 'Le domaine spatial d'un code européen de droit international privé. Émergence et modalités de règles de caractère universel', in M. Fallon, P. Lagarde, and S. Poillot-Peruzzetto (eds), *Quelle architecture pour un code européen de droit international privé?* (2011) 137, at 148–171; 'Les frontières spatiales du droit privé européen selon le droit de l'Union européenne', in E. Poillot and I. Rueda (eds), *Les frontières du droit privé européen—The Boundaries of European Private Law* (2012) 65, at 108–121.

[26] For instance, in *Österreichischer Rundfunk*, much of the discussion concerned the substantive scope of the directive, but the Court admitted the applicability of a directive to an internal situation, while the directive was based on the free movement of workers: 'the applicability of Directive 95/46 cannot depend on whether the specific situations at issue in the main proceedings have a sufficient link with the exercise of the fundamental freedoms guaranteed by the Treaty, in particular, in those cases, the freedom of movement of workers', Case C-465/00, C-138/01 and C-139/01, *Rechnungshof v. Österreichischer Rundfunk and Others*, [2003] ECR I-4989, para. 42; in the *Tobacco IV* case, when answering the argument that the directive was incorrectly based on Art. 95 EC since it related only to local products lacking cross-border effects, the Court found that: '[r]ecourse to Article 95 EC as a legal basis does not presuppose the existence of an actual link with free movement between the Member States in every situation covered by the measure founded on that basis' (Case C-380/03, *Federal Republic of Germany v. European Parliament*, [2006] ECR I-11573, para. 80).

[27] M. Fallon, for instance, considers that primary law, after Lisbon, does not condemn the universal scope of regulations on conflict of laws; see Fallon, *supra* note 25, at 170.

[28] For a more detailed analysis of this issue, see: S. Francq, *L'applicabilité du droit communautaire dérivé au regard des méthodes du droit international privé* (2005), at 515–527.

[29] For instance, see in *Tobacco II*: Case C-491/01, *The Queen v. Secretary of State for Health*, [2002] ECR I-11453, paras 82–91 and 213 (admitting the use of Art. 95 EC for regulating exported goods).

[30] Ibid. For more examples of instances of secondary law presenting a spatial scope not matching the prerequisites of their legal basis, see: Francq, *supra* note 28, at 527–537.

the state. States are, indeed, subject to no limitation regarding the geographical reach of domestic laws.[31]

Analysing the reach of Rome I and Rome II reveals the clear resemblance between the role of the EU with regard to conflict of laws in the field of obligations and the role formerly occupied by Member States in the same field. The EU behaves likes a complete and autonomous legal order. In relation to third states, as a result of its exclusive external competence in relations to matters falling within the scope of Rome I and Rome II, the EU will conduct negotiation with third states, for instance, at the Hague Conference. Member States retain, however, the power to negotiate (or renegotiate) international agreements with third states when they have a 'specific interest in . . . the agreement due to economic, geographic, cultural, historical, social or political ties' with them.[32] Of course, the potential negotiations and the following international agreement are to be assessed in light of the effectiveness of EU law and of 'the Community's external relations policy'.[33] Allowing Member States to conduct specific negotiations under the supervision of the Commission may simply be a result of sound administrative management: the Commission just does not have the staff or resources to renegotiate every international agreement entered into by Member States, nor the possibility to be informed of every local situation that would trigger the need for more intensive cooperation with specific third states.[34] As such, the procedure established by Regulation 662/2009 is similar to the delegation of power model and shows that the universal scope of Rome I and II has not been enacted in ignorance of its implications with regard to relations with third states.

B. Neutral and Universal Conflict Rules

1. Neutrality, Universality, and Fairness

With respect to their universal scope, European conflict rules in the field of obligations resemble national or conventional conflict rules formerly enacted by states.

[31] Of course, limits have long been sought in public international law, but beyond minor indications such as the interdiction to interfere systematically in another state's internal affairs, effective limitations stemming from public international law have never been demonstrated. See: P. de Vareilles-Sommières, *La compétence internationale de l'État en matière de droit privé. Droit international public et droit international privé* (1997). Much of the debate on the prohibition of extraterritoriality is thus ill-founded.

[32] Regulation 662/2009 of 13 July 2009 of the European Parliament and the Council establishing a procedure for the negotiation and conclusion of agreements between Member States and third countries on particular matters concerning the law applicable to contractual and non-contractual obligations, OJ 2009 L 200/25, Art. 4(2)(a). This regulation follows the model of Regulation 664/2009 in the field of alimony, solving the same kind of issues in regards to the external competence of the EU due to Regulation 4/2009 on jurisdiction, applicable law, recognition, and enforcement of decisions and cooperation in matters relating to maintenance obligations, OJ 2009 L 7/1.

[33] Ibid., Art. 4(2)(c).

[34] Micklitz and Patterson, *supra* note 15, at 76 (proposing another explanation: according to them, the reason behind Regulation 662/2009 is that private international law issues 'do not rank high on the political agenda').

This is true as well with respect to their content. This similarity is partly the result of history. The existence of the Rome Convention had a strong influence on the structure and content of the Rome I Regulation and Rome II Regulation. Rome I is actually a mere recast of the Rome Convention, adapting the text regarding the transformation of the Brussels Convention into a regulation and responding to a few difficulties encountered by national and European courts in implementing the Brussels and the Rome Convention.[35] Rome II, even if enacted before Rome I, presents many similarities to the latter due to the dominant model of the Rome Convention in the field of contractual obligations that Rome II was due to complement for extra-contractual obligations.[36] As the Commission phrased it in the Rome II Regulation Proposal, the goal was to 'standardize' the conflict rules of Member States in order to promote legal certainty and reduce litigation costs within the Union, not to develop a new model of conflict rules tailored to the specific values and policies of the European Union, let alone to encapsulate a particular external policy supported by European conflict rules.[37] Moreover, the project for a convention on the law applicable to non-contractual obligations elaborated by the European Group for Private International Law (GEDIP) (on the basis of which the Commission later proposed the Rome II Regulation) was itself based on a comparative law study of national conflict rules.[38] Academics have thus been quite influential with regard to the Rome Convention (the negotiation committee was mostly composed of academics) and later Rome I and Rome II. Unsurprisingly, the conflict rules of Rome I and Rome II are thus characterized by the traditional features of national and conventional conflict rules: neutrality and universality.

Universal conflict rules cover a different, yet related, reality than the 'universal scope' of the regulations. As explained earlier, Rome I and Rome II are said to have universal scope because they apply to every situation pending before European courts irrespective of the potential links of this situation with the EU. This is the first aspect of universality, that of the situations covered. Rome I and Rome II also offer so-called universal conflict rules, that is, conflict rules that can be used to designate the law of a third state as well as the law of a Member State. The designation operated by those conflict rules is thus not limited to Member States' law. This is the second aspect of universality: universality with regard to the potentially designated law. The two aspects of universality are not necessarily related: the scope

[35] Garcimartín-Alférez, 'The Rome I Regulation: Much Ado about Nothing?', 2 *European Legal Forum* (2008) 61, at 77; Francq, 'Loi applicable aux obligations contractuelles (matière civile et commercial)', *Répertoire Communautaire Dalloz* (2013), n° 7.

[36] Rome II was indeed conceived as the '*pendant*' of the Rome Convention: see Proposal for a Regulation of the European Parliament and the Council on the law applicable to non-contractual obligations (Rome II), COM (2003) 427 final, at 3, point 1.2, *in fine*.

[37] COM (2003) 427 final, at 4–5, point 2.1.

[38] The GEDIP is a think-tank of professors of private international law, independent of EU institutions, but which often anticipated Commission proposals in its exploratory work. See: M. Fallon and P. Lagarde, 'Commentaire de la proposition pour une convention européenne sur la loi applicable aux obligations non-contractuelles', available at: <http://www.gedip-egpil.eu/documents/gedip-documents-8cf.html> (last accessed 16 May 2015).

of a regulation harmonizing conflict rules can be limited to situations presenting specific links with the EU (for instance, one of the parties being established in the EU), while the conflict rules of such a regulation could designate the law of a third state as being the applicable law (a general connecting factor like the place of performance of a contract could, for instance, designate the law of a third state). In practice, however, the two aspects of universality have often been linked.[39] Such is the case of Rome I and Rome II, which are universal in both respects: in their scope and in regards to the potentially applicable law. The provisions of the two regulations are indeed intended to designate as applicable the law of any state, 'whether or not it is the law of a Member State'.[40]

Neutrality is probably the most important feature of bilateral conflict rules as they are perceived since Savigny. Savigny is said to have set the foundations of bilateralism, the currently dominant theory and practice of private international law. At the cost of oversimplification, bilateral conflict rules can be presented as rules attempting to identify the 'seat' of a situation or relationship in regards to the essence of the relationship. In contemporary terms, situations and relationships are anchored in a legal system with which they have the closest connection. Savigny anchored relationships within legal systems with the help of connecting factors designed for each type of legal relationship. The search for the 'seat' of legal relationships (considered, by Savigny, as extensions of individuals) mirrors the way in which individuals were themselves located within a community on the basis of their domicile.[41] The process of designation of the applicable law through the identification of the 'seat' of a relationship is described as neutral because it does not pursue any specific substantive policy (such as choosing the law which will render the relationship valid or furthering environmental protection), and it generally disregards the content of the designated law and its impact on the relationship or on the community of the forum as a whole.[42] In short, the goal is not to promote fairness or any substantive policy but instead to respect the close relationship with a specific legal order. This goal also explains why foreign law and forum law (in our case, third state law and Member State or European law) are treated as equal. In line with the traditional role of bilateral conflict rules, Rome I and Rome II identify, through predetermined connecting factors, the 'seat' of a relationship on the basis of its proximity with a legal system.[43] Ultimately, the goal of the general

[39] For instance, the 1956 Hague Convention on the law applicable to maintenance obligations towards children designates the law of the place of residence of the child (Art. 1) and foresees that the Convention applies only when the designated law is that of a contracting state (Art. 6). The scope of the convention is thus limited to children residing in a contracting state whose conflict rules designate the law of a contracting state.

[40] Art. 3 Rome II; Art. 2 Rome I. The two provisions are entitled 'universal application'.

[41] For more detail: Gothot, 'Simples réflexions à propos de la saga du conflit de lois', in *Le droit international privé: esprit et méthodes—Mélanges en l'honneur de Paul Lagarde* (2005) 343, at 349–354.

[42] See, amongst others: P. Mayer and V. Heuzé, *Droit international privé* (11th edn, 2014) 92, para. 114; D. Bureau and H. Muir Watt, *Droit international privé—T. I Partie générale* (3rd edn, 2014) 400–401, n° 348.

[43] Art. 4 Rome I proposes fixed connecting factors for various types of contracts (for instance, for the sale of goods, the law applicable is the one of the country where the seller has his habitual

conflict rules of these two regulations is to identify the country with which the situation presents the closest connection: the escape clause enshrined in Article 4(3) of the two regulations shows that if the general connecting factors fail to designate the law of the country with which the situation is most closely connected, they should be derogated from in order to follow the designation operated by the 'closest connection' test.

Neutrality does not exclude any consideration of fairness. Fairness is implicated in the identification of the relevant connecting factor. Here, fairness is applied in the sense of respecting the parties' legitimate expectations *in regard of the law potentially applicable*, rather than in regard of the content of this law and of the outcome of the litigation.[44] In other words, by identifying the law most closely related to the situation, conflict rules should match the need for predictability and thereby reach a fair solution for both parties.[45] Considerations of predictability can even take precedence over the search for a close connection when parties are allowed to designate the applicable law.[46] Another relevant dimension of fairness is the aim of balancing the relationship; some conflict rules tend to protect the weak party by designating the law best known to this party. Such is the case for consumer and employees' protection matters.[47] As a result, conflict rules can pursue specific policies of private international law (different from substantive policies) and nevertheless remain neutral: the search for a close connection matching the expectation of both parties or of the party deserving special protection remains detached from the content of the designated law and from the final outcome of the case. We will explore a few exceptions where some substantive policies do have an impact on the designation process in section C.

residence; for contracts for services, the law of the place where the service provider has his habitual residence, etc.). In Rome II, Art. 4 establishes general connecting factors for torts (i.e. the law of the country where the damage occurred or of the country where the victim and tortfeasor have their habitual residence), before presenting a set of rules for specific torts (for instance, Art. 9, which specifies that for damages emerging from instrustrial action, the law applicable is the law of the country where the action took place).

[44] The proposals for the two regulations contain multiple references to balancing the interests of the parties and to predictability. See for instance, in Rome II Proposal, the comment of the general conflict rule, Art. 3: 'The Commission's objectives in confirming the *lex loci delicti commissi* rule are to guarantee certainty in the law and to seek to strike a reasonable balance between the person claimed to be liable and the person sustaining the damage.' And further: 'The rule also reflects the need to strike a reasonable balance between the various interests at stake. The Commission has not adopted the principle of favouring the victim as a basic rule, which would give the victim the option of choosing the law most favourable to him. It considers that this solution would go beyond the victim's legitimate expectations and would reintroduce uncertainty in the law, contrary to the general objective of the proposed Regulation. The solution in Article 3 is therefore a compromise between the two extreme solutions of applying the law of the place where the event giving rise to the damage occurs and giving the victim the option' (COM (2003) 427 final, at 11–12).

[45] A good example is Art. 4(2) Rome II designating the law of the country where both victim and tortfeasor have their habitual residence, even if the damage occured in a different country.

[46] Art. 3 Rome I; Art. 14 Rome II.

[47] Arts 6 (designating for consumer contracts, the law of the country where the consumer habitually resides) and 8 (designating for employment contract, the law of the country of habitual performance) of Rome I.

2. Neutrality, Universality, and External Policy

With regard to these two features—universality and neutrality—the EU conflict rules hardly pursue any external policy, and yet they do reach external situations. As explained earlier, due to their universal scope, Rome I and Rome II apply even to entirely foreign situations pending in front of a Member State court. As a result of the formulation of the current conflict rules, these situations are treated exactly as 'European' situations for the purpose of determining the applicable law (neutrality), and laws of third states are treated exactly as laws of Member States (universality).

A few provisions of the two regulations are noteworthy in this respect. Provisions dealing with public policy and overriding mandatory rules touch on topics that can be at the heart of special policies regarding external situations, but do not distinguish between 'European' and 'external' situations or Member States' law and third states' law. Article 26 of Rome II and Article 21 of Rome I state that 'the application of a provision of the law of *any* country' designated by the regulations' conflict rules may be refused if it would result in effects manifestly contrary to the public policy of that forum. Article 9(3) of the Rome I and Article 16 of the Rome II allow for the application of the overriding mandatory rules of the forum even if they are not designated by the conflict rules of the respective regulation. Furthermore, while Article 16 of Rome II does not provide for this possibility, Article 9(3) of Rome I allows the court of a Member State to take into consideration the overriding mandatory rules of another country (so-called foreign mandatory rules) in certain situations. In all these situations, be it in order to displace the applicable law incompatible with values or overriding mandatory rules of the specific forum, or in order to consider the application of foreign mandatory rules not designated by the general conflict rules, no distinction is made with regard to the connection of the situation with the EU or the origin of the law applicable or to be applied as a foreign mandatory rule. Third state laws and external situations are treated as equal to Member States law and 'European' situations.

Of course, distinctions will be made in the implementation process of public policy or overriding mandatory rules: public policies of Member States apply depending on how the given situation is connected to the Member State concerned (through '*ordre public de proximité*' and '*ordre public atténué*'), and overriding mandatory rules of the forum are triggered as a result of the connection between the situation and the forum, which justifies the need for mandatory rules to cover the situation. At the EU level, however, no specific consideration is given to external situations or the status of third state law. It is particularly striking that overriding mandatory rules of Member States and of third states are placed on equal footing under Article 9(3) Rome I. According to this provision, the judge of a Member States considers a potential reference to the overriding mandatory rules of another Member States (whose law has not been designated as applicable to the contract) under the same conditions as overriding mandatory rules of third States. Shouldn't Member States have more consideration for their sister states' policies expressed in overriding mandatory rules than for third states' policies? With regard to the relationship of 'trust' and 'solidarity' established among Member States, reciprocal help in furthering each other's most important policies (as expressed in overriding mandatory rules) might be expected. For this reason, it is also particularly surprising that the possibility of taking into consideration foreign mandatory rules has been rejected in Rome II, even for those of other Member States. These crucial provisions tend to show that when turning to the conflict of laws (in the field of obligations at the least), we are still deprived of a sense of community resting on a specific solidarity, and of a clear understanding of the impact of the special relationship existing among Member States. Interestingly, the particularity of the relationship among Member States extends well beyond Rome I and Rome II. For instance, when applying its overriding mandatory rules, a judge of a Member State needs to respect the 'mutual recognition exception'.[48] This obligation does not derive from Rome I or Rome II but, rather, from EU substantive law.[49]

In addition, the very symbolic provisions on public policy and overriding mandatory rules thus express neutrality and universality, which, as mentioned earlier, are characteristic of the conflict rules formulated by the EU and formerly by Member States. Conflict rules of Member States once treated all foreign laws as equal and placed foreign countries on equal footing (with the exception of particular rules that might be enshrined in bilateral agreements). The deeper roots of this attitude deserve to be remembered as they shed a positive light on what may otherwise appear as a failure in the conception of EU conflict rules. Putting all states on equal footing and treating their laws alike can be characterized as an 'internationalist' attitude, in contrast to the 'nationalist' attitude (or the parochial attitude) favouring national interests (or the *lex fori*). Internationalism is said to bring more favourable results in terms of harmony of solutions, because (i) it is not centred on interests of the forum, and (ii) it is often linked with the search for coordinated solutions.[50] As already emphasized regarding the universal scope of the regulations, neutrality and universality of conflict rules, as such, represent a policy choice: whether or not to treat foreign and 'European' situations alike, and foreign and Member State laws alike.

C. Taking the External Dimension into Account?

Despite the fact that the effect of the general policy choice behind Rome I and Rome II has been to erase the difference between external and 'European'

[48] The intervention of overriding mandatory norms of the forum is submitted to mutual recognition. That is, application of this overriding mandatory law is prohibited if it creates an obstacle to one of the fundamental freedoms (trade, services, etc.) unless it rests on valid justification grounds and is proportionate. The measure cannot be considered proportionate if the law applicable to the case is the law of another Member State which provides for equivalent protection in regard of the measure's aim and justification. See: Joined Cases C-369/96 and C-376/96, *Arblade*, [1999] ECR I-8453, para. 39; C-165/98, *Mazzoleni*, [2001] ECR I-2189, para. 22. The exact reach of the mutual recognition exception remains, however, controversial.

[49] For further considerations on the role of substantive EU law in the distinction between internal and external situations see section 2, this chapter.

[50] For more detail on nationalism and internationalism and their links with the universal and particular conceptions of private international law: Mayer and Heuzé, *Droit international privé*, *supra* note 42, at 65–67, paras 69–72.

situations and to treat all laws on an equal footing, Rome I and Rome II have not been negotiated in ignorance of the outside world. Some provisions reveal that the EU institutions sometimes take into consideration relationships with third states (section 1 below) and the need to further certain EU substantive policies (section 2 below).

1. In Relations with Third States

Relations with the outside world were taken into consideration with respect to pre-existing international agreements in the fields covered by Rome I and Rome II.

First, for potential conflicts between international instruments (the regulations versus former international conventions), the two regulations differentiate between pre-existing conventions concluded by one or more Member States with third countries and pre-existing conventions concluded exclusively among Member States.[51] In line with Article 351(1) TFEU, the regulations take precedence over the conventions in force exclusively between Member States but not over those concluded with third states. The latter are dealt with by Member States according to Regulation 662/2009 (section 1.A.2, earlier).

Second, the substantive scope of the two regulations has been drafted with the aim of avoiding unnecessary overlap with existing conventions providing for uniform substantive laws or dealing with conflict of laws. For instance, in light of the 1950 New York Convention on arbitral awards and of the 1930 and 1931 Geneva Conventions on bills of exchange, promissory notes and cheques, the substantive scope of Rome I excludes arbitration agreements and negotiable instruments.[52] Similarly, Rome II does not apply to nuclear damage, because other conventions already cover this issue.[53]

2. In Imposing some EU Policies

Several provisions of Rome I and Rome II show consideration for EU policies:

(i) Intra-EU matters as domestic situations

The most striking example is Article 3(4) Rome I concerning purely 'European' situations. In cases where all the relevant factors of the case are located in the EU, the parties' choice of a third state's law may not prejudice the application of EU mandatory laws (rules 'which cannot be derogated from by agreement'). As stated in the proposal, the provision tends to avoid 'fraudulent evasion of Community

[51] Art. 28 Rome II; Art. 25 Rome I. The first paragraph of these provisions concerns conventions concluded with third states and the second paragraph conventions concluded exclusively among Member States.

[52] Art. 1(2)(d) and (e). See the explanations in COM (2005) 650 final, at 5. These exclusions date back to the Rome Convention: Report (Giuliano-Lagarde) on the Convention on the law applicable to contractual obligations, OJ 1980 C 282/1, at 11.

[53] COM (2003) 427 final, at 9 referring to the Paris Convention of 29 July 1960 and the conventions and protocols supplementing it.

law'.[54] The provision has been conceived in view of the growing number of mandatory rules in EU secondary law concerning contracts.[55] The most obvious examples concern consumer directives, in principle dealt with under another provision of the regulation (Article 6).[56] However, other examples can be found in the field of commercial transactions.[57] Article 3(4) of Rome I gives priority to any mandatory rule of EU law (i.e. 'provisions of Community law...which cannot be derogated from by agreement') over a third state's law chosen by the parties. If parties have chosen a Member State's law, that chosen law is supposed to reflect all mandatory EU provisions contained in regulations or directives.[58] Article 3(4) Rome I is interesting in two (related) respects. First, it obviously entails a restriction of party autonomy: the opportunity to select the applicable law is restricted to areas not governed by EU mandatory rules. Second, this limitation rests on a double assimilation: (i) intra-EU relationships are assimilated to domestic situations; (ii) for those specific situations, party autonomy in the sense of private international law is assimilated to private autonomy in the sense of internal law. Indeed, with regard to domestic matters, the legitimacy of party autonomy in the sense of private international law, which allows parties to escape from the legal system where the situation is entirely localized in a single jurisdiction, is debatable.[59] A compromise was reached under the Rome Convention which limits party autonomy for purely domestic contracts, by merely allowing the 'incorporating' of foreign provisions into the contract where no mandatory domestic rules governs the contract (Article 3(3) Rome Convention, now Article 3(3) Rome I). The contract therefore remains, as a matter of principle, subject to the domestic law of the country where all relevant aspects of the situation are located. The same logic now applies to situations entirely located in the EU under Article 3(4). The corresponding assimilation between domestic situations and intra-EU situations is representative of the way the EU conceives itself more and more as a 'state', and its Member States as federal entities.

(ii) The mirror of EU substantive policies

In several provisions of Rome I and Rome II, connecting factors are chosen in order to pursue a particular policy recognized by EU substantive law. Article 6 of Rome I ensures the application of EU consumer protection law when the consumer habitually resides in the EU. Points (e) and (f) of Article 4 also designate the law of

[54] COM (2005) 650 final, at 5.

[55] Art. 3(4) does not solve all problems raised by those directives, since many of them also intend to apply in a mandatory way when the situation is not entirely located in the EU (section 2, this chapter).

[56] For instance: Directive 2008/122/EC of 14 January 2009 on the protection of consumers in respect of certain aspects of timeshare, long-term holiday product, resale and exchange contracts, OJ 2009 L 33/10 (Art. 12).

[57] For instance: Directive 86/653/EEC of 18 December 1986 on the coordination of the laws of the Member States relating to self-employed commercial agents, OJ 1986 L 382/17 (Arts 5 and 19); Regulation 236/2012 of 14 March 2012 on short selling and certain aspects of credit default swaps, OJ 2012 L 86/1 (in particular, Arts 12–14).

[58] For a detailed analysis of Art. 3(4) Rome I, see: Francq, *supra* note 35, at paras 70–75.

[59] Report *Giuliano-Lagarde, supra* note 52, Art. 3, point 8.

the place of habitual residence of franchisees and distributors. For those contracts whose proper connection was controversial, 'the solutions are based on the fact that Community law seeks to protect the franchisee and the distributor as the weaker parties'.[60] Article 6 and Article 4(e)–(f) are inspired by the protective policy pursued in substantive EU law for consumers and distributors, but they offer a private international law perspective on such protection: these conflict rules designate the laws applicable on the basis of the proximity of the situation with a legal system (a method of designation considered favourable to the 'weak' party), rather than in view of their substantive content. Thus, in contracts between a professional or a principal established in a third state and a consumer or a distributor residing in the EU, the law of a Member State is likely to be applied. Rome I presents another specificity derived from the formulation of former directives harmonising conflict of laws rules in the field of insurance: the conflict rule concerning large risks is universal in regard of the situations covered, while the conflict rules relating to so-called mass risk is limited to 'risks situated inside the territory of a Member State'.[61]

In Rome II, two provisions deserve a closer look: Article 6(3) and Article 7. Article 6(3) designates the law applicable to damages actions introduced by the victims of a restraint of competition, as 'the law of the country where the market is or is likely to be affected' (Article 6(3)(a)). In cases where the action is introduced in a Member State where one of the defendants is domiciled, the victim-plaintiff can choose to base his claim on the law of that Member State under two conditions: (i) 'the market in that Member State is amongst those directly and substantially affected by the restriction of competition'; (ii) if there are several defendants to this action, 'the restriction of competition on which the claim against each of these defendants relies directly and substantially affects also the market in the Member State of that court'. Recital 23 provides a definition of restrictions of competition as behaviours producing an anti-competitive effect 'within a Member State or within the internal market' and 'prohibited by [now] Articles [101] and [102] of the Treaty or by the law of a Member State'. Article 6(3) was thus certainly intended to reflect EU competition law policy. Article 6(3) Rome II raises numerous interpretation issues.[62]

Concerning external relations in particular, it is not clear if the provision was intended as a 'universal' provision. In regard to the situations covered, Recital 23 points only to situations that have an adverse effect on the EU market, while Article 6(3)(b) deals only with litigation pending in a Member State court when the defendant is domiciled in the territory of a Member State. With regard to the applicable law, Recital 23 focuses on breaches of EU or Member States'

[60] COM (2005) 650 final, at 6.

[61] See Art. 7 (1) of Regulation Rome I. Mass risk insurances cover the most common insurance types where there is a large need for consumer protection, while large risks are risks occurring in specific field of activity or to which large companies are exposed (see Art. 5(d) Directive 73/239, replaced by Art. 13(27) Directive 2009/138, OJ 2009 L 335/1).

[62] For a comprehensive discussion: Francq and Wurmnest, 'International Antitrust Claims under Rome II', in J. Basedow, S. Francq, and L. Idot (eds), *International Antitrust Litigation—Conflict of Laws and Coordination* (2012) 91.

competition law and Article 6(3)(b) designates the law of a Member State. It therefore seems that the legislative intent was to deal only with situations producing an anti-competitive effect in the EU and to designate the law of a Member State or EU law as the law to apply. Even if the wording of Article 6(3)(a) could be considered universal, this position is difficult to reconcile with the wording of the definition in Recital 23.

Article 6(3) raises a second issue regarding external matters or situations. Competition law (Article 101 TFEU, the Sherman Act, etc.) determines its own scope of application.[63] For this reason, competition law provisions have usually been treated as overriding mandatory rules.[64] Rules on competition dealing with the lawfulness of a behaviour are thus applied only so far as they intend to regulate a specific situation, or, in other words, when the situations falls within their predetermined scope. In contrast, a bilateral conflict rule designating the applicable law for competition law issues disregards the applicability condition unilaterally set by competition law provisions. Consequently, Article 6(3) Rome I could potentially designate the law of a country, whose competition law provisions do not intend to cover the situation, as the applicable law.[65] This is another reason to doubt that Article 6(3) should apply to entirely foreign situations (deprived of anti-competitive effect on the EU market) and be used for designating foreign competition law. Indeed, why should EU conflict rules decide when the Sherman Act applies in the EU, when the Sherman Act itself identifies the situations it intends to cover?

Article 6(3) thus raises all sorts of issues concerning the treatment of external situations and the application of third states' law. The formulation of the provision and of the corresponding recitals mirrors a specific legislative intent: the provision was apparently conceived to further the application of EU law (private law and perhaps competition law provisions) in cases of infringement of EU competition law and, thus, only for situations presenting some connection with the EU. As such, the provision can hardly be considered as neutral, nor as universal. Quite the contrary: the rule could be considered as a disguised unilateral conflict rule made to ensure the application of EU law in case EU law claims its application, that is, in case of infringement of EU competition law.

Article 7 Rome II is a happier example of a conflict rule reflecting substantive EU policy. For non-contractual claims based on environmental damages, the claimant can choose between the law of the country where the damage occurred and the law of the country where the event giving rise to liability occurred. The claimant can thus choose the law most favourable to him within a predetermined set of possibilities. Recital 25 underlines that EU principles in regard of environmental protection justify 'discriminating in favour of the person sustaining the

[63] See, among others: T. C. Hartley, *International Commercial Litigation* (2009), at 853; Wagner-von Papp, '§ 11 Internationales Wettbewerbsrecht', in C. Tietje (ed.), *Internationales Wirtschaftsrecht*, (2009) 455, at 468 *et seq*.

[64] Idot, 'Les conflits de lois en droit de la concurrence', *Journal de Droit International* (1995) 321. National Competition Law is cited in the *Giuliano-Lagarde Report* as an example of overriding mandatory rules: *Giuliano-Lagarde Report*, at 28 (comment on Art. 7, para. 4).

[65] For more details, see: Francq and Wurmnest, *supra* note 61, at 107–119.

damage'. As such, Article 7 offers an example of a conflict rule truly embodying a substantive policy (applying the law most favourable to the protected party), rather than a private international law policy of protection (applying the law most closely connected to a protected party). Beyond the uncertainties linked to the definition of the environmental damages,[66] the provision raises one efficiency concern illustrated, for instance, by the Shell case. After the oil spill in Nigeria, Shell Netherlands and Shell Nigeria were sued in the Netherlands by Nigerian farmers supported by an NGO.[67] Rome II did not apply to the case for temporal reasons but it would have probably led to the same result as the Dutch conflict rule applied to the case: Nigerian law would be applicable under Rome II since both the event giving rise to liability (understood in a strict sense) and the damage occurred in Nigeria. Under Article 7 Rome II, the Dutch company thus escapes the application of EU environmental standards. There are only two ways of applying EU environmental standards. On the one hand, the decisions taken by the parent company could be considered an 'event giving rise to liability' within the meaning of Article 7 Rome II, leading to the application of Dutch law. The chances are limited for such a large interpretation of the 'event giving rise to liability' to be adopted. On the other hand, EU environmental law standards could be considered as overriding mandatory rules applicable to EU companies irrespective of the place of their activity. All in all, even if Article 7 is probably the sole provision in Rome II that pursues a true EU substantive policy, the limits to its efficiency become clear in a cases where, as in the Shell case, the event giving rise to liability and the damage are localized in the same country and this country has rather low environmental standards.

The analysis of Article 7 in light of the *Shell* case can lead to two opposite interpretations. First, Article 7 could be interpreted as a clear external policy choice against an extraterritorial application of EU environmental standards. Article 7 does not promote the extraterritorial application of EU environmental law to activities of EU companies abroad, and treats foreign and EU environmental law equally. Second, one could also consider that the drafters of Article 7 did not anticipate how the wording of the provision could turn in favour of polluters in cases like Shell, allowing EU companies to benefit from the lower environmental standards of third states. Article 7 could be amended in order to offer other options to the victims (for instance, the possibility of choosing the law of the place of incorporation of the mother company).

In the end, if the EU legislature was willing to submit EU companies to EU environmental standards even for their conduct abroad, this concern could most efficiently be dealt with in European regulations and directives concerning the environment. EU substantive law could work as a set of overriding mandatory

[66] See the wording of Recital 24 casting doubt on the possibility for private persons to base a claim on Art. 7.

[67] Information on the case can be found at: <https://milieudefensie.nl/english/shell/oil-leaks/courtcase> (last accessed 16 May 2015). More precisely, that case has been brought against Shell Nigeria and Royal Dutch Shell whose principal place of business is in the Netherlands but whose registered office is in the UK.

rules imposed on all EU companies irrespective of the place of their activity. A clear policy choice regarding external situations, and in particular the environmental impact of EU companies abroad, would first need to be reached.

D. Conclusion: Part 1

Rome I and Rome II do have an impact on external matters and situations owing to their universitality. They aim to cover external situations and they designate third state law under the same conditions as they designate EU or Member State law. They do not, however, pursue any specific external policy: foreign and intra-EU situation are treated equally, as are foreign and EU/Member State law. Rome I and Rome II can thus be said to pursue a 'Swiss policy' of neutrality. In many ways, the EU has enacted new conflict rules very similar to those formerly existing at the Member States' level.

As highlighted above, this does not mean that they have been drafted in disregard of the rest of the world, nor that their provisions are entirely deprived of any policy concern. What is lacking, however, is a conception of the EU as a unique entity where Member States entertain special relationships (based on trust and solidarity), different from the relations the EU can have with the rest of the world. Also, specific concern for the implementation of EU substantive policies are not (convincingly) reflected in the bilateral conflict rules of Rome I and Rome II.

The only signs in the opposite direction are Article 3(4) Rome I (dealing with situations where all relevant connecting points are located in the EU), Article 6(3) Rome II (dealing apparently with infringements of EU competition law) and Article 7 Rome II (dealing with environmental damages). Yet, as illustrated by the example of Article 7 Rome II, bilateral conflict rules do not implement on the international scene a true EU substantive policy. The example of Article 6(3) shows, in addition, that bilateral conflict rules, when conceived for implementing EU substantive law, raise all sorts of interpretation issues with regard to external situations and third states law.

In contrast to these findings, EU substantive law offers a radically different picture of EU external policy in private law. First, the treatment of external situations is clearly addressed in so far as EU law requests its application to those situations. Second, the bilateral method, and the corresponding neutrality principle, are superseded by a massive use of the unilateral method.

2. EU Substantive Law: Balanced Unilateralism

EU substantive law in the field of obligations (contractual or non-contractual), broadly understood as encompassing rules on the legality of behaviours, offers a surprisingly different picture, opposite to the 'neutrality' characterizing the conflict rules adopted by the EU in the same field. In EU substantive law, the treatment of external situations is directly addressed in and results from the policy objectives of particular directives and regulations. In essence, EU substantive law fixes its own scope of application in a unilateral fashion and thereby states which situations are covered (both internally and externally) with regard to its (substantive) policy objectives. Since this has been demonstrated at length in earlier writings, only a few examples in the case law and secondary law shall be pointed out.[68] Other chapters in this book, notably Chapters 6 and 7, illustrate similar phenomena. Directives and regulations that identify their own scope of application over external situations are often propounded as a way of securing the application of EU standards over third states' standards. However, they can hardly be qualified as 'extraterritorial' since they always cover situations presenting a close link with the EU and rarely correspond to any aggressive policy in disregard of the needs of cooperation with and consideration for third states' policies.[69] For this reason, they offer a positive picture of a 'balanced' unilateralism. Unilateralism is meant here as it is understood in private international law. Unilateralism covers a theory and a corresponding method in private international law opposed to bilateralism (used for instance in Regulation Rome I and Rome II).[70] Generally speaking, unilateralism supports the idea that substantive rules determine their own scope of application, as a result of the legislative intent. Therefore private international law should be based on the respect of the way in which relevant substantive rules (of different legal systems) identify the situations to which they intend to apply. This approach is opposite to the one used in Rome I and Rome II, where bilateral conflict rules locate a situation within a legal system and thus identify the applicable law, irrespective of the content and scope of the relevant substantive laws, that is, they do so in a neutral way.

By identifying their external/international reach, EU secondary law indicate that projecting EU policies internationally rests on a specific method of private international law that contrasts and potentially clashes with the method used in Rome I and Rome II.

[68] See Francq, *supra* note 28; 'The Scope of Secondary Community Law in the Light of the Methods of Private International Law—Or the Other Way Around?', 9 *Yearbook of Private International Law* (2007) 333.

[69] For similar observations in other contexts, see: Scott, 'Extraterritoriality and Territorial Extension in EU Law', 62 *American Journal of Comparative Law* (2014) 87. In fields like the emissions trading scheme, import of timber and timber products, export of electrical and electronic waste, training for seafarers, ship inspections, security standards for third country air cargo, bans on air carriers, regulation of credit rating agencies, and alternative investment funds, she observes that secondary law fixes its scope of application according to a principle of 'territorial extension'. Being often concerned with access to the EU market, those instruments quite naturally need to determine their addressees, but Scott shows that in doing so, the EU manages to impose its standards, for instance on credit rating agencies who would wish to be relied upon by EU financial institutions. In addition, as she proves, the delimitation of EU law's territorial scope is never made without consideration for foreign law or international standards. Quite the contrary; it is often conceived as a way to further the implementation of some international standards as compliance with those would be considered as a valid reason to have access to the EU market. Her analysis thus confirms, in a different context, the findings made in earlier publications, where I showed that EU law determines its scope unilaterally without corroborating the '*lex-forism*' prejudices usually associated with unilateralism in private international law: S. Francq, *supra* note 28, at 616–621.

[70] For a general overview of unilateralism as a general theory and method of private international law: Francq, 'Unilateralism', in J. Basedow, F. Ferrari, and G. Rühl (eds), *European Encyclopedia of Private International Law* (forthcoming, 2016). See also *infra* section 2.B.

A. Secondary Law: Projecting EU Policies on the International Scene

Examples of directives or regulations fixing their own scope of application and therefore submitting to their provisions some situations partially located in third states can be found in various fields and can take different forms.

For instance, provisions reflecting the mandatory character of EU consumer protection directives are common. Even if the parties contracted for the law of a third country as applicable to the contract, rights provided for by directives nevertheless apply, so long as the situation presents close contacts with EU or one or more Member States.[71] Such provisions have a direct impact on conflict of laws, since they limit party autonomy but also state the (territorial) scope of application of the directive. In doing so, they identify the situations in which rights provided by the directives should apply—namely, situations presenting a close link with the EU or one or more Member States.[72] As such, these provisions solve the conflict of laws issue in a unilateral way by setting their own criteria of applicability (the 'close link'). They are thus difficult to reconcile with bilateral conflict rules of Rome I and II, which designate the law applicable to the contract without specific concern for EU substantive law.

With regard to this difficulty, several directives have been amended in order to reserve the issue of the applicable law to the Rome I Regulation. Interestingly, those efforts show how difficult it is to separate the substantive policy concern from the definition of the scope of application of a directive. Directive 2011/83 provides for a recast of several directives,[73] which used to establish their own scope with a 'close connection test'. Under Article 25 of Directive 2011/83, if the law of a Member State applies, this directive cannot be derogated from. In essence, Rome I is assigned to determine the applicable law and if the applicable law happens to be that of a Member State, then Directive 2011/83 is mandatory. The Directive thus gives priority to Rome I. However, Recital 58 states that 'where the law applicable to the contract is that of a third country, Regulation (EC) No 593/2008 should apply, in order to determine whether the consumer retains the protection granted by this Directive'. This recital implies that even if the law applicable is that of a third state (under Rome I), the directive could potentially still apply. But how exactly can that be if the general provisions of Rome I designate the law of a third state? This is only possible via Article 9 Rome I concerning overriding

[71] For instance: Directive 2008/48 of the European Parliament and the Council of 23 April 2008 on credit agreements for consumers and repealing Council Directive 87/102, OJ 2008 L 133/66, Art. 28(4).

[72] On the interpretation of the close link, see: Case C-70/03, *Commission v. Kingdom of Spain*, [2004] ECR I-7999, para. 33.

[73] Directive 2011/83/EU of the European Parliament and the Council of 25 October 2011 on consumer rights, amending Council Directive 93/13/EEC and Directive 1999/44/EC of the European Parliament and of the Council and repealing Council Directive 85/577/EEC and Directive 97/7/EC of the European Parliament and of the Council, OJ 2011 L 304/64.

mandatory laws.[74] Considering this possibility implies that the directive amounts to an international mandatory law and thus more broadly delineates its scope of application.[75] The latest version of the timeshare directive is another example of a directive fixing its own scope of application: if third state law applies under Rome I, the directive shall nevertheless apply if the immovable property is located in the EU or if the trader conducts professional activities in or directs these activities towards a Member State.[76] The same clarification is not necessary for cases where the law of a Member State applies, because in such a case, respect for the directive is guaranteed as part of Member State law.

Examples can also be found outside EU consumer law. For instance, Article 2 of Regulation 392/2009 on the liability of carriers of passengers by sea in case of accident expressly lists the situations covered,[77] as do Article 1 of Regulation 236/2012 on short selling and certain aspects of credit default swap[78] and Article 2 of Regulation 285/2014 setting technical standards for over-the-counter (OTC) derivative contracts having a 'direct, substantial and foreseeable effect' within the Union.[79] Of course, such is the case as well with directives relating to the taking-up of a professional activity: they usually refer to the professional's establishment or his or her pursuit of an activity on the territory of a Member State.[80] All these instruments of EU secondary law (and many others) expressly state which

[74] Arts 3 and 4 concerning the application of mandatory EU law in regard of purely intra-European situations where parties have chosen a third state's law is not an option since in consumer contracts Art. 6 applies.

[75] See the definition of overriding mandatory rules under Rome I (Art. 9(1)): 'Overriding mandatory provisions are provisions the respect for which is regarded as crucial by a country for safeguarding its public interests, such as its political, social or economic organisation, to such an extent that *they are applicable to any situation falling within their scope*, irrespective of the law otherwise applicable to the contract under this Regulation.' (emphasis added).

[76] Directive 2008/122/EC of the European Parliament and the Council of 14 January 2009 on the protection of consumers in respect of certain aspects of timeshare, long-term holiday product, resale and exchange contracts, OJ 2009 L 33/10, Art. 12(2). By stating that the directive applies when the property is located in the EU, the directive goes beyond Rome I. Under Rome I, the directive would apply only when 'the trader conducts professional activities or directs these activities to a Member State' (see Art. 6 Rome I designating the law of the country where the consumer habitually resides when the professionals conducts or directs its activity towards this country).

[77] Regulation 392/2009 of the European Parliament and the Council of 23 April 2009 on the liability of carriers of passengers by sea in the event of accidents, OJ 2009 L 131/24, Art. 2 (applies to international transport or to certain transports within a Member State when: '(a) the ship is flying the flag of or is registered in a Member State; (b) the contract of carriage has been made in a Member State; or (c) the place of departure or destination, according to the contract of carriage, is in a Member State'.)

[78] Regulation 236/2012 of the European Parliament and the Council of 14 March 2012 on short selling and certain aspects of credit default swaps, OJ 2012 L 86/1, Art. 1 (applying to financial instruments traded on a trading venue in the Union and to debt instruments issued by a Member State or the Union and the derivatives relating to such a debt instrument).

[79] Commission Delegated Regulation 285/2014 of 13 February 2014 supplementing Regulation (EU) No. 648/2012 of the European Parliament and of the Council with regard to regulatory technical standards on direct, substantial, and foreseeable effect of contracts within the Union and to prevent the evasion of rules and obligations, OJ 2014 L 85/1, Art. 2.

[80] For instance, Art. 2 Directive 2009/138 of the European Parliament and the Council of 25 November 2009 on the taking-up and pursuit of the business of Insurance and Reinsurance (Solvency II), OJ 2009 L 335/1.

situations partially located in a third state fall within their scope. In doing so, they delimit their own scope of application (or geographical scope) in a unilateral way and clearly reveal the EU legislature's view on the relationship of its law with the law of other states.

B. CJEU: Translating Silent Unilateralism

When the law-maker has not clearly expressed his view on the relationship between EU law and third states' law in its secondary law instruments, the CJEU (when questioned on this issue) identifies the scope of application of EU secondary law (and its potential priority over third states' law) in regard to the provisions and purpose of the regulation or directive in question. In doing so, the CJEU takes over the role of 'translator' in the dialogue between EU law and third states' law.[81]

1. Ingmar versus Eaton Leonard Tech

The *Ingmar* case is well known in this respect.[82] In that case, the Court considered the EU directive on commercial agents applicable to a contract between a principal established in California and a commercial agent carrying out his activities in the UK, despite the party's express choice in favour of the law of the state of California in the contract. The directive intends to 'protect commercial agents' and thus 'to eliminate restrictions on the carrying-on of the activities of commercial agents, to make the conditions of competition within the Community uniform and to increase the security of commercial transactions'.[83] For the Court, these objectives of the directive require its application 'throughout' the EU and 'where the situation is closely connected with the Community, in particular where the commercial agent carries out her activity in the territory of a Member State, irrespective of the law by which the parties intended the contract to be governed'.[84] In terms of private international law, this decision deals with two aspects of the directive. On the one hand, the Court fixes the (geographical) scope of application of Directive 86/653: the directive applies to situations closely connected with the EU and this connection is deemed to exist when the agent carries on his activities in the EU. On the other hand, for situations where the directive aims to apply, general conflict rules, and in particular party autonomy, are subordinated. Of course, the combination of these two elements led some to consider that the directive was turned into an overriding mandatory rule,[85] but, more interestingly in regards to external

[81] See on the paradigm of law as translation and its application to EU law: A. Bailleux et al. (eds), *Traduction et droit européen, Enjeux d'une rencontre—Hommage au Professeur Michel van de Kerchove* (2009) (and in particular the contribution of Azoulaï, 'La jurisprudence de la Cour de justice et le paradigme de la traduction', at 181); F. Ost, *Le droit comme traduction* (2009).

[82] Case C-381/98, *Ingmar GB Ltd v. Eaton Leonard Technologies Inc.*, [2000] ECR I-9305.

[83] Ibid., paras 20 and 23.

[84] Ibid., paras 24 and 25.

[85] Idot, 'Note sous CJCE, 9 novembre 2000', *Revue Critique de Droit International Privé* (2001) 112, at 117 (wondering whether after *Ingmar*, every directive should be considered as an overriding mandatory rule).

relations, the need to apply this directive despite the choice of a third state law and the establishment of the defendant on the territory of a third state is derived from the objectives of the directive. Since the directive is silent as to its territorial scope, the reasoning of the Court is entirely based on the analysis of the recitals. In the end, the most important reason to apply the directive in this case seems to be the need to protect the agent for the purpose of ensuring the functioning of the internal market.[86]

Ingmar thus establishes a link between the purpose of secondary law and the treatment of situations partially located in third states. There are potentially two lessons to be learned from *Ingmar*. First, *Ingmar* suggests that achieving the goals of EU law necessarily implies to deal also with external situations, at least in determining whether and how far EU law applies to those situations.[87] Second, in doing so, EU secondary law resolves a conflict of laws issue: it imposes the application of its laws to the covered situations and displaces the potential application of third states' law. In *Ingmar*, party autonomy had been used to choose the law of a third state,[88] but even such a designation of a third state's law resulting from the objective provisions of Rome I and Rome II or national conflict rules must be displaced. This has recently been illustrated again in the *Google* case.

2. *Google versus AEPD*

In this case, the Court had to consider whether the EU directive on the protection of personal data was applicable in a litigation between a Spanish national and resident and Google Spain and Google Inc.[89] Google Inc. has its seat in the US and operates a search engine offered worldwide. Google Spain is the Spanish subsidiary of Google Inc. in charge of selling, in Spain, advertising space available on the Google website.[90] Mr Costeja González wanted to effect the removal of information concerning him that had been published in a Spanish newspaper and was accessible when entering his name in the Google search engine. He had

[86] Indeed, the other aims of the directive (combating distortion of competition and favouring freedom of establishment) are hardly at stake in the factual situation of *Ingmar*: see Francq, *supra* note 28, *at* 405–416; Michaels and Kamann, 'Grundlagen eines allgemeinen gemeinschaftlichen Richtlinienkollisionsrechts—'Amerikanisierung' des Gemeinschafts-IPR?', *EWS* (2001) 301).

[87] As highlighted in the *Tobacco II* case, the treatment of 'external' or partially 'external' situations can be necessary in secondary law based on Art. 114 TFEU: Case C-491/01, *The Queen v. Secretary of State for Health, ex parte British American Tobacco (Investments) Ltd and Imperial Tobacco Ltd*, [2002] ECR I-11453, paras 85 and 127.

[88] The fixing of the spatial scope of application of secondary EU law does not always mean that party autonomy is excluded. Party autonomy is excluded only in so far as secondary law not only determines its own scope, but additionally has the highest degree of imperativity (i.e. constitutes an overriding mandatory law where the application of the foreign law undermines the result intended by EU law). On the distinction between applicability and imperativity, see: Francq, *supra* note 28, at 328–334, 432–441, and 575–576.

[89] Case C-131/12, *Google Spain and Google Inc. v. AEPD and Mario Costeja González*, judgment of 13 May 2014; Directive 95/46/EC of the European Parliament and of the Council of 24 October 1995 on the protection of individuals with regard to the processing of personal data and on the free movement of such data, OJ 1995 L 281/31.

[90] For more details, see: Case C-131/12, *supra* note 89, para. 43.

filed a request against the newspaper and against Google. The Spanish authority on data protection refused the request in regard to the newspaper but considered that operators of the search engine were subject to the data protection legislation (meaning the implementation of the directive), which required the withdrawal of data or the prohibition of access to such data in the circumstances of the case. The Court delivered its preliminary ruling during the appeal lodged by Google and Google Spain against this decision. Interestingly, Article 4 of Directive 95/46 had been identified by the Spanish court, and later by the CJEU, as the provision determining the 'territorial scope of the directive',[91] since it is titled 'applicable law' and formulated as a set of the conditions under which each Member State will apply its implementing legislation.[92] The Court had thus to assess whether the 'processing' of the data of Mr Costeja González had been 'carried out in the context of the activities of an establishment of the controller on the territory of the Member State' under Article 4(1)(a) of the directive. According to the Court, Google Spain can be considered as an establishment of Google Inc. (the 'controller') since it 'engages in the effective and real exercise of activities of an establishment of the controller on the territory of a Member State'.[93] The Court also considered that the processing of the personal data of Mr Costeja González had been carried out in the context of the activities of this establishment. Indeed, 'processing of personal data for the purposes of the service of a search engine such as Google Search, which is operated by an undertaking that has its seat in a third State but has an establishment in a Member State, is carried out "in the context of the activities" of that establishment if the latter is intended to promote and sell, in that Member State, advertising space offered by the search engine which serves to make the service offered by that engine profitable'.[94] The activities of Google Search and those of its Spanish establishment were thus considered to be 'inextricably linked'.[95]

Of course, the findings of the Court are open to debate.[96] First, Google Spain is not in direct contact with Mr Costeja González: Google France is in fact in the same position towards the claimant as Google Spain is, since neither of them is engaged in data searching. Second, the case raises the issue of who can actually rely on the directive. It is now certain that the European establishments of Google are considered establishments per se, and that the data available in the search engine are processed in the context of the activities of such establishments, which triggers the application of the directive. However, this is only one side of the spectrum; on the other lies the question of who is protected. Can a Japanese national and resident claim that the directive applies because Google has an establishment in Spain, or is the nationality or residence (or even European citizenship) of the victim also a factor

[91] Ibid., see the title between paras 41 and 42.

[92] Art. 4 is entitled: 'National law applicable'. The CJEU also relied on Art. 4 to determine whether Spanish law applied (rather than any other Member States' law). This aspect of the case will not be discussed here.

[93] Case C-131/12, *supra* note 89, para. 49 (see Recital 19 of Directive 95/46).

[94] Ibid., para. 55 [95] Ibid., para. 56.

[96] See for a comprehensive analysis: Hardy, 'Application dans l'espace de la directive 95/46/CE: la géographie du droit à l'oubli', *Revue Trimestrielle de Droit Européen* (2014) 879.

of applicability? This latter aspect is not discussed explicitly in the case, but it seems difficult to imagine that the Court would have delivered the same opinion in favour of a victim presenting no connection with the EU and suing in Europe in the hope of benefitting from the directive.[97] Third, the decision also leaves questions open about the implementation of the 'right to be forgotten'. If Google has to withdraw access to some information, does it have to do so everywhere throughout the world, meaning that third states' residents would also be deprived of access to that information?

Many issues are thus left open in the decision, but most importantly, the general approach of the Court deserves attention and is relevant for conflict of laws and external relations: the decision gives the data protection directive teeth. The directive, based on Article 100A EC (now Article 114 TFEU), was aimed at removing the obstacles to the flow of personal data in the internal market due to heterogeneous developments of Member States' legislation regarding this sensitive topic.[98] However, like many other directives taking over general interests formerly defended by national legislators, Directive 95/46 also had to ensure a high level of data protection in the 'European Community'.[99] The processing of personal data on the Internet (a phenomenon not fully considered at the time of enactment of the directive) can hardly be regulated at local level and the protective objective of the directive inevitably calls for the directive to be applied also to 'controllers' established outside the EU. The directive had already anticipated this problem in its Chapter IV concerning the 'transfer of personal data to third countries'. The wording of Chapter IV shows, however, that the directive was concerned with the physical transfer of data and not adapted to the activities of worldwide search engines. The Court explains its approach of the scope of the directive in the following terms: 'in the light of the objective of Directive 95/46 of ensuring effective and complete protection of the fundamental rights and freedoms of natural persons, and in particular their right to privacy, with respect to the processing of personal data, those words cannot be interpreted restrictively', and further, 'the European Union legislature sought to prevent individuals from being deprived of the protection guaranteed by the directive and that protection from being circumvented, by prescribing a particularly broad territorial scope'.[100] The Court relies on this objective, namely the protection of privacy, to determine the scope of the text and the necessity to cover companies located in third countries. Taking stock of the link between the protection of privacy and the scope of the directive should help answer some of the issues left open by the decision.[101]

The *Google* decision thus confirms the findings from *Ingmar*. The (territorial) scope of application of EU secondary law stems from its policy objectives: a direct correlation can be established between the achievement of EU policies and the

[97] Under Art. 2 Brussels I (or Art. 4 Brussels I *bis*) for instance, at the place of domicile of the Spanish subsidiary.

[98] Recital 8 of Directive 95/46. [99] Recital 9 of Directive 95/46.

[100] Case C-131/12, *supra* note 89, para. 53.

[101] For instance, the directive probably does not aim at protecting the privacy rights of third countries' nationals established outside the EU.

potential need to cover situations partly located in third states. As a result, EU policy objectives offer an answer to the conflict of laws question: EU substantive law states when and how foreign situations should be submitted to its provisions, irrespective of the law potentially designated by Rome I, Rome II, or national conflict rules. In the *Google* case, since privacy is excluded from the material scope of Rome II, national conflict rules had to determine the law applicable to the damages potentially claimed by the victims. But as far as the establishment of liability is concerned—was the processing lawful? Should the data have been removed?—the directive applies irrespective of whether the general conflict rules (here, the national ones) designate the law of a Member State or of a third state to be applicable.

C. Conclusion: Part 2

The analysis of EU substantive law enacted in the field of obligations offers an interesting contrast with the picture of Rome I and Rome II. Directives and regulations do affect external situations but, in contrast with Rome I and Rome II, this is not done in a neutral manner. Quite the contrary, EU substantive law actively pursues its policies on the international scene. The question is to determine how far external (or semi-external) situations are subject to EU substantive policies. This observation, put in the technical vocabulary of private international law, reveals a strong revival of unilateralism at the EU level.[102]

The 'Swiss' policy of neutrality pursued by Rome I and Rome II is here replaced by a substantive policy. Rome I and Rome II Regulations and substantive law are guided by opposing logic regarding the treatment of external matters and situations, and this is for good reasons: substantive law is not neutral. On the contrary, substantive EU law has a strong sense of what the European values are and of their impact on external situations.

3. Lessons from Schizophrenia?

A comprehensive analysis on the reasons for the divergence opposing the EU regulations on private international law and EU substantive law with regard to external situations and third state law exceeds the limits of this chapter.[103] In conclusion, however, a few explanations can be contemplated, together with some comments on the lessons to be learned from the observations made earlier.

A. The Weight of Tradition in Private International Law

Neutrality and universality (with regard to the scope of conflict rules and of the law designated by them) can be explained by the weight of tradition in private

[102] Francq, *supra* note 28, at 577–640; Francq, *supra* note 68, at 333–378.

[103] Again, explanations have been sought in a more thorough fashion in the contributions cited *supra* in note 101.

international law. As explained earlier, the Rome I Regulation is a mere recast of the Rome Convention, and the Rome II Regulation was conceived as its mirror for extra-contractual obligations. In addition, the drafting of the instruments was influenced by academics, specialists in private international law rather than EU law. Beyond a few particular provisions, the philosophy of those instruments was not to consider a different role for private international law, a specific treatment of European situations as opposed to 'external' situations, or to focus on specific European substantive policies.

At the time, the shift of power resulting from the adoption of EU regulations on private international law was significant. The regulations replaced former national conflict rules (leading to the abrogation of their national '*pendant*'); the EU was beginning to take over the role of the Member States in negotiations with third states and was about to become a member of the Hague Conference. The EU endorsing the role of the 'state' in the domain of private international law has led to fierce controversies and it was probably wise at the time to refrain from further (and more complex) debates over the role and fundamental principles of private international law.

Indeed, more importantly, the traditional conception of private international law (or rather, the post-Savignian conception) is deeply rooted in the ideas of neutrality and universality. If the purpose of private international law is to identify the seat of a relationship, or in contemporary terms, the country of the closest connection, its rules can hardly be formulated in detailed consideration of special external policies (beyond a few interesting exceptions discussed above). These principles also result from the history of private international law: much effort was dedicated to distinguish the question of private international law from the question of sovereignty.[104] The idea of private international law impacting on sovereignty had a lasting and deep influence on its tools and solutions, and this still surfaces today in the debate on 'extra-territoriality'.[105] The major adaptations towards flexibility, functionalism, and the introduction of some substantial consideration of fairness occurred only after a clear distinction was made between issues of private international law and the respect for sovereignty.[106] Those adaptations were echoed in the formulation of Rome I and Rome II: escape clauses for flexibility, party autonomy on a large scale for functionalism, and eventually a few provisions pursuing (in a more or less direct way) some consideration of fairness (consumer protection, for instance) or substantive policy (Article 7 Rome II and Article 3(4) Rome I). The sole provision offering a clear vision of a potential 'external policy' of the Rome

[104] For a solid account of history of the links between sovereignty and private international law, see for instance: Audit, 'Le droit international privé en quête d'universalité', 305 *Recueil des Cours de l'Academie de Droit International* (2003) 9, at 161–210.

[105] See for instance the decision of the US Supreme Court in the *Kiobel* case: *Kiobel v. Royal Dutch Petroleum Co.*, 133 S.Ct. 1659 (2013).

[106] For a clear account of these adaptations, see: Audit, *supra* note 104, at 288–357; Symeonides, 'Private International Law at the End of the 20th Century: Progress or Regress?—General Report', in S. Symeonides (ed.), *Private International Law at the End of the 20th Century: Progress or Regress?* (2000) 3, at 21–62.

I and Rome II Regulations is Article 3(4) Rome I, which limited party autonomy in purely 'intra-European' situations.

In sum, Regulations Rome I and Rome II are the direct heirs of a long tradition of neutral and universal conflict rules. Even if those principles have been subject to some adaptations, as conflict of laws was progressively distinguished from the conflict of sovereignties, they remain the core foundations of private international law. When the EU took over the role of Member States in the field of private international law, it did so without reconsidering its foundations. As a result, external and internal situations, Member State law and third states law, are generally placed on an equal footing. EU substantive law illustrates, however, the need for some specific consideration of the reach of EU law and policies in regard to external situations.

B. Efficiency in Substantive Law

Deprived of any long-standing tradition, EU substantive private law is driven by the search for efficiency and it shows a strong sense of identity internationally. There is something essentially pragmatic about EU law, drafted by technocrats rather than academics. New substantive policies are being formulated at the EU level and their effective implementation also requires determining to what extent external (or rather, partially external) situations should be subject to those policy choices. As explained earlier, the external policy of EU substantive law appears as the natural extension of an internal substantive policy.

The reasons for this 'external' side of the internal policies can be debated. They could be identified in the special nature of EU private law and of the EU legal order. H.-W. Micklitz has shown how EU private law was about building and shaping markets and thus had a strong regulatory character.[107] As a law driven by the needs of a specific market, a reality also prompted by the limitation of power (and the formulation of legal basis), EU substantive law might be more prone to identify its addressees, and thus to clarify its territorial scope.[108] Moreover, the EU is a legal order in constant evolution and on a quest for its own identity; the need for targeting those submitted to its norms might then be a mere reflection of this state of uncertainty regarding its own limits.

The necessary link between substantive policies and the territorial scope of norms, however, has also been identified, beyond EU law, in national law.[109] Therefore,

[107] H.-W. Micklitz's chapter in this book moves in this direction when he shows that regulatory private law accompanies regulating international markets by extending its own standards beyond the internal market or engaging in international negotiation. Also: Micklitz, 'The Visible Hand of European Regulatory Private Law', 28 *Yearbook of European Law* (2009) 3, at 9–12. Although he doubts that EU private law really is about social justice or about providing a chance to benefit from the Internal Market (at 13), I tend to think that market access is often the prism (imposed by the limitation of power and the formulation of Art. 114 TFEU) through which some European values can be seen.

[108] Considering the specifities of regulatory private law in the field of private international law, see: Basedow, 'Conflict of Economic Regulation', 42 *American Journal of Comparative Law* (1994) 423.

[109] See, for instance, the writings of Brainerd Currie (B. Currie, *Selected Essays on the Conflict of Laws* (1963)) and Rolando Quadri (R. Quadri, *Lezione di diritto internazionale privato* (5th edn, 1969)) and the formulation of § 6 of the US Restament (Second) on conflict of laws.

explanations for the external dimension of regulations and directives can be found outside the specific nature of the EU legal order or of EU private law, notably in private international law theory. According to the founders of contemporary unilateralism, the necessary link between the legislative intent and the scope of the legislative product is best explained by the nature of law as the result of social experience and as a tool to guide human action.[110] If substantive law aims at influencing private behaviours and is animated by a policy resulting from the accumulation of social experience in a given society, it necessarily identifies those it seeks to address. As such, laws of a given society thus inevitably determine how far they apply to the outside world. As mentioned earlier, unilateralism proposes a radically different vision of private law, and of private international law, than the one supported by the (dominant) bilateralist doctrine. Suffice it here to recall that the way in which European substantive law treats external situations and pursues its policies on the international scene reflects the fundamental elements of unilateralism. As already pointed out, the unilateralist theory presupposes (i) that each law determines its own (territorial or extra-territorial) scope as a result of its substantive content and purpose, and (ii) that conflict of laws issues should be resolved by paying respect to this self-determination rather than attempting to locate legal relationships, irrespective of the scope of application of the laws in conflict.[111] It is thus unsurprising that unilateralists have strongly opposed the (almost paternalistic) idea that the identification of the applicable law can be solved on the basis of neutral and universal conflict rules, as if the foreign state's sovereign conception of its laws were irrelevant.

Unilateralism considers that laws always identify their own scope (territorial and extraterritorial) as a result of their normative purpose and of the social experience from which they derive. Accordingly, this doctrine raises the question whether from a conflict of laws perspective there is something really new about (EU) regulatory private law. Regulatory private law, given its specific purpose, surely needs to identify its international reach, but the insight from unilateralism is that this is true for any law, since every law necessarily has an own purpose and thus a scope.[112] As Pilenko put it, the internal and external aspects of laws are necessarily intertwined.[113] The 'external dimension' of private law is, for unilateralists, a matter of course: all of private law has—and has always had—a regulatory function.

[110] See Francq, *supra* note 28; Francq, *supra* note 68 (where several explanations for the presence of a clear definition of the territorial scope of EU substantive law are discussed, before reaching the conclusion that the only valid explanation is to be found in the unilateralist conception of the nature of law as a guide for action).

[111] Ibid. For a general overview of unilateralism as a general theory of private international law: Francq, *supra* note 70.

[112] Pillet, for instance, was identifying in every law a 'but social' on the basis of which conflict of laws should be solved (Pillet, 'Theorie continentale des conflits de lois', 2 *Recueil des Cours de l'Academie de Droit International* (1924) 44, at 467–482; *Principes de droit international privé* (1903), at 22, 249–264, and 285 *et seq.*) thereby echoing the old statutist school which dominated private international roughly between the thirteenth and the nineteenth centuries. Quadri's and Currie's conceptions of law present laws as an attempt to shape a society even more clearly.

[113] Pilenko, 'Droit spatial et droit international privé', 5 *Jus Gentium* (1954) 35–59; 'Le Droit spatial et le Droit international privé dans le projet du nouveau Code Civil français', 6 *Revue Hellénique de Droit International* (1953) 319–355.

C. European Conflict of Laws as a Tool for External Policy?

This chapter necessarily raises the issue of the interaction between these opposite ways of addressing external situations in private international law regulations and in EU substantive law, and that of shaping an external policy (neutral versus substantive) in the field of obligations in the EU. How is the tension resulting from Rome I and Rome II and EU substantive law to be addressed in practice, and what does it tell us about the role of EU private international law?

In practice, many issues are solved by Articles 23 Rome I and 27 Rome II giving priority to special conflict rules disseminated in EU regulations and directives. Since, as shown above, the EU solves a conflict of laws issue when determining the territorial scope of EU substantive law, the general (and neutral) conflict rules of Rome I and II are set aside in favour of the policy-oriented rules of secondary law.

However, despite this peaceful solution, it sometimes feels very odd to consider the discrepancies between Rome I and II on the one hand and the rest of EU private law on the other. EU regulations on private international law hardly reflect the substantives policies defended by EU secondary law on the international scene. In those regulations on conflict of laws, (almost) no trace can be found of the special relationship existing among Member States. Up to now, the task of building and taking stock of that special relationship Member States have developed over the last 60 years has been left to EU substantive law. Interestingly, when commenting on the EU conflicts revolution, and in particular on the introduction of a distinction between internal and external conflicts, Michaels' examples relate almost exclusively to the impact of EU substantive law on conflict of laws issues.[114] Would the revolution have occurred beyond and in spite of EU core instruments on private international law?

A different approach, though, raises several concerns if based on discrimination between Member States and third states, between external situations and internal situations, between third states law and Member States law, and more generally on the achievement of specific substantive policies. First, since the EU has taken over the role of the Member States and thus the task of avoiding denial of justice, it has to offer private international law solutions for every situation falling within the substantive scope of its private international law regulations. As the source of a complete set of conflict of laws solutions in specific areas (i.e. here contractual and non contractual obligations), the EU law-maker cannot merely identify cases when EU law applies to internal and external situations. There is a need for some process of designation of the applicable law when EU law does not apply. The means to answer this question are, however, open for consideration. Second, a system of private international law that is more in tune with specific EU policies and their impact internationally would imply a substantial departure from the current conception of private international law and of its historically acquired wisdom. As mentioned earlier, the reasons for treating all foreign laws and international situations as equal deserve consideration: the equal treatment of all laws

[114] Michaels, 'The New European Choice of Law Revolution', 82 *Tulane Law Review* (2008) 1607, at 1635–1638.

mirrors the international spirit of private international law, its openness towards foreign systems and its aim of favouring international harmony of solutions for conflict of laws issues, traditionally opposed to a more 'nationalist' or 'particularist' trend, which insists on the coherence of the *lex fori*.[115] Unilateralism has often been attacked on this front: the method is regularly considered as synonymous with parochialism rather than cosmopolitanism (the contemporary expression of internationalism). The European experience with unilateralism is, however, as shown above, rather sensible and mirrors a 'moderate and restrained approach' of extraterritoriality:[116] when EU regulations and directives apply to partly external situations (i.e. apply extraterritorially), this is as a result of their protective aim, and the situations covered always have a strong connection with the EU.

The question of the role of European private international law with regard to the 'outside' world can hardly be avoided and does not simply replicate the old debates about nationalism and internationalism. Rather, the questions—and the way they are addressed—have been transformed by globalization as well as over 60 years of European integration, both of which make evident, or even trigger, the tensions between cosmopolitanism and respect for local values.

The question is, first, not so much to ascertain whether European private international law is a policy tool but rather to determine how it can be a balanced and efficient policy tool. As the EU experience in private law shows, policies *are* formulated in private international law terms, but we still need to reconsider our general tools of private international law in this regard.[117] This is a vast programme, which might lead us to reconsider the role of Rome I and Rome II and the convenient place for unilateralism and bilateralism in the EU.

Second, the reason why we need to address this issue is not eurocentrism or some modern version of nationalism. It is, rather, based on a true transnational reality, something that can happen once nationalisms have been overcome without denying local identities. Over the past 60 years, Member States have developed a special relationship based on trust, solidarity, and cooperation. Together, they have formulated substantive policies and defined common values, reflected in the charter, the treaties, and secondary substantive law, which cannot be ignored at the private international law level, all the more so since these policies and values aim at having direct implications for conflict of laws.[118]

[115] J.-L. Halperin, *Entre nationalisme juridique et communauté de droit* (1999) 180, warning that globalization might paradoxically come up with a regionalist conception of private international law, more focused on local interests.

[116] The expression 'moderate and restrained approach' is borrowed from B. Currie (*supra* note 109, at 759; 'The Disinterested Third State', 28 *Law and Contemporary Problems* (1963) 754, at 763–764) but applies here to the normative choice of the legislature as well as the interpretation proposed by the CJEU, while Currie used it to qualify the interpretation process endeavoured by judges. Concurring on the moderate version of extraterritoriality, see: Scott, *supra* note 69.

[117] The traditional conflict tools have been adapted towards flexibility and substance, but only to a certain extent: Audit, *supra* note 104, at 291–359.

[118] The recent Communication from the Commission to the European Parliament, the Council, the European Economic and Social Committee, and the Committee of the Regions entitled 'the EU Justice Agenda for 2020—Strengthening Trust, Mobility and Growth within the Union' (COM (2014) 144 final) discusses external relations in those terms: 'The objective should be that what has been achieved at EU level in the justice areas for defending rights and setting standards, such as in the field of personal data protection, finds supports and rives EU relations with third countries.' The sole

Mutual trust, in particular, is acknowledged as a foundational principle for the EU legal system and especially, for its area of freedom, security, and justice.[119] As such, it is particularly suited to guide the specific conception of EU conflict of laws, both in its internal and external dimension, and perhaps introduce some differentiation in their respective treatment. Up until now, the concept of trust, more specifically mutual trust, has mainly served as a justification for the free circulation of judgments among Member States, and more generally the system of resolving conflicts of jurisdiction among Member States.[120] The impact of trust on the conflict of laws, however, has not been greatly considered beyond mutual recognition deriving from the four freedoms.[121] Inquiring whether and how far mutual trust could or should structure the conception of common conflict rules is a far-reaching and difficult enterprise. Particularly from a critical EU law perspective, the notion of mutual trust is notorious for its indeterminate content, and its implications deserve closer scientific inquiry.[122] Generally speaking, the notion of trust as a guiding principle for conceiving legislative action is open to many interpretations. For instance, depending on the parties involved in the 'trust' relationship (relations among Member States, relations between citizens and State or the Union, relations among the institutions, between national and European institutions, relations among administrative/transnational authorities, etc.), mutual trust can have various meanings, result from different factual settings, and be subject to different dynamics. As regards conflict of laws, trust could at first sight be considered totally alien to the usual reasoning used to choose the applicable law. The traditional conception of conflict of laws approaches the relationship between legal systems at a somewhat abstract level by automatically putting them on equal footing: the compatibility of values between systems is a priori taken for granted and only exceptionally addressed at the stage of the public policy exception. In contrast, the EU experience shows that mutual trust, if it were to inform conflict of laws, has a substantive and dynamic nature: dynamic because it is both a precondition to the

consequence clearly derived by the Commission from this objective is 'more efficient cooperation with the Hague Conference' (point 4.3, p. 9). No mention is made of a possible evolution of the current provisions of PIL regulations such as Rome I and Rome II.

[119] The conclusion of the European Council in Tampere based the development of cooperation in the field of civil (and criminal) justice on mutual recognition, and later summits linked mutual recognition to the mutual trust (considered at the same time as established and to be developed): see para. 33 of the Presidency Conclusions (Tampere European Council 15 and 16 October 1999, available at: <http://aei.pitt.edu/43337/1/Tempere_1999.pdf>; last accessed 16 May 2015) and point III.3.2 of the Hague Program approved by the European Council on 5 November 2004, available at: <http://ec.europa.eu/home-affairs/doc_centre/docs/hague_programme_en.pdf> (last accessed 16 May 2015).

[120] For an excellent account of the impact of trust on the jurisdiction issues and consideration for the way forward in this respect: Weller, 'Mutual Trust: In Search of the Future of European Private International Law', 11 *Journal of Private International Law* (2015) 64.

[121] Ibid., concurring on this point. The recent Communication from the Commission (COM (2014) 144 final, *supra* note 118) offers a relatively poor vision of the implications of trust in the field of civil justice (point 3, p 4; point 4.3, pp. 8–9).

[122] On trust as a source code for the development of the Union's method based on cooperation, see: D. Gerard, *Managing Diversity in the European Union: Cooperation, Convergence and Mutual Trust* (PhD Thesis, UCLouvain). The thesis explores the concept of mutual trust, relying partially on Luhmann's work (*Trust and Power* (1979)), and its limits and conditions.

relationship between legal systems and a result thereof, and substantive because it apparently derives from sharing common values.

Mutual trust, or trust generally speaking, could nevertheless explain specific phenomena that already exist and perhaps help to identify what is wrong with our current conflict of laws rules. For instance, the need to impose the data protection directive on third country operators derives directly from the absence of trust in foreign legal systems. In the case of *Google*, the current terms of the US Patriot Act (and its Section 215) might justify why trust is currently questioned.[123] Furthermore, some specific conflict of laws tools, such as the so-called method of recognition, operate best in a context where legal systems develop a specific trust relationship.[124] Eventually, as mentioned earlier, trust (and its corollary, solidarity) potentially justifies a more collaborative approach towards, and thus a more open application of, fundamental policies of sister states as embodied in their international mandatory rules, as opposed to third states policies.[125]

Even if fundamental, trust certainly is not the only guiding principle for European conflict of laws rules, especially in its external dimension.[126] Considering the external dimension of conflict of laws obviously leads to facing the 'substantive' side of the discipline and to open it up to the general discussion on the role of the EU, and, in particular regard to its conflict tools, for global governance.[127] This discussion will have a deep impact on the traditional understanding of conflict of laws rules and also, as mentioned earlier, on the balance between unilateralism and bilateralism. Reality, however, does not wait for theories. Irrespective of the theoretical debate, EU substantive law, as shown above, is de facto already implementing external policies in private international law terms.

[123] Interestingly, under the data protection directive, the transfer of personal data to third states is limited to countries which ensure 'an adequate level of protection' (Directive 95/56, Art. 25(1)). The impact of this provision on private situations and on relations with third states is illustrated by the case *Maximilian Schrems v. Data Protection Commissioner* (C-362/14; see the Opinion of Advocate General Yves Bot delivered on 23 September 2015; the ECJ decision was delivered on 6 October 2015. The Court declares void Decision 2000/520 of the Commission, which considered the US as offering an adequate level of protection under the 'Safe Harbour Privacy Principles', and criticizes a system where interferences with privacy protection are authorized 'on a generalized basis' as incompatible with Art. 7 of the Charter (paras 93 and 94).

[124] On the method of recognition, see: P. Lagarde (ed.) *La reconnaissance des situations en droit international privé* (2013).

[125] For more detail: Francq, 'Unilatéralisme v. Bilatéralisme: une opposition ontologique ou un débat dépassé? Quelques considérations de droit européen sur un couple en crise perpétuelle', in T. Azzi and O. Boscovic (eds), *Quel avenir pour la théorie générale des conflits de lois? Droit européen, droit conventionnel, droit commun* (forthcoming, 2015).

[126] For instance, in his contribution, Timmermans, in line with Art. 3(5) TEU, rightly points out fundamental rights as a guide for external policy.

[127] Interestingly, there is no chapter on private international law in the very stimulating book recently dedicated to the EU's role in global governance; see B. Van Vooren, S. Blockmans, and J. Wouters, *The EU's Role in Global Governance: The Legal Dimension* (2013). Private international law scholars have already started inquiring how far their field could take its share in the global governance debate, but have not necessarily done so form an EU perspective (Muir Watt, 'Private International Law Beyond the Schism', 2 *Transnational Legal Theory* (2011) 347; H. Muir Watt and D. Fernández Arroyo, *Private International Law and Global Governance* (2014); see also Volume 7 Issue 3 (November 2014) of the online *Erasmus Law Review*, gathering contributions on 'The Role of Private International Law in Contemporary Society: Global Governance as a Challenge', introduced by L. Carballo Piñeiro and X. Kramer).

5

The External Dimension of Private International Family Law

Etienne Pataut

Family law is not—to say the least—at the heart of the European Union (EU). The EU does not have any competence in family law, which remains in the hands of the Member States. Therefore, if EU law modifies family law, and it does, it is only indirectly.

Immigration law is one field where EU affects family law. The EU is now an area permitting freedom of movement to all its citizens. Citizens have an unconditional right to move from one country to another, including with their families. Based on this principle, secondary law and case law have provided a great many solutions in order to promote freedom of movement, such as the recognition of 'family status' and access to national social benefits. Those rules frequently concern nationals of third countries who have a family link with a European citizen or a long-term residence in the EU. Therefore, freedom of movement of EU citizens has an important impact both on family law and on immigration rules applicable to third country nationals.

The second field is private international law. According to Article 81 TFUE, the EU possesses the competence to adopt rules on private international law. On the basis of this competence, over the last 15 years the EU has adopted many regulations in the area of private international law in general, and in family matters in particular. In doing so, the fundamental goal of the EU was to build a legal regime which allows for close cooperation between Member States, closer than exists between Member States and third states.

Third states, however, cannot be entirely disregarded.[1] Families can and often do have connections with third countries, either by nationality or domicile, and their concerns therefore are rightly subject to EU law. The EU's attempts to tackle those issues are twofold, and raise separate questions that are addressed in this chapter. First, the EU attained the competence to enter into international conventions with third countries, the so-called external competence. As discussed in the first part of

[1] See A. Malatesta, S. Bariatti, and F. Pocar (eds), *The External Dimension of EC Private International Law in Family and Successions Matters* (2008). See also Chapter 4 and Chapter 6 in this book.

this chapter, the exercise of this competence raises difficulties in family law. Second, EU instruments on private international family law, although primarily designed for use by EU judges and EU citizens, have an impact on third country nationals. The second part of this chapter considers the uncertain scope of this impact.

1. The EU's External Competence in the Field of Family Law

A. Treaty-Making Power

The first question raises nothing more than the private international aspect of traditional treaty-making powers: who has the power to negotiate, sign, and finally ratify an international convention? Of course, these questions are not unique to family law. However, experience shows that as far as private international law is concerned, most of them were raised in family matters.

As a general rule, established in the famous *ERTA* case,[2] the EU's external competence depends on the exercise of its internal competence. This rule has been applied to private international law by the Court of Justice (CJEU) in its equally famous 1/94 opinion about the Lugano Convention.[3] In this opinion, the Court stated that external competence in private international law should be given to the EU and not to Member States because the EU exercised its internal competence in the field by adopting, among others, the Brussels I Regulation.

This issue has raised some new difficulties concerning the legal relations between Member States, the EU, and third states. A good illustration of those difficulties can be seen in the EU's participation in the Hague Conference on private international law.[4] Those who follow the work of the Conference might recall the effect the entry into force of the Amsterdam Treaty had on the negotiations of the worldwide convention on jurisdiction, discussed in The Hague.[5] Indeed, the Commission took over those negotiations in spite of objections voiced by Member States delegations, some expressing these with considerable vehemence. The Commission did so because it considered that under Article 65 EC (now 81 TFEU), the EU had sole competence in private international law matters.

This shift of power resulted in a modification of the very statute of the Conference, adopted in 2005 and entered into force in 2007: Article 3 of the statute now allows that a 'Regional Economic Integration Organisation' may become a member of the Conference. Although drafted in general terms, this provision was clearly designed to

[2] Case 22/70, *Commission v. Council*, [1971] ECR 263. This chapter is based on the Court of Justice's case-law until May 2015.

[3] Opinion 1/03, *Lugano Convention*, [2006] ECR I-1145. For a thorough analysis, see F. Pocar (ed.), *The External Competence of the EU and Private International Law* (2007).

[4] Warlet, 'La participation de l'Union européenne à la conférence de La Haye', in M. Benlolo-Carabot, U. Candas, and E. Cujo (eds), *Union Européenne et droit international, mélanges en l'honneur de P. Daillier* (2012) 785.

[5] These negotiation eventually failed due to lacking consensus among the negotiating states; the work of the Conference, nevertheless, led to the adoption of the 2005 choice of forum Convention.

allow for the EU's accession to the Conference.[6] Indeed, the EU became a member of the Conference on 3 April 2007.[7] Subsequently, the EU has ratified the 2007 texts on maintenance and signed the 2005 convention on choice of forum.[8] Therefore, it is now clear that Member States have competence to sign/ratify conventions adopted before 2007, whereas the EU has competence for those adopted thereafter.

However, this solution is not as simple as it seems, and it raises some further problems which are diplomatic and/or political, as much as legal, particularly in family matters.

The following sections will discuss three of these problems briefly.

B. Forcing Ratification: The 1996 Child Convention

Between 1999 (entry into force of the Amsterdam Treaty) and 2007 (modification of the Hague Conference status and accession of the EU to the Conference), the situation regarding the Hague conventions was ambiguous. On the one hand, the ratification of pre-2007 conventions was in the hands of the individual Member States, as discussed above. On the other hand, ratification of those conventions also required at least pan-European coordination since the EU had gained competence over private international law issues.

A good example of how this ambiguous situation affected the ratification process of the Hague conventions can be seen in the fate of the 1996 Child Protection Convention. This convention had been negotiated and signed at a time when the EU had not yet assumed competence on private international law. At the same time, the political decision was taken in the EU to address questions of international jurisdiction in family matters in a convention, the 1998 Brussels II Convention,[9] which was transformed into a regulation even before it entered into force.[10] As

[6] Art. 3 of the Statute, available at <http://www.hcch.net> (last accessed 21 May 2015):

(1) The Member States of the Conference may, at a meeting concerning general affairs and policy where the majority of Member States is present, by a majority of the votes cast, decide to admit also as a Member any Regional Economic Integration Organisation which has submitted an application for membership to the Secretary General. References to Members under this Statute shall include such Member Organisations, except as otherwise expressly provided. The admission shall become effective upon the acceptance of the Statute by the Regional Economic Integration Organisation concerned.

(2) To be eligible to apply for membership of the Conference, a Regional Economic Integration Organisation must be one constituted solely by sovereign States, and to which its Member States have transferred competence over a range of matters within the purview of the Conference, including the authority to make decisions binding on its Member States in respect of those matters.

[7] Council Decision 2006/719/EC of 5 October 2006 on the accession of the Community to the Hague Conference on Private International Law, OJ 2006 L 297, at 1–14.

[8] For details, see Hague Conference on Private International Law, *Choice of Forum Convention*, available at <http://www.hcch.net/index_en.php?act=states.details&sid=220> (last accessed 21 May 2015).

[9] Convention on Jurisdiction and the Recognition and Enforcement of Judgments in Matrimonial Matters and Protocol on its Interpretation by the Court of Justice, OJ 1998 C 221.

[10] Council Regulation 1347/2000 of 29 May 2000 on the jurisdiction, recognition and enforcement of judgements in matrimonial matters and in matters of parental responsibility for joint children,

both texts (the 1996 Hague Convention and the then Brussels II Convention) concerned international child protection, the simultaneity of the negotiations of those conventions led to some diplomatic turmoil in The Hague. The members of the Hague Conference felt that EU Member States did not negotiate in good faith because the EU negotiations were secret, whereas the Hague discussions were transparent and public. Indeed, the criticism from The Hague was largely justified: as the EU did not have any internal competence at the time, as far as international convention are concerned, the 100-year-old Hague experience gave the organization strong legitimacy to lead international discussion on the topic.

Anyway, both texts were eventually adopted and the question of ratification arose. According to the Statute of the Hague Conference and EU law at the time, it was clear that the competence to ratify the Child Protection Convention lay in the hands of the Member States. However, this competence started to shift shortly thereafter: in 1999, the competence in private international law issues was transferred to the EU, and in 2000, the EU exercised this competence by adopting the Brussels II Regulation. Even though the CJEU had not yet rendered its *Lugano* opinion, discussed above, it could already be argued at that time that, since internal competence had been exercised, external competence should follow.

Such was indeed the view of the European Council. It adopted a specific decision the title of which is telling: Council Decision of 19 December 2002 authorizing the Member States, in the interest of the Community, to sign the 1996 Hague Convention.[11] Recital 4 of this decision states:

> [t]he Community has exclusive competence for the relevant provisions of the Convention insofar as those articles affect Community rules adopted in this area. The Member States should retain their competence in the areas covered by the Convention which do not affect Community law.

However, the legal situation was less clear than this strong wording might suggest. Indeed, only Member States could become parties to the 1996 Convention (as stated in recital 5 of the above-mentioned decision by the EU Council). Accordingly, the decision concerning ratification ultimately also lay in the hands of the Member States, not just the EU. While the political need for a unified European action had thus become obvious, the legal basis for such a common action was far less clear.

It took some political pressure being applied to the Member States to obtain ratification from all from them. In particular, political difficulties concerning Gibraltar polluted the whole discussion. Because of the territorial dispute between the UK and Spain relating to the status of Gibraltar, both countries were unable

OJ 2000 L 160 (Brussels II Regulation), now replaced by the so-called Brussels II *bis* Regulation, Regulation 2201/2003, OJ 2003 L 338.

[11] Council Decision 2003/93/EC of 19 December 2002 authorizing the Member States, in the interest of the Community, to sign the 1996 Hague Convention on jurisdiction, applicable law, recognition, enforcement, and cooperation in respect of parental responsibility and measures for the protection of children, OJ 2003 L 48.

to agree upon the applicability of the 1996 Children Convention to that territory. The situation created an impasse and led to an unusually firmly worded letter from the Secretary General of the Hague Conference to the President of the Council of the European Union of 25 October 2005.[12] In the letter, the Secretary General urged all the Member States to come to an agreement so as not to jeopardize the entry into force of the 1996 Convention. Eventually, both the UK and Spain ratified the 1996 Convention, albeit with some reservations. Other Member States also took their time in ratifying. The 1996 Convention finally entered into force in September 2014 in Belgium. Italy has still not ratified it.[13]

The course of events shows that the ratification issue was not as clear cut as indicated by the European Council in its 2002 decision. Theoretically, the EU could take legal action against the last reluctant Member State (Italy), but in practice it has not done so. This shows that there is still some remaining uncertainty about the exact scope of the external competence of the EU in this field. Politics, here, is difficult to distinguish from law.

C. Expanding the External Competence: The 2007 Maintenance Convention

Maintenance is an area of law where lack of international texts is not to be feared. The Hague Conference adopted three sets of conventions, all of which are still in force today: (i) two conventions on maintenance obligations toward children (1956 and 1958); (ii) two conventions on maintenance in general, applicable law and recognition and enforcement (1973); and (iii) two conventions on recovery and applicable law, the second called the Hague Protocol (2007).[14] Meanwhile, the EU decided to follow its own legal path and adopted a specific text, the Maintenance Regulation 4/2009.[15]

Such an abundance of texts necessarily creates the risk of overlaps and other difficulties relating to the coordination of those instruments.[16] Those problems are addressed in the instruments themselves, which contain various provisions on the relations between those legal instruments. The discussion here will focus more specifically on the relationship between EU Regulation 4/2009 and the 2007 Hague Protocol on the law applicable to maintenance.

[12] Hague Conference on Private International Law, *Letter from the Secretary General of the Hague Conference to the President of the Council of the European Union*, available at <http://www.hcch.net/upload/tb_e.pdf> (last accessed 16 August 2015).

[13] Hague Conference on Private International Law, *Status Table*, available at <http://www.hcch.net/index_en.php?act=conventions.status&cid=70> (last accessed 21 May 2015).

[14] This last text is called 'Protocol of 23 November 2007 on the law applicable to Maintenance obligations'. Use of the term 'protocol' rather than the usual 'convention' is due to political and practical reasons, and has no impact on its legal nature.

[15] Council Regulation 4/2009 of 18 December 2008 on jurisdiction, applicable law, recognition and enforcement of decisions and cooperation in matters relating to maintenance obligations, OJ 2009 L 7, at 1.

[16] For a general survey, see P. Beaumont, B. Hess, L. Walker, and S. Spancken (eds), *The Recovery of Maintenance in the EU and Worldwide* (2014).

The first project for the Regulation by the Commission, in 2005, contained several detailed provisions on the law applicable to maintenance obligations.[17] However, in 2007, when the Hague Protocol on applicable law was adopted, the Commission decided to modify the structure of the draft regulation: while the draft regulation still contained rules on jurisdiction, recognition and enforcement provisions on the applicable law were deleted. Instead, the Regulation refers to the Hague Protocol in its very original Article 15, which states:

> The law applicable to maintenance obligations shall be determined in accordance with the Hague Protocol of 23 November 2007 on the law applicable to maintenance obligations in the Member States bound by that instrument.

This solution is striking since it incorporates into European legislation a text that has been adopted at international level, external to the EU's legislative procedures.[18] It is not, however, without difficulties. The most important one, in practice, concerns the entry into force of both instruments.

The Hague instruments, like other international treaties or conventions, have their own procedure for entry into force. For instance, Article 25 of the Hague Protocol states that '[t]he Protocol shall enter into force on the first day of the month following the expiration of three months after the deposit of the second instrument of ratification, acceptance, approval or accession referred to in Article 23.' For that reason, the Protocol entered into force in August 2013, three months after Serbia ratified the text, following EU ratification in 2010.

On the other hand, EU instruments also regulate their entry into force. Article 76 of the 4/2009 Regulation states that: 'this Regulation shall apply from 18 June 2011, subject to the 2007 Hague Protocol being applicable in the Community by that date. Failing that, this Regulation shall apply from the date of application of that Protocol in the Community.'

Accordingly, whether or not the EU Regulation entered into force depended, in part, on the Hague Protocol, that is, an international treaty, the entry into force of which did not depend on EU procedures. This is the reason why the Regulation contains a further provision in the Preamble which provides for the possibility that the Regulation may enter into force before the Hague Protocol does so, or at least for the possibility that the Hague Protocol may enter into force in some Member States only. As stated in recital 20 of the text:

> It should be provided in this Regulation that, for Member States bound by the 2007 Hague Protocol, the rules on conflict of laws in respect of maintenance obligations will be those set out in that Protocol. To that end, a provision referring to the said Protocol should be inserted. The 2007 Hague Protocol will be concluded by the Community in time to enable this Regulation to apply. To take account of a scenario in which the 2007 Hague Protocol does not apply to all the Member States a distinction for the purposes of recognition,

[17] Proposal for a Council Regulation on jurisdiction, applicable law, recognition and enforcement of decisions and cooperation in matters relating to maintenance obligations of 15 December 2005, COM (2005) 649 final, Articles 12 *et seq.*

[18] More generally on this issue, see Scott, 'Extraterritoriality and Territorial Extension in EU Law', 62 *American Journal of Comparative Law* (2014) 87. See also Chapter 4, this book.

enforceability and enforcement of decisions needs to be made in this Regulation between the Member States bound by the 2007 Hague Protocol and those not bound by it.[19]

To provide for this possibility, the recognition and enforcement section distinguishes between decisions rendered in a Member State which is bound by the 2007 Hague Protocol (Articles 17 *et seq.*), on the one hand, and decisions rendered in a Member State which is not bound by the 2007 Hague Protocol (Articles 23 *et seq.*) on the other.

This cautious approach proved necessary since, as has just been seen, the Regulation entered into force in 2011 and the Protocol only in 2013. Therefore, there should have been a two-year gap during which the European instrument was in force, but not the Protocol, leaving the resolution of choice of law issues to each Member State.

Such a solution was indeed complex, and the European institutions decided it could be avoided. They decided to adopt an original and more radical approach. This approach is probably the best, in terms of efficiency, uniformity, and simplicity. It is, however, questionable from a legal point of view. The solution is twofold.

First, the Council, as has been seen, decided to ratify the Hague Protocol in 2010.[20] The competence to do so, however, was not obvious. The *ERTA* doctrine laid down by the CJEU links external competence to the actual exercise of internal competence. Therefore, the EU must have adopted a text dealing with the same questions as the international instrument at stake. This is the reason why, in recital 4 of its 2010 decision, the Council states that:

> [m]atters governed by the Convention are also dealt with in Council Regulation (EC) No 4/2009 of 18 December 2008 on jurisdiction, applicable law, recognition and enforcement of decisions and cooperation in matters relating to maintenance obligations. The Union should decide, in this particular case, to sign the Convention alone and to exercise competence over all the matters governed by it.

But this assertion could be challenged since, precisely, *there is no choice of law rule in the Regulation*. Instead, as discussed above, Article 15 merely refers to the Hague Protocol in this context. Accordingly, the Hague Protocol and the Regulation each have a different scope. The use of the word 'matter' in the decision is misleading because both texts concern broadly speaking the same 'matter', that is, maintenance. However, the rules are completely different since the Hague Protocol deals with choice of law issues, while the European Regulation deals with the other private international law issues. Therefore, the rationale behind the *ERTA* doctrine—that is, the risk of jeopardizing a European policy if external competence was exercised by Member States—is not respected. Since there is no autonomous choice of law

[19] Another difficulty needs to be mentioned: the peculiar situation of Denmark and the UK regarding texts in matters of freedom, security, and justice (see Recitals 47 and 48 of Regulation 4/2009 and the declaration by the EU with the ratification decision of the Hague Protocol). This question will not be addressed here.

[20] Council Decision 2011/220 of 31 March 2011 on the signing, on behalf of the European Union, of the Hague Convention of 23 November 2007 on the International Recovery of Child Support and Other Forms of Family Maintenance, OJ 2011 L 93/9.

rule in the Regulation, there is no risk of discrepancy if Member States decide or not to ratify the Hague Protocol.

However, Article 15, which provides that the EU will follow the rules of an international instrument, was deemed to be sufficient to exercise external competence. Since there is no substantive rule in Article 15, this solution appears to be nothing other than a self-awarded exclusive external competence[21] or, as other authors elegantly put it, 'a competence by parthenogenesis'.[22]

Second, to avoid the time-lag problem, EU stated in a declaration made when it ratified the Protocol:[23]

> [t]he European Community declares that it will apply the rules of the Protocol provisionally from 18 June 2011, the date of application of Council Regulation (EC) No 4/2009 of 18 December 2008 on jurisdiction, applicable law, recognition and enforcement of decisions and cooperation in matters relating to maintenance obligations, if the Protocol has not entered into force on that date in accordance with Article 25(1) thereof.

This declaration creates a rather strange legal creature: a set of European choice of law rules, adopted by reference to an international instrument, which is not in force, but nevertheless is applicable in Europe. Such a solution is beyond legal analysis.

Of course, legal criticisms have to be weighed against the obvious political will of both Member States and European institutions. Moreover, the solution that has been followed was probably the most reasonable and simplest one, since it allowed for a global and simultaneous entry into force of the Hague Protocol in all the Member States. The downside of such a course of action is that that the legality of the Regulation could be challenged before the CJEU. Such legal action, however, is doubtful with regard to such a narrow and technical matter. The aim of the analysis conducted here is therefore not to express some kind of legal bitterness or regret but instead to confirm the impression that the question of the scope and exercise of external competences is more political than legal in nature.

D. Authorizing the Accession of Third States: The 1980 Convention

Another question to ponder concerns the exact scope of the EU's external competence. This matter has been raised before the CJEU in relation to the accession of Russia to the 1980 Hague Child Abduction Convention.

It is usual practice of the Hague Conference to distinguish between two groups of states: those which were a party to the Conference when the convention was

[21] Kohler, 'Le nouveau régime transfrontalier des obligations alimentaires en Europe: interrogations sur le règlement (CE) 4/2009 du Conseil', 6 *Annuaire de Droit Européen* (2008) 1175, at 1183.

[22] Kohler and Pintens, 'Entwicklungen im europaïschen Familien- und Erbrecht 2008-2009', 56 *Zeitschrift für das Gesamte Familienrecht* (2009) 1529, at 1531.

[23] Hague Conference on Private International Law, *Maintenance Protocol—Declarations and Notifications*, available at <http://www.hcch.net/index_en.php?act=status.comment&csid=1065&disp=type> (last accessed 21 May 2015).

adopted, and those which were not, and became a member of the Conference only thereafter. The states in the first group participated in the negotiations and thus ratification is sufficient for a convention to enter in force. In other words, no specific agreement or consent from the other states is required. To the contrary, if a state from the second group wishes to accede to a convention, every other state and member of the Conference that is already party to the convention must give its consent to this accession. For the 1980 Child Abduction Convention, the model is followed in Articles 37 and 38 which state respectively that '[t]he Convention shall be open for signature by the States which were Members of the Hague Conference on Private International Law at the time of its Fourteenth Session', and that '[t]he accession will have effect only as regards the relations between the acceding State and such Contracting States as will have declared their acceptance of the accession.'

Russia has been a member of the Hague Conference since 2001. It wished to accede to the 1980 Convention in 2011. Therefore, Russia's accession needs to be accepted by the other Conference member states, already party to the 1980 Convention. Inside the EU, some Member States granted their consent. Between those Member States and Russia, the 1980 Convention is now in force.[24] However, other Member States, including Germany, Italy, Poland, and the UK, have not yet accepted Russia's accession and the Convention therefore is not in force between Russia and those Member States.

Such a situation is unsatisfactory, particularly in a case where, as in child abduction matters, the Union is now governed by a completely unified set of rules since the adoption of the Brussels 2 *bis* regulation.[25] As a matter of policy, a unified solution with third states would be preferable.

However, such a unified solution requires an external competence of the EU. Once again, the existence and scope of this external competence are questionable. The external competence certainly exists today: Article 81 TFUE gives internal competence to the EU and such internal competence has been exercised by the adoption of the Brussels II *bis* Regulation, which sets out a particular legal regime for intra-EU child abduction. However, the Hague Child Abduction Convention was adopted in 1980 and entered into force in 1983 in some Member States, long before the EU's internal (and thus external) competences existed. Accordingly, regarding the accession of third states, it is unclear who, the EU or the Member States, must provide their consent to the accession. The background is this issue is again political and relates to the reluctance of certain Member States to accept Russia as part of the legal cooperation on child abduction under the Convention. Had all parties accepted Russia's accession, it is more than likely that no-one would have raised the issue.

This divergence of opinion among Member States and the need for a unified answer led the Commission to put the following question to the Court:

[24] See the exact present state of the convention at Hague Conference on Private International Law, *Status Table*, available at <http://www.hcch.net/index_en.php?act=conventions.status&cid=24> (last accessed 21 May 2015).

[25] Council Regulation 2201/2003 of 27 November 2003 concerning jurisdiction and the recognition and enforcement of judgments in matrimonial matters and the matters of parental responsibility, repealing Regulation (EC) No 1347/2000, OJ 2003 L 338/1.

Does the exclusive competence of the [European] Union encompass the acceptance of the accession of a non-Union country to the Convention on the civil aspects of international child abduction [concluded in the Hague on] 25 October 1980 ['the 1980 Hague Convention' or 'the Convention']?[26]

The answer of the Court, given by the Grand Chamber, has been delivered on 14 October 2014. As suggested by the opinion of Advocate General Jääskinen, the Court gives a positive answer to the question, and states that external exclusive competence does indeed encompass the acceptance of the accession of a third state to the 1980 Convention.

The Court's opinion is not a surprise but its ramification is still uncertain. It will more than likely have an important impact on the conventional relations between EU, Member States, and third states, and not only in relation to accession questions. The opinion of the Court will also influence the possibility that Member States will make declarations and reservations to conventions to which they are already a party. More generally, the specific nature of the question asked is the possibility of a kind of retroactive application of the external competence. EU regulations in private international family law all contain provisions dealing with the applicability of previously adopted conventions. The general principle is that prior conventions remain unaffected by the new rules. After the opinion of the Court was made, granting the EU an absolute and general external competence, this solution has now to be revised or, at least, it has become more nuanced. Given the dense multi- and bilateral network of conventions in force between Member States and third states, the opinion of the Court could have a significant legal and political impact.

The major lesson to be learned from the study of the emergence of an EU external competence in matters of private international family law is therefore that the existence, scope, and exercise of this external competence are political matters as much as they are legal ones. This leads to an uncommon, flexible approach, which leaves room for political compromises and therefore for what lawyers hate most: uncertainty.

2. EU Family Law Instruments and Third States: The Example of Jurisdiction

A. EU or Extra-EU Private International Law

Since 2000, the EU has slowly built up a common body of private international law. More than 15 regulations are now in force in various fields of law, opening the way for a discussion about a possible general codification of European private international law.[27] The specific nature of EU private international law has been

[26] Opinion 1/13, of 14 October 2014, not yet published; Question published in OJ 2013 C 226, at 2.

[27] See Communication from the Commission, 'The EU Justice agenda for 2020—Strengthening trust, mobility and growth within the EU', COM (2014) 144 final, para. 4-2.

under intense doctrinal scrutiny for the past few decades. One of the issues regularly raised is the comparison between private international law inside the EU and private international law regarding relations with third countries. It is still unclear whether distinct private international law rules are needed. Should this requirement be thought to be necessary, a clear line between rules applicable inside and outside the EU must be drawn.[28]

Such a distinction is fairly easy to make when it comes to procedural cooperation. In these situations, an 'outgoing' state and an 'incoming' state are involved. Both of them need to be a Member State for the rules of cooperation to be applicable. That solution is followed in various areas such as proof collecting,[29] service of documents,[30] or recognition and enforcement of judgments.[31] In all these cases, cooperation under the relevant regulation provision is possible if, and only if, it involves two Member States. Third states, therefore, are not involved. The most striking example is to be found in Articles 10 and 11 of the Brussels II *bis* Regulation. These articles deal with child abduction and lay down rules of cooperation that are specific to Member States, but take place inside the functioning of the 1980 Hague Child Abduction Convention. EU Member States have organized closer cooperation between them, but they try to insert this cooperation with the laws set up within the framework of the 1980 Convention.

As far as choice of law is concerned, the difficulty is of a different kind but it is fairly simple to tackle. The fundamental option that has been taken by all the regulations is to treat situations involving Member States only or Member States and third states equally. The choice of law rules are deemed to be universal, by which the law applicable is the law designated by the connecting factor, without making any distinction depending on whether this connecting factor is inside or outside of the EU. The model for such a rule is to be found in Article 2 of the Rome 1 Regulation on contracts[32] which states that '[a]ny law specified by this Regulation shall be applied whether or not it is the law of a Member State.' The same model is followed in all the other Regulations dealing with choice of law: Rome II,[33] or, in family matters, maintenance,[34] divorce,[35] or successions.[36]

Things become much more complicated when it comes to international jurisdiction. In all the previous examples, the question always involved two legal systems which needed to be coordinated. On the contrary, when it comes to jurisdiction, only one legal system is involved: the system of the judge seized. Cases can have various connections to various states, within or outside the EU. Would, for example, a sales contract between a someone domiciled in Germany and someone domiciled in

[28] See A. Nuyts and N. Watté (eds), *International Civil Litigation in Europe and Relations with Third States* (2005).

[29] Art. 1 of Regulation 12096/2001.

[30] Art. 1 of Regulation 1393/2007.

[31] Brussels I Regulation: 44/2001 and 1215/2012, Arts 33 and 36; Brussels II Regulation: 2201/2003, Art. 21; Regulation EET: 805/2004, Art. 1.

[32] Regulation 593/2008.

[33] Regulation 846/2007, Art. 3.

[34] Regulation 4/2009, which, as has been seen, refers to the Hague Protocol of 2007, in which Art. 2 gives universal effect to the choice of law rule.

[35] Regulation 1259/2010 (Rome III Regulation), Art. 4.

[36] Regulation 650/2012, Art. 20.

Argentina with a delivery of goods in Canada be considered to be a contract 'inside the EU'? Would it be different if goods were to be delivered in Italy?

Per se, international jurisdiction issues concern only the tribunal of one state, and it is therefore extremely difficult to make a clear distinction between a legal regime that would concern Member States only and another regime that would concern relations between Member States and third states. The distinction between 'intra-EU' and 'extra-EU' situations is one that is almost impossible to make.[37]

As a policy issue, it can be accepted that there is and should be closer cooperation between Member States than cooperation between Member States and third states. The fundamental European principle of mutual trust and the grid of the European Judicial Network allow for close cooperation between authorities, for the sake of European citizens. However, the question remains of how to implement this policy in jurisdictional matters,[38] taking into consideration that the decision made will have an important impact on the recognition and enforcement of foreign judgments.[39]

Here again, the question is much more a political than a purely technical one. From the family law perspective, if indeed there is a distinction between different private law relationships, it should not lie in the jurisdiction rule itself, and the real difficulty concerns exorbitant grounds of jurisdiction.

As far as jurisdiction is concerned, several models exist, all of them being tested in various EU instruments. The original model was set up in the 1968 Brussels Convention and was unchanged in the provisions of its follower, the Brussels I Regulation. Following Articles 2 and 4 of the text, the very applicability of the rules of jurisdiction, subject to a few exceptions, was based on the fact that the defendant was domiciled in a Member State. Therefore, a distinction was drawn between litigation which involved a defendant domiciled in a third state, for which jurisdiction had to be decided by national rules, and litigation which involved a defendant domiciled in a Member State, for which jurisdiction had to be decided upon by European rules.

This solution, however, was partly abandoned during the recast of the Brussels I Regulation.[40] Moreover, it has never been followed in family matters, for which existing texts hesitate between semi-universal and universal rules. The latter seem

[37] In general, see Pataut, 'Qu'est-ce qu'un litige intracommunautaire?', *Justice et droits fondamentaux, Mélanges J. Normand* (2003), at 365. See also, Chapter 6, section 4, this book.

[38] Bonomi, 'The Opportunity and the Modalities of the Introduction of Erga Omnes EC Rules on Jurisdiction', in A. Malatesta, S. Bariatti, and F. Pocar (eds), *The External Dimension of EC Private International Law in Family and Successions Matters* (2008) 149.

[39] See Fallon and Kruger, 'The Spatial Scope of the EU's Rules on Jurisdiction and Enforcement of Judgments: From Bilateral Modus to Unilateral Universality?', 14 *Yearbook of Private International Law* (2012–2013) 1.

[40] Partly only, unfortunately, and despite the proposal of the Commission, which suggested the deletion of the rule. See the critics in European Commission, *Report on the Application of Council Regulation No. 44/2001*, COM (2009) 174 final, para. 3-2 and the proposal of a new Art. 4 in European Commission, *Proposal for a Regulation on Jurisdiction and the Recognition and Enforcement of Judgments in Civil and Commercial Matters*, COM (2010) 748 final.

preferable, although it leaves open the difficult and political question of the existence of exorbitant grounds of jurisdiction.

B. Semi-Universal Rules: The Brussels II *bis* Approach

The Brussels II *bis* approach is very different from Brussels I because the applicability of the jurisdiction rules is not limited by any connecting factor drawing a specific territorial scope of application. Therefore, once the jurisdiction connecting factor is located in a Member State then the courts of that Member State have jurisdiction, regardless of other connecting factors. Therefore, in divorce cases, if Article 3 of the Regulation gives jurisdiction to the courts of a Member State (because of habitual residence, for example), these courts have jurisdiction, regardless of all the other connecting factors. Member State national rules are not applicable at all.

Such a solution was new and could appear somewhat puzzling for judges. This might explain why, for example, the French *Cour de cassation* affirmed the jurisdiction of the French court pursuant to Article 14 of the French Civil Code and not to the Brussels II Regulation in a case where the members of the family had French and/or Moroccan nationality, where the wife and children were living in France but where the husband was living in Morocco, and where jurisdiction of the French court was challenged in favour of jurisdiction of Moroccan courts, by virtue of a bilateral convention.[41] It is very likely that the Franco-Moroccan nature of the relationship hid the fact that an EU piece of legislation was actually applicable. Applicable it was, nevertheless, and if indeed the French courts had jurisdiction, it was thanks to Article 3 of the original Brussels II Regulation (Regulation 1347/2000) and not to Article 14 of the French Civil Code.

On the contrary, the correct interpretation has been given by the CJEU in one of the first decisions interpreting the original Brussels II Regulation.[42] In that case, resembling the one heard by the French courts, a Swedish national domiciled in France wanted to obtain divorce from her Cuban husband, who had returned to Cuba. She went to the Swedish courts, arguing they had jurisdiction based on her nationality. The argument, however, was dismissed by the CJEU. As the Court clearly said (paragraph 28):

> where, in divorce proceedings, a respondent is not habitually resident in a Member State and is not a national of a Member State, the courts of a Member State cannot base their jurisdiction to hear the petition on their national law, if the courts of another Member State have jurisdiction under Article 3 of that regulation.

This solution is far better than the one in Brussels I. In jurisdiction matters, the question is not to determine whether one or more EU country is concerned with

[41] Civ. 1, 28 March 2006, JCP. 2006. II. 10133; note by A. Devers. The bilateral convention was in fact not applicable to the case.

[42] Case C-68/07, *Sundelind Lopez*, [2007] ECR I-10403. The Brussels 2 *bis* Regulation has kept the same provisions.

the legal relationship challenged before the court, the only question is to select an appropriate connecting factor and, if this connecting factor is directed towards a particular country, give jurisdiction to the courts of that country. The fact that jurisdiction rules are being harmonized at EU level does not make any difference. It does not imply that the legal relationship concerned needs to be connected to two or more Member States. As far as jurisdiction is concerned, there is no theoretical difference between a national rule of jurisdiction and EU rules of jurisdiction, and for third countries, there is no difference between national or European jurisdiction rules. The structure of the rule is the same and the application is the same.

Therefore, as in Brussels I, a distinction between 'intra-EU' and 'extra-EU' cases in order to determine the very applicability of European or national jurisdiction rules seems to add enormous complexity for no satisfying theoretical or practical reason.

Brussels II, however, does not radically exclude all national rules. For divorce cases, Articles 6 and 7 establish a regime where national rules of jurisdiction can be used only when no connecting factor used by the regular jurisdiction rule is located in a Member State. In any case, these national grounds of jurisdiction cannot be used against a defendant habitually resident in the EU, domiciled in the common law sense in the UK or Ireland, or a national of a Member State. Finally, EU nationals habitually resident in another Member State can avail themselves of the national rules of jurisdiction of that state against a defendant who is neither habitually resident in the EU, nor an EU national, nor domiciled in the common law sense in the UK or in Ireland.[43]

Things are simpler when it comes to parental responsibility, since Article 14 simply states that 'where no court of a Member State has jurisdiction pursuant to article 8 to 13, jurisdiction shall be determined in each Member State by the laws of that State'.

Even though the formulation, at least in divorce cases, might seem complicated, the aim is very simple and the text is able to draw a clear line between national and European rules of jurisdiction. The latter are applicable when the former are not, that is, when no connecting factor links the case and the courts of a particular Member State. Therefore, as in Brussels I, national law on international jurisdiction has not completely disappeared, although, as will be shown, its role is completely different.

C. Universal Rules: The Maintenance and Succession Regulations Approach

The Maintenance Regulation (4/2009) and the Successions Regulation (650/2012) have adopted another model, simpler and arguably better.[44]

[43] Borras, 'Art. 6 and 7', in U. Magnus and P. Mankowski (eds), *Brussels II bis Regulation* (2012).

[44] For a close analysis, see also Bonomi, *supra* note 38, at 153.

Articles 3, 4, and 5 of the Maintenance Regulation provide the main connecting factors for a court of a Member State to have jurisdiction. In the main these involve habitual residence, choice of court by the parties, and the mere appearance of the defendant before a given court. Another possibility is to give jurisdiction to the courts of the Member State which has jurisdiction in a connected family matter.

If no Member State court has jurisdiction in that situation, then Article 6 opens the possibility for a subsidiary jurisdiction based on the common nationality of the parties. Finally, if no Member State has jurisdiction pursuant to all these rules, Article 7 offers the opportunity for a *forum necessitatis*, based on the fact that a proceeding cannot be reasonably brought before the courts of a third state. As is obvious, there is no room at all for national rules of jurisdiction.

Although the rules are different, the same model has been adopted in the Succession Regulation. Chapter II (Articles 4 *et seq.*) organizes a complete and closed jurisdiction system. Basically, the competent courts are those of the habitual residence of the deceased (Article 4). In addition, it is possible to have jurisdiction based on choice of forum, choice of law, or mere appearance (Articles 5, 6, and 9). If none of these conditions are met, then a court of a Member State can have specific jurisdiction over goods of the deceased that are located in the forum or general jurisdiction if, in addition, the deceased is either a national of that state or had its former habitual residence in that state (Article 10). Finally, if no Member State has jurisdiction pursuant to all these rules, Article 11 also allows a *forum necessitatis* based, once again, on the fact that a proceeding cannot be reasonably brought before the courts of a third state. Once again, national rules of jurisdiction are completely set aside.

D. Exorbitant Grounds of Jurisdiction

In the Brussels I text, two separate bodies of international rules of jurisdiction are still necessary as when the defendant is domiciled outside the EU, the basic rules of jurisdiction do not apply, even when the connecting factor (e.g. the place of the tort) is located in a Member State. Therefore, the use of national rules of jurisdiction is inevitable and not limited to exorbitant grounds of jurisdiction. In Brussels II *bis*, on the contrary, there is no need for national rules of jurisdiction. The provisions of the Regulation completely supersede national rules and are potentially applicable to every situation.

Therefore, Articles 6 and 7 of Brussels II bis completely differ from Article 4 of Brussels I: whereas Article 4 is a technical necessity, using Articles 6 and 7 comprises a fundamental policy choice. Article 4 is a technical necessity since one needs to know what happens when the defendant is domiciled outside the EU; in addition, it leaves room for exorbitant grounds of jurisdiction. On the contrary, the only objective of Articles 6 and 7 is to allow the use of exorbitant grounds of jurisdiction.

Exorbitant grounds of jurisdiction are difficult to define. In a broad sense, exorbitant grounds can be defined as rules of jurisdiction based on criteria that cannot be considered as consisting of a reasonable link between the dispute and the forum.

Of course, as it is extremely difficult to precisely define what a 'reasonable link' is, the distinction between 'exorbitant' and 'non-exorbitant' grounds of jurisdiction is largely a matter of policy. The choice made in Brussels II *bis* is to base divorce jurisdiction on habitual residence and nationality of both spouses. It could be argued, and indeed it is very often, that the various connecting factors based on habitual residence in Brussels II *bis* are too broad. However, taking the text as it is, from the provisions of the family matters regulations it is clear that every ground that has not been accepted as a basis for jurisdiction is to be considered as exorbitant. The hierarchical relationship between European rules of jurisdiction and national rules of jurisdiction makes that unequivocal.

Brussels II *bis* and the Maintenance and Succession Regulations accept that in some cases, courts of a Member State can be given jurisdiction in a situation where none of the connecting factors of the ordinary rules are located within the EU. In other words, it is only when the jurisdiction rules in the Regulations do not appoint any judge in the EU that national rules can be used. National rules of international jurisdiction are secondary, inferior rules. Moreover, the exceptional nature of these situations is stressed by the fact, in Brussels II, EU nationals, EU residents, and those domiciled in the UK or Ireland are immune from these fora and, in the two other Regulations, the rules are of subsidiary nature.

Therefore, as one can see, two very different issues are at stake here. The first one is to determine whether there should be room for national rules of jurisdiction *in general*, based on the fact that the litigation is located in the EU. The second is to determine whether one needs *exorbitant grounds* of jurisdiction, and if so, if those exorbitant grounds of jurisdiction should be governed by national or European rules.

It is argued that the family law model is far better at answering the first question. Once again, in our view, there is no theoretical nor practical convincing argument in favour of keeping two sets of rules for international jurisdiction. Once the political decision to adopt European rules has been made, these rules should completely replace their national counterparts.

E. Do We Need Exorbitant Grounds of Jurisdiction?

It is far from obvious that exorbitant grounds for jurisdiction are needed and there are strong arguments against such rules today.[45] These arguments seem particularly strong in family matters, where the necessity for a harmonious solution to be arrived at is of utmost importance. Exorbitant grounds of jurisdiction jeopardize recognition abroad and, therefore, should be used only when strong policy arguments favour the attraction of a specific litigation before the courts of a particular Member State.

[45] See in particular, in the Brussels I context Arroyo, 'Exorbitant and Exclusive Grounds of Jurisdiction in European Private International Law: Will They ever Survive?', in H. P. Mansel *et al.* (eds), *Festschrift für E. Jayme* (2004) 169.

Moreover, it is to be regretted that national law cannot be completely left aside. If ever it appeared impossible to refuse exorbitant grounds for jurisdiction in family matters in Europe, then why could such a choice not be made at EU level? If complete unification of ordinary rules of jurisdiction is possible, then it must also be possible to unify exorbitant grounds of jurisdiction. Therefore, the solution eventually adopted in Brussels II *bis*, even if it is better than the one adopted in Brussels I, can be criticized. It seems to allow for unpredictable results and, since every Member State is free to keep any rule it considers useful for whatever reasons, it does not reflect a policy that would be endorsed by the whole EU. Since the 'Europeanization' of jurisdiction has been decided as a worthy goal, a unified approach should be adopted for exorbitant rules.

This analysis is shared by the Commission. A few years ago, a modification of the Brussels II text was proposed.[46] In that proposal, the Commission suggested the adoption of two uniform exorbitant rules: one based on the nationality of one of the spouses, the other based on the fact that the spouses had a common habitual residence on the territory of a Member State for the past three years. Indeed, those rules could be contested as the need of exorbitant grounds can be challenged. Predictability would, however, at the very least be enhanced by unification. This solution has not been yet accepted by Member States for divorce matters[47] but, as we have seen, it has been accepted for in matters of successions and maintenance.

The Brussels II *bis* rules also lead to a strange solution because of the choice that has been made to protect an important class of defendants from national rules: those who are integrated in the EU, either by habitual residence, domicile (UK or Ireland), or nationality. This rule openly discriminates against nationals from third countries living abroad. Such a policy choice can be challenged. The reasons for such discrimination do not appear clear, especially in family matters. Once again, international harmony is of great importance in family matters, and therefore the possibility of international recognition of judgments should always be taken into account. Because of this protection offered to EU nationals and EU residents by Article 6, Member States' courts whose jurisdiction is based on Article 7 will only hear cases with almost no connection at all with their territory. Such a solution seriously challenges the chances of recognition of their decision in third States. It is regrettable that such an important choice is not more fully justified in the regulation for cases where it does not seem that the competence of a Member State court is really justified.

It seems that the *forum necessitatis* which has been adopted in both the Succession and Maintenance Regulations is to be preferred. It allows for exceptional extension of jurisdiction of the courts of a Member State in cases where the foreign forum with the closest connection is unavailable, or when it would be too much of a

[46] European Commission, *Proposal for a Council Regulation Amending Regulation (EC) No 2201/2003 as Regards Jurisdiction and Introducing Rules Concerning Applicable Law in Matrimonial Matters*, COM (2006) 399 final, at 14.

[47] As it has not been accepted for the Brussels I recast, where the Commission also suggested a uniform set of exorbitant rules, including a *forum necessitatis*, which has been rejected by Member States.

burden for the plaintiff. Although the rule leaves room for uncertainty, it is a better approach to the exceptional nature of the intervention of the Member State court.

Therefore, as one can see, it is argued that when it comes to jurisdiction, there is no really convincing reason to make distinctions between European and non-European litigation. The question is not to determine whether there are connections with third states, but only to determine whether the connecting factor adopted by a jurisdiction rule is located in Europe or abroad. When it comes to jurisdiction, the whole European territory should be considered as a single legal order. Legal certainty and simplicity would certainly be gained if the Successions or Maintenance model was followed.

6

The External Reach of EU Private Law in the Light of *L'Oréal versus eBay* and *Google and Google Spain*

*Niilo Jääskinen and Angela Ward**

1. Introduction

Laying down parameters for the external reach of the substantive private law of the EU presents particular challenges in the age of globalization and the Internet. In an increasingly interconnected world, courts everywhere are being compelled to develop principles that are appropriately adapted to reviewing conduct taking place beyond national borders when that conduct impacts within.[1] This entails navigation of a precarious course, given the competing imperative of preserving the established pillars of both public and private international law in cross-frontier situations, while at the same time adjusting the relevant rules to accommodate contemporary circumstances. Determination of the territorial scope of application of substantive provisions of EU private law is intimately bound up with this process.

The challenges are particularly complex in the European Union. This is so because of the absence of explicit primary law provisions from which the EU Court of Justice (CJEU) might draw in developing rules on applying EU law to facts and action taking place outside the EU. The territorial scope of EU law is expressly set out in the Treaty on European Union and the Treaty on the Functioning of the

* Any views expressed are personal to the authors and do not reflect those of any institution or organization. We would like to thank Betül Kas, Joshua Andresen, Mirka Kuisma, and François Vanherck for research assistance. Responsibility for the text lies with the authors.

[1] H. Muir-Watt, 'Private International Law as Global Governance: Beyond the Schize, from Closet to Planet', available at <http://works.bepress.com/horatia_muir-watt/1> (last accessed 12 June 2015); Wai, 'Transnational Liftoff and Juridical Touchdown: The Regulatory Function of Private International Law in an Era of Globalization', 41 *Columbia Journal of Transnational Law* (2002) 209; Michaels, 'Globalizing Savigny? The State in Savigny's Private International Law, and the Challenge of Europeanization and Globalization', Duke Law School Legal Studies Research Paper Series 74/2005.

European Union (TFEU). While these rules cannot be completely set to one side, they are of limited assistance in prescribing the outer parameters of substantive private law of the EU,[2] given that they are silent on this subject.

Thus far there have been two major cases in which the CJEU has been called on to enforce EU legislation regulating horizontal legal relations between private subjects, even though part of the conduct in question took place outside of the EU. These are Case C-324/09 *L'Oréal SA and Others v. eBay International AG and Others*[3] (in the following referred to as '*L'Oréal v. eBay*'), and Case C-131/12 *Google Spain SL Google Inc v. AEPD and Mario Costeja González* (in the following referred to as '*Google*').[4]

Both of these disputes arose as a result of the globalization of markets and the Internet. In each, proceedings were instituted before a national court within the EU, but at the same time the cases were complicated by the existence of an 'external' element of some kind, thereby obliging the CJEU to develop rules justifying the application of substantive EU private law in such circumstances. In *L'Oréal v. eBay*, the Court had to decide whether the protection of EU trade mark law extended to offers for sale of goods from outside the EU by means of eBay's websites. In *Google*, the dispute concerned whether Google Inc., an undertaking established in the United States, was bound by the EU Data Protection Directive[5] when some of its marketing and advertising operations were undertaken by its subsidiary, Google Spain.

This paper will first map the core areas of EU law that are relevant to working out the current status of the external reach of substantive EU private law. These are: the territories in which EU law applies as prescribed by the EU Treaties

[2] It should be added that we have decided to opt for the term 'external reach' due to the doctrinal and political controversies relating to the notion of *extraterritorial effect*.

[3] Case C-324/09, *L'Oréal SA and Others v. eBay International AG and Others*, [2011] ECR I-6011. For examples of commentaries see Riefa, 'The End of Internet Service Providers Liability as We Know it—Uncovering the Consumer Interest in CJEU Case C-324/09 (L'Oréal/eBay)', 1 *Journal of European Consumer and Market Law* (2012) 104; Lievens, 'L'Oréal v. eBay—Welcomed in France, Resented in England', 43 *International Review of Intellectual Property and Competition Law* (2012) 68; Lemarchand and Lampe, 'L'arrêt eBay c/L'Oréal de la CJUE du 12 juillet 2011 revisite les conditions de la qualification de fournisseur d'hébergement au sens de l'article 14 de la directive 'e-commerce', 75 *Droit de l'immatériel: informatique, médias, communication* (2011) 53; Smit and Ligot, 'Arrêt "L'Oréal": clarifications sur le cadre légal des activités et des responsabilités des hébergeurs de sites internet', 42 *Journal de Droit Européen* (2011) 294; Roth, 'Verantwortlichkeit von Betreibern von Internet-Marktplätzen für Markenrechtsverletzungen durch Nutzer: L'Oréal gegen eBay', *Wettbewerb in Recht und Praxis* (2011) 1258; Sujecki, 'Betreiberhaftung für Markenrechtsverletzungen auf Online-Marktplatz', 22 *Europäische Zeitschrift für Wirtschaftsrecht* (2011) 764; Spindler, 'Europarechtliche Rahmenbedingungen der Störerhaftung im Internet', *Multimedia und Recht* (2011) 703.

[4] Case C-131/12, *Google Spain SL Google Inc v. AEPD and Mario Costeja González*, judgment of 13 May 2014. For examples of commentaries see van Calster, 'ECJ in Google Spain confirms reach of EU Data Protection Directive. Right to be forgotten not withheld verbatim but may be realised in practice', Gavc Law, available at <http://gavclaw.com/2014/05/13/ecj-in-google-spain-confirms-reach-of-eu-data-protection-directive-right-to-be-forgotten-not-withheld-verbatim-but-may-be-realised-in-practice/> (last accessed 12 June 2015).

[5] Directive 95/46/EC of the European Parliament and of the Council of 24 October 1995, on the protection of individuals with regard to the processing of personal data and on the free movement of such data, OJ 1995 L 281/31.

(section 2 below); EU public law and the established rules on conduct taking place outside of the EU (section 3 below); the manner in which the CJEU has interpreted the primary EU legislative instrument governing jurisdiction of EU Member State courts when a dispute involves a non-EU element, and material facts taking place outside of the EU,[6] namely Regulation 44/2001 on jurisdiction and the recognition and enforcement of foreign judgments[7] (section 4 below).[8]

Once these preliminaries have been addressed, we will describe and analyse the rulings of the CJEU in *L'Oréal v. eBay* and *Google* (section 5 below), and consider the extent to which the legal principles discussed in sections 2, 3, and 4, have permeated the conclusions reached by the CJEU. In *Google*, the measure at issue, the Data Protection Directive,[9] contained express clauses concerning the Directive's territorial reach.[10] In *L'Oréal v. eBay*, however, the measures at issue, namely

[6] Other regulations of the 'Brussels' family are Council Regulation (EC) 2201/2003 of 27 November 2003 concerning jurisdiction and the recognition and enforcement of judgments in matrimonial matters and the matters of parental responsibility, repealing Regulation (EC) 1347/2000 (Brussels IIa), OJ 2003 L 338/1; Council Regulation (EC) 4/2009 of 18 December 2008 on jurisdiction, applicable law, recognition and enforcement of decisions and cooperation in matters relating to maintenance obligations OJ 2009 L 7, 1. and Regulation (EU) 650/2012 of the European Parliament and Council of 4 July 2012 on jurisdiction, applicable law, recognition and enforcement of decisions and acceptance and enforcement of authentic instruments in matters of succession and on the creation of a European Certificate of Succession OJ 2012 L 201/107. Given, however, the absence to date of any disputes involving the external reach of EU private law that have also entailed application of these measures, have not (yet) lead to case law pertinent to the legal issues we will be addressing.

[7] On 22 December 2000, the Council adopted Regulation 44/2001 on jurisdiction and the recognition and enforcement of judgments in civil and commercial matters, OJ 2012 L 12/1, which replaces the Brussels Convention of 1968 with regard to the territories of the Member States covered by the TFEU, as between the Member States except Denmark. The Brussels Convention of 27 September 1968 on jurisdiction and the enforcement of judgments in civil and commercial matters, which was applicable between the EU countries before the regulation entered into force, continues to apply with respect to those territories of EU countries that fall within its territorial scope and that are excluded from the regulation pursuant to Art. 355 TFEU. On 12 December 2012, the European Parliament and the Council adopted Regulation 1215/2012, OJ 2012 L 351/1, which replaces Regulation 44/2001 but will be applicable only from 10 January 2015. The 1988 Lugano Convention, which was concluded by the then Member States of the European Communities and certain EFTA States in 1988, constitutes a parallel convention to the 1968 Brussels Convention. It was revised by the Convention on Jurisdiction and the Recognition and Enforcement of Judgments in Civil and Commercial Matters, signed at Lugano on 30 October 2007 by the Community, Denmark, Iceland, Norway, and Switzerland.

[8] EU international private law acts accept third country law as *lex causae*. This principle is explicitly stated in Art. 20 of Regulation (EU) 650/2012 of the European Parliament and Council of 4 July on jurisdiction, applicable law, recognition and enforcement of decisions and acceptance and enforcement of authentic instruments in matters of succession and on the creation of a European Certificate of Succession, OJ 2012 L 201/107, where it is provided that '[a]ny law specified by this Regulation shall be applied whether or not it is the law of a Member State.' However, it is also applicable in the context of the Rome regulations, namely Regulation (EC) 593/2008 of the European Parliament and Council of 17 June 2008 on the law applicable to contractual obligations (Rome I), OJ 2008 L 177/6, Regulation (EC) 864/2007 of the European Parliament and Council of 11 July 2007 on the law applicable to non-contractual obligations (Rome II), OJ 2007 L 199/40, and Council Regulation (EU) 1259/2010 of 20 December 2010 implementing enhanced cooperation in the area of law applicable to divorce and legal separation, OJ 2010 L 343/10.

[9] *Supra* note 5. [10] Namely Art. 4.

Directive 89/104/EEC to approximate the laws of the Member States relating to trade marks[11] and Regulation 40/94 on the Community Trade Mark,[12] were silent on the question of their territorial limits. The pertinence of this difference will be addressed in our conclusions.

Furthermore, in the analysis of the rulings in *Google* and *L'Oréal v. eBay*, reference will be made to the approach taken regarding the problem of the attribution of jurisdiction to Member State courts when the facts of a dispute involving interpretation of measures of EU private law traverse more than one EU Member State, particularly but not exclusively due to the trans-border nature of the Internet. This will show that the problem of the external reach of EU private law has a parallel in the challenge the CJEU faces with respect to the determination of the competent Member State courts under Regulation 44/2001 when the facts of a dispute encompass more than one Member State.

It will be our contention that the EU Court of Justice judgment in *L'Oréal v. eBay* rests on a mix of the classical effects doctrine, to be detailed in section 3, on the application of EU (public) competition law to facts arising outside of the EU and the notion of targeted behaviour which had already been deployed by the Court in intra-EU trans-border disputes involving the Internet.[13] On the other hand, the reasoning in *Google* justified the application of EU data protection law on the basis of the establishment of entities within the EU that are subsidiaries or otherwise closely linked to the extra-EU entity that was allegedly in breach of the Data Protection Directive.[14] This rationale also finds its roots in EU (public) competition law in the so-called entity theory, a doctrine stemming, inter alia, from Case C-48/69 *ICI (Dyestuffs) v. the Commission* (hereafter '*Dyestuffs*').[15] It allows the Commission to assert jurisdiction with respect to breach of competition law by extra-EU undertakings working through subsidiaries established in the EU. The same notion has also risen in the context of the interpretation of Regulation 44/2001, so that group structure has also been relevant to determining whether an undertaking established outside of the EU can be caught by the special rules on jurisdiction for consumer contracts appearing in Regulation 44/2001.[16] This will be addressed in sections 3 and 4.

In our view, the better approach would be for the EU legislature to address the external reach of measures of EU private law in the individual measures themselves, whether that be a regulation or a directive, in conformity with the approach adopted under the Data Protection Directive. Given the complexity of

[11] OJ 1989 L 40/1. [12] OJ 1994 L 11/1.

[13] See Joined Cases C-585/08 and C-144/09, *Pammer and Hotel Alpenhof*, [2010] ECR I-12527. Compare, however, Case C-170/12, *Pinckney*, judgment of 3 October 2013, which concerned the role of the Internet in determining the place where a harmful event occurs under Art. 5(3) of Regulation 44/2001 and Case C-387/12, *Hi Hotel HCF*, judgment of 3 April 2014.

[14] *Supra* note 5.

[15] Case C-48/69, *ICI (Dyestuffs) v. the Commission*, [1972] ECR 619. See more recently, e.g. Case C-97/08, *Akzo Nobel and Others v. Commission*, [2009] ECR I-8237, and Case C-440/11 P, *Commission v. Stichting Administratiekantoor Portielje*, judgment of 11 July 2013.

[16] Case C-318/93, *Brenner and Noller*, [1994] ECR I-4275.

the challenges at hand, constraining the CJEU to draw on its case law on extraterritorial effects in parallel fields such as EU public law and the interpretation of Regulation 44/2001 would seem to be an inadequate response to the challenges presented by globalism and the advent of the Internet.

2. The Territories in Which EU Law Applies as Prescribed by the Treaties

The Member States to which the 'Treaties shall apply' is currently set out in Article 52(1) TEU, whereas in the past it appeared in Article 299(1) EC. All twenty-eight Member States of the European Union are listed therein. More detailed rules governing the territorial scope of the Treaties are provided in Article 355 TFEU, and these correspond with former Articles 299(2), first subparagraph, EC and Article 299(3)–(6) EC.[17]

Pursuant to Article 355(2) TFEU, the special arrangements for association set out in Part Four of the TFEU are to apply to the overseas countries and territories listed in Annex II.[18] The special arrangement of association with the EU, as prescribed by Article 355(2) TFEU, has spawned a complex body of case law on the circumstances in which EU law extends to the associated countries, given that they inevitably entail assessment of conduct and legal relations that have occurred outside of EU territory.[19] To date, however, these disputes have not considered issues relating to EU private law, or the impact of EU private international law measures on the association arrangements.

3. EU Public Law and Conduct Taking Place Outside of the EU

General principles of law that have been developed by the CJEU on the circumstances under which EU public law captures legal relations and behaviour that have

[17] Art. 355(1) TFEU provides that in addition to the provisions of Art. 52 of the Treaty on European Union relating to the territorial scope of the Treaties, the provisions of the Treaties shall apply to Guadeloupe, French Guiana, Martinique, Réunion, Saint-Barthélemy, Saint-Martin, the Azores, Madeira, and the Canary Islands in accordance with Art. 349 TFEU. The provisions of the Treaties shall apply to the European territories for whose external relations a Member State is responsible in accordance with Art. 355(3) TFEU.

[18] It is further stated in Art. 355(2) TFEU that the Treaties shall not apply to those overseas countries and territories having special relations with the United Kingdom of Great Britain and Northern Ireland which are not included in the aforementioned list.

[19] For a detailed discussion of this case law see the Opinion of Advocate General Cruz Villalón in Case C-384/09, *Prunus*, [2011] ECR I-3319, and the Opinion of Advocate General Jääskinen in Joined Cases C-24/12 and C-27/12, *X and TBG*, of 16 January 2014, not yet published. See further Ziller, 'The European Union and the Territorial Scope of European Territories', 38 *Victoria University of Wellington Law Review* (2007) 51.

occurred outside of the EU are pertinent to the exploration the external effects of substantive EU private law for a number of reasons. This is, for one thing, due to the effects that EU regulation of public law can have on private legal relations. For another, this is due to the fact that EU competition law stands out as the field in which legal rules on the reach of EU law beyond its frontiers have been long established.[20]

This encompasses the *effects doctrine*, which indexes the applicability of EU law and competence of EU authorities to the effects of extraterritorial conduct restricting competition within the EU territory, and the *entity theory*, according to which, irrespective of differences in terms of legal personality, companies forming an economic unit must be considered to be a single economic entity. This results in imposition of liability on the controlling company with respect to the whole group, and therefore brings third country companies with subsidiaries or other establishments within the EU into the scope of EU competition law.

The leading case on this issue, namely Joined Cases 89/85 *et al., Ahlström Osakeyhtiö and Others v. Commission*[21] (hereinafter referred to as '*Woodpulp*') was elaborated by the CJEU some 25 years ago, and may provide a useful source of inspiration in the development of principles concerning the external reach of EU private law. Moreover, reliance on EU public law by entities located in non-EU countries is currently being addressed in the case law of the CJEU.[22] Cross-fertilization, therefore, between the rules on the reach of EU public law, on the one hand, and EU private law, on the other, is not beyond the realms of possibility.

In *Woodpulp*, the Court held that by applying competition rules in the Treaty to undertakings whose registered offices were situated outside of the Community, the Commission had not made an incorrect assessment of the territorial scope of Article 85 of the EEC Treaty, now Article 101 TFEU.[23] The case came before the CJEU because a series of woodpulp producers and two associations of woodpulp producers, all having their registered offices outside the Community, sought the annulment of a decision of the Commission in which the Commission had established that they had committed infringements of Article 85 of the EEC Treaty, principally through price collusion, and had fined them.

The Court stated that when producers collude on the price to be charged to their customers in the Community, and put that collusion into effect by selling at prices which are actually coordinated, they are taking part in collusion which has the object and effect of restricting competition within the common market

[20] We refer, with a certain nostalgia, to a description on the case law on applicability of EEC competition law to extraterritorial restrictions before the Alhström case in Jääskinen, 'EEC ja ulkomaalaiset yritykset: Euroopan talousyhteisön kilpailunrajoitu soikeuden soveltaminen ulkomaalaisiin yrityksiin', *Suomen Lakimiesliiton Kustannus* (1984).

[21] Cases C-89/85 *et al., A. Ahlström Osakeyhtid v. Commission (Woodpulp)*, [1988] ECR 5193.

[22] See notably Case T-494/10, *Bank Saderat v. Council*, judgment of 5 February 2013. This case has been appealed to the Court of Justice. See also Opinion of Advocate General Sharpston of 26 February 2015 in Case C-176/13 P, *Council v. Bank Mellat*, and Case C-200/13 P, *Council v. Bank Saderat Iran and Commission*.

[23] *Supra* note 21, para 14.

within the meaning of Article 85 of the EEC Treaty[24] (now Article 101 TFEU). The decisive factor that was at play was the place where the (unlawful) agreements were implemented.[25] Unlike the approach taken subsequently by the Court with respect to jurisdiction over consumer contracts (see discussion below of *Brenner and Noller*), it was immaterial whether or not the undertakings concerned had had recourse to subsidiaries, agents, sub-agents, or branches within the Community in order to make contact with purchasers within the Community.[26] Advocate General Darmon in *Woodpulp* made explicit and clear recourse to the effects doctrine.[27] The Court's approach was more nuanced, but nevertheless, implementation of unlawful agreements entered into outside the Community but producing anti-competitive effect within it brought the collusion concerned within the reach of Community competition rules.[28]

There is, however, a competing line of case law on extra-EU reach of EU law. It emerged due to ongoing controversy relating to the acceptability of the effects doctrine in terms of public international law.[29] Thus, in *Dyestuffs*, a concerted practice involving a parent company located outside the Community and its subsidiaries within it fell within the jurisdiction of the European Commission. In considering whether the impugned practices had effects within the common market, the Court held that by 'making use of its power to control its subsidiaries established in the Community, the applicant was able to ensure that its decision was implemented on that market',[30] and that the fact that 'a subsidiary has separate legal personality is not sufficient to exclude the possibility of imputing its conduct to the parent company'.[31] The Court added that this may be the case in particular 'where the subsidiary, although having separate legal personality, does not decide independently upon its own conduct on the market, but carries out, in all material respects, the instructions given to it by the parent company'.[32] The 'unity of the group' was relevant,[33] as was whether the parent company 'was able to exercise decisive influence over the policy of the subsidiary as regards selling prices in the Common Market'.[34]

Beyond the realm of competition law, in Case C-366/10 *Air Transport Association of America and Others*,[35] the Court was called on to consider whether, inter alia, by enacting Directive 2003/87/EC establishing a scheme for greenhouse gas emissions allowance trading within the Community and amending Council Directive

[24] Ibid., para 13. [25] Ibid., para 16. [26] Ibid., para 17.

[27] Ibid., in particular at paras 57 and 58 of his Opinion.

[28] Debate on the effects doctrine often suffers from a misplaced assumption that the 'effect' proving a sufficient link justifying application of a competition law regime would refer to purely economic trans-border causalities. However, in legal terms the effects doctrine refers to situations where extraterritorial restrictions modify the conditions of competition on a certain market, and in the case of the EU, within the common market, in a way which in substance corresponds with the prohibition according to the law of this jurisdiction. See Jääskinen, *supra* note 20, at 57–60.

[29] See, for example, J. Crawford, *Brownlie's Principles of Public International Law* (8th edn, 2012), at 478–485.

[30] *Dyestuffs*, *supra* note 15, para 130. [31] Ibid., para 132. [32] Ibid., para 133.

[33] Ibid., para 135. [34] Ibid., para 137.

[35] Case C-366/10, *Air Transport Association of America and Others*, [2011] ECR I-13755.

96/61/EC,[36] the EU had breached principles of customary international law recognizing the sovereignty of states over their airspace, the prohibition on exertion of sovereignty over the high seas, and the freedom to overfly them. These questions arose because the validity of Directive 2003/87 was questioned. It was argued that the scheme purported to regulate parts of flights taken outside the airspace of the EU Member States, including flights registered in third states, although the Directive only applied to flights which arrived at or departed from an aerodrome situated on the territory of a Member State.

The Court held that EU law could not render Directive 2003/87 applicable to aircraft registered in third states that flew over the high seas or third states. This was so because the EU was bound to respect international law in the exercise of its powers.[37] Directive 2003/87 did not, however, purport to do this. No breach of the principle of territoriality or sovereignty arose since the aircraft concerned were 'physically in the territory of one of the Member States of the European Union' and were 'thus subject on that basis to the unlimited jurisdiction of the European Union'.[38] Furthermore, the Court cited the *Woodpulp* case in finding that the 'fact that, in the context of applying European Union environmental legislation, certain matters contributing to the pollution of the air, sea or land territory of the Member States originate in an event which occurs partly outside that territory is not such as to call into question, in the light of the principles of customary international law capable of being relied upon in the main proceedings, the full applicability of European Union law in that territory'.[39]

The external reach of EU public law, and more particularly the EU Charter of Fundamental Rights,[40] may also feature as an element of an appeal that is currently pending before the CJEU. In Case T-494/10 *Bank Saderat Iran v. Council*,[41] the applicant, an Iranian commercial bank, seeks the annulment of EU measures freezing its funds and economic resources as part of the restrictive measures imposed by the EU in order to apply pressure to the Islamic Republic of Iran to end proliferation-sensitive nuclear activities and the development of nuclear weapon delivery systems. The bank wished to rely on certain provisions of the EU Charter on Fundamental Rights, namely the Article 17 right to property, the Article 41 right to good administration, and the Article 47 right to an effective remedy and a fair trial. However, the Council and the Commission contended that, under EU law, legal persons who were emanations of non-Member countries, like Iran, could not rely on fundamental rights protection and guarantees.[42] The Council and the Commission sought support from Article 34 of the European Convention

[36] Directive 2003/87/EC of the European Parliament and of the Council of 13 October 2003 establishing a scheme for greenhouse gas emission allowance trading within the Community and amending Council Directive 96/61/EC, OJ 2003 L 275/32.

[37] *Air Transport Association of America, supra* note 35, paras 122 and 123.

[38] Ibid., para. 125.

[39] Ibid., para. 129. With regard to hydrocarbons accidentally spilled beyond a Member State's territorial sea the Court cited Case C-188/07, *Commune de Mesquer*, [2008] ECR I-4501, paras 60–62.

[40] Charter of Fundamental Rights of the European Union, OJ 2000 C 364/1.

[41] *Bank Saderat Iran, supra* note 22.

[42] Ibid., para. 33.

of Human Rights (ECHR), the effect of which is that the Court of Human Rights may not accept applications submitted to it by governmental organizations,[43] and the argument that a state is a guarantor of respect for fundamental rights in its territory, and in this case the territory of Iran, but cannot qualify for such rights.[44]

In finding that the applicant Iranian bank 'may take advantage of fundamental rights protection and guarantees'[45] supplied by EU law, the General Court noted that neither in the Charter of Fundamental Rights nor in the Treaties are there any provisions which state that legal persons which are emanations of States are not entitled to the protection of fundamental rights. On the contrary, the provisions of the Charter that were relevant to the pleas raised, namely Articles 17, 41, and 47, guarantee their rights to 'everyone', a wording that includes legal persons such as the applicant.[46]

Article 34 ECHR was dismissed by the General Court as a 'procedural provision which was not applicable to the Courts of the European Union',[47] and concluded that the fact that a state is a guarantor of fundamental rights in its own territory is of no relevance as regards the extent of the rights to which legal persons which are emanations of that same state may be entitled in the territory of other States.[48]

The approach taken by the General Court differs markedly from that of the European Court of Human Rights (ECtHR). The parallel jurisprudence before that Court has been concerned with whether the entity seeking to rely on the ECHR is within the 'jurisdiction' of one of the state parties to the ECHR, within the meaning of Article 1 ECHR.[49]

However, for present purposes, and as we have already noted, leading EU cases on the external reach of EU public law may prove to be a useful source of inspiration as the CJEU grapples with the task of setting parameters for the external reach of EU private law. This applies all the more so, we would argue, given the intimacy of the links between EU public and private law, as exemplified by competition law, and the ramifications for private contracts when prohibitions set by EU public law stand in the way of registration of the transfer of land.[50]

4. The Rules on the Jurisdiction of Member State Courts over Conduct Taking Place Outside of the EU

In assessing the external effects of EU private law, due account needs to be taken of the extent to which the Brussels Convention and Regulation 44/2001 have been

[43] Ibid., para. 35. [44] Ibid., para. 37. [45] Ibid., para. 44.

[46] Ibid., para. 34. [47] Ibid., para. 36. [48] Ibid., para. 38.

[49] For a thorough analysis see M. Milanovic, *Extra-Territorial Application of Human Rights Treaties: Law, Principles, and Policy* (2011). Advocate General Jääskinen has taken the position that Member States are not directly protected by the ECHR or the Charter but can invoke the general principles of law corresponding with provisions of these instruments; see Joined Cases C-106/09 P and C-107/09 P, *Commission v. Government of Gibraltar and United Kingdom*, [2011] ECR I-11113, paras 245–250.

[50] See notably Case C-117/06, *Möllendorf and Others*, [2007] ECR I-8361.

interpreted by the CJEU in relation to extra-EU conduct. The link between the substantive content of EU private law and Regulation 44/2001 is important in all the leading cases that have concerned the interpretation of EU directives governing private legal relations that have featured a cross-border element within the EU. Indeed, in one, the intimacy of the relationship between such Directives and the Regulation prompted a national court to ask the CJEU, in a reference for a preliminary ruling under Article 267 TFEU, whether the Directive concerned was itself a measure governing the conflict of laws.[51]

The basic principle in both the Brussels Convention and its successor Regulation 44/2001 is that persons domiciled in a Member State shall, whatever their nationality, be sued in the courts of that Member State (Article 2(1) of Regulation 44/2001). Persons who are not nationals of the Member State in which they are domiciled shall be governed by the rules of jurisdiction applicable to nationals of that State. According to Article 3 of Regulation 44/2001, persons domiciled in a Member State may be sued in the courts of another Member State only by virtue of the particular rules of competence set out Chapter III of the Regulation. The Regulation does not regulate the issue of third country tribunals in any respects. However, Article 33 of Regulation 1215/2012 replacing 44/2001 will introduce, as of January 2015, limited international *lis pendens* effect to proceedings pending in third country courts.[52]

Thus, unsurprisingly, in Case C-412/98 *Group Josi*,[53] the EU Court of Justice confirmed the primacy of the defendants domicile in triggering the competence of EU Member State courts, and rejected arguments to the effect that it could be displaced by residence of the plaintiff outside of the EU. In that case, a French court had held that it had jurisdiction over a reinsurance contract on the basis that the plaintiff was a company incorporated under Canadian law and without a place of business in the European Community. Thus, even though the defendant was domiciled in Belgium, the Brussels Convention could not be applied to the plaintiff.

The CJEU reiterated that the system of common rules on conferment of jurisdiction set out in the Convention was based on the general rule that persons domiciled in a contracting state were to be sued in the courts of that contracting state.[54] While the Convention contained derogations to this principle, including some which afforded 'a certain influence to the domicile of the plaintiff',[55] it was only 'in quite exceptional cases' that the Convention accorded decisive importance to the plaintiff's domicile in a contracting state for the purposes of conferring jurisdiction,[56] and that none of those specific cases was applicable to the case to hand.[57]

[51] Joined Cases C-509/09 and C-161/10, *eDate Advertising and Others*, [2011] ECR I-10269. This case concerned the interpretation of Directive 2000/13/EC of the European Parliament and of the Council of 8 June 2000, on certain legal aspects of information society services, in particular electronic commerce, in the Internal Market, OJ 2000 L 178/1.

[52] In contrast, Council Regulation (EC) 4/2009 of 18 December 2008 on jurisdiction, applicable law, recognition and enforcement of decisions and cooperation in matters relating to maintenance obligations, OJ 2009 L 7/1, covers third country-related situations.

[53] Case C-412/98, *Group Josi*, [2000] ECR I-5925.

[54] Ibid., para. 34. [55] Ibid., para. 37. [56] Ibid., para. 47. [57] Ibid., para. 48.

The same restrictive approach to exceptions to domicile was followed in Case C-281/02 *Owusu*,[58] where the CJEU answered questions for a preliminary ruling from the UK Court of Appeal on, inter alia, the compatibility of the doctrine of *forum non conveniens* with the Brussels Convention. In the *Owusu* case, one defendant, Mr Jackson, was domiciled in the UK, while three of the remaining defendants were domiciled in Jamaica. In 1997 Mr Owusu, a British plaintiff domiciled in the UK, suffered a serious accident while diving on holiday in Jamaica. Subsequently, he brought an action in the UK for breach of contract against Mr Jackson, who had let him a holiday villa on the private beach where the accident occurred, and an action in tort, still in the UK, against three Jamaican companies running resorts that had access to the beach where the accident occurred.

Mr Jackson and the Jamaican companies argued that an English court should not exercise its jurisdiction on relation to Mr Owusu's claim because the case against them had closer links with Jamaica. The Jamaican courts were said to be a forum with jurisdiction in which the case might be tried more suitably for the interests of all the parties and the ends of justice under the common law doctrine of *forum non conveniens*.[59] On appeal to the UK Court of Appeal, questions for preliminary ruling were sent to the CJEU on this issue.

The CJEU noted that no exception on the basis of the *forum non conveniens* doctrine was provided for by the authors of the Convention, although the question was discussed when the Convention of 9 October 1978 on the Accession of Denmark, Ireland, and the United Kingdom was drawn up, as was apparent from the report on that Convention by Professor Schlosser.[60] Thus, respect for the principle of legal certainty, which was one of the objectives of the Brussels Convention, would not be fully guaranteed if the court, having jurisdiction under the Convention, had to be allowed to apply the *forum non conveniens* doctrine.[61] Moreover, allowing *forum non conveniens* in the context of the Brussels Convention would be likely to affect the uniform application of the rules of jurisdiction contained therein in so far as that doctrine was recognized only in a limited number of Contracting States, whereas the objective of the Brussels Convention was precisely to lay down common rules to the exclusion of derogating national rules.[62]

As mentioned above, Chapter III of Regulation 44/2001 and corresponding provisions in the Brussels Convention provide specific grounds of competence establishing exclusive jurisdiction for courts other than that of the defendant's domicile, or provide concurrent *fora* to the defendant's tribunal. Two prominent

[58] Case C-281/02, *Owusu*, [2005] ECR I-1383.

[59] The defendants relied on the doctrine of *forum non conveniens* as elaborated in In re *Harrods (Buenos Aires)* Ltd [1992] Ch. 72 CA.

[60] P. Schlosser, 'Report on the Convention on the Association of the Kingdom of Denmark, Ireland and the United Kingdom of Great Britain and Northern Ireland to the Convention on Jurisdiction and the Enforcement of Judgments in Civil and Commercial Matters and to the Protocol on its Interpretation by the Court of Justice', OJ 1979 C 59/71, paras 27, 77, and 78.

[61] *Owosu, supra* note 58, para. 38, citing Case C-440/97 *GIE Groupe Concorde and Others*, [1999] ECR I-6307, para. 23, and Case C-256/00, *Besix*, [2002] ECR I-1699, para. 24.

[62] Ibid., para. 43.

examples are the special rules on claims *in rem* with respect to immoveable property, and the rules on competence with respect to consumer contracts.

The Court has issued two important rulings on Article 22(1) of Regulation 44/2001 on disputes featuring a cross-border element. This provision provides for exclusive jurisdiction, regardless of domicile of the defendant, in proceedings which have as their object rights *in rem* in immovable property or tenancies of immovable property, of the courts of the Member State in which the property is situated.[63]

In Case C-420/07 *Apostolides*[64] the CJEU rejected arguments to the effect that Article 22(1) of Regulation 44/2001 should be read in the light of Article 1(1) of Protocol No. 10 on the Act of Accession of Cyprus to the European Union. It provides that application of the *acquis communautaire* shall be suspended in those areas of the Republic of Cyprus in which the government of the Republic of Cyprus does not exercise effective control. Mr and Mrs Orams had argued that the Protocol meant that an English court could not recognize a judgment of a court located in the government-controlled part of the island in the south, with respect to land that the Orams claimed to own in the northern part of the island, because the government of Cyprus lacked effective control in that area. In effect, it was contended that the land was outside of the reach of EU law. The southern Cypriot court had relied on the exclusive jurisdiction vested in it with respect to claims over land located in Cyprus under Article 22(1) of Regulation 44/2001.

A question referred to the CJEU on this point under Article 267 TFEU received a pithy reply. The Court reiterated that provisions in an Act of Accession which permit exceptions or derogations from rules laid down in the EC Treaty must be interpreted restrictively, and must be limited to what is absolutely necessary in order to attain its objectives.[65] The Court then held that the fact that the court issuing the judgment sat in the government-controlled area was decisive,[66] and the fact that the land in question was situated in the northern area was irrelevant.[67]

On the other hand, in Case C-343/04 *ČEZ*,[68] the CJEU declined to allow a Member State court to rely on the antecedent to Article 22(1) of Regulation 44/2001—that is, Article 16(1)(a) of the Brussels Convention—in a case in which it was argued that a nuisance was being created within the EU, namely in Austria, by land located outside it, namely in the Czech Republic, and that the Austrian courts should therefore take jurisdiction over the matter. The nuisance comprised alleged ionizing radiation emanating from a Czech power plant.[69]

[63] For a recent ruling on the meaning of 'proceedings which have as their object rights *in rem* in immoveable property' see Case C-438/12, *Weber*, judgment of 3 April 2014, not yet published.

[64] Case C–420/07, *Apostolides*, [2009] ECR I-3571.

[65] Ibid., para. 35, citing Case 231/78, *Commission v. United Kingdom*, [1979] ECR 1447, para. 13; Case 77/82, *Peskeloglou*, [1983] ECR 1085, para. 12; Case 11/82, *Piraiki-Patraiki and Others v. Commission*, [1985] ECR 207, para. 26; Case C-3/87, *Agegate*, [1989] ECR 4459, para, 39; and Case C-233/97, *KappAhl*, [1998] ECR I-8069, para. 18.

[66] Ibid., para. 37. [67] Ibid., para. 38.

[68] Case C-343/04, *ČEZ*, [2006] ECR I-4557.

[69] At the time the Czech Republic was not a member of the EU and nor was it at the relevant time a party to the Brussels Convention. The fact that Austria, together with Sweden, has rejected

The Court commenced by observing that Article 16 of the Brussels Convention introduced an exception to the general rules of jurisdiction set out in the same Convention. As such, the rules were not given an interpretation broader than was required by their objective.[70] The Court noted that it was clear from both the Jenard Report on the Brussels Convention (OJ 1979 C 59/1) and the consistent case law of the Court that the essential reason for the exclusive jurisdiction of the courts of the Contracting State under Article 16(1)(a) of the Brussels Convention was that the court of the place where the property was situated was best placed to deal with matters relating to rights *in rem* in, and tenancies of, immovable property.[71] The Court further observed that rights *in rem* in immovable property generally had to be decided by applying the rules of the State where the property was situated, and for good reason. Such disputes frequently require checks, inquiries, and expert assessments which have to be carried out on the spot, so that the assignment of exclusive jurisdiction to the court of the place where the property is situated, which for reasons of proximity is best placed to ascertain the facts satisfactorily, satisfies the need for the proper administration of justice.[72]

In light of this, the Court concluded that an action, possibly preventative, for cessation of a nuisance did not fall within the category of actions falling within Article 16(1)(a) of the Brussels Convention.[73] Such an interpretation was supported by neither the Jenard[74] nor the Schlosser Reports.[75] The Court further observed that, in the context of a nuisance action, 'the real and immovable nature of that right' was of only 'marginal significance',[76] and it did not have 'decisive influence'.[77] Further, actions for nuisance generally involved consideration of factors particular to the place where the property concerned was located. To that extent, it appeared to be difficult to consider that a provision of that type was intended to be exclusive even where the distance between the two properties concerned would potentially submit them to local conditions which were usually different.[78]

Finally, in Case C-318/93 *Brenner and Noller*[79] the CJEU was asked whether Articles 13 and 14 of the Brussels Convention on jurisdiction over consumer

nuclear power as an energy form contributed to the inclusion in the Final Act of the Accession Treaty of 1994 of a joint declaration No. 4 on the application of the Euratom Treaty, according to which the Contracting Parties acknowledge that, as Contracting Parties to the Treaty establishing the European Atomic Energy Community, Member States decide to produce or not to produce nuclear energy according to their specific policy orientations.

[70] *ČEZ, supra* note 68, para. 26. See Case C-73/04, *Klein*, [2005] ECR I-8667, para. 15 and the case law cited.

[71] Ibid., para. 28, citing Case 73/77, *Sanders*, [1977] ECR 2383, paras 11 and 12.

[72] Ibid., para 29, citing para 13, and Case C-261/90, *Reichert and Kockler*, [1992] ECR I-2149, para. 10.

[73] Ibid., para. 31. [74] Ibid., para. 32. [75] Ibid., para. 33.

[76] Ibid., para. 34. [77] Ibid.

[78] Ibid., para. 37. It is worth noting, however, that Advocate General Poiares Maduro came to a conclusion in *ČEZ* that differed from that of the Court. In other words, he supported an interpretation of Art. 16(1)(a) of the Brussels Convention that would have brought immovable property located outside EU territory within the exclusive competence of an EU Member State court in the circumstances arising in *ČEZ*.

[79] *Brenner and Noller, supra* note 16.

contracts, now Articles 15 and 16 of Regulation 44/2001, applied when only the consumer is domiciled in the EU, in that case in Germany, while the defendant was not domiciled in a contracting state to the Brussels Convention at all and was in fact domiciled in New York. The CJEU held that the Convention did not apply in these circumstances, at least when the non-EU domiciled party to the contract had no branch, agency, or other establishments in a Brussels Convention contracting state, and the dispute arose out of the operations of such an entity.[80] Thus, *Brenner and Noller* is a clear but relatively rare example of the Court ruling that a private law dispute cannot be heard by EU courts due to the presence of an extra-EU element.

In summary, it can be concluded that the Court has neither maximized nor minimized the circumstances in which legal conflicts with an element that is 'external' to the EU remain within the jurisdiction of EU Member State courts. Rather, its case law represents a moderate approach which draws the interpretation from the wording and context of the relevant conventional or legislative provisions in light of their *travaux préparatoires*.

Once the jurisdictional triggers provided in Regulation 44/2001 have been met or, as the case may be, applicable national law, EU Member State courts are confronted with the additional but not entirely unrelated task of determining whether substantive EU private law can be applied to facts arising out of the EU. This is the issue to which we will now turn.

5. *L'Oréal v. eBay* and *Google*

A. *L'Oréal v. eBay*

L'Oréal v. eBay concerned the external reach of EU trade mark law. L'Oréal (UK) Ltd and several other L'Oréal's corporate entities established outside of the UK instituted proceedings in the High Court of Justice of England and Wales, Chancery Division, alleging that eBay International AG, eBay Europe Group SARL, eBay UK Ltd, and several individuals, had infringed L'Oréal's intellectual property rights through activity on eBay's European web sites. In the UK proceedings L'Oréal argued that sales made through the website www.ebay.co.uk infringed some of its trade mark rights under EU law. This was so because some of the items were counterfeit, others were goods that were not intended for sale such as testers, or were trade mark-protected goods intended for sale outside the European Economic Area (EEA). The goods were offered for sale from locations outside the EU.

The High Court referred a series of question to the CJEU under Article 267 TFEU in order to help it resolve the disputes. One question probed the consequences arising from advertising and offering goods for sale on eBay's website that

80 Ibid., paras 18 and 19.

had not been put on the market in the EEA by or with the consent of L'Oréal. The High Court wondered whether it was sufficient that the advertisement or offer of sale was targeted at consumers in the territory covered by that trade mark in order for them to attract the protection of Article 5(1)(a) of Directive 89/104 to approximate the laws of the Member States relating to trade marks[81] and Article 9(1) (a) of Regulation 40/94 on the Community trade mark,[82] or whether the trade mark proprietor had to show that the advertisement or offer for sale necessarily entailed putting the goods in question on the market within the territory covered by the trade mark.

eBay argued that the proprietor of a trade mark registered in a Member State or of a Community trade mark could not properly rely on the exclusive right conferred by that trade mark as long as the goods bearing it and offered for sale on an online marketplace were located in a third state and would not necessarily be forwarded to the territory covered by the trade mark in question. L'Oréal, the UK government, the Italian, Polish, and Portuguese governments, and the European Commission contended, however, that the rules of Directive 89/104 and Regulation 40/94 applied as soon as it was clear that the offer for sale of a trade-marked product located in a third state was targeted at consumers in the territory covered by the trade mark.[83]

The CJEU held that the latter contention had to be accepted. If it were otherwise, operators that used electronic commerce means such as Internet websites to sell EU customers trade mark-protected goods from third states would have no obligation to comply with the EU intellectual property rules. Such a situation would have an impact on the effectiveness (*effet utile*) of those rules.[84]

The CJEU added, however, that the mere fact that a website is accessible from the territory covered by the trade mark was not a sufficient basis for concluding that the offers for sale displayed there are targeted at consumers in that territory.[85] The Court applied, by analogy, its ruling in Joined Cases C-585/08 and C-144/09 *Pammer and Hotel Alpenhof*.[86] There it was held that the mere fact that a

[81] First Council Directive of 21 December 1988 to approximate the laws of the Member States relating to trade marks, OJ 1989 L 140/1, now repealed, and replaced by Directive 2008/95/EC of the European Parliament and of the Council of 22 October 2008 to approximate the laws of the Member States relating to trade marks OJ 2008 L 299/25.

[82] Council Regulation (EC) 40/94 of 20 December 1993 on the Community trade mark, OJ 1994 L 11/1, now repealed and replaced by Council Regulation (EC) 207/2009 of 26 February 2009 on the Community trade mark OJ 2009 L 78/1.

[83] *L'Oréal, supra* note 3, para. 61.

[84] Ibid., para. 62. We recall that exhaustion of EU trade mark rights arises when the goods in question are put on the market in the EEA, and not when they are put on the market elsewhere. See Art. 7 of Directive 89/104 and Art, 13 of Regulation 40/94.

[85] Ibid., para. 64.

[86] *Pammer, supra* note 13, para. 69. In Case C-173/11, *Football Dataco and Others*, judgment of 18 October 2012, paras 36–38, where it was held that the mere act of accessibility of date in a particular national territory is not a sufficient basis for concluding that the operator of a website is performing an act of reutilization under Art. 7 of Directive 96/9/EC of the European Parliament and of the Council of 11 March 1996 on the legal protection of databases, OJ 1996 L 77/20. What is required is evidence from which it may be concluded that the act discloses intention on the part of its performer to target persons in that territory. See also Case C-5/11, *Donner*, judgment of 21 June 2012, paras 27–29.

website can be accessed in a Member State was insufficient for a trader to be considered to be directing its activity to that Member under Article 15(1)(c) of Regulation 44/2001 on special rules of jurisdiction for consumer contracts. The Court noted in *L'Oréal* that if the fact that an online marketplace was accessible from that territory was sufficient for the advertisements displayed there to be within the scope of Directive 89/104 and Regulation 40/94, websites and advertisements which, although obviously targeted solely at consumers in third states, nevertheless technically accessible from EU territory, would wrongly be subject to EU law.[87]

It therefore fell to the national courts to assess on a case-by-case basis whether there were any relevant factors on the basis of which it may be concluded that an offer for sale, displayed on an online marketplace accessible from the territory covered by the trade mark, was targeted at consumers in that territory. When the offer for sale was accompanied by details of the geographic areas to which the seller was willing to dispatch the product, that type of detail was of particular importance in this assessment.[88]

B. *Google*

In 2010, a Spanish national resident in Spain (the 'data subject'), lodged with the Spanish Data Protection Agency, the AEPD, a complaint against a daily newspaper *La Vanguardia*, and against Google Spain and Google Inc. The complaint was based on the fact that when Internet users entered the data subject's name in the search engine of the Google group, they obtained links to two pages of *La Vanguardia* of 1998, on which an announcement mentioning the data subject's name appeared for a real estate auction connected with attachment proceedings for the recovery of social security debts.

In July 2010, the AEPD rejected the complaint in so far as it related to *La Vanguardia*, but the complaint was upheld in so far as it was directed against Google Spain and Google Inc, which then brought separate actions against that decision before the National High Court in Spain. The action therefore raised the

[87] *L'Oréal, supra* note 3, para. 64. According to the answer to the preliminary questions in *Pammer*, the following matters, the list of which is not exhaustive, are capable of constituting evidence from which it may be concluded that the trader's activity is directed to the Member State of the consumer's domicile: the international nature of the activity, mention of itineraries from other Member States for going to the place where the trader is established, use of a language or a currency other than the language or currency generally used in the Member State in which the trader is established with the possibility of making and confirming the reservation in that other language, mention of telephone numbers with an international code, outlay of expenditure on an Internet referencing service in order to facilitate access to the trader's site or that of its intermediary by consumers domiciled in other Member States, use of a top-level domain name other than that of the Member State in which the trader is established, and mention of an international clientele composed of customers domiciled in various Member States. On the other hand, the mere accessibility of the trader's or the intermediary's website in the Member State in which the consumer is domiciled is insufficient. The same is true of mention of an e-mail address and of other contact details, or of use of a language or a currency which are the language and/or currency generally used in the Member State in which the trader is established.

[88] Ibid., para. 65.

question of the obligations owed by operators of search engines to protect personal data of persons concerned who did not wish for certain information, which had been published on third parties' websites and contained personal data relating to them that enabled that information to be linked to them, to be located, indexed, and made available to Internet users indefinitely. The answer to that question depended on the way in which the Data Protection Directive fell to be interpreted in the context of technology that emerged after the directive's publication, and whether or not it could be extended to an Internet server located in California in the US.

A series of questions was referred to the CJEU, one concerning the extraterritorial reach of the Data Protection Directive, while the others were concerned with the data subject's substantive rights in EU law. Only the former will be addressed here.

The national referring court asked for an interpretation of Article 4(1) of Directive 95/46, according to which:

> 1. Each Member State shall apply the national provisions it adopts pursuant to this Directive to the processing of personal data where:
>   (a) the processing is carried out in the context of the activities of an establishment of the controller on the territory of the Member State; when the same controller is established on the territory of several Member States, he must take the necessary measures to ensure that each of these establishments complies with the obligations laid down by the national law applicable;
>   (b) the controller is not established on the Member State's territory, but in a place where its national law applies by virtue of international public law;
>   (c) the controller is not established on Community territory and, for purposes of processing personal data makes use of equipment, automated or otherwise, situated on the territory of the said Member State, unless such equipment is used only for purposes of transit through the territory of the Community.
> 2. In the circumstances referred to in paragraph 1(c), the controller must designate a representative established in the territory of that Member State, without prejudice to legal actions which could be initiated against the controller himself.

In the light of this provision and the facts before it, the referring court asked whether an 'establishment' existed within the meaning of Article 4(1)(a) of Directive 95/46. It also asked for an interpretation of the words 'use of equipment' under Article 4(1)(c). Third, it asked whether, in the absence of the connection factors referred to in Article 4(1) of the Data Protection Directive, the Directive had to be applied in the light of Article 8 of the EU Charter of Fundamental Rights on protection of personal data, where the centre of gravity of the conflict was located, thus ensuring more effective protection of the rights of EU citizens.

The CJEU found it necessary to answer only the first of these questions. It noted that the main issues raised by the referring court concerned the notion of 'establishment' within the meaning of Article 4(1)(a) of Directive 95/46.[89] It was further noted that the Spanish court had stated that Google Search was operated and

[89] *Google, supra* note 4, para. 44.

managed by Google Inc., and that it had not been established that Google Spain carried out an activity directly linked to the indexing or storage of information or data contained on third parties' websites in Spain. Nevertheless, according to the Spanish court, the promotion and sale of advertising space, which Google Spain attended to in respect of Spain, constituted the bulk of Google group's commercial activity and may be regarded as closely linked to Google Search.[90]

The Court commenced its reasoning by observing that recital 19 in the Preamble to Directive 95/46 states that 'establishment on the territory of a Member State implies the effective and real exercise of activity through stable arrangements', and that 'the legal form of such an establishment, whether simply [a] branch or a subsidiary with a legal personality, is not the determining factor',[91] but that it was not disputed that Google Spain engages in the effective and real exercise of activity through stable arrangements in Spain. Moreover, as it had a separate legal personality, it constituted a subsidiary of Google Inc. on Spanish territory and therefore amounted to an 'establishment' within the meaning of Article 4(1)(a) of Directive 95/46.[92]

The Court went on to consider whether the processing of personal data by the controller was 'carried out in the context of the activities' of an establishment of the controller on the territory of Spain. Google Spain and Google Inc. argued that since the processing of personal data at issue was carried out exclusively by Google Inc., that operated Google Search without any intervention on the part of Google Spain, the latter's activity was limited to providing support to the Google group's advertising activity which is separate from its search engine service.[93]

Nevertheless, the Court held that Article 4(1)(a) of Directive 95/46 does not require the processing of personal data in question to be carried out 'by' the establishment concerned itself, but only that it be carried out 'in the context of the activities' of the establishment.[94] Further, in the light of the fact that the objective of Directive 95/46 was to ensure effective and complete protection of the fundamental rights and freedoms of natural persons, and, in particular, their right to privacy, with respect to the processing of personal data, these words could not be interpreted restrictively.[95]

The Court noted that it was clear in particular from recitals 18 to 20 in the preamble to Directive 95/46 and Article 4 thereof that the EU legislature sought to prevent individuals from being deprived of the protection guaranteed by the directive and that protection from being circumvented, by prescribing a particularly broad territorial scope.[96] It was therefore concluded that the processing of personal data for the purposes of the service of a search engine such as Google Search, which was operated by an undertaking that had its seat in a third State but had an establishment in a Member State, is carried out 'in the context of the activities' of that establishment if the latter is intended to promote and sell, in that Member State,

[90] Ibid., para. 46. [91] Ibid., para. 48. [92] Ibid., para. 49.
[93] Ibid., para. 51. [94] Ibid., para. 52. [95] Ibid., para. 53.
[96] Ibid., para. 54.

advertising space offered by the search engine which serves to make the service offered by that engine profitable.[97]

The activities of the operator of the search engine in the US and those of its establishment in Spain were considered to be inextricably linked, since the activities relating to the advertising space constituted the means of rendering the search engine in the US economically profitable, and the engine was also the means enabling those activities to be performed.[98] The Court relied on *L'Oréal v. eBay*[99] in asserting that the conclusion reached avoided compromising the directive's effectiveness and the effective and complete protection of the fundamental rights and freedoms of natural persons which the directive sought to ensure, in particular the right to privacy.[100] It can be noted that the Court based its appreciation of the questions in issue more on the real business model of Google than technicalities relating to how data processing was physically organized within the Google group.

6. Analysis

The first point to note is that in neither of these judgments was there any dispute as to whether the Member State courts concerned had jurisdiction under Regulation 44/2001 or otherwise. In the case of *L'Oréal v. eBay*, this was so because one of the defendants was a UK company. In *Google*, the proceedings were of an administrative law nature, even though in substance they concerned private law. This situation arose because Google was seeking relief against a decision of the national data protection authority in Spain requiring it to take action it did not wish to take.

However, it is interesting to note that the absence of any live issues related to jurisdiction did not prevent the influence of legal principles developed within the rubric of Regulation 44/2001 from being felt in the judgments. Moreover, legal concepts with their roots in EU public law, as discussed above in section 3, were prominent.

Prior to *L'Oreal v. eBay* and *Google*, the notion of 'targeted' or 'directed behaviour' had been called on to resolve problems relating to jurisdiction over, amongst others, consumer contracts that had been concluded across Member State borders by means of the Internet,[101] while the CJEU also had to consider whether mere accessibility of information emanating from outside of the Member State via the

[97] Ibid., para. 55. [98] Ibid., para. 56.

[99] And in particular paras 62 and 63 of the judgment *L'Oréal, supra* note 3.

[100] *Google, supra* note 4, para. 58, citing Art. 1(1) of the Directive 95/46/EC on the protection of individuals with regard to the processing of personal data and on the free movement of such data and recitals 2 and 10 in its Preamble and Joined Cases C-465/00, C-138/01 and C-139/01, *Österreichischer Rundfunk and Others*, [2003] ECR I-4989, para. 70; Case C-553/07, *Rijkeboer*, [2009] ECR I-3889, para. 47; and Case C-473/12, *IPI*, judgment of 7 November 2013, para. 28 and the case law cited.

[101] See notably *Pammer, supra* note 13, which concerned interpretation of Council Directive 90/314/EEC of 13 June 1990 on package travel, package holidays and package tours OJ 1990 L 158 p. 59 and concerned facts arising in both Germany and Austria.

Internet was a 'harmful event' under Article 5(3) of Regulation 44/2001, thereby satisfying its special basis for jurisdiction provided by that provision.[102] Equally, the Court had had occasion to address whether an act, not involving the Internet, taken outside of the Member State asserting jurisdiction (but still within the EU), can amount to an act of infringement of a trade mark pursuant to Article 93(5) of Regulation 40/94 on the Community Trade Mark[103] because it produces effects within that jurisdiction.[104]

Thus, as has already been mentioned in *L'Oréal v. eBay*, the CJEU drew heavily from *Pammer*[105] which concerned the interpretation of one of the rules on special jurisdiction for consumer contracts under Regulation 44/2001. In addition to this, Advocate General Jääskinen, in his Opinion in *L'Oréal v. eBay*, drew, and specifically so, on the effects doctrine and the judgment of the Court in *Woodpulp*[106] in rejecting the argument of eBay to the effect that trade market protection did not apply to L'Oréal products offered to customers from outside of the EU unless and until these products are put on the market in the EU. He noted that, in the light of the effects doctrine applied in the field of EU competition law, behaviour outside the territory of the EU but directly producing legally relevant effects on the subject matter of EU legislation cannot escape the application of EU rules merely because the acts causing such effects take place outside Union territory.[107]

The influence of the legal principle elaborated in the context of Regulation 44/2001 and the external reach of EU public law is also evident in the scope of the questions put to the CJEU by the national referring court in *Google*. These encompassed corporate structures along the lines of the *Dyestuffs* case law on entity theory in EU competition law, which is reflected in the Data Protection Directive itself.

That said, in cases where there is a public policy interest relating to the internal market, as is the case with intellectual property rights or to fundamental rights such as the right to data protection, the Court seems to be sympathetic to granting wide applicability to substantive EU law provisions, even if this extends the reach of EU law to conduct originating in third countries. It is no wonder that the problems in this respect related to provision of services and goods over the

[102] See, for example, *eDate Advertising, supra* note 51. This case concerned the interpretation of Directive 2000/31/EC of the European Parliament and of the Council of 8 June 2000 on certain legal aspects of information society services, in particular electronic commerce, in the Internal Market, OJ 2000 L 178/1, and facts traversing Germany and Austria and France and the United Kingdom. See also, in the context of copyright law, *Pinckney, supra* note 13, which concerned the protection of copyright under Directive 2001/29/EC of the European Parliament and of the Council of 22 May 2001 on the harmonization of certain aspects of copyright and related rights in the information society, OJ 2001 L 167/10.

[103] Council Regulation (EC) 40/94 of 20 December 1993 on the Community trade mark, OJ 1994 L 11/1.

[104] Case C-360/12, *Coty Germany*, judgment of 5 June 2014.

[105] *Pammer, supra* note 13, para. 69.

[106] *Ahlström, supra* note 21.

[107] Para. 125 of the Opinion of Advocate General Darmon in *Ahlström, supra* note 21.

Internet, whose ubiquitous nature breaks the traditional legal criteria relating to territoriality.[108]

In EU case law concerning transactions that are purely internal to the EU, there seem to be two basic approaches to Internet-related cross-border disputes. As to the applicability of substantive provisions and, in certain situations, jurisdiction, targeting of a Member State territory or market seems to be relevant. However, in the context of competence of courts in matters relating to tort, delict or quasi-delict, the Court in Case C-170/12 *Pinckney*[109] explicitly rejected this criterion and based the jurisdiction of a Member State court to protect against an alleged infringement of copyright on the mere accessibility of the relevant goods or services in that Member State through offers for sale on the Internet. It remains to be seen if this distinction will be extended to cases based on torts and the Internet with an extra-EU element.

In the case of third countries, targeting EU territory as the ground for applicability of substantive EU private law provisions is sourced in a philosophy similar to that of the effects doctrine in competition law. In other words, if economic activity outside the EU produces effects in the internal market, then EU law must become applicable. On the other hand, an approach akin to the *Dyestuffs* entity theory has been applied in a situation where a third country undertaking is clearly active within the EU, but its presence in construed through corporate structures.

7. Conclusion

As this chapter has shown, in view of the great variety of different factual constellations and policy considerations relating to the external reach of substantive EU private law, along with the pace of technological developments, the CJEU faces an unenviable task of developing a solid matrix of rules to resolve the manifold legal problems that are beginning to burgeon. Therefore, in our view, each individual measure of EU private law should contain provisions governing their external reach, in the same way as the Date Protection Directive, and which define, as far as possible, the boundaries of the territorial applicability of the measure in question. Otherwise, difficult legal issues of the kind that emerged in *L'Oréal v. eBay* and *Google Spain* will be dealt with by the CJEU on a case-by-case basis, leaving the Court to draw on neighbouring fields of law to resolve the problems as they emerge, such as territories to which EU law applies as prescribed by the EU Treaties (section 2 above), EU public law, and the established rules on conduct taking place outside of the EU (section 3 above), and Regulation 44/2001, both with regard to the circumstances in which an extra-EU factual element will affect the jurisdiction

[108] For a discussion see, for example, Peukert, 'Territoriality and Extraterritoriality in Intellectual Property Law', in G. Handl and J. Zekoll (eds), *Beyond Territoriality: Transnational Legal Authority in an Age of Globalization* (2011); and De Souza and Waelde, 'Moral Rights and the Internet: Squaring the Circle', 3 *Intellectual Property Quarterly* (2002) 265.

[109] *Pinckney, supra* note 13.

of EU Member State national courts (section 4 above), and the manner in which Regulation 44/2001 has been interpreted in disputes involving the Internet, and which traverse the borders of one or more EU Member States (section 6 above). Given the enormity of the task at hand, we query whether continuation of an ad hoc approach for addressing the legal issues generated by globalization, the Internet, and other emerging technologies is the optimal way forward.

7

Do EU Contract and Company Law have Global Reach?

Stefan Grundmann

1. The Topic

Before 2008, simple local contracts such as loan contracts did not have a visibly global effect. After that time they were found to have triggered the deepest and most wide-reaching financial and economic crisis since the Second World War.[1]

The global company—or rather, in practice, the global group of companies, often called the 'multinational enterprise'[2]—existed and had its global dimension well before 2008. A truly international regulatory regime for this phenomenon has, however, not been seriously considered, at least not in relation to group relationships in a going concern within the same large multinational, until perhaps 2011[3] (accounting law forms one exception, which will be touched upon later, and financial services supervision another, which will not be discussed here).

[1] On the chain of adverse effects which triggered the financial crisis, see, for instance Acharya *et al.* in V. Acharya and M. Richardson (eds), *Restoring Financial Stability—How to Repair a Failed System* (2009), at 1–7 and 12–25; Grundmann, Hofmann, and Möslein, in S. Grundmann, Ch. Hofmann, and F. Möslein (eds), *Finanzkrise und Wirtschaftsordnung—Grundsatzfragen und Politikverantwortung* (2009) 1, at 3–15; and Hellwig, 'Gutachten E', *66. Deutscher Juristentag* (2010), E1, at E41–46, E56 *et seq*. On sub-prime loan contracts and their role in this process in particular, see Avgouleas, 'The Global Financial Crisis—Behavioural Finance and Financial Regulation—In Search of a New Orthodoxy', 9 *Journal of Corporate Law Studies* (2009) 22, at 35 *et seq*.; A. Turner, *The Turner Review—A Regulatory Response to the Global Banking Crisis* (2009), at 106 *et seq*.; Bar-Gill, 'The Law, Economics and Psychology of Subprime Mortgage Contracts', 94 *Cornell Law Revue* (2009) 1073.

[2] For the concept and term see, for instance, P. Muchlinski, *Multinational Enterprises and The Law* (2nd edn, 2007); J. Dunning, *Multinational Enterprises and the Global Economy* (1992); B. Köhler, *Strukturen und Strategien transnationaler Konzerne* (2004); Ch. Pitelis and R. Sugden, *The Nature of the Transnational Firm* (2000); Ch. Römer, *Multinationale Unternehmen—Eine theoretische und empirische Bestandsaufnahme* (2008); see also *OECD Guidelines for Multinational Enterprises* (last update 2011); on the legal regime in Europe, see summary in S. Grundmann, *European Company Law—Organization, Finance and Capital Markets* (2nd edn., 2012), §§ 30 *et seq*.

[3] *Report of the Reflection Group on the Future of EU Company Law* of 5 April 2011, at 59–75; earlier, however, frequently perceived as a merely 'Germanic' enterprise: Forum Europaeum Konzernrecht, 'Corporate Group Law for Europe', 1 *European Business Organization Law Review* (2000) 165 ('Konzernrecht für Europa', 27 *Zeitschrift für Unternehmens- und Gesellschaftsrecht* (1998) 672).

Contract and company—market transactions and the firm[4]—would both seem to have gained or considerably increased a global dimension over the last five years. This raises the question of a global perspective for European private law. The questions asked in this chapter are twofold: (i) to what extent does EU private law in the two paradigmatic fields of contract and company law already respond to sets of problems globally? and (ii) in which respect could or should a more global reach of these fields of law be expected or desired? In answering both questions, we adopt a very broad concept of contract and company law which includes market regulation (for contracts) and financial markets (for companies).[5]

The answer to these questions depends on an analysis both at the level of conflict of laws and at the level of substantive law design. Both levels are linked more or less intimately depending on the question of which type of rules is at stake, namely to which extent the rule is inspired for reasons of public interest regulation or not (i.e. to what extent 'government interests' are involved). There is, however, a considerable difference in approach between the EU and the US concerning the question of how far global dimensions are taken into account. The US is paradigmatic in this respect and will be contrasted with the EU approach because of its active approach to policing cases of different fact patterns around the world. The framework set by the conflict of laws regime will be discussed first, including the regime of fundamental freedoms which produces very similar effects as conflict of laws (see section 2 following). Single pieces of substantive law will then be analysed on this basis (see section 3 following).

2. The Conflict of Laws Framework

A. Differing Starting Points in Contract and in Company Law and One Core Parallel

The starting point both for the harmonization (or unification) of contract law in the EU and, in a less far-reaching way, for company law was (proposals for) conflict of laws regimes. This is quite evident for contract law, as the EEC's (Rome) Convention on the Law Applicable to Contractual Obligations of 1980[6] was

[4] Groundbreaking for the alternative, see Coase, 'The Nature of the Firm', 4 *Economica* (1937) 386; then Williamson, 'Transaction-Cost Economics: The Governance of Contractual Relations', 22 *Journal of Law & Economics* (1979), 233; Williamson, 'Corporate Governance', 93 *Yale Law Journal* (1984) 1196. These pioneering works triggered a host of literature namely in governance research; from a legal perspective, see Grundmann, 'On the Unity of Private Law—From a Formal to a Substance Based Concept of Private Law', 10 *European Review of Private Law* (2010) 1055.

[5] In this sense, the two main textbooks or commentaries are Grundmann, *supra* note 2; S. Grundmann, *Europäisches Schuldvertragsrecht—das Europäische Recht der Unternehmensgeschäfte (nebst Texten und Materialien zur Rechtsangleichung)* (1999).

[6] (Rome) Convention 80/934/EEC of 19 June 1980 on the law applicable to contractual obligations, OJ 1980 L 266/1, in force, however, only as of 1 April 1991, OJ 1991 C 52/1; consolidated version (in force in then all Member States) in OJ EC 1998 C 27/34; replaced today by Regulation 593/2008 of the European Parliament and of the Council of 17 June 2008 on the law applicable to contractual obligations (Rome I), OJ EC 2008 L 177/6.

drafted and signed earlier than any substantive law harmonization, its beginnings stemming from the EC Doorstep and the EC Consumer Credit Directives in the 1980s.[7] With respect to company law, the picture is more diffuse. Among the core measures already envisaged in the EEC Treaty of 1958, however, two were outstanding. The first was in good measure related to conflict of laws, on cross-border mergers of companies created under different Member States' laws, while the second was oriented more towards substantive law, the European Company Statute. Both were to be finalized some four or almost five decades later.[8] By this early stage, however, resolving conflicts of laws in contract law at EU level was seen as a fundamental requirement and indeed even as the starting point of the development of all EU law in this area,[9] while in company law it was conceived as an annex to substantive law regulation of mergers rather than something that encompassed company law (or even company *and* capital market law) in its entirety. Therefore, in contracts, it is possible to speak of a conflict of laws framework (or even 'constitution'), while in company law it still is not.

Today, however, this picture is different in so far as there is at least a partial substitute for a convention or regulation on conflict of laws. This is the CJEU's case law based on the freedom of establishment, and aiming at a greater freedom of choice of applicable laws for companies and their decision makers. This increased freedom of choice of laws applies to structural measures—those affecting the overall structure of the company—such as freedom of incorporation, freedom of cross-border merger (with a change of applicable law for the assets and the shareholders of (at least) *one* company), and freedom of transfer of seat (albeit with some uncertainties).[10] The freedom of choice of laws may not go quite so far as

[7] Council Directive 85/577/EEC of 20 December 1985 to protect the consumer in respect of contracts negotiated away from business premises, OJ EC 1985 L 372/31; and Council Directive 87/102/EEC of 22 December 1986 for the approximation of the laws, regulations and administrative provisions of the Member States concerning consumer credit, OJ EC 1987 L 42/48 respectively. These two measures have also been replaced today, see Directive 2011/83/EU of the European Parliament and of the Council of 25 October 2011 on consumer rights, amending Council Directive 93/13/EEC and Directive 1999/44/EC of the European Parliament and of the Council and repealing Council Directive 85/577/EEC and Directive 97/7/EC of the European Parliament and of the Council (Consumer Rights Directive), OJ 2011 L 304/64; and Directive 2008/48/EC of the European Parliament and of the Council of 23 April 2008 on credit agreements for consumers and repealing Council Directive 87/102/EEC (Consumer Credit Directive), OJ 2008 L 133/66 respectively.

[8] Directive 2005/56/EC of the European Parliament and of the Council of 26 October 2005 on cross-border mergers of limited liability companies, OJ 2005 L 310/1; Council Regulation 2157/2001 of 8 October 2001 on the Statute for a European Company (SE), OJ 2001 L 294/1; with Council Directive 2001/86/EC of 8 October 2001 supplementing the Statute for a European Company with regard to the involvement of employees, OJ 2001 L 294/22. On the outstanding importance attributed to these measures in 1958 and on the long history of both measures (and the many forerunners/proposals), see Grundmann, *supra* note 2, §§ 28 *et seq.* and 33 respectively.

[9] For some authors, the only requirement for a functioning internal market see, for instance, Koch, 'Private International Law—a "Soft" Alternative to the Harmonization of Private Law?', 3 *European Review of Private Law* (1995) 329; Taupitz, 'Privatrechtsvereinheitlichung durch die EG—Sachrechts- oder Kollisionsrechtsvereinheitlichung?', 48 *Juristenzeitung* (1993) 533, at 539.

[10] See Case C-212/97, *Centros*, [1999] ECR I-1459 and Case C-167/01, *Inspire Art*, [2003] ECR I-10155 (cross-border incorporation); Case C-411/03, *SEVIC Systems AG*, [2005] ECR I-10805 (cross-border merger); Case C-208/00, *Überseering*, [2002] ECR I-9919; and Case C-210/

they do in contract law; it may be oriented only towards the internal market (see below section 3). Yet, it is worthwhile to take these developments into consideration when contrasting contract and company law. The conflict of laws in the company law arena is no longer a completely blank slate. Moreover, if one conceives capital market law as an integrative and indeed highly important part of EU company law,[11] there is not only a second fundamental freedom to consider (i.e. the free movement of capital), but also some specific genuine conflict of law rules in EC/EU secondary law: These rules can be found, for instance, in the EC Takeover and in the EC Market Abuse Directives,[12] and they may even possess the potential to combine to form a coherent picture or a general principle (see section 3 following).

One structural parallel between contract and company law, despite all their differences, is of particular importance. This is the existence of the effect principle which decides on the application of public regulatory regimes. It does so both in contract law (explicitly, in this sense, Article 9 Rome I Regulation) and in company law, as shown in various specific legal measures at the EU level (see sections B.2 and C.2 following). The effect principle is very general, as can be seen in the application of antitrust law, which was highly influential in this respect.[13] In other words, the global reach of at least the regulatory aspects both of contract and of company law—and, more generally, private law—has a clear guiding principle and a global orientation. Acts committed worldwide which have a considerable impact in the EU come within range of EU public interest regulation. In time, Articles 4(1) and 6 of the Rome II Regulation recognized this connecting factor (the impact principle) explicitly and formulated a more general principle in this respect.[14]

In the following section, both regimes are considered in turn with a particular view to the question of how far they lend themselves to fostering transactions and policies with a global perspective or scope. More precisely, it looks at how far EU norms take global interests into account ('importation') and how far EU norms are imposed in third states ('exportation').

06, *Cartesio*, [2008] ECR I-9641 and Case C-378/10, *Vale*, judgment of 12 July 2012 (cross-border transfer of seat/re-incorporation).

[11] On the concepts and on the reasons for such an integrative view, see, more extensively Grundmann, *supra* note 2, § 1.

[12] Art. 4 of the Directive 2004/25/EC of the European Parliament and the Council of 21 April 2004 on takeover bids, OJ 2004 L 142/12; and Art. 10 of the Directive 2003/6/EC of the European Parliament and of the Council of 28 January 2003 on Insider Dealing and Market Manipulation (Market Abuse), OJ 2003 L 96/16, as of 2016 Market Abuse Regulation 596/2014/EU.

[13] Antitrust law is the paradigm of market regulation. In the EU it is also the example which came into being earliest and which moreover was integrated in the EEC Treaty of 1958, i.e. that it has been elevated to the 'constitutional' level. For the effect principle as the core connecting factor in this area of the law, see references, *infra* note 22.

[14] Regulation 864/2007 of the European Parliament and of the Council of 11 July 2007 on the law applicable to extra-contractual obligations (Rome II), OJ 2007 L 199/40.

B. A Fully Fledged Conflict of Laws Framework in Contract Law

1. Traditional Contract Law (Primarily Default Rules)

While the Rome I Regulation ((EC) No. 593/2008)—or its almost identical predecessor, the Rome Convention of 1980—can be seen as a quasi-constitutional framework for the whole of *internal market* contract law, two decisions stand out with respect to the question of global reach.

First is Article 3 of this Regulation. More clearly than national conflict of laws regimes or international treaties on the conflict of laws that existed prior to it, this rule formulates an unrestricted freedom of choice of laws. It may not cover all contract law—namely, questions of public interest regulation (see below sub-section B.2)—, but for the rest ('traditional contract law' and primarily default rules), the freedom is unrestricted. Any law throughout the world can be chosen and no material link to that law is required. The parties do not need to justify a particular choice.[15] The only precondition is that the case has a non-trivial cross-border element, that it is not a purely domestic case (see Article 3(3) Rome I Regulation) or, with respect to the application of harmonized EC/EU law standards, that it is not a case which has links only to EU Member State laws (see Article 3(4) Rome I Regulation, 'EU domestic cases'). Thus, from the perspective of EU law (i.e. the Rome I Regulation), both for actors within the EU and for actors outside the EU, the choice is unlimited: in the first case, the choice of third countries' laws, in the second, the choice of EU private law. Typically, however, EU private law can be chosen only in its transposed form, that is, as a Member State law based on EU harmonization (transposed into this national law).

The second decision taken by the EU legislature has already been touched upon implicitly: the Rome I Regulation has been conceived as a so-called *loi uniforme* (as had the Rome Convention of 1980). Indeed, Article 2 specifies that the law chosen or applicable can be any law throughout the world, not just a law of one of the Member States. Thus, while the Convention had been conceived as a constitutional framework for internal market contract law in 1980, it was not limited to this, nor is the Rome I Regulation. It is completely open globally.

Both decisions with respect to global reach—unlimited freedom of choice of laws and formulation as a *loi uniforme*—should be seen, however, in the light of three (potential) modifications or restrictions. The first is not particularly important in the area of contract law: a characteristic of the EU Rome Regulations is that they claim application only in subsidiarity to other—pre-existing—international treaties on the conflict of laws, for instance in Article 25 Rome I Regulation.[16]

[15] A. Briggs, *The Conflict of Laws* (2nd edn, 2008) 154 *et seq.* and 165 *et seq.*; G.-P. Calliess, *Rome Regulations*, (2011), Rome I Art. 3 para. 23; Martiny in Ch. Reithmann and D. Martiny, *Internationales Vertragsrecht* (7th edn, 2010), para. 85.

[16] Thus, while the Rome Convention (now Rome I Regulation) was oriented to internal market in so far as it wanted to create a level playing field for contract drafting, at least with respect to conflict of laws, there is now a remarkable openness to global acts in the regulations based on Art. 81 TFEU, while most other legal bases in the EU Treaties ask for a much more focused internal market orientation. On this issue, see in more detail Chapter 3 in this book.

In theory, although not in practice, other treaties could, for instance, restrict the freedom of choice of laws more stringently than the Rome I Regulation does. In contract law, however, such treaties are extremely rare.

The second modification or restriction is much more important. Even under the Rome I Regulation, after extended policy debates about this exact question, sets of rules which are not based on state law but are universally accepted continue to fall outside the scope of application (and the 'privileges') of the Regulation. They are not laws which can be chosen under the Rome I Regulation. Under this Regulation, they are treated like private party-made 'law', that is, like standard contract terms if indeed chosen.[17] Thus, the Rome I Regulation is not open to recognizing such a body of 'law' as a *lex mercatoria.*[18]

Third, with respect to the freedom of choice of laws and with respect to the current state of EU contract law, it has to be borne in mind that this freedom does not apply, or is at least seriously restricted, where rules are at stake which have been drafted with a view to preserving a public interest and, indeed, most EU contract law is precisely of this kind. Therefore, in summary, Article 3 Rome I Regulation gives full freedom of choice of laws, but more so in the case of third countries' contract laws and for Member States' contract laws where these are not harmonized. The areas of harmonization, that is, of EU contract law, are mostly designed to protect a public interest and therefore fall into the area which will now be discussed.

2. *Public Interest Regulation: The Effect Principle*

The *public interest* is the core criterion for the second area for which Article 9 Rome I Regulation formulates the general principle: the furtherance of any form of public interest—for the political, social, or economic overall order—is 'privileged' in so far as the forum (Member) state may apply regulation with such a scope without being restricted by the Regulation. The (Member) state, if it applies this type of public interest regulation, may do so despite diverging choice of laws made by the parties or diverging choice of laws rules contained in the Rome I Regulation (see Article 9(2) Rome I Regulation). National law is allowed to disregard EU regulation in this area.[19] With respect to public interest regulation by states other than that of the forum, the court may—but need not—apply them, at least with

[17] On this—much disputed—issue, see for instance G.-P. Calliess, *supra* note 15, Rome I Art. 3 para. 29; Martiny, *supra* note 15, paras 127 *et seq.*

[18] There is a host of literature on *lex mercatoria* and its application (which is not really problematic in arbitration). For my own view on how *lex mercatoria* is applicable in state courts (if chosen) at least in internal market relationships see Grundmann, 'Law merchant als lex lata Communitatis—insbesondere die Unidroit-Principles', in U. Diederichsen, G. Fischer, and D. Medicus (eds), *Festschrift for Walter Rolland* (1999), at 145.

[19] What remains, however, is a control under fundamental freedoms; see Grundmann, 'Internal Market Conflict of Laws—From Traditional Conflict of Laws to an Integrated Two Level Order', in A. Fuchs, H. Muir Watt, and É. Pattaut (eds), *Les conflits de lois et le système juridique communautaire* (2004), 5; Freitag's chapter on Art. 9 Rome Regulation in Ch. Reithmann and D. Martiny *Internationales Vertragsrecht*, (7th edn, 2010), (Art. 9 Rom-I-VO) para. 534; D. Martiny, *Münchener Kommentar BGB*, Vol. 10 (5th edn, 2010), Art. 9 Rom I-VO para. 62.

respect to the nullity of contracts violating such regulation (Article 9(3) Rome I Regulation). Thus, the public interest concept defines the scope of application where a fundamentally different conflict of laws regime applies.

The most important question is left open by the regulation and it is up to the forum state to decide. This is the question of the *connecting factor* which applies in the area of public interest, that is, under which circumstances the forum state *wants* to apply such public interest regulation of its own sphere. The core criterion named in the Regulation is that the forum state considers the application of a particular rule important enough for the furtherance of public interests that it wants to apply the rule. Case law and most authors today point to the substantive law rule itself and its law aims when assessing whether application of this particular rule is considered to be so important as to discard choice of laws.[20] Therefore, in the area of furtherance of the public interest, the substantive law rule and its aims are intimately linked to the question of applicable law, contrary to what is the case in the area of freedom of choice of laws discussed earlier. In the substantive law rule, the substantive solution is to be found as well as the criterion of the intensity of the interest pursued, which decides about the applicability of this rule. This is, of course, very similar to the 'governmental interests' theory which in some US jurisdictions is used as a general conflict of laws rule, and which—for any rule, not only for 'public interest' regulation—looks for the 'governmental interests' enshrined in it in order to assess whether it should be applied.[21] When we say that the national substantive law rule decides on its willingness to be applied and that in this respect national law displaces the EU regulation, one proviso needs to be made. In many substantive law areas in the EU, the 'public interest' regime itself is of EU origin, that is, it is to be found in EU harmonization so that the 'national' rule is in essence one which only transposes the EU policy regime into the national regime. Thus, it is the finality of the EU rule which decides the question as to how strong the 'governmental interests' enshrined in it are in order to assess whether it should be applied internationally. Such 'European' policies will be illustrated in the last sub-section of part 3 devoted to substantive law.

The criterion of the intensity of the interest pursued is formulated in the most prominent specifications as the 'effect' principle. If the act or contract reaches the market, constituency, or institution which a substantive law rule is aimed to protect, any other connecting factor is of minor importance compared to this 'place of effect'.[22] In antitrust law, it is not the place where the enterprises participating

[20] Calliess, *supra* note 15, Rome I Art. 9 para. 30; Freitag, *supra* note 19, paras 651 *et seq.*

[21] Groundbreaking, Currie, 'The Constitution and the Choice of Law—Governmental Interest and the Judicial Function', 26 *The University of Chicago Law Review* (1958) 9. The leading textbook in this respect is still D. Currie et al., *Conflict of Laws* (9th edn, 2013), 118–204.

[22] Joint Cases 89, 104, 114, 116, 117, and 125–129/85, *Woodpulp*, [1988] ECR 5193. For German law with its emphasis on antitrust law see Bundesgerichtshof (Supreme Court), Official Reports (BGHZ) 40, 391, at 396 *et seq.* (17 *Neue Juristische Wochenschrift* (1964) 969, at 971 ('Stahlexport')); and similar for its law against unfair competition (for competitors from different states), Official Reports (BGHZ) 35, 329, at 333 *et seq.* = 15 *Neue Juristische Wochenschrift* (1962) 37, at 38 *et seq.* ('Kindersaugflaschen').

in a cartel are registered, nor where the cartel has been formed that is decisive, but the market for which, for instance, prices have been fixed.[23] In capital market law, again, it is not the place where the company whose shares are at stake is registered that is decisive, but the market to which the shares are admitted as the place which guarantees transparency and honesty of the trade.[24] In the law against unfair competition (as far as it protects competitors), not the place where the decision has been taken to engage in an act of competition or where the strategy has been developed is decisive, but the place where the interests of the competitors meet, that is, where they compete for clients.[25] All this, however, may have been decided by the CJEU in some cases, as the substantive law rule was European as well. This is a question of the substantive law rule at stake, not of Article 9 Rome I Regulation, and substantive law rules need not be of EU origin, in which case national private law rather than the (global) reach of EU private law is at stake.

Before giving examples from EU contract law, one last specification may be helpful. The specific conflict of laws rules for consumer and labour contracts contained in Articles 5 to 8 Rome I Regulation can also reasonably be understood as more specific emanations of Article 9 Rome I Regulation, with three important differences: (i) the connecting factor is specified (the place of the most important effect is defined); (ii) among all 'places of effect' only one (i.e. the most important) is chosen; (iii) Articles 5 to 8 Rome I Regulation are symmetrically formulated, rendering foreign law applicable under the same circumstances as the law of the forum.

The case in which this overarching principle is probably illustrated most strikingly (outside the old and settled areas of 'public interest' regulation, such as competition law and capital market law) is the *Ingmar* case.[26] This case falls outside consumer law (two commercial actors were involved) and formally also outside labour law (the two actors were independent). Thus, Articles 5 to 8 Rome I Regulation could not be applied, or at least not directly. The case turned around the question whether the regime contained in Articles 17 to 19 of the (Independent) Sales Agents Directive applied,[27] a regime

[23] Ibid.

[24] M. Ooi, *Shares and Other Securities in the Conflict of Laws* (2003) 38 *et seq*. In Germany, see Grundmann, 'Deutsches Anlegerschutzrecht in internationalen Sachverhaltsgestaltungen—vom internationalen Schuld- und Gesellschaftsrecht zum internationalen Marktrecht', 54 *Rabels Zeitschrift für Ausländisches und Internationales Privatrecht* (1990) 283, at 305–308; and many others, such as K. Hopt, *Die Verantwortlichkeit der Banken bei Emissionen* (1991) 121 and 123–125; H.-D. Assmann, *Großkommentar Aktiengesetz* (4th edn, 2004), Introduction, paras 703 and 705–711; in principle also D. Zimmer, *Internationales Gesellschafisrecht—das Kollisionsrecht der Gesellschaften und sein Verhältnis zum Internationalen Kapitalmarktrecht und zum Internationalen Unternehmensrecht* (1996) 50–73.

[25] See *supra* references note 22.

[26] Case C-381/98, *Ingmar*, [2000] ECR I-9305; case notes, for instance, by Idot, *Revue Critique de Droit International Privé* (2002) 112; Jayme, 'Zum internationalen Geltungswillen der europäischen Regeln über den Handelsvertreterausgleich', 21 *Praxis des internationalen Privat- und Verfahrensrechts* (2001) 190; Kruger, 8 *Columbia Journal of European Law* (2002) 85; Reich, *Europäisches Zivil- und Wirtschafisrecht* (2001) 51; Roth, 39 *Common Market Law Review* (2002) 369; Staudinger, 45 *Neue Juristische Wochenschrift* (2001) 1974; Verhagen, 51 *International & Comparative Law Quarterly* (2002) 135.

[27] Council Directive 86/653/EEC of 18 December 1986 on the coordination of the laws of the Member States relating to self-employed commercial agents, OJ 1986 L 382/17.

which gives the sales agent a right to compensation for the clients whom he newly acquired and whom, after termination, he can no longer 'use' (a right which the agent cannot renounce before termination). Under Article 3 Rome I Regulation, California law, which does not contain such a compensation rule, could validly be chosen (as had been done). There were, in addition, 'reasonable' contacts to California—not even needed under Article 3 Rome I Regulation—given that the contract partner of the sales agent (the enterprise whose goods were to be marketed) had its headquarters there. The Court nevertheless decided that there was a strong enough 'public interest' enshrined in the EU contract law rule—the interest in protecting the sales agent as the weaker party—to justify the mandatory application. As a result, the 'place of effect' was, of course, where the sales agent had acquired his clients: in this case, the United Kingdom (which had transposed the Directive). The interesting point regarding the case is, first, that even a rule aimed primarily at protecting an individual interest (of the sales agents) can be characterized as also protecting an institution or function (a 'public interest'), the market of sales agents. In this respect, the similarity to a labour relationship—despite the independence of the sales agent—has perhaps played a role. Second, via this line of reasoning, the 'place of effect' principle is applied to core contract law as well—as traditional contract lawyers would categorize it—while it has been developed for antitrust and other public interest regulatory regimes which influence contract drafting but which traditionally have not been considered as being 'contract law' in the proper sense. At least formally, these are clearly placed beyond contract law regimes and differ from them considerably in style and structure.

One last remark on the place of effect principle and the link between substantive law interests and questions of applicable law is worth making, the former guiding the solution for the latter. Although this chapter is not about competences, the parallels are evident. Indeed, the most important line of arguments justifying implied external competences of the EU is about the furtherance of substantive law interests which create the need for global reach. If an interest vested in a substantive law measure based on an internal market competence requires, for its effective realization, that there also be a treaty-making power with respect to third state relationships, this latter competence has been implied in the CJEU case law (see also Article 216 TFEU).[28]

[28] Groundbreaking for implied (external) competences: Case 22/70, *AETR*, [1971] ECR 263. Stressing the efficiency aspect that substantive law interests may require extension to third state relationships (parallelism of internal and external competences) even more directly see Opinion 2/91, *International Labour Organization*, [1993] ECR I-1061; Opinion 1/94, *WTO*, [1994] ECR I-5267; see also Joined Cases C-466/98 *et al.*, *Open Skies*, [2002] ECR I-9427. The question whether this competence is exclusive or not is then assessed on the basis of an overall in-depth analysis of the single norm, see Opinion 1/03, *Lugano Convention*, [2006] ECR I-1145.

3. *Public Interest Regulation, Governmental Interests, and Long-Arm Statutes*

The application of 'public interest' regulation under the effect principle has a global reach. This dimension can be made more explicit by contrasting it to the alternative approaches which are mostly followed in the US. The application of 'public interest' regulation under the effect principle neither reaches out as extensively as the governmental interest theory named above, nor as so-called long-arm statutes. The former stretches out more broadly in that it applies a (substantive law) 'public interests' analysis to all contract law, not only to that part of contract law in which the protection of a public interest is the dominant motive.[29] Conversely, long-arm statutes known mainly from US case law seize fact patterns which are 'more removed'; that is which have less significant contacts to the US than the effect principle would require. Although most cases of the long-arm reach of US law turn on jurisdiction extended to defendants outside the US on the basis of connecting factors of a rather exceptional kind, there are a few cases that concern conflict of laws as well.[30] In these cases, similarly weak links to the US (or the US state affected) are invoked as a basis for applying US law (or the law of that state). Most cases are about liability rules which typically are much more favourable for plaintiffs in the US, namely for tort victims. The typical feature of the long-arm application of US law in these cases is that the tort as such did not have any genuine link with the US, but that the tortfeasor—often a multinational enterprise—has some economic interests in the US (section 302 CPLR New York requires only 'transacting any business in New York'), and that the US want to police the case for policy interests. Thus, for instance, for the alleged crime of financing a terrorist attack between Lebanon and Israel, a Lebanese bank was deemed to fall under US jurisdiction and US liability standards were deemed to apply—in this case the Anti-Terrorism 'Alien Tort Statute'—on the basis of an account which the Lebanese bank owned in the US and via which it transacted with US banks.[31] Application of US law does not require that the matter itself which is tried has an impact or 'effect' on the US—here the terrorist attack—but only that subjecting the case to US law does not violate 'traditional notions of fair-play', often conceived very broadly.[32]

[29] See references *supra* note 21.

[30] Leading cases rendered by the U.S. Supreme Court are *International Shoe v. Washington*, 326 US 310 (1945) and *World-Wide Volkswagen Corp. v. Woodson*, 444 U.S. 286 (1980). For the development of the case law on (long-arm) jurisdiction (not discussed here), see Currie, *supra* note 21, at 97 *et seq.*, 388–423, and 646–648; worth reading, Casad, 'Long Arm and Convenient Forum', 20 *Kansas Law Review* (1971) 1 and the monograph by J.-P. Schmidt-Brandt, *Zu den long-arm statutes im 'Jurisdiktions-Recht' der Vereinigten Staaten von Amerika und zu ihrer Bedeutung für wirtschaftsrechtliche Streitigkeiten* (1991).

[31] *Licci v. Lebanese Canadian Bank*, SAL, No. 183 N.Y. of 20 November 2012; the contact was also rather fortuitous in *Deutsche Bank Securities, Inc. v. Montana Board of Investments*, 7 N.Y.3d 65, 850 N.E.2d 1140 (mere use of a New York-based messaging wire sufficient to apply New York law/jurisdiction).

[32] See references in the last two notes. Developing a set of five (rather general) criteria *Asahi Metal Industry Co. Ltd. v. Superior Court*, 480 US 102 (107 S.Ct. 1026 (1987)).

The EU has a parallel case to the Lebanese Canadian Bank case, which structurally diverges from the traditional concept of place of effect principle as well. In *Möllendorf*, the CJEU conveyed anti-terrorism rules as a spill-over effect on private law too, by declining the transfer of land titles because of alleged links to terrorist acts worldwide.[33]

C. A Company Conflict of Laws Regime with Segmented Reach

1. Fundamental Freedoms as Inchoate Conflict of Laws Regime

It may well be that the fundamental freedoms—namely freedom of establishment—do not contain conflict of law rules proper. In any case, they would apply only to internal market transactions, but even with respect to internal market transactions, it is unclear whether they give just as much freedom of choice of laws as does Article 3 Rome I Regulation. For this reason, there are at least practical problems with cross-border transfers of seat, because a directive on this phenomenon, giving procedural certainty to the regime established by the fundamental freedoms (see footnote 10), is still absent. In principle, however, it is clear that all structural measures are potentially applicable across borders, at least between the Member States. This freedom also guarantees that all laws for the internal organization can be freely chosen, when incorporating and when re-incorporating: the transfer of the registered seat changes the applicable law.[34] In the context discussed here, however, it is paramount that all this is not the case in the relationship to third states: the global perspective is missing.

2. The Transactional Side of Company Law, with Capital Market Laws and Effect Principle

One area of, and one perspective on, European company law remains distinct. Where transactions are concerned, the reach of European company law is generally broader than in other aspects, namely in EU capital market law. This is the case even at the level of fundamental freedoms (primary law) because the fundamental freedom relevant in this respect, the freedom of capital movements, also protects the freedom of commerce with third countries (Article 64 TFEU). The competence contained in Article 65(2) TFEU allows for treaties concluded with third countries and concurs with the more general competence contained in Article 207 TFEU. This fundamental freedom under which effects of company law which may discourage investment must be scrutinized, something that reaches deep into company organization law,[35] does not only apply to capital market law and capital transfers.

[33] See Case C-117/07, *Möllendorf*, [2007] ECR I-8361.

[34] On the transfer of statutory seat—as opposed to real seat (headquarters)—see survey in Grundmann, *supra* note 2, § 27 (also on the change of applicable law triggered by such transfer).

[35] See the summary and survey ibid., § 19 paras 32–39 and § 25 para. 30.

At the level of EU secondary law, the perspective of transaction related rules in EU company law is truly global in situations which are related both to the transfer of capital and to the organizational side of company law. At the level of the company as a whole, there is a conflict of laws rule illustrating this global reach for the situation which affects a company most profoundly, that is, a change of control via a (hostile) takeover. For Article 4 of the EC Takeover Directive subjects takeovers of companies whose shares are admitted to regulated markets, in principle, to the law of this regulated market, both with respect to the bid to be made to the investors and to the powers which company organs have during the bidding phase (and also shortly after). The connecting factor is again the place of effect, but now with respect to the interests of investor protection, and all this irrespective of where the companies have their seat and where decisions, namely the decision to make a bid, have been taken. There is a similar conflict of laws rule with respect to the single transactions at the level of the single investor(s). This rule deals with one important case, namely the prohibition of insider dealing and market manipulation. In this respect, Article 10 of the Market Abuse Directive subjects transactions to the market of admission, the regulated market to which the security has been admitted—again, independent of where the single decisions have been taken. Thus, EU standards have to be complied with if an analyst acquires securities which he then recommends with the scope to influence prices accordingly (scalping). As of 2016, the Market Abuse Regulation applies. Again, the reach of the rule is global, under the effect principle, and this constitutes probably a general connecting factor which applies also to matters other than insider dealing and market manipulation (see footnote 24).

3. Substantive Law Measures—Designed for a Global Scope?

After the framework set by conflict of laws, that is, after a general view on the extent to which EU private law or Member States' private laws are applicable, some paradigmatic sets of rules of substantive law should be analysed in order to give some colour to this overall picture. Substantive law measures typically do not concentrate on questions of (global) reach or application but rather concentrate on the substantive solutions to the questions raised. EU company law and EU contract law, however, contain paradigmatic examples which are also telling with respect to the overall subject of how hard the legislator of European private law, more specifically of EU company and of EU contract law, considers these factors. The first section below concentrates on genuine European models in company and in contract law and on their potential to circulate worldwide. The second section looks at a set of rules in which the EU helped solve problems of global interest (importation of the global dimension). The third section, conversely, analyses rules where one might ask whether the EU should not impose 'European' standards on the third countries (exportation to the global sphere).

A. EU 'Codifications' as Global Models? The Cases of the European Company and of CESL

1. *The Most Prominent Self-Sufficient EU Measures in Company and Contract Law*

Genuine EU private law models are rare. In general, EU private law measures need to be transposed into Member States' laws and can then be applied to cases in third countries only as an 'integral part' of those national laws. Genuine EU private law models of considerable importance are even rarer; in company law and in contract law there are only two (one still at proposal stage): the Statute of the European Company (with the directive on schemes of labour co-determination on the board level),[36] and the proposed Regulation on a Common European Sales Law (CESL),[37] now withdrawn and to be changed into a more narrow instrument on digital contacts. Both measures differ considerably in the level at which each addresses the matter to hand. While the European Company Statute regulates one set of problems in some detail (i.e. the different ways of creating a European company), and otherwise contains only islands of regulation and thus cannot be seen as a fully fledged codification of (public) limited company law at the EU level,[38] the CESL is different. CESL regulates most sets of problems within the scope of its application which comprises sales contracts (and closely related services contracts) and contracts on digital contents. It can indeed be seen as a fully fledged, or almost fully fledged, codification of sales contracts (with closely related services contracts) and contracts on digital contents at the EU level. The lacunae are not so great that they would necessarily obstruct a largely self-sufficient application of this regulation, that is, an application of the regulation (typically) not requiring additional national rules in order to solve cases. Conversely, in the case of the European Company, most problems are resolved via reference to the national law of the Member State of the seat (see Articles 9 and 15 of the Statute).

[36] See references *supra* note 8. Other European models have not gained real importance. This is true for the European Economic Interest Grouping and even more so for the European Cooperative Society; see Grundmann, *supra* note 2, § 34, and conversely, for the rather high success of the European Company, § 33 para 7.

[37] European Commission Proposal for a Regulation of the European Parliament and of the Council on a Common European Sales Law of 11 October 2011, COM (2011) 635 final. On this proposal see, for instance, the broad survey in the special issue of the 50 *Common Market Law Review* (2013) 1.

[38] Therefore, the European Company has also been called the 'European Company of national imprint'. See on this terminology and on the problems associated with it C. Jaeger, *Die Europäische Aktiengesellschaft—europäischen oder nationalen Rechts?—eine rechtsvergleichende Untersuchung* (1994), at 215 *et passim* ('nicht zu verantworten'); critical still today, Bouloukos, 'The European Company (SE) as a Vehicle for Corporate Mobility within the EU: A Breakthrough in European Corporate Law?', 18 *European Business Law Review* (2007) 535, at 536; Ebert, 'The European Company on the Level Playing Field of the Community', 14 *European Business Law Review* (2003) 183, at 191 *et seq.*; Casper, 'Erfahrungen und Reformbedarf bei der SE—Gesellschaftsrechtliche Reformvorschläge', 173 *Zeitschrift für das Gesamte Handels- und Wirtschaftsrecht* (2009) 181, at 185 *et seq*. Conversely, some other authors highlighted the chances of this design: Fleischer, 'Supranational Corporate Forms in the European Union: Prolegomena to a Theory on Supranational Forms of Association', 47 *Common Market Law Review* (2010) 1671, at 1674–1681; Grundmann, *supra* note 2, § 33 para. 8.

2. *Reduced Scope of Application: Solely for Cases with Internal Market Dimension*

Although these are the two outstanding genuinely European models in company and in contract law, they are not designed in a way that they could easily be applied throughout the world as sets of rules 'made in Europe' which could be chosen or 'imported' globally.

This is obvious in the case of a European Company Statute. All forms of creating a European Company Statute, as listed and then further specified in Article 2 of the European Company Statute ((EC) No 2157/2001), require participation of one or two public limited companies created under the laws of one Member State (i.e. with at least registration there), all admitted forms being listed in annex I of that statute, all being creations of the laws of the Member States. In most cases, the actual seat (of the core decision body) has to be in the Union. Therefore, the European Company Statute is not an instrument to be adopted worldwide. This may coincide with the fact that EU company law, even on the conflict of laws levels, is directed only towards the internal market. The core reason for such a restrictive application is, however, that the EU legislature (namely the Council and thereby the Member States) did not want to allow for unlimited competition of this legal form with their own public limited liability company forms.[39] This intention may be obsolete to a certain extent because of the case law of the CJEU which, on the basis of the freedom of establishment, opens up competition in any event (see above, footnote 10), albeit only between forms of public limited companies under Member States' laws. In any case, this limitation was never based on sound policy considerations with respect to companies founded in third countries, if that country allowed for the creation of a public limited company under foreign law (unrestricted incorporation theory). For such companies, the Member States' legislatures could not seriously fear that the existence of the European Company Statute and an extended freedom of choice of this statute (in the third country) would reduce their own regulatory powers. They would not possess nor could they claim such powers with regard to the third country anyway.

The restrictions are less severe in the case of CESL. This can be chosen under EU standards on the basis of Article 4 of the proposed regulation if one of the contracting parties resides in the EU (or if a similar connecting factor is in the EU, such as the place to which the good is to be delivered). The regime is more open because the second party can reside in a third country. Under Article 4 of the Regulation, however, the CESL cannot be chosen, for instance, for a contract between two parties from two (different) South American countries, even if these countries follow the approach of Article 3 of the Rome I Regulation and grant unlimited freedom of choice of laws to the parties. This is worth mentioning because under circumstances such as these, English or German contract law could be chosen, as could all other contract laws of Member States. Therefore, even in contract law, where the

[39] See short comments in Grundmann, *supra* note 2, § 33 para. 16.

conflict of laws regime is open to a global choice of laws, the genuinely European model seems strangely constrained by the ties of the internal market and less open to a 'global' perspective than the laws of the Member States which form only part of the EU! Odd as this may seem, the reason for restricting the scope of application in this way would seem to be that the EU Commission wanted to avoid the requirement of a vote by unanimity, and therefore it chose Article 114 TFEU as the legal basis for the regulation, not Article 352 TFEU.[40] Whether this is a valid legal basis need not be discussed here. In our context, it is more important that Article 114 TFEU was considered to require a link with the internal market. This was apparently seen to imply that the European model could no longer be created as a model made in Europe for the world, but only as a model largely made in Europe for Europe alone, nor as a model code in which European policy considerations and a paradigmatic architecture of contract law are expressed and as such can be 'sold' worldwide, but as an exclusively internal market oriented and thus limited instrument.

3. *Summary and Comparison with Harmonized Member State Law*

Summarizing the main findings made so far and adding some comparison with Member State law, including those aspects which have been harmonized, is a good way to highlight the most striking features of genuinely European models from a global perspective: CESL—as the EU model for contract law—contains a mixture of traditional contract law and regulatory elements aimed at protecting public interests. Because it is designed for the protection of the weaker party,[41] it will not always be easy to tell which part is public-interest oriented and which part is not. In the traditional contract law parts—virtually non-existent in traditional EU secondary law, at least in the harmonization measures adopted thus far—CESL would seem to be a set of rules of reduced global dimension compared with any Member State law. Any Member State law can be freely chosen, even between partners in third countries beyond the EU. CESL, as has been highlighted, can only be chosen if one party resides in the EU (or in case of similar connecting factors). Conversely,

[40] On the problems of this choice and legal basis, see, for instance, Fleischer, Optionales europäisches Privatrecht ('28. Modell'), 76 *Rabels Zeitschrift für Ausländisches und Internationales Privatrecht* (2012) 235, at 243–244; Gutman, 'The Commission's 2010 Green Paper on European Contract Law: Reflections on Union Competence in Light of the Proposed Options', 7 *European Review of Contract Law* (2011) 151, at 158–163; Riesenhuber, 'Der Vorschlag für eine Verordnung über ein "Gemeinsames Europäisches Kaufrecht": Kompetenz, Subsidiarität, Verhältnismäßigkeit; Stellungnahme für den Rechtsausschuss des Deutschen Bundestages', 23 *Europäisches Wirtschafts- und Steuerrecht* (2012) 7; also Grundmann, 'Costs and Benefits of an Optional European Sales Law', 50 *Common Market Law Review* (2013) 225, at 230 *et seq.* (problematic also because introduction of a fully fledged optional code is a 'constitutional' question, since a legal basis for harmonizing all private law—non-existent in the Treaty—would de facto be created).

[41] COM (2011) 635 final, recital 11 ('should maintain or improve the level of protection that consumers enjoy under Union consumer law [as it really is in place in the EU Member States]'); even more explicitly Staudenmayer, 'Der Kommissionsvorschlag für eine Verordnung zum Gemeinsamen Europäischen Kaufrecht', 55 *Neue Juristische Wochenschrift* (2011) 3491, at 3496 *et seq.*

with respect to regulatory aspects, the differences as compared with Member States laws appear to be minor. Application of these parts requires an impact (a place of effect) in that Member State or in the EU in order to render that Member State law or CESL applicable. If this is the case, Member State law applies if it is the forum, and if it is not, it applies only if the forum is ready to apply foreign rules aimed at protecting public interests as well. In the case of CESL, the requirements of Article 4 of the proposed CESL Regulation would have to be satisfied in addition, but if the/a place of effect is in the EU, this will probably be the case in virtually all instances. Even in this case, however, application of the CESL requires the parties explicitly to choose it. Thus, in cases occurring solely in third countries, CESL will play no role as it cannot already have been chosen to deal with the traditional contract law aspect of a case (this is different with Member State law; for example, English common law). In mixed EU and third country cases, CESL can be chosen. In addition, the place of effect will be in the EU if the interest protected is in the EU (Member State laws apply on the basis of the same connecting factors but also if Article 4 Rome I Convention renders applicable the Member State law to be most closely related to the case and no choice of law has been made by the parties). In pure internal market cases, the question of global reach does not pose itself. The CJEU case law on conventions limiting recognition rules similarly to internal market cases would seem to imply that the Court is not willing to get around such limits of scope of application formulated in the EU legal measures.[42]

Much more dramatic is the difference between the genuine EU model and Member State laws in the area of company law. The model of the European Company Statute cannot be chosen in third countries even where a third country follows the incorporation theory in a radical way and allows the creation of a company under foreign law without limits, and also if all business is to be done in that country and the headquarters are based there. In this type of situation in third countries, a company can be created under the laws of particular Member States (e.g. in England and lately also in Germany),[43] but it cannot be created as a European company, or it can but only indirectly via being created as a company under Member State laws first. Similarly, the freedom of choice of laws in company law, as far as it is granted at the EU level, only gives access to another Member State's laws, not to a third country's laws, because it is based on the (internal market)

[42] See, for the Brussels Convention, Case C-129/92, *Owens v. Bracco*, [1994] ECR I-117. Further developed in Case C-412/98, *Group Josi Reinsurance*, [2000] ECR I-5925; and Case C-281/02, *Owusu v. Jackson*, [2005] ECR I-1383; see also Case C-420/07, *Apostodolides v. Orams*, [2009] ECR I-3571 (requiring that the effect of the judgment abroad be the same as in the country of origin).

[43] English law has long allowed that limited liability companies having their shareholders, business, and headquarters elsewhere to incorporate (register) in England, see Briggs, *supra* note 20, at 265 *et seq*. For incoming companies, German law now follows this same approach ('exporting' German law), see Gesetz zur Modernisierung des GmbH-Rechts und zur Bekämpfung von Missbräuchen (MoMiG) 'Limited Liability Companies' Modernization Act' of 23 October 2008, *Bundesgesetzblatt* (Official Journal) part I p. 2614, in force as of 1 November 2008 (abolishing the old section 4a(2) GmbHG and section 5(2) AktG which had prescribed for all limited liability companies that registration was possible only at the place of the headquarters); see also *Bundestags-Drucksache* (Parliament Protocols) 16/6140, at 29.

freedom of establishment. A freedom to choose a third country's company law as governing a company doing its business and having its headquarters in a Member State can be granted only by Member State conflict of laws, such as, for instance, under the English incorporation theory. Thus, in company law, it is not the EU but—if they opt to do so—the Member States that claim genuine global reach.

B. The EU Engaging Globally in Regulatory Regimes ('Importation'): The Case of IAS/IFRS

Accounting law is, although neglected, a core area of company law with strong ties to capital market law because it regulates the core periodical information tool on companies. The link to the 'public good' is evident—to creditors, the general public, and investors and capital markets. Differences in accounting law played a major role in companies seeking international standing, namely in the 1990s when many non-US companies sought listing on the New York Stock Exchange. These differences triggered attempts to permit such listing to German and European companies without imposing the duty to submit accounts under several accounting regimes, at home and on the US market. The core rule at EU level today—having its predecessor in German law (section 292a of the Commercial Code)—is Article 4 of the EC IFRS Regulation. Consolidated accounts in groups of companies with at least one company admitted to a regulated market have to be submitted according to International Accounting Standards/International Financial Reporting Standards (IAS/IFRS) and solely according to them (the liberating effect with respect to the requirements established by the EC Accounting Directives), and for all other accounts, the same option is given to the Member States (Article 5 IFRS Regulation). In other words, with a view to fostering globalization strategies of the enterprises, a global set of rules has been referred to and the EU has collaborated in adopting it as a legal standard; this set of rules exhausts the requirements demanded, both within the EU and beyond.

Such a set of rules can be found in the IAS/IFRS which, in content and approach, are closer to the much less systematic and hopelessly abundant US-GAAP (generally accepted accounting principles) than to the EC directives in this field which, however, also constitute a more concise and indeed virtually 'codified' version of them but with modernized content.[44] What is of interest in our context are three points: the rule-setting procedure; the recognition within the EU and the US which is paramount for achieving the core goal; and also some idea about what could happen in the future application of the rules.

[44] Dewing and Russel, 'Financial Integration in the EU: the First Phase of EU Endorsement of International Accounting Standards', 46 *Journal of Common Market Studies* (2008) 243, at 257; Ballwieser, 'Grenzen des Vergleichs von Rechnungslegungssystemen—dargestellt anhand von HGB, US-GAAP und IAS', in K.-H. Grunewald *et al.*, *Festschrift für Bruno Kropff* (1997), 371, at 379; K. Born, *Rechnungslegung nach IAS, US-GAAP und HGB im Vergleich* (2nd edn, 2001), at 24; detailed comparison in Financial Accounting Standards Board, *The IASC-US Comparison Project: A Project on the Similarities and Differences between the IASC Standards and US GAAP* (1996).

The elaboration of the IAS (today, the IFRS), is in the hands of the International Accounting Standards Board (IASB). Its composition is characterized by the particularly broad representation of both the constituencies affected and the expertise in the area (members of supervisory authorities, accounting firms, of law and economics), as well as the mechanisms for a particularly broad inclusion of public discussion in the norm-setting process. This constitutes an effort to narrow the gap which arises from a perspective of democratic legitimacy (legitimacy by procedure).[45] This is particularly important because IAS/IFRS go far in that they propose not only general principles but also fully fledged sets of rules, or genuine codes, to be modified only in very narrow exceptional cases. Therefore the de facto binding force is particularly far reaching, and democratically legitimized organs have a very limited role to play.

In a second step, IAS/IFRS must be recognized in the different states or in the EU. While accounting law is seen in the US less as an area of parliamentary prerogative, and while the SEC has now recognized IFRS as 'equivalent' to US-GAAP,[46] recognition in the EU is linked to the 'endorsement' procedure which is seen as highly important and controversial.[47] While IFRS have been recognized as a whole set of rules in order to gain equivalence with the requirements contained in the accounting law directives under Article 3 IFRS Regulation, the actual endorsement of the individual rules comes in a separate step. Each new rule can be accepted or rejected given that IFRS are developed in continuity. For this, the European legislature also specified some prerequisites besides the comitology procedure which the EU Commission has to follow, namely requirements of transparency and compliance with the standard of 'true and fair view' (Article 3(2) IFRS Regulation). The sense of this procedure is, among others, to convey official, namely democratic, legitimacy to these 'privately' adopted sets of rules ('private ordering'). As parties can choose any national contract law as the applicable law in most jurisdictions—and increasingly also company laws— this procedure indirectly also conveys democratic legitimacy globally, at least for those IFRS which have been endorsed by the EU.

A similar spill-over effect could theoretically be expected at the level of application because a court like the CJEU speaks for such a large economic bloc and thus its practice may contribute to legal certainty with respect to IFRS. This, however, would seem to constitute a somewhat theoretical possibility because, on the one hand, the IFRS are interpreted by the IASB itself as well (limiting the need of additional guidance) and, on the other, the CJEU, due to its personnel—cannot be expected to render a high number of path-breaking decisions in accounting law.

[45] See more in detail on this aspect, Renner, 'Occupy the System! Societal Constitutionalism and Transnational Corporate Accounting', 20 *Indiana Journal of Global Legal Studies* (2013) 941; also Kirchner and Schmidt, 'Private Law-Making—IFRS: Problems of Hybrid Standard Setting', in P. Nobel (ed.), *International Standards and the Law* (2005) 67.

[46] See releases by the SEC: *Release No.* 33-8818 and 34-55998; and R. Buchholz, *Internationale Rechnungslegung—die Vorschriften nach IAS, HGB und US-GAAP im Vergleich—mit Aufgaben und Lösungen,* (2009) 20.

[47] On the procedure, see Grundmann, *supra* note 2, § 18 paras 6–8.

IAS/IFRS are not the only set of rules drafted by private rule-setters outside a national or a supranational legislative procedure. Important other examples are standards on banking supervision, namely own-funds requirements, which the Basel Committee develops,[48] the standards established by the International Organization of Securities Commissions (IOSCO) with respect to capital market information, namely prospectuses,[49] as well as the standards developed by the International Conference of Drug Regulatory Authorities (ICDRA) on questions of health techniques and pharmaceuticals.[50] With regard to the question of the global reach of EU private law, these sets of rules are comparable to IFRS. Some of these standards may no longer fall into the realms of contract or company law even in the very large sense, and not even into private law. More important in our context, however, are the following two points. The procedure of drafting these sets of rules—outside a legislative procedure set up by state or inter- or supranational institutions—is indeed similar, therefore comparable questions arise with regard to the legitimacy and due representation of the groups affected and the incorporation into (supra-)national law. On the other hand, the differences are also quite significant, in a way which would seem to give the IFRS the status of a truly paradigmatic case, which is why they have been chosen as an example here. With IFRS, drafting is still more exclusively in the hands of the 'private' rule-setter than in the other cases. In the Basel Committee and IOSCO, texts are not formulated and presented to the Member States or the EU in a similarly 'unmodifiable' way. Instead, both institutions formulate standards and principles, for banks' own capital requirements or for prospectuses, which are still to be elaborated into a binding text by the EU institutions. Important matters of content are also awaiting formal incorporation into such a text, even though these standards, set via private ordering, serve as the guideline. There is no simple endorsement of sets of rules composed by independent and private parties. The IFRS are special, however, also with respect to its internal rule-setting procedure because the IASB is composed of all groups affected (businesses and related counselling) and those which have particular expertise in the field (regulators and scholarship), and its procedures and standards must be transparent. Therefore, at a global level, IASB and IFRS serve even more directly than the other examples given as a 'substitute' for state or supranational parliaments and private law with fully fledged codifications of a certain area, and they apply directly to the accounts of the firms which are subject

[48] Above all, Basel Committee on Banking Supervision, *Guidance for National Authorities Operating the Countercyclical Capital Buffer* (2010); Basel Committee on Banking Supervision, *International Framework for Liquidity Risk Measurement, Standards and Monitoring* (2010); Basel Committee on Banking Supervision, *A Global Regulatory Framework for More Resilient Banks and Banking Systems* (2010, revised June 2011); Basel Committee on Banking Supervision, *The Liquidity Coverage Ratio and liquidity Risk Monitoring Tools* (2013).

[49] For shares and debentures respectively, IOSCO, *International Disclosure Standards for Cross-Border Offerings and Initial Listings by Foreign Issuers* (1998); IOSCO, *International Disclosure Principles for Cross-Border Offerings and Listings of Debt Securities by Foreign Issuers* (2005); for all this and for the annual reports, see <http://www.iosco.org> (accessed 18 August 2015).

[50] See, for instance, *Recommendations of the XVth International Conference of Drug Regulatory Authorities* (2012).

to these standards (of course, once these standards have been endorsed by the EU legislature).

C. The EU Enforcing its Regulatory Regimes Globally ('Exportation'): The Effect Principle Further Developed

If the genuinely European models are not designed for export at all, the question of the global reach of European private law is reduced to those areas where EU law transposed into national laws most directly aims to subject cases worldwide to its application. Such a scope can most largely be found where EU private law, under the effect principle, requires its own application because application is necessary to achieve the goals which the substantive law rule intends to protect.

In this area, further development seems to be required, as can be shown with respect to aspects of the 2008 financial crisis which was primarily triggered by the US subprime loans crisis and the bankruptcy of the Lehmann Brothers (and its group), but had huge knock-on effects in the EU market. Examples from the causation chain beautifully illustrate how far the effect principle reaches or should reach.

The crisis was triggered by sub-prime loans; loans given to debtors who could not pay back their loans from their income but only from rising prices of the properties purchased (see footnote 1). Assuming that this type of loans violated principles of responsible lending, the question arises whether an EU regime formulating such a principle as a (mandatory) duty of (loan) contract law could reach or could have reached sub-prime lending in the US. Apart from the fact that such a duty has only been proposed but finally not, or only partly, been adopted in the (second generation) EC Consumer Credits Directive (5),[51] such global reach should not be favoured in the case at hand. The effect principle, in the cases involving a lending to consumers (individual protection), has been formulated in more detail and not just as a principle, namely in Articles 5 *et seq.* Rome I Regulation. These rules show that the scope of a duty of responsible lending would not have protected consumer borrowers in the US, neither would the prime rationale of the decision rendered in the Ingmar case have done so, as the effect of this decision was to protect a party that had invested into an EU market (domicile or habitual residence). Moreover, such global reach was also not necessary to keep consumer credit markets in the EU 'fair' and 'consumer friendly' (functional protection). Mortgage markets in Europe and the US are too separate from each other. A possible remote effect—via additional steps and links—is not sufficient to justify global application of an EU substantive law regime under the Rome I Regulation and under the CJEU case law. This is also preferable from a policy perspective given that the effects are very

[51] See Arts 8–9 of the Proposal for a Directive of the European Parliament and of the Council on the harmonization of the laws, regulations and administrative provisions of the Member States concerning credit for consumers, COM (2002) 443 final; not taken over into Directive 2008/48/EC of the European Parliament and of the Council of 23 April 2008 on credit agreements for consumers and repealing Council Directive 87/102/EEC (Consumer Credit Directive), OJ 2008 L 133/66 (see, however, recital 26 there); since then, there has been some reversal in COM (2009) 114 final, at 7 and in Art. 18 of Directive 2014/17/EU on credit agreements relating to residential immovable property.

indirect and that other conditions were needed to trigger the crisis, conditions which were much more directly linked or even addressed to EU markets.

Next, these loans were accumulated and securitized, creating a financial product which aimed to liberate the initiator (the credit institution which was the original lender) from any responsibility (see footnote 1). Assuming that there is (and was) an EU policy decision to impose responsibility on initiators of products which are to be marketed via a distribution chain, a policy awarding a mandatory right of redress against these initiators to the final sellers of the product (no immunization against risks stemming from defects),[52] once again the question arises about the kind of reach such a policy should have, that is, whether it could be applied globally. In this case, an application of the law of the target market—in the EU (see footnote 24)—is much more justified than with respect to the loans. This is particularly so if these mandatory rules of redress are primarily aimed to protect final purchasers and their claims against final sellers. In this case, the practice named—securitization and selling off the risks without requirement for redress—has quite obviously a direct effect within the EU where the product was actively marketed.

In a similarly direct way, a third element contributing to the financial crisis is related—and even addressed—to the EU market (as the 'place of effect'). If under the EU financial services regime (at least), the full and clear disclosure of relevant conflicts of interests is a core requirement, recurring in the core market segments,[53] the following line of argument, based on an assessment of the substantive law interests, would seem to impose itself. This rule under EU law seeks to protect the investor—reached in the EU as the targeted market—by warning him to be aware that the information given may by no means be neutral but is instead tainted by bias, and to take appropriate additional measures of precaution. If, for instance, US ratings agencies did not disclose in their (triple-A) ratings that they had been actively engaged in the design of the financial products rated (and compensated typically more than for the rating itself), the EU rule violated would seem to

[52] There is indeed such a policy approach in real economy, namely with respect to the marketing/distribution of goods. See the rule contained in Art. 4 of the EC Sales Directive, installing a right of redress between members of the distribution chain, i.e. commercial players. The mandatory character of this rule was justified by the consideration that such a right of redress guaranteed to the final seller may enhance the chances of the final purchaser to enforce his legal warranties under the directive against the final seller (and certainly the special purpose vehicles installed by initiators, i.e. by the originators of the 'toxic papers' as financial products, were particularly weak when guarantees should be enforced against them). For this scope of Art. 4, see, for instance, COM (1995) 520 final, 15; Bridge, in M. Bianca and S. Grundmann (eds), *EU Sales Directive—Commentary* (2002), Art. 4 para. 7.

[53] For EU Primary Market Law (namely prospectuses), see, in this sense, point VIII of the annex and also Art. 21(2) of the EC Prospectus Directive (Directive 2003/71/EC of the European Parliament and of the Council of 4 November 2003 on the Prospectus to be published when securities are offered to the public or admitted to trading, and amending Directive 2001/34/EC, OJ 2003 L 345/64). For EU Secondary Markets Law, namely for investment services (among others, advice), see, in this sense, Arts 13 and 18 EC Market in Financial Instruments Directive—MIFID (Directive 2004/39/EC of the European Parliament and of the Council of 21 April 2004 on markets in financial instruments amending Council Directives 85/611/EEC and 93/6/EEC and Directive 2000/12/EC of the European Parliament and of the Council and repealing Council Directive 93/22/EEC (MiFID), OJ 2004 L 145/1 and 2005 L 45/1), similar, as of 2016, MiFID2.

apply to any such non-disclosure with respect to products marketed on EU markets, irrespective of where they had been designed elsewhere and from where they originated. It was investors in the EU who were targeted by offers of products thus (inadequately) rated. Again, the effect principle would require application of the EU regime, and therefore liability for intentional violation of disclosure rules, which amounts to a common law tort in most jurisdictions (see, for example, section 826 Civil Code in Germany).

4. Conclusion

Meditating on the global importance of EU private law, the first astounding feature is the degree of global openness to be found in contract law (and the law of transactions) and, conversely, the restriction to internal market cases which can be found in company (organization) law. The latter can be seen both at the level of EU primary (fundamental freedoms) and secondary law. This finding reminds one of the old truism that companies (and groups) 'live globally, but die locally/nationally' (in insolvency).[54] The reason is that companies' lives are made up of transactions while their winding-up concerns the organization.

The strongest 'will to global reach' can be found in those rules on transactions which are primarily aimed at the public good; for instance, a smooth functioning of the markets. Here, the effect principle makes EU substantive law applicable also to rules—in order to reach their substantive law goals—which the parties did not choose to apply and this also in cases where the relevant decisions have been taken outside the EU. The core criterion is whether the protected interests have been affected directly within the EU. Such direct impact within the EU can be found in all the different single steps which lead to the financial crisis. This particularly speaks in favour of developing the effect principle in this context still further.

[54] For instance A. Cairns, *The Wall Street Journal* of 14 May 2009.

PART III

THE MAKING OF INTERNATIONAL PRIVATE REGULATION AND THE ROLE OF THE EU

8

International Banking Standards, Private Law, and the European Union

Jan Wouters and Jed Odermatt

1. Introduction

The European Union (EU or Union) is home to many globally systemically important banks (G-SIBs) which in recent years have grown in size and importance and have become ever more interconnected with the global financial system. Since the 2008/9 global financial crisis and Europe's sovereign debt crisis, the EU has taken steps to improve financial governance at the regional level, introducing bodies such as the European Banking Authority (EBA) and the European Systemic Risk Board (ESRB), and it introduced a Single Supervisory Mechanism (SSM) to undertake supervisory tasks regarding the banking sector.[1] This reform at the regional level has not taken place in a vacuum, however. The financial crisis exposed weaknesses in the global financial system and failures of the regulatory framework. The response to this crisis led to a proliferation and intensification of regulation regarding the financial system at many levels. Much of the EU's regulatory reform has taken place in the context of expanded efforts at the international level, primarily in the context of the Group of 20 (G20) and Financial Stability Board (FSB). This has called for the EU to engage, or re-engage, with the multitude of organizations and bodies at the international level that deal with the regulation of banking and the financial system. While the EU is engaged with a large number of international organizations (IOs) and is deeply involved in negotiating and entering into bilateral and multilateral treaties, it had been less internationally active in the field of banking and finance.

This chapter illustrates some of the processes that take place between global norm-generating bodies in the field of financial regulation and the EU. It first examines some of the features of global financial regulation which make it a unique area of global governance. Whereas the EU is an effective international actor in the

[1] European Commission, *A Comprehensive EU Response to the Financial Crisis: Substantial Progress Towards a Strong Financial Framework for Europe and a Banking Union for the Eurozone (Press Release)*, 28 March 2014.

field of trade, the nature of global financial law, based on soft law and informal bodies, presents a challenge to the Union to exert the same level of influence. The chapter then examines the wide variety of norm-generating bodies that are active in the field of banking and financial regulation and the extent to which the EU is represented in these bodies. While the EU is active in 'agenda-setting bodies' such as the G20 and FSB, it will be seen that the Union has not been able to translate its economic weight into global influence in many of the financial standard-setting and regulatory bodies at that level. The chapter then discusses the extent to which these bodies have influenced EU regulation in practice, focusing on the Union's main regulatory efforts since the crisis. These reforms have been highly influenced by non-binding commitments made in informal bodies at the international level. The aim of the chapter is not to give an in-depth examination of regulation that has taken place at the EU or global levels; rather, it seeks to provide an insight into the dynamics that take place between the EU and international standard-setting bodies, providing thereby a case study of the Union's contribution to (regulatory) private law through its external actions.

2. Why Financial Regulation is Unique

The EU is not only a globally significant trading power; it is also home to a large and globally significant banking sector. Although the Union has become a highly influential actor in the field of trade and commercial policy, it has so far not lived up to its international ambitions in the area of financial regulation. There are several reasons that may explain this. First, in the field of international financial law the EU finds itself in an international environment that is very different from that of international trade. Global finance is not regulated by 'traditional' international bodies such as the World Trade Organization (WTO) or the Bretton Woods institutions, but it is increasingly being dealt with by informal networks and other standard-setting bodies.[2] This includes 'agenda-setting' bodies that meet at the leaders' level, such as the G20, or at the level of central banks or supervisory agencies, such as the FSB. While the EU has developed tools and methods to participate in bilateral and multilateral trade negotiations and to work within formal bodies such as the WTO, its relationship with this array of informal bodies remains less defined. Whereas the EU Treaties set out the legal framework for the EU's negotiation and ratification of international agreements, there is far less guidance on the issue of the EU's role in IOs and other informal bodies. The legal and political constraints that have hampered the Union's representation in traditional IOs have been discussed extensively elsewhere.[3] The obstacles that the EU encounters in

[2] Gadbaw, 'Systemic Regulation of Global Trade and Finance: A Tale of Two Systems', 13 *Journal of International Economic Law* (2010) 51.

[3] See Wouters, Odermatt, and Ramopoulos, 'The European Union in the World of International Organizations' in M. Smith, S. Keukeleire, and S. Vanhoonacker (eds), *The Diplomatic System of the European Union: Evolution, Change and Challenges* (2015); Wouters, Odermatt, and Ramopoulos, 'The Status of the European Union at the United Nations General Assembly' in I. Govaere,

being an active member of IOs are also manifested in the Union's relationship with global regulatory and standard-setting bodies.

Second, whereas international trade law involves binding treaties and formal dispute resolution methods, finance is dominated by global 'soft law'.[4] Global finance is generally only the subject of international treaties in so far as they touch upon issues of removing barriers to trade in financial goods. International financial law includes a range of best practices, guidelines, and other 'commitments' made by states, but it rarely involves enforceable legal obligations. There is less emphasis on harmonization of laws, and more on coordination, oversight, and transparency. Financial regulation has also long been dominated by a 'hands-off approach'[5] where regulation, especially at the global level, is seen as an intrusion into the free market. In contrast to the field of trade, which is associated with opening access to markets and removing barriers, much of recent financial law is associated with 're-regulating' the financial markets in order to establish a more stable financial system.

In standard-setting and other bodies, it is not the head of state or ministries that are necessarily represented. Rather, central banks, supervisory and regulatory agencies often take centre stage. The involvement of administrative agencies and technocrats can make it easier to come to an agreement, especially since the parties are not involved in the negotiation of legally enforceable instruments.[6] As Brummer argues, 'most of the sources of international financial law are informal, intergovernmental institutions that set agendas and standards for the global regulatory community'.[7] Again, the EU has developed extensive practice regarding formal treaty negotiation and the ratification and implementation of binding norms. The way it deals with these other forms of 'soft law' remains ill defined,[8] and it is not always clear how these soft-law commitments should be implemented within the EU legal order. Whereas international agreements are binding on the Union and its Member States from the moment they enter into force,[9] soft law commitments require transposition, often via technical EU legislation. This process

E. Lannon, and P. Van Elsuwege (eds), The *European Union in the World: Liber Amicorum Professor Marc Maresceau* (2014) 211.

[4] Brummer, 'Why Soft Law Dominates International Finance—and not Trade', 13 *Journal of International Economic Law* (2010) 623.

[5] Cottier and Lastra, 'The Quest for International Law in Financial Regulation and Monetary Affairs', 13 *Journal of International Economic Law* (2010) 527. 'The regulatory hands-off approach, which has dominated recent decades of international relations in these fields, contrasts with other areas of international economic law. International trade regulation witnessed an increased number of international rules and the reinforcement of a rule-oriented, if not rule-based, approach.'

[6] Brummer, *supra* note 4, at 631: 'Instead, agreements can be entered into between administrative agencies and technocrats—with relatively little interference by outsiders.'

[7] Brummer, *supra* note 4, at 627.

[8] See Wouters and Odermatt, 'Norms Emanating from International Bodies and Their Role in the Legal Order of the European Union' in R. A. Wessel and S. Blockmans (eds), *Between Autonomy and Dependence: The EU Legal Order under the Influence of International Organisations* (2012) 47.

[9] Case 181/73, *Haegeman*, [1974] ECR 449, para. 5.

of transposition can be time-consuming, however, and in some cases may mean that the Union implements commitments in ways that deviate from international standards.

The EU's presence in the field of global financial regulation is also affected by internal constraints. In the field of trade, the Union has, for decades, exercised exclusive competence as part of the common commercial policy. The EU Member States benefit from a unified trade policy, backed up by a central actor, the European Commission. Financial regulation, on the other hand, remains a competence that is shared between the Union and the various Member States and various Union bodies. Some Member States, particularly the UK, Germany, and France, where banking is a large part of the economy, have remained internationally active in their own right. There are also differing views among Member States about the appropriate approach to take on a number of issues, such as the financial transaction tax.[10]

In the regulation of global finance the Union's influence does not yet match its global ambitions. It has been argued, for instance, that 'the EU has failed to create a consistent system of external representation that might enable it to play a more prominent role on the global stage, considering its overall economic might and the competences that supranational bodies have acquired in the European policy process'.[11] It has been observed that the Union has been unable to translate economic power into policy influence: 'the Commission plays an active role in these bodies but there is no evidence that it is able to take the lead or exercise an influence that is stronger than the role of the specialised agencies such as central banks and supervisory authorities'.[12] This relates in part to 'its unsatisfactory presence in supranational fora oriented towards cooperation in matters of economic regulation'.[13] The next section examines the role that the EU plays within the array of standard-setting and other bodies, many of which have become much more influential since the global financial crisis of 2008.

[10] In September 2011, the European Commission tabled a proposal for an EU-wide Financial Transaction Tax. However, it soon became clear that the unanimity required under Art. 113 TFEU could not be reached. A smaller group of 11 Member States decided to pursue the FTT through the enhanced cooperation procedure. See Council Decision 2013/52/EU of 22 January 2013 Authorising Enhanced Cooperation in the Area of Financial Transaction Tax, OJ 2013 L 22/11. In April 2014, the Court of Justice rejected a challenge to the Council Decision authorising enhanced cooperation. See Case C-209/13, *United Kingdom v. Council*, judgment of 30 April 2014. In May 2014 ten EU Member States, all part of the euro area, agreed to introducing a limited financial transaction tax by 2016. See A. Barker, 'Eurozone divided over financial transaction tax deal', *Financial Times* of 6 May 2014.

[11] Rommerskirchen, 'Keeping the Agents Leashed: The EU's External Economic Governance in the G20', 35 *Journal of European Integration* (2013) 348.

[12] See Ohler, 'Back in Balance? The EU and the Challenges of International Financial Regulation', in D. Kochenov and F. Amtenbrink (eds), *The European Union's Shaping of the International Legal Order* (2014) 290.

[13] A. Hervé, 'The Participation of the European Union in Global Economic Governance Fora', 18 *European Law Journal* (2012) 143.

3. EU Engagement with International Banking Standard-Setting Processes

Brummer distinguishes two types of bodies in international financial law: agenda-setting and standard-setting bodies.[14] The G20 and FSB fit primarily in the former category, and are much more focused on setting out broad goals and targets for members. The G20 sets out non-binding declarations which are viewed as global 'soft law' or 'informal law'.[15] However, these declarations are highly influential and impact upon the regulatory work done in various other standard-setting bodies. These include various trans-governmental networks and formal IOs as well as private standard-setting bodies.[16] This section gives an overview of this vast array of bodies, and gives some insight into the EU's presence and influence in them. Whereas the Union has a seat at the table and has been relatively influential in the FSB and G20, its role in standard-setting bodies is less defined.

A. Agenda-Setting Bodies

1. The Group of 20

The Group of 20 (G20) has emerged from the 2008 financial crisis as the main international body spearheading reform of the international financial system, especially in the banking sector.[17] It is now viewed as the world's premier body for international economic cooperation.[18] The 2009 Declaration on Strengthening the Financial System set out some of the main steps that G20 members were to take in order to further strengthen the global economy.[19] This included strengthening international frameworks for prudential regulation as well as improving oversight of systemically important financial institutions. By the 2010 Toronto Summit, the G20 leaders had identified four key pillars of reform. These are to develop: (i) a strong regulatory framework, (ii) effective supervision, (iii) resolution and addressing systemic institutions,

[14] Brummer, 'How International Financial Law Works (and How It Doesn't)', 99 *Georgetown Law Journal* (2011) 275.

[15] See Wouters and Geraets, 'The G20 and Informal International Lawmaking', in J. Pauwelyn *et al.* (eds), *Informal International Lawmaking: Case Studies* (2013) 19.

[16] See Pan, 'Challenge of International Cooperation and Institutional Design in Financial Supervision: Beyond Transgovernmental Networks', 11 *Chicago Journal of International Law* (2010) 243, characterizing regulators into five different groups: IOs, state-to-state contact groups, trans-governmental networks, bilateral and regional networks, and private standard-setting bodies.

[17] Wouters, Sterckx, and Corthaut, 'The International Financial Crisis, Global Financial Governance and the European Union', in A. Antoniadis, R. Schuetze, and E. Spaventa (eds), *The European Union and Global Emergencies: Law and Policy Analysis* (2011) 141.

[18] See Giovanoli, 'The International Financial Architecture and Its Reform After the Global Crisis', in M. Giovanoli and D. Devos (eds), *International Monetary Law and Financial Law: The Global Crisis* (2010).

[19] G20, *Global Plan Annex: Declaration on Strengthening the Financial System Leaders, London,* 2 April 2009.

and (iv) transparent international assessment and peer review. The February 2014 Communiqué of the Meeting of Finance Ministers and Central Bank Governors called for a renewed focus on 'building resilient financial institutions; ending too-big-to-fail; addressing shadow banking risks; and making derivatives markets safer'.[20] The ambitious reform of the system of global economic and financial regulation is therefore centred on the G20. Moreover, the Union has identified the G20 as a forum where it can persuade others to follow its agenda on a number of issues.[21] EU presence and effective participation in this global forum is important if the Union seeks to influence global developments in the financial sector.

The Union is a full member of the G20. It sits alongside other EU Member States France, Germany, Italy, and the UK, while Spain and the Netherlands have been regularly invited to G20 meetings. From 2008 onwards, the G20 has met at the level of head of state or government. Although the EU Treaties provide for the Commission to ensure the Union's external representation,[22] it was decided that there would be a joint representation of the Commission and the Council. At the leaders' level, both the President of the Commission and the President of the European Council (currently Jean-Claude Junker and Donald Tusk) attend the G20 leaders meeting.[23] For the meeting of finance ministers and central bank governors, the Commissioner for Economic and Monetary Affairs, the rotating Council presidency, and the President of the European Central Bank (ECB) represent the Union. This has led to a division of labour in practice, depending on the issue under discussion. The Commission is generally responsible for EU representation on issues of macroeconomic policy.[24]

G20 communiques are highly influential in EU legislation and other activity. As discussed in section 4 below, G20 commitments are referred to consistently in the preambular language of Union legislation and their associated explanatory reports. The preamble to the Regulation establishing the ESRB, for example, states that the board 'should contribute, inter alia, towards implementing the recommendations of the IMF, the FSB and the Bank for International Settlements (BIS) to the G-20'.[25] The activity of the G20 remains in the realm of soft law or informal law, and its commitments are not strictly binding on the Union and its Member States.

[20] G20, *Communiqué of the Meeting of Finance Ministers and Central Bank Governors, Sydney*, 22–23 February 2014.

[21] Wouters and Van Kerckhoven, 'The EU's Internal and External Regulatory Actions after the Outbreak of the 2008 Financial Crisis,' 8 *European Company Law* (2011) 201.

[22] See Art. 17(1) Treaty on European Union (TEU). There is an exception regarding the European Common Foreign and Security Policy (CFSP) and 'other cases provided for in the Treaties'.

[23] For a more elaborate discussion on how they distribute the tasks, see Debaere, 'The Output and Input Dimension of the European Representation in the G20', 63 *Studia Diplomatica* (2010) 141, at 148–149.

[24] For issues of coordination and the drafting of the EU agenda, see Wouters, Van Kerckhoven, and Odermatt, 'The EU at the G20 and the G20's Impact on the EU', in B. Van Vooren, S. Blockmans, and J. Wouters (eds), *The EU's Role in Global Governance: The Legal Dimension* (2013) 259.

[25] Regulation 1092/2010 of the European Parliament and of the Council of 24 November 2010 on European Union Macro-Prudential Oversight of the Financial System and Establishing a European Systemic Risk Board, OJ 2010 L 331/53.

Moreover, much of the G20's reform agenda is 'outsourced' to technical standard-setting and supervisory bodies, discussed below.

2. *The Financial Stability Board*

Established through a decision of the G20 leaders at their London summit in the wake of the 2008 crisis, the FSB is the major institutional innovation of the G20.[26] The establishment of the FSB has been described as 'potentially the most significant change in the organizational structures of global financial regulation'.[27] It is the successor to the Financial Stability Forum, established by the G7 finance ministers and central bank governors in 1999 in the wake of the Asian financial crisis. G20 leaders decided that there was a need 'to establish the much greater consistency and systematic cooperation between countries, and the framework of internationally agreed high standards, that a global financial system requires'.[28] The FSB has been described as the 'fourth pillar' of global economic governance, along with the International Monetary Fund, World Bank, and WTO, and in its short life has become an important institution in the field of economic and financial stability.[29] The aim of the FSB is to coordinate work at the international level by the national regulatory agencies and international standard-setting bodies. It has not been established to develop and enforce binding legal rules on its members; rather, it is concerned with coordination at multiple levels.

The FSB has been highly influential in regulatory reform of banking and finance since the crisis. It has identified key standards for sound financial systems which 'are broadly accepted as representing minimum requirements for good practice that countries are encourages to meet or exceed'.[30] These are international standards developed by the IMF, the Basel Committee on Banking Supervision (BCBS), and other bodies identified as being relevant and critical to a well-functioning financial system. They are standards that are viewed as universal, flexible, broadly endorsed, and accessible by national authorities and international financial institutions (IFIs). These include the IMF's Code of Good Practices on Transparency in Monetary and

[26] Helleiner, 'What Role for the New Financial Stability Board? The Politics of International Standards after the Crisis', 1 *Global Policy* (2010) 282.

[27] E. Wymeersch, K. J. Hopt, and G. Ferrarini, *Financial Regulation and Supervision: A Post-Crisis Analysis* (2012), at 1.41.

[28] G20, *Global Plan Annex: Declaration on Strengthening the Financial System Leaders*, 2 April 2009: 'We have agreed that the Financial Stability Forum should be expanded, given a broadened mandate to promote financial stability, and re-established with a stronger institutional basis and enhanced capacity as the Financial Stability Board (FSB).'

[29] Stressing the importance of the newly established FSB in the global economic governance architecture, US Treasury Secretary Timothy Geithner, at a press conference at the G20 Pittsburgh summit in September 2009, stated that '[a]fter the second world war, we came together and established the IMF, the World Bank, the GATT which became the WTO. But the Financial Stability Board is, in effect, a fourth pillar of that architecture.' See Wouters and Odermatt, 'Comparing the 'Four Pillars' of Global Economic Governance: A Critical Analysis of the Institutional Design of the FSB, IMF, World Bank, and WTO', 17 *Journal of International Economic Law* (2014) 49.

[30] FSB, *Key Standards for Sound Financial Systems*, available at <https://www.financialstability-board.org/cos/key_standards.htm> (last accessed 16 June 2015).

Financial Policies,[31] BCBS's Core Principles for Effective Banking Supervision,[32] and the Financial Action Task Force's Recommendations on Combating Money Laundering and the Financing of Terrorism and Proliferation.[33] The key standards are regularly reviewed and updated by the FSB. Among the key standards developed are the *Key Attributes of Effective Resolution for Financial Institutions.*[34] These Key Attributes set out the basic requirements the FSB considers necessary for a resolution regime. The FSB has urged jurisdictions to converge their resolution regimes through legislative changes in order to incorporate the Key Attributes. These standards have proven to be highly influential in EU legislation on banking recovery and resolution, as discussed in section B below.

One of the key roles of the FSB is to monitor the implementation of commitments made at the G20 summits. It recently pointed to four main elements of regulatory reform that still need to be addressed by the G20 membership. These are: (i) building resilience of financial institutions; (ii) ending too-big-to-fail institutions; (iii) transforming shadow banking to transparent and resilient market-based financing, and (iv) making derivatives markets safer.[35]

The FSB is also involved in peer review of member jurisdictions, which helps fulfil the G20's fourth pillar of reform: 'transparent international assessment and peer review'. It undertakes thematic and country peer reviews, examining the implementation and effectiveness of standards developed by standard-setting bodies and FSB policies.[36] Peer review is a condition of FSB membership.[37]

Unlike the other key pillars of global economic governance, such as the IMF and WTO, the FSB is not a formal IO.[38] Its founding charter is a memorandum of understanding, which unlike a treaty, does not impose international legal obligations upon its members.[39] G20 leaders have decided to establish the FSB 'on an enduring organisation footing',[40] and have endowed the FSB with legal personality

[31] IMF, *Code of Good Practices on Transparency in Monetary and Financial Policies* (2000), available at <http://www.imf.org/external/np/mae/mft/index.htm> (last accessed 16 June 2015).

[32] BCBS, 'Core Principles for Effective Banking Supervision', available at <http://www.bis.org/publ/bcbs230.pdf> (last accessed 16 June 2015).

[33] FATF, *International Standards on Combating Money Laundering and the Financing of Terrorism & Proliferation—The FATF Recommendations*, 16 February 2012, available at <http://www.fatf-gafi.org/recommendations> (last accessed 16 June 2015).

[34] FSB, *Key Attributes of Effective Resolution Regimes for Financial Institutions*, available at <https://www.financialstabilityboard.org/publications/r_111104cc.pdf> (last accessed 16 June 2015).

[35] FSB, *FSB Chair's Letter to G20 Ministers and Governors on Financial Reforms*, available at <https://www.financialstabilityboard.org/publications/r_140222.htm> (last accessed 16 June 2015). See also G20, *Communique Issued by the Group of 20 Finance Ministers and Central Bank Governors*, 22–24 February 2014, point 10.

[36] See FSB, *Peer Reviews*, available at <http://www.financialstabilityboard.org/activities/peer_reviews.htm> (last accessed 16 June 2015).

[37] Art. 6 Charter of the Financial Stability Board.

[38] Wouters and Odermatt, *supra* note 29.

[39] IMF, *IMF Membership in the Financial Stability Board (prepared by the Legal and Monetary and Capital Markets Departments, approved by José Viñals and Sean Hagan)*, 10 August 2010.

[40] FSB, *Report to the G20 Los Cabos Summit on Strengthening FSB Capacity, Resources and Governance*, 12 June 2012, available at <http://www.financialstabilityboard.org/publications/r_120619c.pdf> (last accessed 16 June 2015).

under Swiss law.[41] The FSB, however, is striking in terms of its fluid structure and low level of formality. The FSB charter sets out the structure of the organization and the mandate of the different bodies. The FSB consists of the plenary, the steering committee, standing committees, working groups, the regional consultative groups, the chair, and the secretariat. The plenary is the sole decision-making body for all matters governed by the FSB charter, including the FSB budget and work programme and the appointment of the FSB chair. Not much is known, however, about the way in which FSB decision-making works in practice. The plenary generally takes decisions by consensus. This means that every member has a de facto veto over the decision-making process. It has been argued that the FSB is different from other bodies involved in financial regulation due to the fact that a large part of its plenary consists of state finance ministries and treasury secretaries. This contrasts with other bodies that are made up of central bank governors or economic experts. Gadinis argues that 'it is the presence of the politicians that distinguishes the FSB from the other international bodies in financial regulation'[42] such as the International Organization of Securities Commissions (IOSCO) or BCBS, which are more technical in nature. For this reason, it has been argued that the FSB may be less likely to make politically unpopular decisions.[43]

The FSB consists of three types of members: member jurisdictions, international organizations, and international standard-setting bodies and other groups. The Union is represented via the ECB and the Commission, which are grouped among other IOs such as the IMF, Organisation for Economic Co-operation and Development (OECD), and the World Bank. Six EU Member States are also represented by their respective national authorities: France (Banque de France, Autorité des Marchés Financiers, Ministry of Economy and Finance), Germany (Deutsche Bundesbank, Bundesanstalt für Finanzdienstleistungsaufsich, Bundesministerium der Finanzen), Italy (Banca d'Italia, Commissione Nazionale per le Società e la Borsa and Ministero dell'Economia e delle Finanze), the Netherlands (De Nederlandsche Bank and the Ministry of Finance), Spain (Banco de España and Ministerio de Economía y Competitividad), and the UK (Bank of England, Financial Conduct Authority, HM Treasury).

The FSB has played an important role in monitoring commitments made by G20 members and is a major part of the G20's success in driving reform. Its mandate is broad: it includes promoting implementation of Member commitments; advising on and monitoring best practice in meeting regulatory standards; coordinating the work of different standard-setting bodies; and assessing vulnerabilities affecting the global financial system. The FSB, which is housed at the Bank for

[41] The FSB has now been established as an association under Art. 60 of the Swiss Civil Code.

[42] See Gadinis, 'The Financial Stability Board: The New Politics of International Financial Regulation', 48 *Texas International Law Journal* (2013) 157, at 167.

[43] '[I]n the case of the FSB, if it is to perform its countercyclical role properly, it will be very difficult to avoid politically unpopular messages'. Baker, 'Mandate, Accountability and Decision Making Issues to be faced by the FSB', in S. Griffith-Jones, E. Helleiner, and N. Woods (eds), *The Financial Stability Board: An Effective Fourth Pillar of Global Economic Governance?* (2010) 19, at 22.

International Settlements (BIS) in Basel, relies upon and cooperates with a variety of IOs and standard-setting bodies.

B. International Organizations

1. *The International Monetary Fund*

The IMF also plays an important role in financial governance at the international level. It is a member of the FSB, with which it cooperates on numerous tasks, including collaboration on the Early Warning Exercises (EWE).[44] It has developed key standards, including the IMF Code of Good Practices on Transparency in Monetary and Financial Policies (MFP),[45] a code of transparency practices for monetary and financial policies. Likewise, the 2007 Code of Good Practices on Fiscal Transparency,[46] which sets out principles to ensure government fiscal transparency, is part of the FSB's key standards. The IMF's Special Data Dissemination Standard (SDDS)[47] and General Data Dissemination System (GDDS) deal with the dissemination of economic and financial data, and the provision of comprehensive, accessible, and reliable economic, financial, and socio-demographic data.

The EU's relationship with the IMF has evolved considerably since the 2008 financial crisis and the European sovereign debt crisis.[48] All EU Member States are IMF Member countries, however neither the EU nor the euro area are members of the IMF. The ECB enjoys observer status at the IMF Executive Board on items concerning euro policy whereas the Commission has observer status at the Development Committee.[49] The Union has therefore had to rely on the EU Member States to represent the Union within the Fund.[50] However, it has been observed that Member State coordination remains rather weak.[51] This has been explained by issues of competence (monetary policy and economic policy), the scattering of EU Member States among different IMF constituencies, and the mix of euro- and non-euro-area Member States.

[44] Charter of the Financial Stability Board, Art. 2(1)(h). [45] IMF, *supra* note 31.

[46] IMF, *Code of Good Practices on Fiscal Transparency*, available at <http://www.imf.org/external/np/pp/2007/eng/051507c.pdf> (last accessed 16 June 2015).

[47] IMF, *Data Quality Assessment Framework*, available at <http://dsbb.imf.org/Pages/DQRS/DQAF.aspx> (last accessed 16 June 2015).

[48] Wouters, Van Kerckhoven, and Ramopoulos, 'The EU and the Euro Area in International Economic Governance: The Case of the IMF', in D. Kochenov and F. Amtenbrink (eds), *The European Union's Shaping of the International Legal Order* (2014) 306.

[49] See see M. Emerson *et al.*, *Upgrading the EU's Role as a Global Actor: Institutions, Law and the Restructuring of European Diplomacy* (2011) 70–74.

[50] On the EU's representation at the IMF, see Wouters and Van Kerckhoven, 'International Monetary Fund', in K. E. Jørgensen and K. Verlin Laatikainen (eds), *Routledge Handbook on the European Union and International Institutions: Performance, Policy, Power* (2013) 221.

[51] Wouters, Van Kerckhoven, and Ramopoulos, *supra* note 48, at 310; Bini Smaghi, 'A Single EU Seat? In the IMF?', 42 *Journal of Common Market Studies* (2004) 221.

2. The World Bank

Despite the fact that it does not have a specific mandate to deal with the regulation of international finance, the World Bank plays a limited role in financial regulation. Like the IMF, it is a member organization of the FSB. It has developed the Insolvency and Creditor Rights (ICR) Standard,[52] which sets out international best practice on effective and efficient insolvency and creditor rights systems. The World Bank also plays a role by providing finance and advice to countries that reform their economies, including their financial sectors. The World Bank undertakes Financial Sector Assessment Programs (FSAP), comprehensive and in-depth assessments of a country's financial sector, jointly with the IMF. Whereas the IMF is responsible for financial stability assessment, the World Bank is responsible for development assessment. FSB members' adherence to standards is also monitored by their publication of detailed assessments prepared by the IMF and World Bank as a basis for the Reports on the Observance of Standards and Codes (ROSCs). The Union is not a member of the World Bank and does not have observer or similar status. Although the case for an EU seat is probably much stronger in the case of the IMF, the Union does play a major role in the field of development and aid, and could seek observer status in the future.[53]

3. The Bank for International Settlements

The Bank for International Settlements (BIS) is an IO comprising 60 central banks. Based in Basel, the BIS houses the FSB, of which the BIS is a member organisation. Established in 1930, the BIS is one of the oldest of the international financial institutions. Originally established to deal with reparations following the First World War, the BIS has evolved over time, and its current goals are to 'serve central banks in their pursuit of monetary and financial stability, to foster international cooperation in those areas and to act as a bank for central banks'.[54] The BIS decision-making bodies consist of the general meeting of member central banks, the board of directors, and the management of the bank. The ECB and the central banks of most EU Member States are members of the BIS. Much of the regulatory work is undertaken through its committees, such as the Basel Committee on Banking Supervision and the Committee on the Global Financial System (see section 3C).

[52] Insolvency and Creditor Rights (ICR) Standard, based on The World Bank Principles for Effective Creditor Rights and Insolvency Systems and UNCITRAL Legislative Guide on Insolvency Law, December 2005. Available at <http://siteresources.worldbank.org/GILD/Resources/FINAL-ICRStandard-March2009.pdf>.

[53] Emerson, Balfour, Corthaut, Wouters, Kaczynski, and Renard, *supra* note 49, 75.

[54] BIS, *About BIS*, available at <http://www.bis.org/about/> (last accessed 16 June 2015).

4. The World Trade Organization

Although the WTO is primarily focused on the liberalization of global trade, its work has also touched upon issues relating to financial regulation. The General Agreement on Trade in Services (GATS) is a multilateral agreement administered by the WTO[55] and is binding on all WTO members, including the EU and its Member States. The agreement relates to internationally traded services, including the banking and financial services sector. Unlike the other types of regulation discussed in this chapter, GATS is not prudential in nature, but 'relates to the treatment of foreign investment by national authorities and does not so much coordinate specific regulatory actions as define the limits of regulatory authority'.[56] The scope and the application of GATS in the field financial services is set out in the Annex on Financial Services.[57] Article 2(a) of the Annex stipulates that:

> a Member shall not be prevented from taking measures for prudential reasons, including for the protection of investors, depositors, policy holders or persons to whom a fiduciary duty is owed by a financial service supplier, or to ensure the integrity and stability of the financial system.[58]

However, this provision adds that prudential measures which do not conform with GATS obligations shall not be used as a means of avoiding GATS commitments and obligations. It is acknowledged that in some cases measures taken by WTO members to ensure financial stability, including those agreed to in other international fora, may infringe upon certain GATS commitments.[59] This tension stems in part from the different overarching goals. Whereas the FSB and similar bodies are concerned primarily with the stability and integrity of the international financial system as a whole, the GATS is concerned with the progressive liberalization of trade in services, especially through limiting or removing government regulation. While these are not necessarily mutually exclusive goals, it is debatable whether GATS rules provide enough flexibility to WTO members to regulate their financial sectors following the global financial crisis. As states seek to re-regulate their banking and financial sectors, these steps can touch upon issues covered by international trade agreements.[60] There is little

[55] Agreement Establishing the World Trade Organization 1994, 1867 UNTS 154.

[56] Brummer, *supra* note 4, at 627.

[57] General Agreement on Trade in Services, Annex on Financial Services.

[58] Art. 2(a) Annex on Financial Services. For a thorough analysis, see B. De Meester, *Liberalization of Trade in Banking Services. An International and European Perspective* (2014), at 102–104 (paras 239–241) and at 206–216 (paras 450–471).

[59] On the tensions between trade liberalization and global financial stability see Wouters and Odermatt, *supra* note 29, Wouters and Coppens, 'International Economic Policy-Making: Exploring the Legal Linkages between the World Trade Organization and the Bretton Woods Institutions', 3 *International Organizations Law Review* (2006) 267; Bismuth, 'Financial Sector Regulation and Financial Services Liberalization at the Crossroads: The Relevance of International Financial Standards in WTO Law', 44 *Journal of World Trade* (2010) 489.

[60] See De Meester, 'The Global Financial Crisis and Government Support for Banks: What Role for the GATS?' 13 *Journal of International Economic Law* (2010) 27.

cooperation between the WTO and international regulatory and standard-setting bodies, however, and the WTO is an important organization that remains absent from the FSB.

C. International Standard-Setting and Other Bodies

The next section turns to the various other bodies that play a role in standard setting in the field of banking and finance. The first three, the Basel Committee on Banking Supervision (BCBS), the Committee on the Global Financial System, and the Committee on Payment and Settlement Systems, are committees hosted at the BIS, and the BIS secretariat prepares for meetings and draws up background papers. The International Association of Insurance Supervisors and the International Association of Deposit Insurers, along with the FSB, have their secretariats at the BIS, but are independent bodies in their own right. The final bodies discussed are all self-standing bodies.

1. The Basel Committee on Banking Supervision

The BCBS is a forum for cooperation on banking supervisory matters and is a global standard setter in prudential regulation. Its mandate is 'to strengthen the regulation, supervision and practices of banks worldwide with the purpose of enhancing financial stability'.[61] Hosted by the BIS, the BCBS membership is composed of organizations with direct banking supervisory authority and central banks.[62] BCBS decisions do not have legal force as such,[63] and it relies on members' commitments. Its goals include promoting financial stability, enhancing the quality of banking regulation and supervision, contributing to the development of BCBS standards, guidelines, and sound practices, and the timely implementation of BCBS standards in their domestic jurisdictions.[64] The BCBS charter stresses that its members should promote the interests of *global* financial stability and not solely national interests of the members.[65] Although non-binding, its guidelines and supervisory standards are highly influential and are implemented in members' systems, either through domestic legislation or other means.

Nine EU Member States are members of the BCBS: Belgium, France, Germany, Italy, the Netherlands, Luxembourg, Spain, Sweden, and the UK. Other members are: Argentina, Australia, Brazil, Canada, China, Hong Kong SAR, India, Indonesia, Japan, Korea, Mexico, Russia, Saudi Arabia, Singapore, South Africa, Switzerland, Turkey, and the US.[66] Jurisdictions are represented by their central bank (e.g. the Bank of England) and/or prudential regulation authority (e.g. the Prudential Regulation Authority). The Union is not represented in its own right at

61 BCBS Charter 2013, available at <http://www.bis.org/bcbs/charter.htm> (last accessed 16 June 2015).

62 BCBS Charter, Art. 4.

63 BCBS Charter, Art. 3.

64 BCBS Charter, Art. 5.

65 BCBS Charter, Art. 5(g).

66 See BIS, *Jurisdictions and Institutions Represented on the Basel Committee on Banking Supervision*, available at <http://www.bis.org/bcbs/membership.htm> (last accessed 16 June 2015).

the BCBS, however the Commission, ECB, and EBA are observers alongside the IMF and Financial Stability Institute (FSI). Being an observer means that the EU is involved in task forces and working groups, and may contribute comments on consultative papers.[67]

The main regulatory standard developed by the BCBS is the Basel III accord, a comprehensive package designed 'to strengthen the regulation, supervision and risk management of the banking sector'.[68] The accord includes standards on capital adequacy[69] and the liquidity coverage ratio (LCR).[70] These increased capital requirements are designed to 'significantly reduce the probability and severity of banking crises in the future'.[71] BCBS has taken on an important role since the 2008 financial crisis, and the implementation of banking standards has been a topic stressed by the G20 leaders. G20 leaders endorsed the Basel III regulatory framework at their 2010 summit in Seoul[72] and continue to stress the importance of full and timely implementation of Basel III and other financial sector reforms.[73] In August 2013, the BCBS delivered a report to the G20 for the St Petersburg Leaders' Summit on the implementation of Basel III reforms, noting that 11 members had implemented Basel III measures on capital requirements. The implementation of these standards by the Union is discussed further in section 4 below.

2. *The Committee on the Global Financial System*

The Committee on the Global Financial System (CGFS) monitors developments in global financial markets for central bank governors. The CGFS's mandate, approved by the governors of the G10 central banks on 8 February 1999,[74]

[67] De Meester, 'Multilevel Banking Regulation: An Assessment of the Role of the EC in the Light of Coherence and Democratic Legitimacy', in A. Follesdal, R. A. Wessel, and J. Wouters (eds), *Multilevel Regulation and the EU: Interplay between Global, European and National Normative Processes* (2008) 117.

[68] BIS, *International Regulatory Framework for Banks (Basel III)*, available at <http://www.bis.org/bcbs/basel3.htm> (last accessed 16 June 2015).

[69] BCBS, *Basel III: A Global Regulatory Framework for More Resilient Banks and Banking Systems*, December 2010 (revised June 2011).

[70] BCBS, *Basel III: The Liquidity Coverage Ratio and Liquidity Risk Monitoring Tools*, January 2013.

[71] BIS, *Basel III: A Global Regulatory Framework for More Resilient Banks and Banking Systems (Press Release)*, 16 December 2010, available at <http://www.bis.org/publ/bcbs189_dec2010.htm> (last accessed 16 June 2015).

[72] G20, *Summit Leaders' Declaration (Seoul, South Korea)*, 11–12 November 2010, point 29: 'We endorsed the landmark agreement reached by the BCBS on the new bank capital and liquidity framework, which increases the resilience of the global banking system by raising the quality, quantity and international consistency of bank capital and liquidity, constrains the build-up of leverage and maturity mismatches, and introduces capital buffers above the minimum requirements that can be drawn upon in bad times.'

[73] See G20, *Leaders Declaration (St Petersburg, Russia)*, 6 September 2013, point 67: 'We reiterate our commitment to implement Basel III according to internationally agreed timelines and welcome the progress that has been made since Los Cabos. It is imperative that the Basel III standards are consistently applied.'

[74] BIS, *Committee on the Global Financial System: Mandate, as approved by the Governors of the G10 Central Banks on 8 February 1999*, available at <https://www.bis.org/cgfs/mandate.htm> (last accessed 16 June 2015).

includes identifying and assessing potential stress in the global financial market and the promotion and development of well-functioning and stable financial markets and systems. It aims to establish policy recommendations to central banks in order to support them in fulfilling their responsibilities in the field of monetary and financial stability. The ECB is represented alongside the central banks of nine EU Member States. Although not a standard-setting body, the CGFS produces influential publications on issues such as international banking, financial crises, financial statistics, credit risk transfer, derivatives, market infrastructure, monetary policy, and disclosure practices. For example, its report on the macro financial implications of alternative configurations for access to central counterparties in over-the-counter (OTC) derivatives markets[75] has been influential in the field of OTC derivatives.[76]

3. *The Committee on Payment and Settlement Systems*

The Committee on Payment and Settlement Systems (CPSS) seeks to contribute to the strengthening of the financial market infrastructure through 'promoting sound and efficient payment, clearing and settlement systems'.[77] It undertakes studies in the field of payment and settlement systems. Together with IOSCO it has developed the Principles for Financial Market Infrastructures[78] which are part of the FSB's Key Standards.[79] The ECB is represented alongside the central banks of several EU Member States. Benoît Cœuré, a member of the ECB Executive Board, is the current Chair of the Committee.

4. *The International Organisation of Securities Commissions*

The International Organisation of Securities Commissions (IOSCO) is an international association of the world's securities regulators responsible for standard setting in the securities area. IOSCO's institutional set-up, decision-making process, and the role of the EU in the organization are discussed in more detail by Marcacci in Chapter 11 of this volume. IOSCO has worked closely with other international standard-setting bodies, including the FSB and G20 on regulatory reform following the crisis. It has developed the 2010 Objectives and Principles of Securities Regulation[80] and the corresponding

[75] Committee on the Global Financial System, 'The Macrofinancial Implications of Alternative Configurations for Access to Central Counterparties in OTC Derivatives Markets', CGFS Papers 46/2011.

[76] Whiteley, 'G20 Reforms, Hedging and Covered Bonds', 7 *Capital Markets Law Journal* (2012) 151.

[77] BIS, Committee on Payment and Settlement Systems, information available at <http://www.bis.org/cpss/> (last accessed 16 June 2015).

[78] Committee on Payment and Settlement Systems, Technical Committee of the International Organization of Securities Commissions, *Principles for Financial Market Infrastructures*, available at <http://www.bis.org/publ/cpss101a.pdf> (last accessed 16 June 2015).

[79] FSB, *supra* note 30.

[80] IOSCO, *Objectives and Principles of Securities Regulation*, available at <http://www.iosco.org/library/pubdocs/pdf/IOSCOPD323.pdf> (last accessed 16 June 2015).

Methodology for Assessing the Implementations of the IOSCO Principles.[81] It has undertaken work on OTC derivatives,[82] financial market infrastructures,[83] and credit rating agencies,[84] in many cases upon the request of the G20 and FSB. Since the global financial crisis the scope of IOSCO's work has expanded, especially as the regulation of hedge funds has been added to the global agenda.[85]

IOSCO currently comprises 205 members, of which there are three categories: ordinary, associate, and affiliate. Ordinary members are generally the national securities commissions of member jurisdictions, whereas associate members are other government branches that exercise competence in the field of securities market regulation. Affiliate members include bodies such as self-regulatory organizations (SROs), securities exchanges, financial market infrastructures (including clearing and settlement agencies), and international bodies other than governmental organizations with an appropriate interest in securities regulation.[86] The Commission and the European Securities and Markets Authority (ESMA) are associate members. The European Fund Asset Management Association, the representative association for the European investment management industry, is an affiliate member. It has been argued that the EU's non-membership in IOSCO 'is likely to have hampered the EU ability to project its regulatory preferences internationally'.[87]

5. *The International Association of Deposit Insurers*

The International Association of Deposit Insurers (IADI) was established in 2002 to enhance the effectiveness of deposit insurance systems. It has developed, along with BCBS, core principles for effective deposit insurance systems which have been identified as an FSB Key Standard.[88] IADI comprises 73 members, represented by the body responsible for deposit insurance. The European Bank for Reconstruction and Development and the European Forum of Deposit Insurers are among the IADI's 'partners', international institutions that have entered into a cooperative arrangement with IADI in the pursuit and furtherance of it objectives.[89]

[81] IOSCO, *Methodology for Assessing Implementation of the IOSCO Objectives and Principles of Securities Regulation*, September 2011 (revised August 2013), available at <http://www.iosco.org/library/pubdocs/pdf/IOSCOPD359.pdf> (last accessed 16 June 2015).

[82] IOSCO, Report on Trading of OTC Derivatives.

[83] Committee on Payment and Settlement Systems, *supra* note 78.

[84] See IOSCO, *Code of Conduct Fundamentals for Credit Rating Agencies—Consultation Report.*

[85] European countries, particularly, France and Germany pushed for the addition of hedge funds in the G20's regulatory agenda; Quaglia, 'The Sources of European Union Influence in International Financial Regulatory Fora', 21 *Journal of European Public Policy* (2014) 327, at 336.

[86] IOSCO, 'Membership Categories and Criteria', available at <http://www.iosco.org/about/index.cfm?section=membership> (last accessed 16 June 2015).

[87] Quaglia, *supra* note 85, 339.

[88] FSB, *supra* note 30.

[89] IADI, 'List of IADI Members', available at <http://www.iadi.org/aboutIADI.aspx?id=48> (last accessed 16 June 2015).

6. *The International Association of Insurance Supervisors*

The International Association of Insurance Supervisors (IAIS) was established in 1994 in order to 'promote effective and globally consistent supervision of the insurance industry'[90] and contribute to global financial stability. Its membership includes insurance supervisors and regulators from more than 200 jurisdictions. The IAIS has developed the Insurance Core Principles, Standards, Guidance and Assessment Methodology,[91] which provide a globally accepted framework for the supervision of the insurance sector. The IAIS is also responsible, alongside other global standard setters and central banks, for identifying global systemically important financial institutions under the auspices of the FSB. IAIS does so by identifying insurers 'whose distress or disorderly failure, because of their size, complexity and interconnectedness, would cause significant disruption to the global financial system and economic activity'.[92] The Commission is one of the IAIS members.[93] It has been observed that the EU has been able to exercise a relatively high level of influence in standard setting in the field of insurance, particularly compared to the US.[94]

7. *The International Accounting Standards Board*

The London-based International Accounting Standards Board (IASB) is an independent accounting standard-setting body of the IFRS foundation. It is responsible for developing international financial reporting standards,[95] part of the FSB Key Standards. It is a private, non-profit organization consisting of 16 full-time board members. The standards are adopted within the Union through regulations[96] upon undergoing a process of endorsement within the EU, including approval by the Accounting Regulatory Committee (ARC).[97] Although the EU is not formally represented at the IASB, the Commission does cooperate with the IASB.[98]

[90] See IAIS, 'About the IAIS', available at <http://www.iaisweb.org/About-the-IAIS-28> (last accessed 16 June 2015).

[91] IAIS, *Insurance Core Principles, Standards, Guidance and Assessment Methodology*, 1 October 2011 (amended 19 October 2013), available at <http://www.iaisweb.org/view/element_href.cfm?src=1/20567.pdf> (last accessed 16 June 2015).

[92] IAIS, *Financial Stability & Macroprudential Policy & Surveillance*, available at <http://www.iaisweb.org/Supervisory-Material/Financial-Stability-Macroprudential-Policy-Surveillance-988> (last accessed 16 June 2015).

[93] IAIS, *supra* note 89.

[94] Quaglia, *supra* note 85, at 335.

[95] International Financial Reporting Standards Foundation, 'About the IFRS Foundation and the IASB', available at <http://www.ifrs.org/IFRSs/Pages/IFRS.aspx> (last accessed 16 June 2015).

[96] Commission Regulation (EU) 1375/2013 of 19 December 2013 amending Regulation (EC) 1126/2008 adopting Certain International Accounting Standards in Accordance with Regulation (EC) 1606/2002 of the European Parliament and of the Council as regards International Accounting Standard 39.

[97] See European Commission, *International Accounting Standards and Interpretations Endorsement Process in the EU*, available at <http://ec.europa.eu/internal_market/accounting/docs/ias/endorsement_process.pdf> (last accessed 16 June 2015).

[98] See European Commission, *Accounting—Financial Reporting*, available at <http://ec.europa.eu/internal_market/accounting/index_en.htm> (last accessed 16 June 2015).

8. The International Auditing and Assurance Standards Board

The International Auditing and Assurance Standards Board (IAASB) issues standards in the fields of auditing, assurance, and other related fields. The IAASB consists of 18 members, including both practitioners and non-practitioners, who sit in their personal capacity and do not represent their jurisdiction. It is an independent body under the auspices of the International Federation of Accountants (IFAC). They have developed the International Standards on Auditing (ISA), dealing with the standards of independent auditors' responsibilities when conducting an audit of financial statements, which are another FSB Key Standard.

9. The Financial Action Task Force

The Financial Action Task Force (on Money Laundering) (FATF) was established in 1989 by the G7 states to combat the threat of money laundering. The FATF is not a formal IO founded in a treaty or other legal document; rather, it is a 'partnership' established by the Ministers of the member jurisdictions. The FATF comprises 34 member jurisdictions and two regional organizations. The Gulf Cooperation Council is a full member, but its constituent countries (Bahrain, Kuwait, Oman, Qatar, Saudi Arabia, and the United Arab Emirates) are not. The Commission is a member alongside 15 EU Member States: Austria, Belgium, Denmark, France, Finland, Germany, Greece, Ireland, Italy, Luxembourg, Portugal, the Netherlands, Spain, Sweden, and the UK. The other EU Member States are not members of the FATF but are members of the Council of Europe Committee of Experts on the Evaluation of Anti-Money Laundering Measures and the Financing of Terrorism (MONEYVAL), a regional body established in 1997 to combat money laundering measures.[99] MONEYVAL currently enjoys associate member status at the FATF, alongside other regional bodies and task forces on money laundering, including the Asia/Pacific Group on Money Laundering (APG) and the Financial Action Task Force on Money Laundering in South America (GAFISUD).

According to the FATF membership policy, the jurisdiction must be considered as 'strategically important', taking into account factors such as the jurisdiction's GDP, the size of its banking sector, and its impact on the global financial system.[100] In addition to the FATF members, there is also a long list of associate members, including other regional task forces on money laundering. The list of observers includes regional banks (African Development Bank, ECB), international financial institutions (IMF, World Bank), as well as UN (United Nations Office on Drugs and Crime (UNODC)) and other international bodies (the Organization

[99] Council of Europe, Committee of Experts on the Evaluation of Anti-Money Laundering Measures and the Financing of Terrorism (MONEYVAL), 'MONEYVAL in brief', available at <http://www.coe.int/t/dghl/monitoring/moneyval/about/moneyval_in_brief_EN.asp> (last accessed 16 June 2015).

[100] FATF, 'FATF Membership Policy', available at <http://www.fatf-gafi.org/pages/aboutus/membersandobservers/fatfmembershippolicy.html> (last accessed 16 June 2015).

for Security and Co-operation in Europe (OSCE), the Organisation for Economic Co-operation and Development (OECD)).

A key aspect of the FATF is the development of its 'recommendations', setting international standards for combating of money laundering and the financing of terrorism. These recommendations have been updated in 1996, 2001, 2003, and, most recently in 2012.[101] The FATF also follows up on the implementation of the recommendations, assessing the compliance of the standards through a process of mutual evaluation.

D. The Diverse World of Financial Governance

Global financial regulation is characterized by a loose network of actors whose mandates in some way relate to the broader goal of maintaining financial stability. While there is no central regulatory body at the international level, the G20 and the FSB have taken up the role of agenda-setting and monitoring bodies. They have identified key standards developed by various bodies, requested studies and reports on various issues of financial stability, and consistently monitored the implementation of these standards in member economies. The G20 and the FSB sit at the centre of this loose and somewhat overlapping network of actors, each of which are comprised of a mix of public and private bodies, finance ministries, central banks, regulators, and IOs. It should also be noted that the framework not only includes bodies involved in the regulation of banks but also from the securities and derivatives markets, insurance and other sectors. This reflects the fact that since the crisis the G20 has expanded its purview to include other fields that may present systemic risk, including hedge funds and shadow banking. It is for this reason that the bodies discussed are involved in 'financial stability' broadly construed, rather than just banking regulation.[102] Whereas the Union is a member of the FSB and G20, its presence at the level or standard-setting and other bodies is mixed. Even where the EU is not a full member, however, it has been a 'net importer' of norms based in these bodies. This is in part due to the fact that they represent internationally-recognized best practices in many fields: '[t]he reason why the EU (and not particularly the rest of the world) accepted the work of the standard setters—without a legal obligation thereto—is to be seen in the ideas of technical craftsmanship, political independence and effective harmonization.'[103] The next section examines how the EU has sought to implement these standards developed at the global level in its own legal order. It looks at the extent to which the EU's ambitious reform following the global financial crisis has been influenced by developments within these bodies.

[101] FATF, *supra* note 33.

[102] 'A common trend in the understanding of systemic risk and in the pernicious TBTF problem is the fact that systemic risk is as likely to arise from securities and derivatives markets as it is from banking markets. This makes systemic risk prevention a fundamental goal of securities regulation (IOSCO plans to expand in this area) and of financial regulation generally, and not 'simply' of banking regulation.' Lastra, 'Systemic Risk, SIFIs and Financial Stability', 6 *Capital Markets Law Journal* (2011) 197.

[103] See Ohler, *supra* note 12.

4. The Impact of International Financial Standards on EU Law- and Policy-Making

Unlike a treaty, which is binding upon the Union and the Member States from the moment it enters into force, commitments made at international summits, or technical standards developed by international bodies, require transposition into the legal order of the EU. This can be complicated by the fact that financial regulation remains a field in which Member States, particularly those with large and influential banking sectors, continue to play an influential role. This section examines how commitments made at the international level and standards developed in international bodies are being implemented in the EU. Through this process of implementation, the EU contributes to the 'hardening' of soft law of international standards.[104] Since the onset of the global economic crisis, the Union has undertaken ambitious reform in the field of financial governance in order to increase the resilience of its banks and financial sector. This includes steps to improve transparency, to bolster capital and liquidity requirements, and to end the problem of 'too-big-to fail'. Much of this reform has been highly influenced by developments at the global level.

A. 'Too-Big-To-Fail' Institutions

One of the key issues to be addressed by the international financial system is the problem of systemcally important financial institutions (SIFIs), or institutions that are 'too big to fail'. It has been acknowledged that inadequate systemic risk control played a central role in the global economic crisis.[105] Dealing with SIFIs and the moral hazard associated with them was therefore a key priority of the G20.[106] The London Summit set out priorities of restoring the economy, which included strengthening financial supervision and regulation and 'to extend regulation and oversight to all systemically important financial institutions'.[107] In Seoul, the G20 leaders 'reaffirmed [their] view that no firm should be too big or too complicated to fail and that taxpayers should not bear the costs of resolution'.[108] The FSB, at the request of the G20, publishes an annually updated list of institutions deemed to be globally systemically important financial institutions.[109] They are defined as financial institutions whose distress or failure 'because of their size, complexity

[104] 'Across multiple issues in global finance, the European Union (EU) acts as a legalization mechanism that transforms soft law from informal transnational best practice into embedded rules backed by domestic law.' Newman and Back, 'The European Union as Hardening Agent: Soft Law and the Diffusion of Global Financial Regulation', 21 *Journal of European Public Policy* (2014) 430, at 431.

[105] Lastra, *supra* note 102.

[106] G20, *Summit Leaders' Declaration (Seoul, South Korea)*, 11–12 November 2010, para. 30.

[107] G20, *Summit Leaders' Declaration (London, United Kingdom)*, 2 April 2009, point 15.

[108] G20, *Summit Leaders' Declaration (Seoul, South Korea)*, 11–12 November 2010, para. 30.

[109] FSB, *2013 Update of Group of Global Systemically Important Banks (G-SIBs)*, available at <https://www.financialstabilityboard.org/publications/r_131111.pdf> (last accessed 16 June 2015).

and systemic interconnectedness, would cause significant disruption to the wider financial system and economic activity'.[110] They are determined with reference to methodology determined by the BCBS.[111] European Union-based institutions that have been determined as systemically important include HSBC, Barclays, Deutsche Bank, BNP Paribas, Crédit Agricole, ING Bank, the Royal Bank of Scotland, and Santander.[112]

It is precisely due to their global and inter-connected nature that global systematically important financial institutions (G-SIFIs) are difficult to deal with at the national level. It has been argued that 'finding "common ground" with regard to major cross-border bank insolvencies is one of the most challenging tasks that the international financial community will have to meet in the future'.[113] Problems continue to exist in areas such as the definition of SIFIs, their regulation and supervision, as well as issues related to their resolution in periods of crisis.[114]

The G20 has endorsed a 'multi-pronged' framework for dealing with the TBTF issue. First, this involves establishing a framework so that financial institutions may be resolved quickly, safely, and without destabilizing the wider financial system. It has also been stressed that SIFIs, especially globally important ones, should also have a higher loss absorbency capacity, reflective of the risks they pose to the global financial system. G-SIFIs should also be subject to more intensive supervisory oversight. This policy framework should also include 'robust core financial market infrastructure to reduce contagion risk from individual failures'.[115] This approach acknowledges that G-SIFIs, due to the risk they pose to the global financial system, should be subject to specialized rules. For instance, national insolvency rules have been deemed inadequate for the resolution of globally important financial institutions, requiring a *lex specialis* resolution regime.[116] In 2010, the FSB released a series of recommendations and time lines on reducing the moral hazard posed by systemically important financial institutions.[117] It seeks to improve the ability of member state authorities to resolve SIFIs in an orderly manner while still allowing these institutions to fulfil their key functions in the economy. It recommends that SIFIs have a higher loss absorbency capacity than Basel III requirements, and that SIFIs are subject to more intensive supervision and resolution planning. In 2013, the FSB published its report, 'Progress and

[110] FSB, *Policy Measures to Address Systemically Important Financial Institutions*, 4 November 2011, para. 3.

[111] BCBS, *Global Systemically Important Banks: Assessment Methodology and the Additional Loss Absorbency Requirement*, available at <http://www.bis.org/publ/bcbs255.pdf> (last accessed 16 June 2015).

[112] FSB, *supra* note 109.

[113] Weber, 'Multilayered Governance in International Financial Regulation and Supervision', 13 *Journal of International Economic Law* (2010) 697.

[114] Lastra, *supra* note 102.

[115] G20, *Summit Leaders' Declaration (Seoul, South Korea)*, 11–12 November 2010, para. 30.

[116] Lastra, *supra* note 102, at 212.

[117] FSB, *Reducing the Moral Hazard Posed by Systemically Important Financial Institutions: FSB Recommendations and Time Lines*, available at <http://www.financialstabilityboard.org/publications/r_101111a.pdf> (last accessed 16 June 2015).

Next Steps Towards Ending "Too-Big-to-Fail" (TBTF)'. While it acknowledges that progress has taken place in putting together an international policy framework, detailed technical work is still required 'to give real teeth to the application of policies to individual SIFIs'.[118]

B. Bank Recovery and Resolution

One of the key issues regarding SIFIs has been the development of a system of bank resolution in the event of their failure. In 2014, the EU Bank Recovery and Resolution Directive (BRRD)[119] was adopted along with other legislation towards establishing a banking union.[120] Having entered into force on 1 January 2015, the BRRD seeks to establish a framework to deal with unsound or failing credit institutions and investment firms and seeks to minimize the costs of resolution of failing institutions on taxpayers.[121] It seeks to establish EU-wide rules for bank recovery and resolution. It requires banks to draw up recovery plans for times of distress and for authorities to prepare resolution plans for dealing with banks in critical condition.[122] The directive refers to the G20's 2009 call for 'review of resolution regimes and bankruptcy laws in light of recent experience to ensure that they permit an orderly wind-down of large complex cross-border institutions'.[123] It also refers to the FSB's key attributes of effective resolution regimes for financial institutions,[124] which the FSB considers to be the core elements necessary for an effective resolution regime. It requires each member jurisdiction to set up a 'resolution regime' which provides authorities with powers to resolve failing financial intuitions in an orderly manner without disruption to the financial system or

[118] FSB, *Progress and Next Steps Towards Ending 'Too-Big-To-Fail' (Report of the Financial Stability Board to the G-20)*, 2 September 2013, at 23.

[119] Directive 2014/59/EU of the European Parliament and of the Council of 15 May 2014 establishing a framework for the recovery and resolution of credit institutions and investment firms and amending Council Directive 82/891/EEC, and Directives 2001/24/EC, 2002/47/EC, 2004/25/EC, 2005/56/EC, 2007/36/EC, 2011/35/EU, 2012/30/EU, and 2013/36/EU, and Regulations (EU) 1093/2010 and (EU) 648/2012, of the European Parliament and of the Council Text with EEA relevance, OJ 2014 L 173/190.

[120] 'Super Tuesday for EU bank regulation', Financial Times of 15 April 2014. See European Commission, 'Finalizing the Banking Union: European Parliament backs Commission's proposals (Single Resolution Mechanism, Bank Recovery and Resolution Directive, and Deposit Guarantee Schemes Directive)', Statement/14/119 of 15 April 2014.

[121] See European Commission, *EU Bank Recovery and Resolution Directive (BRRD): Frequently Asked Questions,* Memo/14/297 of 15 April 2014, available at <http://europa.eu/rapid/press-release_MEMO-14-297_en.htm> (last accessed 16 June 2015).

[122] See European Commission, *New Crisis Management Measures to Avoid Future Bank Bail-Outs (Press Release)*, available at <http://europa.eu/rapid/press-release_IP-12-570_en.htm?locale=en> (last accessed 16 June 2015).

[123] Proposal for a Directive of the European Parliament and of the Council establishing a framework for the recovery and resolution of credit institutions and investment firms and amending Council Directives 77/91/EEC and 82/891/EC, Directives 2001/24/EC, 2002/47/EC, 2004/25/EC, 2005/56/EC, 2007/36/EC, and 2011/35/EC and Regulation (EU) 1093/2010, Explanatory Memorandum, para. 3.

[124] FSB, *supra* note 34.

exposing taxpayers to loss. The FSB states that the adoption of the BRRD 'will be an important step towards implementation of the Key Attributes in EU Member countries'.[125]

C. Capital Requirements

Capital requirements are seen as one of the main instruments used to ensure financial stability.[126] The issue of capital requirements has been a key focus of international regulatory efforts since the 2008 financial crisis. In 2009, Timothy Geithner stressed the importance of capital adequacy, stating that 'capital requirements for banks simply must be higher across the board. Bringing more capital into the banking system is vital. It is equally crucial to hold the largest, most interconnected institutions, whether or not they own banks, to tougher standards than others.'[127] The implementation of Basel III, developed by the BCBS in December 2010, has also been a key priority of the global agenda-setting bodies, such as the G20 and FSB. In October 2012, the BCBS delivered its preliminary report on 'Basel III regulatory consistency assessment' for the EU.[128] On 14 key components, the BCBS found the proposed EU rules to be 'compliant' or 'largely compliant'. However, it notes that the EU approach 'falls substantially short of the Basel framework in two areas: Definition of capital and the Internal Ratings-based (IRB) approach for credit risk'.[129]

In 2013, the Union adopted a legislative package, the so-called CRD IV to strengthen further the banking sector. It implements, via a directive[130] and regulation,[131] the global standards developed as part of Basel III. The package entered into force on 1 January 2014, and certain provisions will be implemented progressively during a phase in period. Their purpose is 'to transpose into EU law an international agreement approved by the G20 in November 2010—the so-called Basel

[125] FSB, *supra* note 118, at 11.

[126] Howarth and Quaglia, 'Banking on Stability: The Political Economy of New Capital Requirements in the European Union', 35 *European Integration* (2013) 333.

[127] T. Geithner, 'Financial Stability Depends on More Capital', available at <http://www.ft.com/intl/cms/s/0/638b9eb2-98ba-11de-aa1b-00144feabdc0.html#axzz2uuirqk00> (last accessed 16 March 2014).

[128] BCBS, *Basel III Regulatory Consistency Assessment (Level 2) Preliminary Report: European Union* (October 2012).

[129] Ibid., at 7. Commissioner Michel Barnier responded to the preliminary assessment, stating that the preliminary findings 'do not appear to be supported by rigorous evidence and a well-defined methodology'. See European Commission, *Commissioner Michel Barnier's reaction to the Basel Committee's preliminary 'Regulatory Consistency Assessment*, Memo/12/726 of 1 October 2012, available at <http://europa.eu/rapid/press-release_MEMO-12-726_en.htm> (last accessed 16 June 2015).

[130] Directive 2013/36/EU of the European Parliament and of the Council of 26 June 2013 on Access to the Activity of Credit Institutions and the Prudential Supervision of Credit Institutions and Investment Firms, amending Directive 2002/87/EC and repealing Directives 2006/48/EC and 2006/49/EC.

[131] Regulation (EU) 575/2013 of the European Parliament and of the Council of 26 June 2013 on Prudential Requirements for Credit Institutions and Investment Firms and Amending Regulation (EU) 648/2012.

3 Agreement—concluded by the Basel Committee on Banking Supervision'.[132] The CRD IV is not merely a cut-and-paste exercise, however. Certain adaptations have had to take place to transpose Basel III into EU law, and to fit within existing EU and Member State arrangements.[133] For example, the EU package is wider in scope, applying to all banks, rather than just those that are 'internationally active' as required in Basel III. The EU regulation also goes further in several respects, touching upon issues such as remuneration,[134] corporate governance, and transparency. However, it has been argued that the package 'involved watering down or modifying the Basel III guidelines in ways to meet EU member state demands'.[135] The CRD IV package, which establishes the 'single rule book' on prudential rules across all EU Member States is one of the most important regulatory reform packages implemented by the Union since the crisis. Implementation of Basel III by the EU also takes upon global significance due to the fact that the Union is a major economic player in the banking sector, and is home of some of the world's important financial institutions.[136]

D. Proprietary Trading

On 29 January 2014, the Commission tabled proposals[137] that would require large and complex banks to refrain from engaging in proprietary trading. The rule is loosely based on the Volcker Rule in the United States, which was approved by regulators on 10 December 2013.[138] It generally seeks to split a bank's potentially risky trading activities from its more traditional deposit-taking and lending activities. The Commission's proposal takes into account the report by the High Level Working Group chaired by the governor of the Bank of Finland, Erkki Liikanen.[139] The proposal notes that the issue of structural reform has not been

[132] Council of the European Union, *3227th Council Meeting: Economic and Financial Affairs (Press Release)*, 5 March 2013.

[133] See European Commission, *Capital Requirements—CRD IV/CRR—Frequently Asked Questions*, 16 July 2013, available at <http://europa.eu/rapid/press-release_MEMO-13-690_en.htm> (last accessed 16 June 2015).

[134] European Commission, *Commission Adopts New Standards to Increase Transparency Over Bankers' Pay and Risk Profiles (Press Release)*, 4 March 2014, available at http://europa.eu/rapid/press-release_IP-14-210_en.htm?locale=en> (last accessed 16 June 2015).

[135] Howarth and Quaglia, *supra* note 126.

[136] According to the European Commission, 'Europe will be leading on this matter, applying these rules to more than 8000 banks, amounting for 53% of global assets.' See European Commission, *Commission Wants Stronger and More Responsible Banks in Europe (Press Release)*, 27 July 2009.

[137] European Commission, *Structural Reform of the EU Banking Sector (Press Release)*, 29 January 2014, available at <http://europa.eu/rapid/press-release_IP-14-85_en.htm> (last accessed 16 June 2015).

[138] 'Regulators approve Volcker Rule Regulators Vote to Back Volcker Rule', Wall Street Journal of 10 December 2013, available at <http://online.wsj.com/news/articles/SB10001424052702303560204579249732841592834> (last accessed 10 December 2013). The 'Volcker Rule' refers to Section 619 of the Dodd–Frank Wall Street Reform and Consumer Protection Act.

[139] Proposal for a Regulation of the European Parliament and of the Council on structural measures improving the resilience of EU credit institutions, COM (2014) 43 final, 3rd Recital: 'The HLEG [High-Level Expert Group] recommended the mandatory separation of proprietary trading and other

the subject of international cooperation, such as via the G20.[140] Rather, the issue has been addressed through initiatives adopted at the national level, including in EU Member States (Germany, France, the UK, Belgium) and the US. This has led to overlapping and incompatible measures, which can cause difficulties for compliance for internationally active banks. At the G20 meeting in St Petersburg, the leaders' declaration called for the issue to be addressed: '[G20 leaders] recognize that structural banking reforms can facilitate resolvability and call on the FSB, in collaboration with the IMF and the OECD, to assess cross-border consistencies and global financial stability implications, taking into account country-specific circumstances, and report to our next Summit'.[141]

E. Credit Rating Agencies

Credit rating agencies (CRAs) also play an important role in the stability of international financial markets, and their activities came under examination following the global economic crisis. At the G20 London Summit, leaders decided 'to extend regulatory oversight and registration to Credit Rating Agencies to ensure they meet the international code of good practice, particularly to prevent unacceptable conflicts of interest'.[142] At the 2012 Los Cabos Summit, G20 leaders called for accelerated progress by national authorities and standard-setting bodies on 'ending the mechanistic reliance on credit ratings and encourage steps that would enhance transparency of and competition among credit rating agencies'.[143] In August 2013, the FSB published its progress report to the G20, Credit Rating Agencies: Reducing Reliance and Strengthening Oversight,[144] which states that member authorities still need to work to reduce reliance on external ratings. The FSB has drawn up its Principles for Reducing Reliance on CRA Ratings. According to these principles, standard setters and authorities should assess references to CRAs in laws, standards, and regulations, and replace them with alternative standards of creditworthiness.

Since 2009 the EU has taken steps to reduce the reliance on CRAs.[145] In June 2013 new rules came into force in order to reduce reliance on CRAs and to improve the rating process, the so-called CRA III. According to the Commission, '[i]n line with our G20 commitments, the new rules will reduce reliance on external ratings, requiring financial institutions to strengthen their own credit risk

high-risk trading activities into a separate legal entity within the banking group for the largest and most complex banks.'

140 Ibid., Explanatory Memorandum, para. 5: 'Structural reform has so far not been part of the international reform agenda agreed by the G20.'

141 G20, *Leaders' Declaration (St. Petersburg)*, Russia, 5–6 September 2013, para. 68.

142 G20, *Leaders' Declaration (London, United Kingdom)*, 2 April 2009, point 15.

143 G20, *Leaders' Declaration (Los Cabos, Mexico)*, 19 June 2012, para. 43.

144 FSB, *Credit Rating Agencies: Reducing Reliance and Strengthening Oversight (Progress report to the St Petersburg G20 Summit)*, 29 August 2013, available at <http://www.financialstabilityboard.org/publications/r_130829d.pdf> (last accessed 16 June 2015).

145 Regulation (EC) 1060/2009 of the European Parliament and of the Council of 16 September 2009 on Credit Rating Agencies.

assessment and not to rely solely and mechanistically on external credit ratings.'[146] The package seeks to implement the FSB principles, which are referred to in the legislation.[147] In 2011, the Commission undertook a mapping exercise to identify EU financial services legislation that referred to ratings with a view to reducing the reliance on CRA ratings. For example, the EBA, the European Insurance and Occupational Pensions Authority, and the ESMA may not refer to credit ratings 'in their guidelines, recommendations and draft technical standards where such references have the potential to trigger sole or mechanistic reliance on credit ratings by the competent authorities'.[148] The FSB has described the EU's reforms as 'significant progress'.[149]

F. Hedge Funds

In their 2009 Declaration on Strengthening the Financial System at the London Summit, G20 leaders stated that 'hedge funds or their managers will be registered and will be required to disclose appropriate information on an ongoing basis to supervisors or regulators, including on their leverage, necessary for assessment of the systemic risks that they pose individually or collectively'.[150] In this way, the G20 extended its scope beyond traditional financial institutions to include a greater range of financial actors.[151] IOSCO delivered a report to the G20 on hedge funds oversight,[152] which set out six high-level principles on the regulation of hedge funds in order to allow for internationally consistent regulation.

The Union adopted the Directive on Alternative Investment Funds Managers (AIFM) in 2011.[153] EU Member States were due to transpose the directive into national law by 22 July 2013.[154] At the time the directive was adopted, Commission President Barroso stated that it 'is another example of how the EU is leading the way in implementing our G20 commitments'.[155] The directive aims to provide

[146] European Commission, *Stricter Rules for Credit Rating Agencies to Enter into Force.*

[147] Regulation 462/2013 of the European Parliament and of the Council of 21 May 2013 amending Regulation (EC) 1060/2009 on credit rating agencies, OJ 2013 L 146/1, Recitals 3 and 4.

[148] Ibid., Art. 5(b).

[149] FSB, *Thematic Review on FSB Principles for Reducing Reliance on Credit Rating Agency Ratings Interim Report*, 29 August 2013, at 3.

[150] Statement Issued by the G20 Leaders, *Declaration on Strengthening the Financial System (London, United Kingdom)*, 2 April 2009.

[151] See G20, *Leaders' Statement (London, United Kingdom)*, 2 April 2009, point 40. G20 leaders agreed 'to extend regulation and oversight to all systemically important financial institutions, instruments and markets. This will include, for the first time, systemically important hedge funds.'

[152] IOSCO, *Technical Committee of the International Organization of Securities Commissions, Hedge Funds Oversight*, June 2009.

[153] Directive 2011/61/EU of the European Parliament and of the Council of 8 June 2011 on Alternative Investment Fund Managers and amending Directives 2003/41/EC and 2009/65/EC and Regulations (EC) 1060/2009 and (EU) 1095/2010, OJ 2011 L 174/1.

[154] Ibid., Art. 66.

[155] European Commission, *European Commission Statement at the Occasion of the European Parliament Vote on the Directive on Hedge Funds and Private Equity (Press Release)*, 11 November 2010, available at <http://europa.eu/rapid/press-release_MEMO-10-573_en.htm?locale=en> (last accessed 16 June 2015).

an EU-wide common framework for supervising and authorization of alternative investment fund managers. The term 'alternative investment fund' encompasses hedge funds, private equity funds, real estate funds, and a range of other types of institutional fund. However, by the end of 2013, only 16 of the 28 EU Member States had met the deadline.[156] Moreover, hedge fund managers have also been slow in implementing the new requirements, which cover issues such as disclosure and governance.[157]

G. Money laundering

Money laundering is yet another field where international cooperation and coordination is required in order to combat the issue fully. The Union has noted that '[m]oney laundering and terrorist financing are frequently carried out in an international context. Measures adopted solely at national or even Community level, without taking account of international coordination and cooperation, would have very limited effects.'[158] It also notes that measures at the EU level should therefore 'take particular account of the Recommendations of the Financial Action Task Force... which constitutes the foremost international body active in the fight against money laundering and terrorist financing'.[159]

In 2013, the Commission adopted two proposals in order to reform and reinforce the EU's rules on anti-money laundering and fund transfers. The proposed directive[160] seeks to implement *International Standards on Combating Money Laundering and the Financing of Terrorism & Proliferation* (FATF Recommendations), adopted by the FATF on 16 February 2012. The proposed regulation[161] also seeks to ensure that Recommendation 16 on wire transfers is transposed uniformly in the Union.[162] According to the Commission, 'both proposals fully take into account the latest Recommendations of the Financial Action Task Force... and go further in a number of fields to promote the highest standards for anti-money laundering and counter terrorism financing'.[163]

156 Kenchington, 'Hedge Fund Rules Absent in 16 EU States', Financial Times of 25 August 2013, available at <http://www.ft.com/intl/cms/s/0/f3ad2d00-0a60-11e3-aeab-00144feabdc0.html#axzz2suskLQLa> (last accessed 16 March 2014).

157 S. Grene, 'AIFMD: Hedge funds drag their feet over EU regulation deadline', Financial Times of 26 January 2014, available at <http://www.ft.com/intl/cms/s/0/5be36af8-838b-11e3-86c9-00144feab7de.html#axzz2yHnwxJtZ> (last accessed 16 June 2015).

158 Directive 2005/60/EC of the European Parliament and of the Council of 26 October 2005 on the prevention of the use of the financial system for the purpose of money laundering and terrorist financing, OJ 2005 L 309/15, 5th recital.

159 Ibid.

160 Proposal for a Regulation of the European Parliament and of the Council on information accompanying transfers of funds, COM (2013) 44 final, Explanatory Memorandum, point 2.

161 Ibid. 162 Ibid., point 2.

163 European Commission, *Anti-Money Laundering: Stronger Rules to Respond to New Threats (Press Release)*, 5 February 2013, available at <http://europa.eu/rapid/press-release_IP-13-87_en.htm?locale=en> (last accessed 16 June 2015).

5. Conclusion

It is perhaps an understatement to say that '[d]ecisions by financial services companies impinge strongly on overall economic growth and have far-reaching political and social implications, both domestically and internationally.'[164] The 2008 global economic crisis has exposed the risks to global financial stability that can be caused by the activities of the banking and financial services sector, and exposed the deficiencies in existing regulatory frameworks at the regional and international levels. Given its economic power and the size of its financial industry in the world economy, the Union has been one of the key players in global financial regulation since the crisis. Indeed, global regulation in this field has remained a 'transatlantic affair',[165] dominated by the US and Europe, despite predictions that it would become more global. However, regulation of global finance is another field where the EU's influence does not yet match its global ambitions. Several issues may explain this discrepancy between the EU's role in the global economy and its influence in global regulation of finance. The main explanatory factor is the coherence of the EU's position in international fora. Where Member State preferences are aligned, and the EU is able to present a cohesive position internationally, the EU has been influential in global standard setting.[166] Yet we have argued that another explanatory factor is the type of governance that dominates global financial regulation, which employs soft law mechanisms developed in informal standard-setting bodies. Until recently the Union has mostly focused on participation in formal bodies such as the WTO and the negotiation of binding international agreements. However, the EU is still developing tools to allow it to undertake a similar role in the various regulatory and standard-setting bodies that have become increasingly important in recent years.

In 2012, Commission President Barroso and Vice-President Ashton issued a strategy for the Progressive Improvement of the EU Status in International Organisations and Other Fora in line with the Objectives of the Treaty of Lisbon.[167] It set out ways to improve the EU's involvement in a number of IOs and other

[164] Posner, 'Making Rules for Global Finance: Transatlantic Regulatory Cooperation at the Turn of the Millennium', 63 *International Organization* (2009) 666.

[165] Mügge, 'Europe's Regulatory Role in Post-Crisis Global Finance', 21 *Journal of European Public Policy* (2014) 316, at 317.

[166] 'The cohesiveness of the EU position is the main explanatory variable for the influence of the EU in international standard setting.' Quaglia, *supra* note 85, at 339.

[167] Communication to the Commission from the President in Agreement with Vice-President Ashton, Strategy for the progressive improvement of the EU status in international organisations and other fora in line with the objectives of the Treaty of Lisbon, COM (2012) 9420 final, on file with the authors. The Communication is no longer available in the public domain. On the implementation of this Strategy in other IOs, see Wouters, Odermatt, and Ramopoulos, 'The EU in the World of International Organizations: Diplomatic Aspirations, Legal Hurdles and Political Realities', in M. Smith, S. Keukeleire, and S. Vanhoonacker (eds), *The Diplomatic System of the European Union: Evolution, Change and Challenges* (2015); and Wouters *et al.*, 'Improving the EU's Status in the UN and the UN System: An Objective Without a Strategy?', in C. Kaddous (ed.), *The European Union in International Organisations and Global Governance* (2014).

fora. It is striking that the document focuses almost entirely on intergovernmental bodies such as the International Maritime Organization and International Civil Aviation Organization. There is no strategy regarding engagement in other types of bodies where the Union may still play a significant role, however, especially international standard-setting and other bodies. Despite their informal character, these bodies exert significant normative influence.

The fact that regulation of global finance is in the form of soft law or informal law need not be an obstacle for the Union. The use of non-binding commitments instead of treaty obligations, or the use of informal bodies such as the G20 and FSB rather than formal bodies such as the IMF, can allow parties to reach agreement more easily, and allows regulation to adapt quickly in response to the constantly evolving field of global finance. It allows the Union to influence the development of global standards, best practices, and guidelines. Unlike many formal intergovernmental bodies, which only allow participation by states, informal bodies such as the G20 and FSB have allowed the EU to play a role in its own right on the global stage. In order for the Union to take advantage of this, however, it must develop a strategy for better engagement with and representation at these various bodies. Otherwise, the Union will remain an importer of regulatory norms, rather than a key agenda setter.

9

The EU in the Transnational Financial Regulatory Arena

The Case of IOSCO

Antonio Marcacci

1. The Legal Grounds for the EU to be an International Player in Financial Markets Law

A. Are there any Explicit Powers for an EU External Action on Financial Services?

The European Economic Community Treaty and its successors do not provide the Community/Union with a patent, clear and exclusive competence for financial markets.[1] This implies that the EU law of financial markets and services must be grounded on more general legal bases, like that concerning the internal market. More precisely, in the Treaty context, the legal *lender of last resort* was, and still is, Article 2 of the Treaty Establishing the European Community (TEC),[2] largely replaced by Article 3 of the Treaty on European Union (TEU). More concretely, the European Community/European Union law on financial markets is entrenched in the so-called free movement of capital, free provision of services and freedom of establishment, as provided for by Article 14 TEC[3] now Article 26 of the Treaty of the Functioning of the European Union (TFEU). Whenever it has not been possible to use the *freedoms*, harmonizing measures were adopted in order to build the single European market on common harmonized rules.[4]

[1] Art. 67(1) of the Treaty of Rome 1957, 298 UNTS 3, simply stated that 'during the transitional period and to the extent necessary to ensure the proper functioning of the common market, Member States shall progressively abolish between themselves all restrictions on the movement of capital belonging to persons resident in Member States and any discrimination based on the nationality or ca the place of residence of the parties or on the place where such capital is invested'.

[2] N. Moloney, *EC Securities Regulation* (2nd edn, 2008) 6. [3] Ibid., at 6.

[4] Ibid., at 8. Former Art. 3(1)(h) Treaty Establishing the European Communities (TEC) 1997, OJ C 340, was substantially replaced by Arts 3 and 6 Treaty on the Functioning of the European Union (TFEU) 2007, OJ C 306.

Practically all the legislation concerning financial markets enacted over the years has been based on Article 50 TFEU (former Article 44 TEC) on freedom of establishment, Article 53 TFEU (former Article 47 TEC) on the taking up and pursuing of activities by self-employed persons, and Article 114 TFEU (former Article 95 TEC) on measures for the approximation of Member States' rules. An important role has also been played by Article 62 TFEU (former Article 55 TEC) on services, and Article 115 TFEU (former Article 94 TEC) on approximation of laws.[5]

Due to the fact that financial services may fall into the macro category of services, it would be easy to assume that they are covered by EU's internal and external competence on trade, the so-called Common Commercial Policy (CCP).[6] Before the entry into force of the Lisbon Treaty, the EC had exclusive competence on trade in goods and shared competence on trade in some services and commercial aspects of intellectual property (former Article 133(5) and (6) TEC). In its Opinion 1/94 on the competence of the then EC to conclude the General Agreement on Trade in Services/World Trade Organization (GATS/WTO) Agreement, the European Court of Justice (CJEU) clarified the relationship between the pre-Lisbon CCP and the provision of services in general. The Court said that only those services provided on a cross-border basis by a supplier established in one Member State to a consumer resident in another Member State could fall within the remit of trade in services as envisaged by the CCP.[7] The reasoning behind this decision was the fact that services provided across borders are sufficiently similar to the trade in goods covered by then Article 113.[8] The CJEU followed a more restrictive approach than that adopted by Article 1(2) of the GATS,[9] which defines the 'trade in services' as:

> the supply of a service:
> (a) from the territory of one Member into the territory of any other Member;
> (b) in the territory of one Member to the service consumer of any other Member;
> (c) by a service supplier of one Member, through commercial presence in the territory of any other Member;
> (d) by a service supplier of one Member, through presence of natural persons of a Member in the territory of any other Member.[10]

The third case seems to be that of Member State A allowing banks and financial firms coming from Member State B to acquire domestic firms or open their own branches in its jurisdiction in order to provide services to the citizens of Member State A. However, according to the CJEU, in the pre-Lisbon regime, for a service to fall inside the CCP its provision had to be inherently cross-frontier (thus only the first case). Further, on a factual basis, financial services are normally provided by branches of financial firms of a Member State legally established in another

[5] *supra* note 2, at 8. [6] Art. 207 TFEU, ex Art. 133 TEC.

[7] Opinion 1/94, *re WTO Agreement*, [1994] ECR I-5267, at para. 44, as reported by Cremona, 'External Relations and External Competence of the European Union The emergence of an integrated policy' in P. Craig and G. De Bùrca (eds), *The Evolution of EU Law* (2nd edn, 2011), at 228.

[8] Opinion 1/94, as reported by Ibid., at 228. [9] Ibid., at 228.

[10] GATS 1994, OJ 1994 L 336/191.

Member State, then financial services legislation could not automatically fall within the remit of the CCP.

With the entry into force of the Lisbon Treaty, the EU has been endowed with an exclusive competence for trade in goods and in services, commercial aspects of intellectual property and foreign direct investment (not assimilable to financial services though). This reform aims at giving the EU full powers on international agreements regarding trade in services and does so by shifting from shared to exclusive competence, and putting an end to many mixed agreements.[11]

It might be thought that this new, solid legal basis could be used to conclude international agreements concerning financial services. However, as regards services, the Lisbon Treaty modifies the depth of competences (from shared to exclusive) *without* modifying the subject matter of these competences. The TFEU, indeed, only refers to 'trade in services' and this does not seem to automatically overturn the more restrictive approach followed by the CJEU in its Opinion 1/94.

Importantly, another key aspect must be considered. Financial markets law covers a wide range of issues, such as financial activities and services; regulation of intermediaries; supervision of financial markets and players; etc. Financial services are only one slice of a big cake and they cannot be treated separately but instead only as part of the goal of building up and ensuring the correct functioning of financial markets. So, the CCP (both *pre-* and *post-*Lisbon regimes) cannot cover financial services for two main reasons: 1) because of the way financial services are supplied—usually within the same jurisdiction and not across borders; 2) because the provision of financial services is just one of the features of Financial Markets Law, which was (and still is) ultimately based on legal grounds other than those related to CCP.

The only explicit external competence regarding financial markets is still the prohibition of free movements of capital between the Member States and third countries (which does not cover financial services). Thus, if the EU wishes to enter into international binding agreements concerning the provision of financial services, it must do so by supporting its external activity through implied external powers arising from Articles 50, 53, 62, 114, and 115.

B. The Doctrine of Implied External Powers ...

It was in 1971 in the *AETR* case concerning the European agreement on transport[12] that the CJEU first mentioned the possibility that the then EEC could act externally on the basis of implied powers deriving from explicit competences granted by the Treaties.[13] The Court stated that once a piece of European legislation is

[11] 'Mixed agreements' are accords concerning areas of shared competence between the EC and Member States. Such a shared competence implied that an agreement had to be ratified both at European and national levels, thus granting any Member State unhappy about the content of an agreement the power to entirely veto it. See M. Bungenberg, 'The Common Commercial Policy after Lisbon' (paper presented at the Hebrew University Jerusalem, 14 July 2008), at 7.

[12] Case 22/70, *Commission v. Council*, [1971] ECR 263.

[13] For a complete and exhaustive review and analysis of this topic, see Cremona, *supra* note 7.

adopted with the aim of developing a common policy as prescribed by the Treaties, then, on the one hand, the EEC has the power to act externally in order to preserve the integrity of the harmonizing rules, and, on the other hand, the Member States 'no longer have the right, acting individually or even collectively, to undertake obligations with third countries which affect those rules'.[14] The 1976 *Kramer* case pushed the boundary a little further by stating that the Community has implied external powers even when common rules are yet to be adopted.[15]

Two other Opinions help give a clearer overview: the already mentioned Opinion 1/94[16] and Opinion 1/2003[17] on the competence of the Community to conclude the new Lugano Convention on jurisdiction and the recognition and enforcement of judgments in civil and commercial matters. These two Opinions use two different grounds to justify the competence of the Community to enter into international agreements. Opinion 1/94 follows the so-called *effet utile* approach,[18] which means that the EC/EU has the authority to undertake international obligations when this is needed in order to achieve a specific Treaty objective even in the absence of an expressed provision. Conversely, Opinion 1/2003 follows the so-called *pre-emption* approach,[19] which means that the competence of the EC/EU to enter into international agreements can arise directly from legislative measures (such as directives or regulations) adopted by the European institutions, as happened in the *AETR* case where internal policy had already been developed and the EEC was recognized as having the power to act externally in order to preserve the integrity of the harmonizing internal rules.[20]

However, both approaches highlight one important feature of the implied powers: these are unavoidably connected either to an internal objective or an internal policy, but such strong connections also represent the limits to the EU's implied external powers. This is because the EU can act externally only on internal bases, so that an *external* policy independent of the necessities and functioning of an *internal* regime is just not possible. An independent external policy is possible only when explicit powers are conferred.[21]

Crucially, the level of normative harmonization has always affected the *depth* of EC external action, thus determining whether the EC/EU has shared or exclusive competence. In particular, when a high degree of harmonization in all sectors covered by an international agreement is not achieved, then the Commission and Member States can only conclude *mixed agreements*, like the WTO/GATS agreement, which must be ratified at both the European and national levels.[22]

However, the new Article 3 TFEU seems to overcome the implied shared competence and, hence, eliminate the issue of mixed agreements altogether,[23] if read

[14] *Supra* note 12.
[15] Cases 3, 4, and 6/76, *Cornelis Kramer and Other*, [1976] ECR 1279.
[16] Opinion 1/94, *supra* note 7.
[17] Opinion 1/03, *re Lugano Convention*, [2006] ECR I-1145.
[18] Cremona, *supra* note 7, at 221. [19] Ibid., at 221.
[20] For a complete and exhaustive analysis of these two different approaches see ibid.
[21] Ibid., at 222. [22] Bungenberg, *supra* note 11, at 7.
[23] P. Craig and G. de Bùrca, *EU Law: Text, Cases, and Materials* (5th edn, 2011) 82; Cremona, 'Defining Competence In EU External Relations: Lessons from the Treaty Reform Process', in

in combination with Article 216 TFEU,[24] which summarizes the implied powers principle and *constitutionalizes* this doctrine. Finally, the picture is completed by Article 218 TFEU establishing the procedure to be followed when the EU negotiates and concludes this kind of agreements.

C. … and its Application to the EU Law of Financial Services

So far, we have verified that under the Lisbon Treaty, on the one hand, the EU financial services law still falls outside the CCP, hence, it does not enjoy any *explicit* external competence. On the other hand, the EU does enjoy *implied exclusive* external competence stemming from Article 3 and Article 216 TFEU, no matter the degree of harmonization. From this standpoint, we may test whether a situation similar to that which occurred in the Open Skies cases may also occur in international financial law agreements.

The Open Skies cases[25] concerned air transport agreements between several Member States and the US. Before the Commission made the decision to take these Member States before the CJEU, it had requested, unsuccessfully, three times to have the right to negotiate international air transport agreements while several Member States were negotiating their own bilateral agreements.[26] The Commission grounded its action on three points: the bilateral agreements breached the principles of freedom of persons and corporations as set up by Article 49 TFEU (former Article 43 TEC); the Member States had lost their negotiating power due to the fact that the then EC had already legislated on the field at issue; finally, those bilateral agreements were likely to violate not only the EC competition law, but also undermine the freedom to provide services throughout the Union.[27]

In November 2002, the Court decided that: many of the bilateral agreements under examination breached several aspects of both EC primary treaty law and secondary legislation; the bilateral agreements breached the principle of freedom of establishment of corporations because these agreements gave other Member States' airlines a treatment different from that reserved for the signatory Member States' airlines (the so-called nationality clauses); once EU legislation has been enacted to implement an internal policy, then the EU's jurisdiction is projected externally.[28]

A. Dashwood and M. Maresceau (eds), *Law and Practice of EU External Relations—Salient Features of a Changing Landscape* (2008) 61.

[24] Cremona, ibid., at 62.

[25] Case C-466/98, *Commission v. United Kingdom*, [2002] ECR I-9427; Case C-467/98, *Commission v. Denmark*, [2002] ECR I-9519; Case C-468/98, *Commission v. Sweden*, [2002] ECR I-9575; Case C-469/98 *Commission v. Finland*, [2002] ECR I-9627; Case C-471/98, *Commission v. Belgium*, [2002] ECR I-9681; Case C-472/98, *Commission v. Luxembourg*, [2002] ECR I-9741; Case C-475/98, *Commission v. Austria*, [2002] ECR I-9797.

[26] A. De Mestral, 'The Consequences of the European Court of Justice's 'Open Skies' Decisions' (Proceedings of the ICAO International Air Transport Conference, 2003), at 23.

[27] Ibid., at 23. [28] Ibid., at 23.

The Open Skies cases are particularly important because they implicitly, but clearly, stated that it is not possible for a Member State to seek to obtain advantages exclusive to it when negotiating bilateral agreements with foreign states.[29] If we apply the same patterns to financial law, we may imagine a bilateral agreement between a Member State and the US concerning, for instance, the opportunity for a signatory Member State's financial firm to operate in the US enjoying a competitive advantage with respect to other Member States' financial firms. The same would be true for a US financial firm operating in the signatory Member State and enjoying a competitive advantage with respect to other Member States' financial firms.

Nevertheless, what must be noticed about international financial law is the legal nature of the 'agreements' signed by the contracting parties. Indeed, unlike fields such as aviation, trade or monetary affairs, international financial law is established through networks made up of domestic public bodies which enter into non-binding soft-law commitments.[30] As a matter of fact, the question here is not about whether the EU can use implied powers to enter into binding agreements; but, rather, whether the Commission can freely 'negotiate' non-binding soft-law commitments without complying with the procedure set up by Article 218 TFEU.

In this respect, the CJEU has drawn a clear line between hard- and soft-law regulatory agreements. As regards the first type of agreements, characterized by having binding[31] effects and likely to generate liability at the international level in case of non-performance,[32] in Case C-327/91[33] the CJEU clearly stated that the authority of the Commission was tempered by the formal procedures set down by the Treaty (Article 218 TFEU, ex 300 TEC and original 228 EEC Treaty), which provide for a primary role of the Council in the field of international agreements, with the Commission's negotiating powers limited to the extent of the authorization granted to it by the Council. The CJEU additionally specified that the institutional balance between the Council and the Commission was not susceptible to being modified even in cases of exclusive competences of the EC. Conversely, in Case C-233/02,[34] the CJEU clearly held that the Commission is endowed with the power to negotiate and conclude soft-law regulatory agreements with no binding effects on the contracting parties.

Thus, the leeway left to the Commission to enter into international financial law commitments and 'negotiate' the contents of non-binding agreements is much broader than the discretion it would have under the implied powers doctrine. Furthermore, even if a struggle between the Commission and some Member

[29] Ibid., at 23.

[30] Brummer, 'Why Soft Law Dominates International Finance—And Not Trade', 13 *Journal of International Economic Law* (2010) 623.

[31] As the Court held in Opinion 1/75 of 11 November 1975: 'in its reference to an "agreement", the second subparagraph of Art. 228(1) of the treaty uses the expression in a general sense to indicate any undertaking entered into by entities subject to international law which has binding force, whatever its formal designation' (Opinion 1/75, *OECD*, [1975] ECR 1355).

[32] C-327/91, *French Republic v. Commission*, [1994] ECR I-3641.

[33] Ibid.

[34] C-233/02, *French Republic v. Commission*, [2002] ECR I-2759.

States, such as the one occurred in the Open Skies cases, was to appear as regards international financial regulatory agreements, the Commission would be likely to win—not because of the implied powers doctrine but because of the primacy of EU law, formalized via harmonization rules. Indeed, once the content of these soft-law regulatory agreements is incorporated into harmonized European rules, the Member States cannot avoid being bound to it and any soft-law commitments to third countries end up being empty shells.

2. The Transnational Financial Regulatory Arena: The International Organization of Securities Commission

A. IOSCO: Origin, Mission, and Membership

The International Organization of Securities Commissions (IOSCO) is the only global quasi-public body entitled to set up standards for transnational financial markets.[35] Founded in 1974 as the pan-American forum of national securities regulators coming from the Americas and called the 'Inter-American Association of Securities Commissions',[36] it very soon turned into a world organization with the accession of France, Indonesia, Korea, and the UK in 1983. Currently, IOSCO has 124 ordinary members, 15 associate members, and 64 affiliate members from all around the world.[37] The official website states that IOSCO's 'membership regulates more than 95% of the world's securities markets in more than 115 jurisdictions'.[38]

As regards the legal nature of IOSCO, this is quite 'controversial' in the sense that it is not a typical international organization grounded on a formal international public-law treaty. For the first decade of its life, IOSCO was completely informal. In 1984 the organization members adopted the still-standing by-laws,[39] organizing the Organization's functioning, and in 1987 IOSCO was formally incorporated as a non-profit organization[40]—a 'personne morale sans but lucrative'[41]— under

[35] See Brummer, 'Post-American Securities Regulation', 98 *California Law Review* (2010) 327, at 338.

[36] Also called the 'Inter-American Association of Securities Commissions' in Sommer Jr., 'IOSCO: Its Mission and Achievement Symposium: Internationalization of Securities', 17 *Northwestern Journal of International Law & Business* (1996) 15.

[37] See IOSCO, *Ordinary Members of IOSCO* (2015), available at <https://www.iosco.org/about/?subsection=membership&memid=1> (last accessed 20 May 2015); IOSCO, *Associate Members of IOSCO* (2015), available at <https://www.iosco.org/about/?subsection=membership&memid=2> (last accessed 20 May 2015); IOSCO, *Affiliate Members of IOSCO* (2015), available at <https://www.iosco.org/lists/index.cfm?section=general> (last accessed 20 May 2015).

[38] IOSCO, *About IOSCO—Scope of Activities* (2015), available at <https://www.iosco.org/about/?subsection=about_iosco> (last accessed 20 May 2015).

[39] Zaring, 'International Law by Other Means: The Twilight Existence of International Financial Regulatory Organizations', 33 *Texas International Law Journal* (1998) 281, at 292.

[40] Sommer, *supra* note 36, at 15.

[41] *Préambule de la Loi concernant l'Organisation Internationale des Commissions de Valeurs*, 1er Décembre 1987, Assemblée Nationale du Québec, 33e législature, 1re session, 1987, chapitre 143, Loi n° 243, Bulletin de l'Assemblée Nationale du Québec, 1987, 2453–2456. Art. 1 states that: 'Une personne morale sans but lucratif est constituée sous la dénomination sociale "Organisation internationale des commissions de valeurs".'

Quebec law,[42] and its Secretariat was formally set up in Montreal. Significantly, Article 8 of the Quebec Act leaves an enormous leeway to IOSCO internal by-laws.[43]

In 1999, the headquarters of the IOSCO General Secretariat were moved to Madrid.[44] With the act *Ley 55/1999, de 29 de Diciembre*[45] IOSCO was incorporated under the Spanish Law as an '*asociación de utilidad pública*' without '*ánimo de lucro*'—a non-profit legal person—whose goals are the '*cooperación para el desarrollo*' (cooperation for the development) and '*fomento de la economía social*' (to nurture the social economy). Thus, IOSCO has neither a charter nor a formal founding treaty[46] and it can be classified as multilateral regulatory network of (usually public) regulators with the formal structure of a private law-based non-profit entity incorporated by a statutory act.

As regards the official goals, the 2010 Resolution on IOSCO's Mission, Goals and Priorities[47] states the Organization works to:

- promote 'internationally recognized and consistent standards of regulation, oversight and enforcement... to protect investors, maintain fair, efficient and transparent markets, and seek to address systemic risks';
- strengthen information exchange and supervision cooperation;
- reinforce market infrastructure and regulation through 'exchange information at both global and regional levels'.[48]

As regards membership, the IOSCO has three different kinds of members: full, associate, and affiliate members. Full members enjoy the right to be part of IOSCO's most important organs, like the Emerging Market Committee and the IOSCO Board. Article 6 of the by-laws states that: '[a] securities commission or a similar governmental body that is not a member is eligible for ordinary membership of the Organization.' The public nature requirement is further strengthened by Articles 7.1 and 7.2 recognizing that a self-regulatory organization (SRO) is

[42] *Loi concernant l'Organisation Internationale des Commissions de Valeurs*, 1er Décembre 1987, Assemblée Nationale du Québec, 33e législature, 1re session, 1987, chapitre 143, Loi n° 243, Bulletin de l'Assemblée Nationale du Québec, 1987, 2453–2456.

[43] *Article 8 de la Loi concernant l'Organisation Internationale des Commissions de Valeurs*, 1er Décembre 1987, Assemblée Nationale du Québec, 33e législature, 1re session, 1987, chapitre 143, Loi n° 243, Bulletin de l'Assemblée Nationale du Québec, 1987, 2453–2456.

[44] IOSCO, *A Resolution on the Relocation of the IOSCO General Secretariat to Madrid* (1999). Alongside Madrid, other cities presented their candidature: Amsterdam, Basel, Frankfurt, London, Paris, and Singapore. See lasindustrias.com, *Madrid, elegida sede del IOSCO* (1999), available at <http://www.lasindustrias.com/madrid-elegida-sede-del-iosco.html> (last accessed 20 May 2015). The reason why Madrid was chosen is linked to the generosity of the Spanish Government, willing to provide the most attractive solution. See R. Bismuth, La coopération internationale des autorités de régulation du secteur financier et le droit international public (PhD Thesis on file at University Paris 1 Panthéon-Sorbonne, 2009) 231.

[45] *Ley 55/1999, de 29 de Diciembre, de Medidas fiscales, administrativas y del orden social*, Boletìn Oficial del Estado, 30 Diciembre 1999, n° 312, p. 46095, n° 24876.

[46] Slaughter, 'Governing the Global Economy through Government Networks', in M. Byers (ed.), *Role of Law in International Politics* (2000) 177, at 184.

[47] IOSCO, *Resolution on IOSCO's Mission, Goals and Priorities* (2010).

[48] Ibid., at 1–2.

eligible for ordinary membership only when its country of origin does not have a governmental regulatory body.

Importantly, IOSCO by-laws do not delve into the nature and the depth of the regulatory powers enjoyed by a country's securities commission. This is mainly because this legal aspect varies greatly from country to country, usually on the basis of the administrative law culture underlying their national traditions. However, IOSCO by-laws seem to imply that a securities commission or a similar governmental body must have at least (some) secondary regulatory powers (with the primary regulatory powers remaining with the legislature), and either broad or narrow enforcement mechanisms. A broad enforcement mechanism implies that the national securities commission has all the powers needed to directly enforce securities laws (like the US Securities Exchange Commission (SEC),[49] while a narrow mechanism implies that the national securities commission can only impose administrative sanctions, report a possible breach to another (more powerful) authority, like a Ministry or a Court, and initiate a legal action (like the German Bundesanstalt für Finanzdienstleistungsaufsicht (BaFin).[50]

The concern about the actual dimension of the enforcement powers of its ordinary members has been a constant characteristic of IOSCO. The old preamble to IOSCO's by-laws stated that the organization's members had to 'provide mutual assistance to ensure the integrity of the markets by a vigorous application of the standards and by effective enforcement against offences',[51] while the new one still emphasizes the importance of enforcement powers but puts them within the wider framework of cooperation.[52] Moreover, Principle 8 of the Objective and Principle of Securities Regulation clearly states that '[t]he regulator should have comprehensive enforcement powers', and Principle 9 provides that '[t]he regulatory system should ensure an effective and credible use of inspection, investigation, surveillance and enforcement powers and implementation of an effective compliance program.'[53]

In particular, in November 1997, the Presidents' Committee passed the Resolution on Enforcement Powers concerning information sharing. The point of the Presidents' Committee was that, without the full authority of obtaining information, the entire enforcement mechanism (both domestic and cross-border) could not operate. With this resolution, each ordinary member was asked to ensure that it or another authority in its jurisdiction had the necessary power to obtain

[49] According to the Securities Exchange Act, sec. 30A(d), the SEC can either carry out an enforcement proceeding before a so-called administrative law judge (a figure that does not exist in Europe) or initiate a civil action before a federal court.

[50] According to the German Securities Trading Act (WpHG), sec. 38, 39 I-III., BaFIN can impose fines in cases of administrative offences.

[51] IOSCO, *Objectives and Principles of Securities Regulation* (2003).

[52] IOSCO, *Resolution of the Presidents' Committee on Amendment to IOSCO's By-Laws to reflect change in structure* (2010), available at <http://www.iosco.org/library/resolutions/pdf/IOSCORES33.pdf> (last accessed 20 May 2015).

[53] IOSCO, *Objectives and Principles of Securities Regulation* (2010).

information relevant to investigating and prosecuting potential violations so that such information could be shared with other members.[54]

As regards associate membership, this has been traditionally reserved for SROs, securities exchanges, international bodies, and associations of public regulatory bodies (i.e. associations with some jurisdiction over a country's market subdivision) from countries whose national regulatory body is already a full member. A clear example of this 'double' nature of the associate membership is given by the US, which sees the North American Securities Administrators Association, Inc. as associate member, with the US being primarily represented by the SEC. Interestingly, the new Article 8.2 makes supranational governmental regulators (like the European Commission and the European Securities and Markets Authority (ESMA)) and intergovernmental international organizations eligible for associate membership.[55]

B. The Distribution of Competences within the Organization

A key aspect of IOSCO governance is the fact that the organization operates through a network of committees,[56] as confirmed by the 'Resolution of the Presidents' Committee on Amendment to IOSCO's By-Laws to reflect change in structure',[57] adopted in 2010. As of the 2012 Annual Meeting,[58] the organization comprises the following bodies:

1. the Presidents' Committee;
2. the IOSCO Board;
3. the Emerging Markets Committee;
4. the General Secretariat;
5. the Regional Committees;
6. the Consultative Committees.

The Presidents' Committee is the IOSCO's formal decision-making body. It meets once a year at the annual meeting and comprises all the presidents of the member agencies,[59] both regular and associate, with each ordinary member having one vote[60] and the associate members having the right to attend and speak.[61] Formally speaking, it 'has all the powers necessary or convenient to achieve the objectives of the Organization',[62] and it adopts important acts such as the resolutions reformulating IOSCO mission aims, amending the by-laws, or setting up the Operational Priorities.

[54] IOSCO, *A Resolution on Enforcement Powers* (1997).

[55] See the newest version of IOSCO by-laws, available at <http://www.iosco.org/library/by_laws/pdf/IOSCO-By-Laws-Section-1-English.pdf> (last accessed 20 May 2015).

[56] Sommer, *supra* note 36, at 18.

[57] IOSCO, *supra* note 52, Annex 1.

[58] The Presidents' Committee conferred upon the Executive Committee the authority to do all it is deemed necessary for the amendments to take effect before the 2012 Annual Meeting. See ibid., at 1.

[59] Ibid., Art. 24.

[60] Ibid., Art. 27.

[61] Ibid., Art. 30.

[62] Ibid., Art. 26.

The Board—constituted for two years and established during the IOSCO Biennial Meeting[63]—recently replaced the Executive[64] and the Technical[65] Committees and the Advisory Board of the Emerging Markets Committee,[66] which were the key bodies within IOSCO for the last two decades. The majority of Board members come from the most developed financial markets, with only few of them coming from emerging economies.

This Board runs the governance, standards setting, and development functions of IOSCO,[67] mainly through the submission of resolutions[68] and the drafting of the Presidents' Committee's agenda[69] (to be both approved by the Presidents' Committee). Furthermore, it prepares the programme of activities and the IOSCO annual budget (approved by the Presidents' Committee),[70] appoints the Secretary General,[71] recommends regional groupings of members for recognition by the Presidents Committee as Regional Committees,[72] recognizes Consultative Committees[73] (which help the Board develop normative documents), and recommends the Presidents' Committee when sanctions should be imposed on members.[74] Finally, the board monitors the organization's activities, regulatory capacity building, market development strategy, membership admission procedure, and outreach and research programmes.[75]

The board is the key executive organ of IOSCO, the only one handling its policy-making outcomes and determining its core activity. In the words of the by-laws: 'Board takes all decisions and undertakes all actions necessary or convenient to achieve the objectives of the Organization.'[76] The legal tool employed by the Board to carry out its activity is the Protocol.[77]

In order to provide emerging securities and futures markets with a body to help refine their peculiar issues, IOSCO set up the Growth and Emerging Markets Committee. This is responsible for establishing principles and minimum standards, preparing training programmes, and 'facilitating the exchange of information and transfer of technology and expertise'.[78] Five working groups covering key

[63] Ibid., Art. 37.1, Part 5.

[64] The Executive Committee was the second key body of IOSCO, acting as its executive arm. See International Organization of Securities Commissions—IOSCO, *2010 IOSCO Annual Report* (2011).

[65] The Technical Committee was established in 1987 by the Executive Committee in order 'to study critical issues affecting countries with developed securities markets'; Lichtenstein, 'Introductory Note to the Bank for International Settlements: Committee on Banking Regulations and Supervisory Practices' Consultative Paper on International Convergence of Capital Measurement and Capital Standards', *30 International Legal Materials* (1991) 967, at 971. For this reason it could be said 'to do the *grunt work* with respect to the most developed markets' (Sommer, *supra* note 36). It was made up of eighteen from the worlds' larger, more developed and internationalized markets.

[66] IOSCO, *supra* note 64, at 4.

[67] IOSCO, *supra* note 52, Part 5.

[68] Ibid., Art. 26(a), Part 4.

[69] Ibid., Art. 40.2(h), Part 5.

[70] Ibid., Art. 40.2(a), Part 5.

[71] Ibid., Art. 40.2(d), Part 5.

[72] Ibid., Art. 40.2(e), Part 5.

[73] Ibid., Art. 40.2(f), Part 5.

[74] Ibid., Art. 40.2(i), Part 5.

[75] IOSCO, *supra* note 64, at. 5.

[76] IOSCO, *supra* note 52, Art. 40.1, Part 5.

[77] Ibid., Art. 41.1, Part 5.

[78] IOSCO, *Fact Sheet* (2014), at 4; available at <http://www.iosco.org/about/pdf/IOSCO-Fact-Sheet.pdf> (last accessed 20 May 2015). The Growth and Emerging Markets Committee has set up working groups in these areas: Disclosure and Accounting; Regulation of Secondary Markets;

topics (such as disclosure and accounting and regulation of secondary markets) drive the work of the Emerging Markets Committee.

Four Regional Committees (Africa/Middle-East; Asia–Pacific; European; and Inter-American) have also been established to focus on specific regional problems. These regional committees behave like forums where IOSCO members exchange information concerning their macro area[79] and discuss topics of special interest.[80]

The value of self-regulation has been long acknowledged by the Objectives and Principles of Securities Regulation, which states that 'the regulatory regime should make appropriate use of Self-Regulatory Organizations (SROs) that exercise some direct oversight responsibility for their respective areas of competence, to the extent appropriate to the size and complexity of the markets'.[81] To improve the involvement of SROs by giving 'a constructive input in the work of IOSCO',[82] an SRO Consultative Committee (SROCC) was established in 1989 and replaced in September 2013 by the Affiliate Members Consultative Committee (AMCC).[83] The current AMCC 'consists of SROs, securities exchanges, financial market infrastructures, investor protection funds, and other organizations'.[84] Significantly, the AMCC works with the Board by providing 'input into the IOSCO policy and standard-setting work'.[85]

As predecessor of the AMCC, the SROCC has always been involved in the law-making process to the extent that it can make its voice heard. Its role was emphasized by the Model for Effective Regulation,[86] highlighting how SROs provide valuable industry input in terms of codes of good conduct, master agreements, and standardization of common practices. Thus, on the one hand, the SROCC had an (informal) consultative role, whereas, on the other, SROs and their normative productions were conceived as tools devised to achieve a 'tighter degree of compliance by the market participants operating within the self-regulatory framework'.[87]

Finally, the General Secretariat in Madrid carries out all the necessary administrative and organizational tasks, such as keeping the records of the organization,[88] monitoring whether the members comply with the by-laws and resolutions or not,[89] and ensuring that the by-laws and resolutions are kept up to date.[90] The current governance of IOSCO, focused on its Board, are illustrated in Figure 9.1.

Regulation of Market Intermediaries; Enforcement and the Exchange of Information; Investment Management.

[79] IOSCO, *supra* note 52, Art. 60(b), Part 8. [80] Ibid., Art. 60(a), Part 8.

[81] IOSCO, *supra* note 51, at 2.

[82] IOSCO, *2008 IOSCO Annual Report* (2009), at 25.

[83] IOSCO, *Affiliate Members Strengthen Consultative Role within IOSCO* (2013), available at <http://www.iosco.org/news/pdf/IOSCONEWS311.pdf> (last accessed 20 May 2015).

[84] Ibid, at 1.

[85] IOSCO, *Affiliate Members Consultative Committee* (2015), available at <https://www.iosco.org/about/?subsection=display_committee&cmtid=2> (last accessed 20 May 2015).

[86] IOSCO SRO Consultative Committee, *Model for effective Regulation—Report of the SRO Consultative Committee of the International Organization of Securities Commissions* (2000).

[87] Ibid., at 3. [88] IOSCO, *supra* note 52, Art. 51(a), Part 7.

[89] Ibid., Art. 51(c), Part 7. [90] Ibid., Art. 51(b), Part 7.

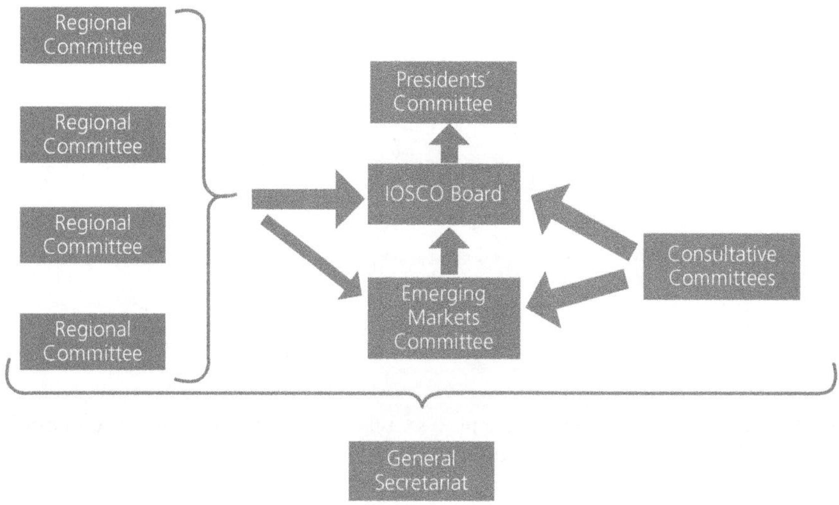

Fig. 9.1 The current governance of IOSCO, as interpreted by the author, makes clear the central role played by the newly established IOSCO Board.

C. The IOSCO Decision-Making Procedure

The preamble to the by-laws officially recognizes that the best way to achieve the organization's aims is through consensus,[91] which generally implies that the final deliberation is based on the 'fairly prevailing opinion' on a particular subject, namely the common views shared by the participants.[92] This is actually the method through which the members' unanimity can be more easily achieved. Within this process an important role is played by the chairperson who facilitates the consensus achievement.

As regards IOSCO, consensus means that before issuing a document, a general accord on its content must be achieved: only if this is achieved can a guideline be supported and adopted by the Presidents' Committee. For that, IOSCO may look pretty democratic due to the fact that each member has one seat and one vote at the Presidents' Committee, in which all the organization's 'sovereign' powers are formally vested. However, the Presidents' Committee only meets once a year and its most important power concerns 'constitutional' amendments.[93] Thus, most of the core 'normative' work is, in practice, carried out by the Board.

Regarding its decision-making process, Article 44.1 of the by-laws states that half of the Board constitutes a quorum, while Article 44.2 provides that if necessary (i.e. when unanimity is not achieved) decisions are put to a vote and must

[91] Ibid, at 3.

[92] See Calliess, 'The Making of Transnational Contract Law', 14 *Indiana Journal of Global Legal Studies* (2007) 469, at 479.

[93] As indicated in Art. 36.3 of the by-laws.

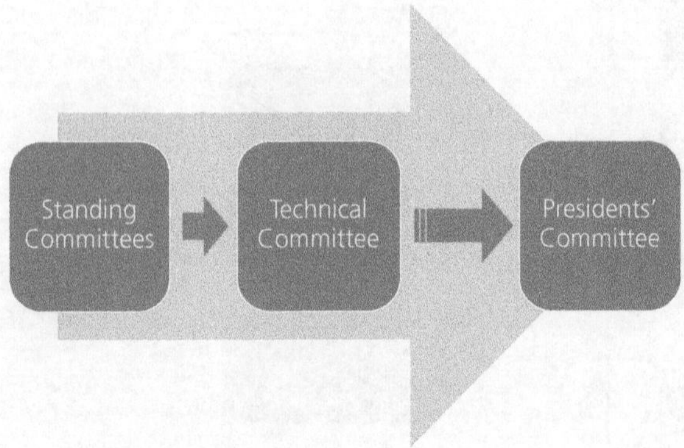

Fig. 9.2 The IOSCO decision-making process, as interpreted by the author, is substantially run by the Board/Technical Committee.

have the support of the majority of the members in attendance. In the event of a tie, the Chairperson has the casting vote. Moreover, the Chairperson is also responsible for reporting the work of the Board to the Presidents' Committee during each Annual Meeting (Article 46) and s/he also has the power to ask other persons to attend the Board's meetings (Article 47). Then, special procedures are followed when conducting public consultations, as stated in the IOSCO Consultation Policy and Procedure.[94]

Another very important aspect of the IOSCO rule-making procedure is the fact that the Board relies heavily on 'working committees'. Indeed, specialized standing committees, made up of experts from full members, carry out the entire normative work. They meet regularly and work according to the instructions they receive from the Board. There are currently nine permanent committees covering several core areas, such as the regulation of secondary markets and investment management.[95]

Alongside the already existing Standing Committees, the Board can establish special task forces focused on particular subjects and responsible for drafting documents, like the 2003 task force on credit rating agencies (CRAs) made up of the Technical Committee's principal representatives,[96] or the Chairmen's Task Force on the Subprime Crisis formed in 2007.[97] Figure 9.2 illustrates the decision-making process.

[94] IOSCO Executive Committee, *IOSCO Consultation Policy and Procedure* (2005).

[95] IOSCO, *General Information* (2012), available at <https://www.iosco.org/about/?subsection=display_committee&cmtid=11> (last accessed 20 May 2015).

[96] IOSCO Executive Committee, *The Role Of Credit Rating Agencies In Structured Finance Markets—Final Report* (2008), at 2.

[97] IOSCO Executive Committee, *Report on the Subprime Crisis—Final Report* (2008).

3. The Legally 'Soft' Involvement of the EU in the Transnational Financial Regulatory Arena and its Growing Informal Influence

Concerning the formal status of the EU in IOSCO, the European Commission is an associate member.[98] It is represented through its Directorate General for Internal Market and Services, and more specifically by Unit G3 of its Directorate G which focuses on financial services policy and financial markets. The 2010-established ESMA is also registered as an associate member and has only recently joint the Board as an 'observer'.[99] However, from a more legalistic viewpoint, we cannot hide the actual legal weaknesses of the EU. This weakness can be found both in the internal aspect (i.e. the legal basis of the European law for financial services), and from the external viewpoint (i.e. the capacity of the EU to conclude international agreements concerning international financial law).

After studying the by-laws, one comes to realize that the big hurdle for the Commission and ESMA to decide whether or not to join IOSCO as full members is not so much about the EU's legal bases concerning financial law, as it is to do with the requirements necessary to become a full IOSCO member. Indeed, the by-laws clearly provide that, in order to become ordinary member, a potential applicant must be either a securities commission or a similar governmental body, and there is no EU body that can fulfil this requirement. In particular, ESMA, established by Regulation 1095/2010,[100] does not have the required regulatory powers. This stems from the fact that, traditionally speaking, European agencies[101] cannot enjoy full decision-making and rule-making powers. Unfortunately, this core deficiency remains even after the important Short Selling case,[102] which granted ESMA a wider regulatory leeway, and despite the fact that ESMA has a recognized legal personality, and is a permanent and relatively independent body.[103]

However, despite all these hurdles, the Commission has played a much more active, although still informal, role in the international financial arena, in particular since the 2007–2008 financial crisis. Elliot Posner claims that the EU had already increased its role in the transnational regulation forum as of the

[98] IOSCO, *Associate Members of IOSCO* (2015), available at <https://www.iosco.org/about/?subsection=membership&memid=2> (last accessed 20 May 2015).

[99] About membership, see ibid. About observer status, see IOSCO, *IOSCO Board* (2015), available at <https://www.iosco.org/about/?subsection=display_committee&cmtid=11> (last accessed 20 May 2015).

[100] Regulation 1095/2010, OJ 2010 L 331/84.

[101] Moreover, it should be noted that 'no one common definition of an agency may be identified' (Everson, 'Independent Agencies: Hierarchy Beaters?', 1 *European Law Journal* (1995) 180) and the literature has not unanimously agreed on it yet.

[102] Case C-270/12, *United Kingdom v. Parliament and Council*, [2014] ECR I-0000.

[103] Griller and Orator, 'Everything under control? The 'way forward' for European agencies in the footsteps of the Meroni doctrine', 35 *European Law Review* (2010) 3.

adoption of the Lamfalussy procedure at the end of the 1990s.[104] Before then, many European countries did not have a proactive approach, adapting their legal frameworks to that of the US without proposing new regulatory principles, and most of them used to remain passive by challenging 'the existing normative framework for regulating securities markets only along the edges, instead demanding better terms of cooperation—without disputing basic principles set under US leadership'.[105] The Lamfalussy law-making process was established to rationalize and, above all, speed up the enactment of the European normative production concerning financial markets and services, and one of the results was, as Brummer claims, that 'Brussels began to take charge of the financial services oversight, [and] the EU increasingly began to resemble a second regulatory *superpower*'.[106]

However, the real watershed for a new role of the EU in the transnational regulatory arena coincides with the elaboration and signature of the Lisbon Treaty at the end of 2007—entered into force 1 December 2009—on the one hand, and the 2007–2008 financial crisis, on the other. It is worth noting that even if the Lisbon Treaty does not confer upon the EU any extra competence as regards financial and banking law, it does introduce changes in the remit of the EU external action,[107] likely to give the EU a more prominent (political) international role. In addition, the essential soft nature of international financial law,[108] a deeper involvement of the EU in the global arena may have important implications for EU financial law.

Before 2007, cooperation between IOSCO and EU bodies was already occurring but it was extremely informal. In 2004, for instance, within the framework of its activity on credit risk transfer, the Joint Forum of Basel Committee on Banking Supervision (BCSB),[109] IOSCO, and the International Association of Insurance Supervisors (IAIS)[110] officially declared that they had 'undertaken efforts to

[104] In his 2008 book, Daniel W. Drezner claims that the real turning point of viewing the EU as a single actor in the regulation of the global economy was the entry into force of the 1992 Maastricht Treaty. *See* D.W. Drezner, *All Politics Is Global: Explaining International Regulatory Regimes* (2008) 37.

[105] Posner, 'Making Rules for Global Finance: Transatlantic Regulatory Cooperation at the Turn of the Millennium', 63 *International Organization* (2009) 665, at 677.

[106] C. Brummer, *Soft Law and the Global Financial System: Rule Making in the 21st Century* (2012) 46.

[107] The Lisbon Treaty has established the High Representative for Foreign Affairs and Security Policy and it provides the EU with 'legal status', consolidated by a reinforced competence on the conclusion of international agreements. On this topic, see Craig, 'The Treaty Of Lisbon, Process, Architecture And Substance', 33 *European Law Review* (2008) 137; and Cremona, 'Coherence Through Law: What Difference Will the Treaty of Lisbon Make?', 3 *Hamburg Review of Social Sciences* (2008) 11.

[108] On this topic, see Brummer, *supra* note 30.

[109] The Basel Committee on Banking Supervision is a forum for global cooperation on banking supervisory matters. See Bank for International Settlements (BIS), *About the Basel Committee* (2014), available at <http://www.bis.org/bcbs/about.htm> (last accessed 20 May 2015).

[110] Established in 1994, the IAIS 'is a voluntary membership organization of insurance supervisors and regulators from more than 200 jurisdictions in nearly than 140 countries'. IAIS, *About the IAIS* (2015), available at <http://iaisweb.org/index.cfm?event=getPage&nodeId=25181> (last accessed 20 May 2015).

coordinate with similar projects initiated in the European Union',[111] in particular, the European Banking Supervision Committee (BSC), the Committee of European Insurance and Occupational Pension Supervisors (CEIOPS), and the Committee of European Securities Regulators (CESR), predecessor of the ESMA.[112]

More specifically, as regards the relationship between IOSCO and the CESR, the latter was explicitly mentioned in the Final Communiqué of the XXXI Annual Conference of the International Organization of Securities Commissions.[113] The Final Communiqué states that IOSCO was planning to establish an *International Financial Reporting Standards Database* and that, for this reason, it was liaising with the CESR because it had already developed and implemented a similar database for use in the European Union.

However, things became much more interesting as the financial crisis loomed. On 6 November 2007, the Trustees of the International Accounting Standards Committee Foundation (IASCF), the oversight body of the International Accounting Standard Board (IASB), announced a strategy to enhance the organization's governance and public accountability by including, among other things, the establishment of a formal reporting link to official organizations.[114] On 7 November 2007, the European Commission, the Financial Services Agency of Japan (JFSA), IOSCO, and the US SEC adopted a joint statement in which they proposed the establishment of a new monitoring body within the IASC Foundation, responsible for reviewing and commenting on the IASB's work programme, participating and having the final approval in the selection of the IASCF Trustees, and reviewing the Trustees' oversight activities.[115] In this joint statement, all the signatories are defined as the 'authorities responsible for capital market regulation', thereby putting the European Commission on the same level of the US SEC.[116]

In May 2008, the IASC Trustees announced the establishment of a round-table discussion for the following weeks.[117] On 18 June 2008, the day before the round

[111] See BIS, *Joint Forum Issues Report on Credit Risk Transfer* (2004), available at <http://www.bis.org/press/p041021b.htm> (last accessed 20 May 2015).

[112] See IOSCO, *Joint Forum Issues Report on Credit Risk Transfer* (2004), available at <http://www.iosco.org/news/pdf/IOSCONEWS76.pdf> (last accessed 20 May 2015).

[113] See IOSCO, *Final Communiqué of the XXXI Annual Conference of the International Organization of Securities Commissions (IOSCO)* (2006), available at <http://www.iosco.org/news/pdf/IOSCONEWS97-English.pdf> (last accessed 20 May 2015).

[114] See International Accounting Standards Committee Foundation, *Press Release of 6 November 2007* (2007), available at <http://www.iasplus.com/pressrel/0711governancepr.pdf> (last accessed 20 May 2015).

[115] See European Commission, *Statement of the European Commission, the Financial Services Agency of Japan, the International Organization of Securities Commissions (IOSCO) and the US Securities and Exchange Commission on work to enhance the governance of the IASC Foundation* (2007), available at <http://europa.eu/rapid/press-release_MEMO-07-451_en.htm?locale=en> (last accessed 20 May 2015).

[116] Also in the IOSCO Open Letter to G-20 Meeting of November 2008 (available at <http://www.iosco.org/library/pubdocs/pdf/IOSCOPD282.pdf> last accessed 20 May 2015) the Commission, the FSAJ, and the SEC are referred as the 'authorities of the three largest securities markets'.

[117] See International Accounting Standards Committee Foundation, *Press Release of 12 May 2008* (2008), available at <http://www.iasplus.com/pressrel/0805iascfproposals.pdf> (last accessed 20 May 2015).

table was held, the increasing importance of the European Commission was again recognized by a joint press release released by IOSCO with the Commission, the JFSA, and the SEC, defined as 'the securities authorities in the world's three largest capital markets'.[118] At the January 2009 meeting of the IASC Trustees, the decision to establish a formal link to the Monitoring Board of public authorities was definitively taken.[119] At the moment, the members of the Monitoring Board are the IOSCO Board, the European Commission, the JFSA, and the SEC. The main responsibilities of the Monitoring Board are to ensure that the IASC Trustees correctly carry out their duties and to approve the appointment or reappointment of the Trustees.[120]

Another important example of the increasing importance of the EU institutions in the international financial regulatory arena is given by the fact that the working group on the review of the Recommendations for Central Counterparties set up by the Committee on Payment and Settlement Systems (CPSS),[121] and the IOSCO was chaired in 2009 by representatives from the European Central Bank and SEC.[122]

However, the great leap forward was made in the very hot regulatory area of over-the-counter (OTC) derivatives through the OTC Working Group (OTCWG). This was established in April 2010 after the G-20 leaders' declaration of September 2009 requesting that, by the end of 2012, all standardized OTC contracts be traded on exchanges or trading facilities and cleared through central counterparties so as to lessen systemic risk.[123] The Group was officially chaired by the CPSS, the IOSCO, and the European Commission and was tasked with setting out 'policy options supporting the consistent implementation of appropriate measures regarding trading, clearing, and reporting across jurisdictions'.[124] The regulatory options

[118] European Commission, *Authorities responsible for regulation of public companies announce next steps regarding the creation of a group to interact with the international accounting standards committee foundation—Press Release of 18 June 2008, IP/08/966* (1998), available at <http://europa.eu/rapid/pressReleasesAction.do?reference=IP/08/966&format=HTML&aged=0&language=EN&guiLanguage=en (last accessed 20 May 2015). Also, Securities and Exchange Commission—*SEC, Authorities Responsible for Regulation of Public Companies Announce Next Steps Regarding the Creation of a Group to Interact with the International Accounting Standards Committee Foundation—Release No. 2008-112, 18 June 2008* (2008), available at <http://www.iasplus.com/usa/sec/0806iascf-monitoring.pdf> (last accessed 20 May 2015).

[119] See International Accounting Standards Committee Foundation, *Press Release of 29 January 2009* (2009), available at <http://www.iasplus.com/pressrel/0901monitoringboard.pdf> (last accessed 20 May 2015).

[120] IFRS, *Monitoring Board* (2009), available at <http://www.ifrs.org/The+organisation/Governance+and+accountability/Monitoring+Board.htm> (last accessed 20 May 2015).

[121] Established by the G10 central banks in 1990, it 'serves as a forum for central banks to monitor and analyse developments in domestic payment, clearing and settlement systems as well as in cross-border and multicurrency settlement schemes'. BIS, *Committee on Payment and Settlement Systems broadens its membership* (2009), available at <http://www.bis.org/press/p090724.htm> (last accessed 20 May 2015).

[122] See BIS, *CPSS-IOSCO working group on the review of the 'Recommendations for Central Counterparties'* (2009), available at <http://www.bis.org/press/p090720.htm> (last accessed 20 May 2015).

[123] G20, *Leaders' Statement: The Pittsburgh Summit—Statement No. 13* (2009), available at <http://www.ft.com/cms/s/0/5378959c-aa1d-11de-a3ce-00144feabdc0.html#axzz3afz2e2Q0> (last accessed 20 May 2015).

[124] IOSCO Executive Committee, *Report on Trading of OTC Derivatives* (2011), at 2.

prepared by the OTCWG were incorporated into a report, and later submitted to the G20 finance ministers and central bank governors in October 2010 in a Financial Stability Board Report.[125]

The OTCWG was quickly followed by the Task Force on OTC Derivatives Regulation. This was established in October 2010 and sought to develop international standards concerning OTC regulation for clearing, trading, trade data collection and reporting, and the oversight of market players, coordinate other international initiatives concerning the regulation of OTC, and serve as an internal IOSCO forum that IOSCO members can consult when dealing with issues concerning OTC regulation.[126] The task force is led by the SEC, the US CFTC, the UK FSA, and the Securities and Exchange Board of India;[127] but ESMA, the European Commission, the CPSS, and the OTC Derivatives Supervisors Group have a formal right to appoint observers to the Task Force.

Thus, what seems to be clear regarding the role of the EU in IOSCO, and in the international financial regulatory arena in general, is the increasing role of the EU Institutions. Importantly, this increasing role has the same legal features characterizing international financial law and IOSCO standards: it is soft, in other words *legally informal*. Indeed, IOSCO's standards are non-binding in so far as any EU external action in the financial services domain is not supported by hard legal grounds. All this leads one to assume that the EU is very likely to play an increasingly prominent role in the global financial landscape, and it will be helped in doing so by the soft law dimension in which it operates and by the new general external powers granted by the Lisbon Treaty.

4. Penetration of IOSCO Normative Production into EU Law: The MiFID as a Case Study

To prove the increasing 'transnational' regulatory power of the EU, a case study on EU legislation, the 2004 Markets in Financial Instruments Directive,[128] will be helpful. It is not groundless, indeed, to infer that IOSCO soft law normative production has influenced EU regulation even on contractual relationships between investment firms and their clients, at least at a philosophical level: consider contractual clauses related to market practices and their transformation into public regulatory measures used for public supervision.

Throughout the 1990s and the early 2000s, IOSCO had been publishing several documents covering key points of the contractual relationships between

[125] Ibid., at 2. See also FSB, *Implementing OTC Derivatives Market Reform* (2010), available at <http://www.financialstabilityboard.org/publications/r_101025.pdf> (last accessed 20 May 2015).

[126] IOSCO, *IOSCO forms Task Force on OTC Derivatives Regulation* (2010), at 2.

[127] Ibid., at 3.

[128] Directive 2004/39, OJ 2004 L 145/1. As emended in 2008 by Directive 2008/10, OJ 2008 L 76/33.

investment firms and their clients and public enforcement practices. In particular, the following four documents are relevant:

- The 1990 Resolution on International Conduct of Business Principles:[129] concerning general principles such as honesty, fairness, diligence, and firm–client information exchange, and committing 'IOSCO members to implement the principles through their regulatory structures and effective supervisory arrangements'.
- The 1994 Operational and Financial Risk Management Control Mechanisms for Over-the-Counter Derivatives Activities of Regulated Securities Firms:[130] one the very first IOSCO documents mentioning 'suitability' in an appendix dedicated to the role of regulators. Public supervisory authorities are invited to make 'inquiries into the existence of management controls (or representations as to their existence) relevant to so-called "suitability," [and] "know your customer"'.
- The 1997 Principles for the Supervision of Operators of Collective Investment Schemes:[131] stating that a market operator must execute a transaction as soon as it is 'reasonably practicable' and 'on terms that were the best available'. The document then reads that supervision should try 'to establish how an operator satisfies itself that its business is conducted at best execution,' and 'to confirm that the services' subject to particular fees are performed 'for the benefit of' a Collective Investment Scheme (CIS), 'have been disclosed to investors, and that transactions carried out are done in accordance with best execution standards'. Thus, IOSCO suggested that a contractual rule concerning the operator–CIS relationship should be used as a supervisory canon.
- Last but not least, the 2001 Transparency and Market Fragmentation Report:[132] focused on trading venue transparency. Regulators were asked to develop regulatory principles on transparency to be applied to different trading methods, by considering the diverse requirements related to different trading venues where the same instrument can be traded. The document highlights the importance of the role played by (public) regulators in assessing the appropriate level of transparency (both pre- and post-trade) in any trading venues.[133]

[129] IOSCO, *A Resolution on International Conduct of Business Principles* (1990), available at <http://www.iosco.org/library/resolutions/pdf/IOSCORES4.pdf> (last accessed 20 May 2015).

[130] IOSCO, *Operational and Financial Risk Management Control Mechanisms for Over-the-Counter Derivatives Activities of Regulated Securities Firms* (1994), available at <http://www.iosco.org/library/pubdocs/pdf/IOSCOPD35.pdf> (last accessed 20 May 2015).

[131] IOSCO, *Principles for the Supervision of Operators of Collective Investment Schemes* (1997), available at <http://www.iosco.org/library/pubdocs/pdf/IOSCOPD69.pdf> (last accessed 20 May 2015).

[132] IOSCO, *Transparency and Market Fragmentation* (2001), available at <http://www.iosco.org/library/pubdocs/pdf/IOSCOPD124.pdf> (last accessed 20 May 2015).

[133] The document recalls a 1992 report named 'Transparency on Secondary Markets: A Synthesis of the IOSCO Debate' and focused on transparency issues for secondary markets against the background of order-driven and quote-driven markets, available at <https://www.iosco.org/library/pubdocs/pdf/IOSCOPD27.pdf> (last accessed 17 October 2015).

Interestingly, all these aspects were further on developed by the 2004 Markets in Financial Instruments Directive,[134] the so-called MiFID I, so that the regulatory philosophy they convey seems to be transposed into this directive. MiFID I was intended to mark a sea change in the EU law of financial markets which they had been expecting for long time. Much broader than its predecessor, MiFID I replaced the Investment Services Directive 93/22/EEC (ISD)[135] with the key aim of boosting market integration in Europe,[136] create a level playing field for market players and, thus, a more competitive cross-border securities market[137] with reduced costs of capital raising.[138]

MiFID I was adopted as the most important step of the Financial Services Action Plan,[139] in a regulatory époque focused on opening up markets through competition and releasing free-market forces.[140] Within this framework, the regulation of the investor–firm relationship is an important element, even though consumer protection was 'certainly not at the heart of this Directive'.[141] The MiFID I was, indeed, based on the 'right of establishment'.

The key issues touching upon or directly dealing with the contractual relationship between firms and their clients regulated by the MiFID I were:

- *Investment services and activities*: definition of the services investment firms can be authorized to provide. On the basis of the investor–firm contractual relationship, a service can be classified as advisory-based (portfolio management and investment advice), non-advisory-based (all other services), or execution-only (reception and transmission of orders and execution of orders).[142]
- *Suitability and appropriateness*: the existence of an information asymmetry between the customer and the service provider hampers the correct functioning

[134] Directive 2004/39, OJ 2004 L 145/1. As emended in 2008 by Directive 2008/10, OJ 2008 L 76/33.

[135] Directive 93/22, OJ 1993 L 141/27.

[136] J.-P. Casey and K. Lannoo, *The Mifid Revolution* (2009), at 45, quoting P. Beres, Chair of the Economic and Monetary Affairs Committee; European Parliament, *European Commission's Public Hearing on Non-Equities Markets Transparency*, 11 September 2007.

[137] Haas, 'The Markets in Financial Instruments Directive: Banking on Market and Supervisory Efficiency', IMF Working Paper 2007/250, at 5.

[138] M. Chlistalla, U. Schweickert, and R. Wittner, 'Markets in Financial Instruments Directive—The Way Forward in European Securities Market Integration?' (2006), at 2; available at SSRN: <http://ssrn.com/abstract=964492>.

[139] European Commission, *Financial Services: Implementing the Framework for Financial Markets: Action Plan*, 11 May 1999, available at <http://ec.europa.eu/internal_market/finances/docs/actionplan/index/action_en.pdf> (last accessed 20 May 2015).

[140] Micklitz highlights this trend by writing that: 'The EC initiatives have in common that the European Commission intends to open up markets in order to create and enhance European-wide competition between national suppliers.' H.-W. Micklitz, *Service Standards: Defining the Core Consumer Elements and their Minimum Requirements*, Study Commissioned by ANEC, the European Voice in Standardisation (2007), at 26; available at <http://www.anec.eu/attachments/anec-r&t-2006-serv-004final.pdf> (last accessed 20 May 2015).

[141] Micklitz, 'The Targeted Full Harmonisation Approach: Looking Behind the Curtain', in R. Schulze and G. Howells (eds), *Modernising and Harmonising Consumer Contract Law* (2009) 47.

[142] Casey and Lannoo, *supra* note 136, at 48.

of financial markets.[143] To tame the effects of this asymmetry, MiFID envisages an exchange of information between clients (concerning their needs) and their investment firms (concerning the characteristics of the services/products provided). Such an information flow formalizes through so-called suitability and appropriate tests,[144] taking place before a service/product is provided, in order for the service/product to be the one that best suits a customer's needs. Both tests are designed as interviews: the suitability test, mandatory only for advisory-based services, is focused on a client's financial knowledge, experience, financial situation, and goals, whereas the appropriateness test, based on a client's financial knowledge and expertise,[145] applies to all other services (apart from the execution-only services on non-complex instruments).[146]

- *Best execution*: requiring investment firms to act in a way that, when executing orders, the best possible result for their customer is ensured. Firms must take all 'reasonable steps to obtain . . . the best possible result for their clients taking into account'[147] several elements. It is, thus, a regulated obligation stemming from the contractual firm–client relationship.
- *Client categorization*: MiFID combines mandatory disclosure[148] with information exchange and it sets forth three categories of clients (retail, professional, and eligible counterparties) by tailoring the level of investor protection around the sophistication of the customer: the lower the sophistication, the higher the level of protection.

MiFID relies heavily on public rather than private enforcement through business and consumer organizations. A confirmation of this public-friendly approach is given by the fact that while Article 52(2) of the MiFID offers a 'rather cryptic provision on collective enforcement'[149] without offering a strong position for stakeholders, the role of supervisory administrative bodies is clarified and reinforced by Articles 48 to 51.

Articles 48 and 49 provide that each Member State must designate one public authority to carry out the supervisory duties,[150] and the very same competent

[143] On the issue of information asymmetry and conflicts of interests see Casey and Lannoo, *supra* note 136, at 91–92.

[144] Directive 2004/39, OJ 2004 L 145/1.

[145] Casey and Lannoo, *supra* note 136, at 48.

[146] Art. 19(6) Directive 2004/39, OJ 2004 L 145/1.

[147] Art. 21 Directive 2004/39, OJ 2004 L 145/1. In particular, Art. 21 lists the elements of the best execution duty: 'price, costs, speed, likelihood of execution and settlement, size, nature or any other consideration relevant to the execution of the order'.

[148] The role played by disclosure has been nicely depicted by Niamh Moloney: 'Disclosure, with its "self-help" connotations, is strongly associated with the empowerment model. It forms a central element of current retail market policy internationally, reflecting the ingrained assumption that disclosure can support better decision-making and stronger market-based saving'; N. Moloney, *How to Protect Investors: Lessons from the EC and the UK* (2010) 288.

[149] Cafaggi and Micklitz, 'Administrative and Judicial Collective Enforcement of Consumer Law in the US and the European Community', EUI Working Paper LAW 2007/22, at 37.

[150] A potential delegation of powers to privately-run organizations is allowed, however this must be done in a way that it does not 'involve either the exercise of public authority or the use of discretionary powers of judgement' (Art. 48(2)).

authorities are to 'exchange any information which is essential or relevant to the exercise of their functions and duties'.[151] Articles 50 and 51 attempt to harmonize domestic administrative laws by providing a whole range of supervisory, investigatory, and sanctioning powers that must be made available to competent authorities.[152]

In other words, on the one hand, MiFID I directly provides for rules shaping the contractual relationship between investment firms and their clients; on the other, it grants public supervisory authorities the necessary powers to check compliance with regulatory contractual rules. Thus, a breach of these regulatory contractual rules may result in both civil and administrative liability.

It is quite evident how close IOSCO normative production is to key elements of MiFID I. However, it is very hard to believe the then practically powerless Committee of European Securities Regulators—the predecessor of the European Securities Markets Authority—had the chance to lobby the IOSCO Technical Committee. Neither is the European Commission likely to have been involved, since it became a mere Affiliate Member only in 2009.[153] Thus, it is quite easy to conclude that, at least when it comes to MiFID I, IOSCO normative production pushed the EU law-maker in a clear direction.

The same seems to hold true for the 2014 MiFID II and the most recent IOSCO's position documents. MiFID II is a post-sub-prime and post-Eurozone crises piece of legislation, focused on what the EU law-maker thought the EU needed to secure the stability of its home financial system. Even if the aim remains unchanged, MiFID II is much larger and more far-reaching than MiFID I.[154] Taking into account what had occurred in financial markets during that time, the increasing role of the EU in the international regulatory arena, and the increased sophistication of EU law of financial markets, it is quite easy to hypothesize that the content of MiFID II was affected by the synergistic exchange between IOSCO and the EU focused, at least, on the regulatory trend affecting the contractual relationship between an investment provider and its clients. Some important changes introduced by MiFID II on the suitability test and the execution-only services clearly reflect this.

MiFID II digs deeper into the single features of the suitability test and its disclosure-related obligations. It now openly requires investment firms to consider the client's ability to bear losses when assessing the suitability of an advised product and ensure that when a package of services or products is being recommended, the overall bundled package is suitable. More importantly, a suitability statement—meant to raise contractual liability—is to be disclosed and handed over to a customer before the transaction is made. The trend is clear: entailing an account of the

[151] Directive 2004/39, OJ 2004 L 145/1.

[152] These include, for instance, the power to access to any document in any form whatsoever, and to obtain copies thereof. Directive 2004/39, OJ 2004 L 145/1.

[153] IOSCO, *Final Update—34th Annual Conference of the International Organization of Securities Commissions* (2009), available at <http://www.iosco.org/library/statements/pdf/statements-6.pdf> (last accessed 20 May 2015).

[154] MiFID II is, actually, a package legislation made up of a Directive and a Regulation (MIFIR).

details making up the suitability requirement—a key aspect of the client-provider fiduciary relationship—through public regulation instead of leaving the issue at contractual level.

Crucially, MiFID II severely reduces the leeway of the provision of execution-only services by decreasing the number of instruments that can be considered as non-complex. Article 19(6) of MiFID I simply listed several 'non-complex' financial instruments, with Article 38 of the implementing directive listing the criteria—for instance, liquidity and public availability of information—available to evaluate whether an instrument not mentioned by Article 19(6) could be considered as 'non-complex'.

Article 25 of MiFID II significantly squeezes the amount of financial instruments considered as 'non-complex' through the introduction of a 'psychological' aspect: Those instruments embedding a derivative or incorporating a structure which makes it difficult for a customer to understand the risk involved must be considered to be complex. The reasons why the European law-maker has paid so much attention to the issue of complexity was clarified by ESMA at the beginning of 2014 with its seminal opinion on complex products,[155] in which it highlighted how, due to a combination of market factors,[156] investment firms had recently shifted towards more sophisticated investment strategies and products—allegedly leading to higher yields—and were offering them to retail clients, often through complex investment products.

Even if characterized by a broader approach, the following recent IOSCO documents share key features with MiFID II:

- The January 2013 Suitability Requirements with respect to the Distribution of Complex Financial Products,[157] stating key principles on suitability requirements for complex products distribution, with the following points further developed by MiFID II: the inconvenience of selling complex products to retail customers, and the need for firms to establish a client classification system to avoid a product–customer mismatching; the necessity of a detailed disclosure of the product advised and/or the services provided in connection with a complex product; and the need to take into account the client's capacity for losses. Moreover, particular attention is paid to the supervisory role of public enforcers.
- The December 2013 Regulation of Retail Structured Products:[158] a very developed, detailed piece of soft-law depicting regulatory options for products

[155] European Securities and Markets Authority (ESMA), *Opinion on MiFID Practices for Firms Selling Complex Products* (2014), available at <http://www.esma.europa.eu/system/files/ipisc_complex_products_-_opinion_20140105.pdf> (last accessed 20 May 2015).

[156] ESMA specifies that such market factors are: (i) low returns from the traditional forms of investments or ordinary deposits, and (ii) markets volatility; ibid.

[157] IOSCO, *Suitability Requirements with Respect to the Distribution of Complex Financial Products* (2013), available at <http://www.iosco.org/library/pubdocs/pdf/IOSCOPD400.pdf> (last accessed 20 May 2015).

[158] IOSCO, *Regulation of Retail Structured Products* (2013), available at <http://www.iosco.org/library/pubdocs/pdf/IOSCOPD434.pdf> (last accessed 20 May 2015).

> always considered to be complex.[159] It provides a broad picture of the phenomenon by trying to harmonize the potential regulatory approaches worldwide. It looks at the design and issuing of such products; their disclosure, marketing, and distribution; and, even, the regulation of post-sales practices. Suitability, which goes hand-in-hand with disclosure, is a main concern, so that local regulations should take into account 'tolerance for capital loss' as an element in determining whether a product is suitable or not.

MiFID II is a considerable piece of legislation and it digs much, much deeper into details compared to IOSCO soft law documents. The level of sophistication is definitely incomparable. However, a common leitmotiv can be easily tracked, to the point that it can be deduced that MiFID II works as the European detailed version of a transnational regulatory trend focused on curbing the offering of contractual-based financial products at retail level through public regulation.

5. Conclusion

At the end of this chapter, the answer to the question 'is there a greater role for Europe to play in the transnational financial regulatory arena' must be 'yes'. Indeed, the European Union has already started playing an increasingly pronounced role in determining rules for transnational financial markets and it has done so not so much as a proper state-like agent, but as a hybrid actor, able progressively to replace its (traditional) Member States in the global regulatory battlefield where soft rules are produced. This trend is corroborated by the very recent appointment of a senior official of the European Commission as the new IOSCO Secretary General. Thus, even in the light of the 'soft law leeway' granted by the CJEU case law, it is highly likely that the years to come will see the EU assuming a leading international role as regards the production international financial standards.

[159] IOSCO, *supra* note 157, at 6.

10

The External Dimension of EU Consumer Law

Jules Stuyck and Mateja Durovic

1. Introduction

European Union consumer law has developed enormously, especially over the last 20 years[1] and today it remains by far the most important part of European private law.[2] It should not be surprising, therefore, that consumer law is the area of EU private law that has most influenced non-European legal systems. There is another reason for this, however: EU consumer protection represents the most developed global system of consumer protection in the world.[3]

The well-established and comparatively strict EU rules on consumer protection undoubtedly constitute non-tariff barriers for cross-border trade between the EU and its trade partners.[4] This is why bridging differences in consumer protection is an important objective of the EU in negotiations of trade and other agreements with third countries. Often the EU requires alignment of third countries with its regulatory model of consumer protection, thus maintaining its own high level of consumer protection but also facilitating cross-border trade. This is in line with the EU's constitutional requirement that all Union policies, including its trade policy, ensure a high level of consumer protection as required by Article 38 of the Charter of Fundamental Right of the European Union.

Consumer law is not the only branch of European regulatory private law that may be subject to external action, be it regulatory cooperation, mutual recognition, or just 'export' of rules. As the case law on the internal market freedoms within the EU has shown, however, regulations to protect consumers can form serious trade barriers. Convergence of consumer protection laws, ensuring a minimum level of harmonization, is an important tool in removing these obstacles. As consumer law

[1] See, for example, J. Stuyck, *1993—Twenty Years Later. The Evolution of Consumer Law in the European Union* (2013).

[2] C. Twigg-Flesner, *The Europeanization of Contract Law* (2nd edn, 2013).

[3] For a recent comprehensive but concise overview of EU consumer law see: H.-W. Micklitz *et al.*, *European Consumer Law* (2nd edn, 2014).

[4] Krstic, 'Regulatory Cooperation to Remove Non-Tariff Barriers to Trade in Products: Key Challenges and Opportunities for the Canada-EU Comprehensive Trade Agreement', 39 *Legal Issues of Economic Integration* (2012) 3.

is both an aspect of (regulatory) private law and of the internal market programme, the external action of the Union in the field of consumer protection is a good example of the Union's external action. In the field of consumer protection, this has an important export dimension: the Union exports its consumer law to countries that, for one reason or another, are forced or inclined to align their consumer law with that of the EU.

The extent to which EU consumer law has been exported is exceptional and is not an example for regulatory law in general. In other fields of the law, the EU has not been so successful at this. Notably in relation to (the export of) competition law, the US has an historic advantage over the EU, and private law in general at the global level is fundamentally divided according to large legal families that also co-exist in the EU (EU consumer law remaining the most important branch of private law that is, to a large extent, harmonized at the EU level). The export success of EU consumer law is certainly closely linked to trade obstacles. Removing such obstacles is the most important aim of the EU's external action in the field of consumer protection.

This chapter will show that within the agreements that the EU has concluded or is negotiating with third countries there is a tension between removing obstacles to trade and maintaining a high level of consumer protection. While the EU can (try to) impose its standard on countries that wish to accede to the Union or to benefit from certain advantages (through various forms of association or other agreements) in negotiations with important trading partners, especially the US, Europe is faced with the question whether it can maintain, in all circumstances, its level of consumer protection in cross-border trade.

The intense external activity of the Union in the field of consumer protection contrasts with the absence of a clear competence in this area. In the next section of this chapter, we will address the Union's external competence in the field of private law and, in particular, in consumer law. In the third section of the chapter, the Union's external action in this field will be examined. It will be shown that the EU's export of its consumer protection policy affects consumer law in countries with very different legal systems and traditions. This phenomenon takes place largely via various types of forms of international agreements concluded between the EU and with third countries. Rules of private international law play an important role in consumer law, but they will be omitted from our discussion because they are dealt with elsewhere in the present book.

2. The External Competence of the EU in the Field of Consumer Law

A. Introduction

The EU is in the process of and has already concluded a wide range of agreements containing consumer law provisions with a number of countries. In doing so, the Union may pursue various objectives. An obvious one, especially in pre-accession association agreements, is to help future Member States and associate members align their consumer legislation with that of the Union as an element of the Union's internal market policy. Another less intrusive approach is the desire to organize regulatory cooperation with third countries as an element of trade liberalization. Other objectives may be linked to multilateral or bilateral agreements, such as disseminating values and regulatory regimes. The example of the Western Balkans, discussed in section 3, shows that several reasons may co-exist.

It is the common commercial policy (CCP) that enables the EU to conclude economic agreements with third countries. The CCP is an exclusive Union competence (Article 207 TFEU) and can be the basis for setting product standards and licensing conditions for importers to and exporters from the EU. External aspects of consumer contract law may or may not belong to the CCP. When it comes to consumer private law, the Treaty on the Functioning of the European Union (TFEU) does not provide for any specific external powers of the Union.

The EU has, however, concluded association and cooperation agreements with certain third countries. These third countries have, to varying degrees, unilaterally undertaken to align their consumer legislation with that of the Union.

There is no express basis in the TFEU for agreements on common standards of consumer protection. One must ask, therefore, whether the Union has an external competence based on internal market powers (so called implied powers) in consumer law. In order to answer this question, it is necessary first to look at the Treaty's provisions on internal and external powers, keeping in mind that the basic principle is one of conferral: the Union shall only act within the limits of the competences conferred upon it (Article 5(2) TFEU).

B. The Treaty System of Powers

1. Union Competence: Articles 3 and 4 TFEU

The Lisbon Treaty (2009) introduced clear provisions on the Union's powers, largely codifying the CJEU's case law on the basis of the EC Treaty.

Articles 3 TFEU confers exclusive competence on the Union in a limited number of areas, including the customs union, the establishment of the competition rules necessary for the functioning of the internal market, and the CCP. Pursuant to Article 3(2), the EU also has exclusive competence for the conclusion of an international agreement when its conclusion is provided for in a legislative act of the Union or it is necessary to enable the Union to exercise its internal competence, or in so far as its conclusion may affect common rules or alter their scope. Thus, a shared competence may become an exclusive Union competence through pre-emption as a result of the adoption of EU action (the *Lugano* Opinion).[5]

Article 4 relates to competences shared between the Union and the Member States in a large number of areas including the internal market, social policy, and

[5] Opinion 1/03, *Lugano Convention*, [2006] ECR I-1145.

consumer protection. Certain shared competences, such as development cooperation, humanitarian aid, technological development, are not subject to pre-emption (see Article 4(3) and (4)).

2. *Express External Powers*

The TFEU contains a certain number of express provisions relating to external powers. First and foremost, the Union has an exclusive competence in the field of the CCP (Article 207 TFEU). Since the advent of the Lisbon Treaty, the CCP expressly includes services. External powers are also vested in the Union in the areas of development cooperation, association agreements, research and development, and the environment. The Union also fosters cooperation with third countries and international organizations in education (Article 165(3) TFEU), vocational training (Article 166(3) TFEU), culture (Article 167(3) TFEU), public health (Article 168(3)), and social policy (Article 153 TFEU).[6] A similar or comparable provision does not appear in the title on consumer protection (XV Part III).

Association agreements concluded by the EU typically include arrangements on consumer protection (see section 3 below). Pursuant to Article 217 TFEU, the Union may conclude an association agreement with one or more third countries or international organizations in order to establish an association involving reciprocal rights and obligations, common actions, and special procedures. Association agreements (especially those preparing for accession) very often contain provisions on consumer protection. In *Demirel*,[7] the CJEU said that the Union has the power within an association agreement to 'guarantee commitments towards non-member countries in all the fields covered by the Treaties'.[8] Today this includes consumer law.

3. *Internal Market*

One of the major objectives of the Treaties is the establishment of an internal market (Article 3(3) TEU). The Union shall adopt measures with the aim of establishing or ensuring the functioning of the internal market (Article 26(1) TFEU). The internal market comprises an area without internal frontiers in which the free movement of goods, persons, services, and capital is ensured (Article 26(2) TFEU).

Under Article 114(1) TFEU (on 'approximation of laws') the EU legislature shall adopt measures for the approximation of the provisions laid down by law, regulation, or administrative action in Member States which have as their object the establishment and functioning of the internal market. The scope of this provision is rather broad. In Case C-58/08 *Vodafone*,[9] regarding the Roaming Regulation, the Court held:

> 32. According to consistent case-law the object of measures adopted on the basis of Article 95(1) EC must genuinely be to improve the conditions for the establishment and

[6] Opinion 2/91, *ILO*, [1993] ECR I-01061.
[7] Case C-12/86, *Meryem Demirel v. Stadt Schwäbisch Gmünd*, [1987] ECR 3719, para. 9.
[8] See K. Lenaerts and P. Van Nuffel, *European Union Law* (3rd edn, 2011) 979.
[9] C-58/08, *Vodafone*, [2010] ECR I-4999.

functioning of the internal market...While a mere finding of disparities between national rules and the abstract risk of infringements of fundamental freedoms or distortion of competition is not sufficient to justify the choice of Article 95 EC as a legal basis, the Community legislature may have recourse to it in particular where there are differences between national rules which are such as to obstruct the fundamental freedoms and thus have a direct effect on the functioning of the internal market (Case C-380/03 Germany v Parliament and Council [2006] ECR I-11573, paragraph 37 and the case-law cited) or to cause significant distortions of competition (Case C-376/98 Germany v Parliament and Council [2000] ECR I-8419, paragraphs 84 and 106).

33. Recourse to that provision is also possible if the aim is to prevent the emergence of such obstacles to trade resulting from the divergent development of national laws. However, the emergence of such obstacles must be likely and the measure in question must be designed to prevent them (Germany v Parliament and Council, paragraph 38 and the case-law cited) ....

36. Moreover, provided that the conditions for recourse to Article 95 EC as a legal basis are fulfilled, the Community legislature cannot be prevented from relying on that legal basis on the ground that consumer protection is a decisive factor in the choices to be made (see, regarding public health protection, Germany v Parliament and Council, paragraph 88 ...).

Within the Treaty rules on the internal market, express reference to an external dimension is to be found regarding the customs union (part of the free movement of goods) and the free movement of capital (Articles 64(3), 65(4), and 31 TFEU). *A contrario*, it would seem that for the other internal market freedoms, external powers that do not fall within the ambit of the CCP can be construed on the basis of implied powers or Article 352 (see hereinafter). It should, however, be observed that the external dimension of many aspects of internal market freedoms, including services, now fall within the CCP. Implied powers, therefore, are less needed in this field.

4. *Residual Power: Article 352 TFEU*

Article 352(1) TFEU provides for a residual power. If action by the Union should prove necessary, within the framework of the policies defined in the Treaties, to attain one of the objectives set out in the Treaties, and the Treaties have not provided the necessary powers, the Council, acting unanimously on a proposal from the Commission and after obtaining the consent of the European Parliament, shall adopt the appropriate measures.

In view of the increased number of Union competences and the requirement of unanimity within the Council, the significance of this residuary legal basis is now considerably reduced.

5. *Implied External Powers*

The notion of implied powers has been developed by the CJEU and now finds expression, in particular as regards its external action, in Article 216(1) TFEU. Where the Treaty has not conferred express powers on the Union, the Court has recognized under certain conditions that a Union power, especially to conclude an international agreement, could be derived from an existing power (e.g. an internal power relating to the subject matter).

In the following situations, the CJEU has recognized the existence of implied powers:

- An external power can flow from internal measures where external power is necessary to ensure the effectiveness of the internal measures (Opinion 2/91 (ILO)), in particular where the international agreement could affect the internal rules or alter their scope;[10]
- An implied external power also exists where the conclusion of an agreement is necessary in order to achieve, within the framework of the Union's policies, one of the objectives referred to in the Treaties. An example may be found in the agreements with third countries on transfers of data between law enforcement bodies;
- Finally, where an internal power cannot be effectively exercised without involving third countries, the Union is entitled ipso facto to act externally, even if the first use made of the power is to conclude an international agreement.[11]

An example of implied powers in the area of private law (procedure) can be found in Opinion 1/03 on the Lugano Convention. This raises the question of to what extent the Union possesses implied powers within the meaning of Article 216(1) TFEU, in the field of private law, such as consumer law? With regard to the situation referred to in Article 216(1) TFEU, namely 'where the conclusion of an agreement is necessary in order to achieve, within the framework of the Union's policies, one of the objectives referred to in the Treaties', it may be remembered that the internal market is a very important objective of the Treaty. But when is the conclusion of an external agreement in this area necessary? As to the second situation, 'where it is provided for in a legally binding Union act', we are not aware of any act of the consumer *acquis* containing such a provision.

As to the last category, 'where the conclusion of an agreement is likely to affect common rules or alter their scope', one may perhaps think of consumer contract private international law. Directive 93/13/EEC on unfair contract terms, for example, provides in its Article 6(2) that Member States shall take the necessary measures to ensure that the consumer does not lose the protection granted by this directive by virtue of the choice of the law of a non-Member country as the law applicable to the contract if the latter has a close connection with the territory of the Member States. External action by the Union could probably render this provision more effective. In the absence of case law to that effect, it remains unclear to what extent implied powers could be construed in the area of consumer law, especially in the field of consumer contract law.

The lack of comprehensive or explicit Union powers to conclude international agreements in the field of consumer private law has not prevented it from 'exporting' its consumer law to third countries with which it has concluded association or cooperation agreements. This issue will be discussed next.

[10] See Case 22/70, *Commission v. Council (AETR/ERTA)*, [1971] ECR 263.

[11] See Opinion 1/76, [1977] ECR 741, and Opinion 1/94, *WTO* [1994] ECR I-5267.

3. The Impact of EU Consumer Law on Other Countries

A. The Reasons Behind the Impact

The impact of EU consumer law is not confined to the borders of the European Union and its 28 Member States, but it is possible to observe the influence of EU consumer law on a number of countries which are not members of the EU. These do not include only the countries which are geographically close to the EU, as is the case, for instance, with Turkey, but also distant countries like, for example, Vietnam. Quite naturally the question arises what is behind this broad tendency of acceptance of EU consumer law, or at least parts of it, in a legal system of a non-EU country. In that sense, three main reasons that lie behind the acceptance of the consumer *acquis* into the national legal systems of these countries may be identified.

First of all, countries have accepted the consumer *acquis* into their national legal systems as a necessary prerequisite for their progress in the integration process towards joining the EU. One of the main conditions of this process of integration is the alignment of the legal system of a country wanting to join the EU with EU law.[12] Consumer law as such represents an important element of EU law and hence a country willing to join EU has to accept it.

Second, EU consumer law is the most advanced system of consumer law in the world.[13] EU consumer law is, accordingly, used, either entirely or partially, as a model for designing consumer protection legislation by countries which decide to develop their own national legal systems of consumer protection.

Third, the existence of different requirements of consumer protection among different countries may typically represent an obstacle for international trade among countries.[14] This is why the EU, as one of the biggest economies in the world, may also require its trading partners to align their national consumer legislation with the appropriate European standards in order to facilitate and increase cross-border commercial relations.

It should, however, be observed that there is seldom one reason alone why EU consumer law was transplanted into the legal system of a country. Very often several reasons are intertwined. For instance, in the case of Western Balkan countries, these three reasons have each played an important role in the reception process. First, all these countries made clear their desire to join the EU, thus they are obliged to align their national laws with EU law. Second, having been part of a socialist legal tradition where consumer law as such did not exist, in the development of their regulatory regimes of consumer protection, EU consumer law has been used as an appropriate model for the design of their national legal frameworks. Finally,

[12] *European Council of Copenhagen of 21–22 June 1993: Conclusions of the Presidency*, SN 180/1/93 REV 1, at 13.

[13] See S. Weatherill, *EU Consumer Law and Policy* (2nd edn, 2013) 188.

[14] Grainger, 'Trade Facilitation: A Conceptual Review', 45 *Journal of World Trade* (2011) 39, at 53–54.

the EU has close economic relations with these countries, so it is in their interest that they have the same standards of consumer protection as the EU, in order to facilitate and improve trade relations.

B. Three Different Degrees of Impact

The impact of EU consumer law is not the same in every country it has affected. On the basis of the degree of impact of EU consumer law on foreign legal systems, it is possible to draw a distinction between three categories of countries. Each of these three groups will be examined in turn: a) countries which are part of the EU enlargement process and the European Economic Area–European Free Trade Area (EEA–EFTA) countries; b) countries benefiting from the European Neighbourhood Policy; and c) other countries that belong to neither of these two groups.

1. Countries Part of the EU Enlargement Process (Candidate and Potential Candidate Countries) and EEA–EFTA Countries

The impact of EU consumer law has the strongest impact on the domestic legal system of countries in the first group. This is a result of the fact that these countries, as part of their European integration processes or as an obligation derived from an international treaty, are obliged to harmonize their national legal systems with EU law, including EU consumer law. This obligation is formalized explicitly, in the area of consumer legislation, in specific provisions of the association agreements that the EU has signed with these countries as part of their accession process: association agreements (Turkey), or the stabilization and association agreements (Western Balkan countries), or as part of the extensive integration into the EU's internal market envisaged by the EEA Agreement (Norway, Iceland, and Liechtenstein).

2. Countries within the European Neighbourhood Policy

This group includes countries which are geographically close to the EU and with which the EU has close political and commercial relations. None of these countries is officially a party to the EU enlargement process. In this second group of countries the impact of EU consumer law seems to be less strong than in the first. Provisions on consumer protection can be found in the different forms of agreements that the EU has concluded with these countries. Those are primarily the association agreements that these countries have signed with the EU in the context of development and liberalization of political and trade relations. However, as will be seen, consumer protection requirements contained in these agreements are heterogeneous.

3. Other Countries

EU consumer law has also influenced the consumer law of countries which are neither party to the enlargement process nor to the European Neighbourhood Policy.

In these countries, European standards of consumer protection may exert influence through the different forms of free trade agreements that they conclude with the European Union (e.g. South Korea), or through diverse law reform projects where the European regime of consumer protection is taken as the model (e.g. Fiji).

C. Consequences of the Particularities of EU Consumer Law on its Impact on Third Countries

A question that can be raised in relation to the impact of EU Consumer Law is its suitability for export, bearing in mind certain characteristics and the nature of EU consumer law, in particular its fragmentary character and the required level of harmonization. When it comes to the question of fragmentation, there is no such things as a European Consumer Code, but consumer protection-related provisions are developed through a dozen directives and regulations.[15] These instruments typically regulate only certain types of consumer contracts depending on their object (e.g. consumer credit), or the mode of their conclusion (e.g. distance contracts). The only two horizontal directives are Directive 2005/29/EC on unfair commercial practices and Directive 93/13/EEC on unfair contract terms.

Despite their fragmentation, however, these directives and regulations, when put together, provide a rather complete regulatory regime of consumer protection. For the missing parts, which have not been regulated by EU consumer law, the same consequence occurs as in the case of any EU Member State: a non-EU country accepts existing EU rules and it is supposed to develop new rules or apply its existing rules in the area which has not been regulated by EU consumer law. However, what may happen in practice, particularly where a country is simply attempting to align itself to the EU *acquis*, is that the country accepting EU consumer law does not develop the required set of correlated rules which would adequately complement the existing rules of EU consumer law. This lack of development of correlated national consumer protection rules may as a result lead to the diminished applicability or even a total inapplicability of EU consumer law as accepted in a particular country.[16]

The required level of harmonization also represents an important issue. At the beginning of the development of common European consumer policy, the prevailing approach was minimum harmonization, leaving countries the possibility of offering a higher level of protection than the minimum required by EU law. By contrast, in the last decade there has been a shift to full (or maximum) harmonization: the level of protection provided for by EU law is not only a minimum but also a maximum. So-called gold plating by Member States is not allowed.[17]

[15] See P. Letto-Vanamo, *Coherence and Fragmentation in European Private Law* (2012).

[16] Durovic 'EU Consumer Law Outside the European Union: The Case of Albania', 36 *Journal of Consumer Policy* (2013) 269.

[17] See Howells, 'European Consumer Law—The Minimal and Maximal Harmonisation Debate and Pro Independent Consumer Law Competence', in S. Grundmann and J. Stuyck (eds), *An Academic Green Paper on European Contract Law* (2002).

The proffered justification for the shift towards maximum harmonization is that minimum harmonization caused significant divergences which represent obstacles for cross-border trade, and thus for the development of the internal market.[18] Be that as it may, the shift towards maximum harmonization facilitates the exportation of EU consumer law into non-EU legal systems as it imposes clearer and more developed standards, thus facilitating the reception of EU consumer law by third countries.

D. Introduction of EU Consumer Law in Countries as Part of the EU Enlargement Process and Countries Party to the EEA Agreement

1. *Harmonization of Consumer Law as a Condition for EU Membership*

This category consists of countries which form part of the EU enlargement process, those that wish to become Member States of the EU and are officially party to the its enlargement process. For these countries, harmonization of their consumer legislation with the EU consumer *acquis* forms part of the general prerequisite of the harmonization of their national legal systems with EU law. Currently, this group consists of Turkey and the Western Balkan countries as potential candidate and candidate countries for EU membership.[19]

Countries seeking membership of the EU are obliged to fulfil all the conditions for EU membership which were defined by the European Council in 1993 held in Copenhagen (the Copenhagen criteria).[20] Consequently, the obligation for these countries to accept the consumer *acquis* and align their national legal system to EU law flows from the Copenhagen criteria.[21] The obligation to adapt to the consumer *acquis* is imposed very widely: it not only imposes a 'black letter' harmonization of consumer legislation, but also the setting up of an adequate institutional mechanism and enforcement and application of consumer law in practice.[22]

2. *Emphasis of the Obligation to Harmonize Consumer Legislation Fully*

The European Commission regularly reminds candidate countries that deploying their efforts to harmonize their domestic legislation with EU law, including EU consumer law, is a prerequisite for their accession. Every calendar year the European Commission issues its annual Progress Report in which the regulatory

[18] European Commission, *Explanatory Memorandum to the Proposal for a Directive on Unfair Commercial Practices*, COM (2003) 356 final, para. 49.

[19] See European Commission, *Communication to the European Parliament and the Council. Enlargement Strategies and Main Challenges 2013–2014*, COM (2013) 700 final.

[20] *European Council of Copenhagen: Conclusions of the Presidency, supra* note 12, at 13.

[21] A. F. Tatham, *Enlargement of the European Union* (2009), at 327–328.

[22] See Micklitz, 'The Law of the Western Balkan Countries in the Mirror of Consumer Law', in M. Karanikic, H. W. Micklitz, and N. Reich (eds), *Modernising Consumer Law—The Experience of the Western Balkans* (2012).

regime of consumer protection of candidate countries and the progress in this area are assessed, and future objectives are identified.[23]

In addition, the obligation for these countries to harmonize their national consumer legislation with EU consumer law, as derived from the Copenhagen criteria, is confirmed in the international agreements that these countries have signed with the EU as part of their process of European integration.[24] Moreover, in the EU negotiation process that each candidate country must undertake, consumer protection is, together with health issues, the subject of one chapter: 'Chapter 28: Consumer and Health Protection'.[25] That chapter can only be closed if sufficient progress has been made.

Importantly, the EU does not leave these countries to perform all required reforms of consumer legislation on their own; significant technical and financial assistance is available in particular through the EU Financial Instrument for Pre-Accession Assistance.[26] In the majority of candidate countries, consumer legislation as it stands now is the outcome of the projects supported by the EU.[27]

Within the group of candidate countries, it is also possible to make a distinction between countries on the basis of the EU's accession policy as well as the type of agreement the EU has concluded with these countries as part of the enlargement process. These differences have resulted in certain particularities of regulatory regime in the area of consumer protection. Accordingly, we may classify the candidate and potential candidate countries in two categories.

The first consists of Turkey, a country with a particularly long and complex relationship with Europe, past and present, with which the EU concluded one of the first association agreements in 1964. The second includes the Western Balkan countries, which are at different stages of the EU integration process and with which the EU has signed stabilization and association agreements.

[23] See, for example: European Commission, *Commission Staff Working Document. Albania 2013 Progress Report*, SWD (2013) 414 final, at 53 *et seq.*; European Commission, *Commission Staff Working Document. Bosnia and Herezegovina 2013 Progress Report*, SWD (2013) 415 final, at 30 *et seq.*; European Commission, *Commission Staff Working Document. Former Yugoslav Republic of Macedonia 2013 Progress Report*, SWD (2013) 413 final, at 54 *et seq.*; European Commission, *Commission Staff Working Document. Kosovo 2013 Progress Report*, SWD (2013) 416 final, at 28–29; European Commission, *Commission Staff Working Document. Montenegro 2013 Progress Report*, SWD (2013) 411 final, at 51–52; European Commission, *Commission Staff Working Document. Serbia 2013 Progress Report*, SWD (2013) 412 final, at 56–57; European Commission, *Commission Staff Working Document. Turkey 2013 Progress Report*, SWD (2013) 417 final, at 71–73.

[24] Art. 97 SAA: Consumer Protection (FYROM), OJ 2004 L84/13; Art. 76 SAA: Consumer Protection (Albania), OJ 2009 L107/166; Art. 78 SAA: Consumer Protection (Montenegro), OJ 2010 L108/3; Art. 78 SAA: Consumer Protection (Serbia), OJ 2010 L28/2; and Art. 76 SAA: Consumer Protection (Bosnia and Herzegovina); Art. 72 of the EEA Agreement (Iceland), OJ 1994 L 1/3.

[25] See, for example, European Commission, *Negotiating Framework with Iceland*, available at <http://ec.europa.eu/enlargement/pdf/iceland/st1222810_en.pdf> (last accessed 22 August 2015).

[26] Regulation 231/2014 of 11 March 2014 establishing an Instrument for Pre-accession Assistance (IPA II), OJ 2014 L77/11.

[27] The reform of consumer legislation and its alignment with EU law, for example, was or is currently performed through the IPA projects in Serbia, Montenegro, Kosovo, and FYROM.

3. *Turkey*

Turkey has a long and complex history of the European integration process. It started negotiations for EU membership in October 2005 and currently Chapter 28 on consumer and health protection is one of the open chapters in the negotiations process on which discussion is pending.

Turkey adopted its first law on consumer protection, No. 4077, in 1995. That was the first Turkish law with a specific set of consumer protection rules that derogate from those of the Civil Code. The main goal of this law was to align the legal regime of consumer protection in Turkey with that existing in the EU. From then on, consumer law in Turkey has developed under the EU's influence.[28]

Law No. 4077 of 1995 was subsequently modified and amended in 2003, again with the aim to remedy existing shortcomings and to adjust Turkish consumer law to the evolution of EU Law. Eventually, in the autumn of 2013, Turkey adopted its new Law on Consumer Protection No. 6502 which entered into force on 28 May 2014. This law shows a high level of alignment with EU consumer law.

4. *The Western Balkans Countries*

The countries of the Western Balkans include FYROM (former Yugoslav Republic of Macedonia),[29] Montenegro,[30] and Serbia.[31] These countries have the status of candidate countries for EU membership. Albania,[32] Bosnia and Herzegovina,[33] and Kosovo[34] have the status of potential candidate country. Croatia also belonged to this group of countries until it became the 28th Member State of the European Union on 1 July 2013. The Croatian success in becoming an EU Member State required hard work on the part of Croatian consumers.[35] Eventually, after the accession, Croatia adopted an entirely new law on consumer protection in 2014, fully aligned with EU law.[36]

[28] Akipek, 'The Developments in Turkish Consumer Protection Law and the Effects of EU Law on These Developments', in B. Akcay and S. Akipek (eds), *Turkey's Integration into European Union: Legal Dimension* (2013) 31.

[29] FYROM has not yet started the negotiations; information available at <http://ec.europa.eu/enlargement/countries/detailed-country-information/fyrom/index_en.htm> (last accessed 22 August 2015).

[30] Montenegro has progressed the most since the negotiations with the EU have officially started in 2012; see <http://ec.europa.eu/enlargement/countries/detailed-country-information/montenegro/index_en.htm> (last accessed 22 August 2015).

[31] Serbia officially started accession negotiation with the EU on 21 January 2014; see <http://ec.europa.eu/enlargement/countries/check-current-status/index_en.htm> (last accessed 22 August 2015).

[32] See <http://ec.europa.eu/enlargement/countries/detailed-country-information/albania/index_en.htm > (last accessed 22 August 2015).

[33] See <http://ec.europa.eu/enlargement/countries/detailed-country-information/bosnia-herzegovina/index_en.htm > (last accessed 22 August 2015).

[34] See <http://ec.europa.eu/enlargement/countries/detailed-country-information/kosovo/index_en.htm > (last accessed 22 August 2015).

[35] Josipovic, 'Enforcement Activity in Consumer Protection Regulation in Croatia', 36 *Journal of Consumer Policy* (2013) 287.

[36] *Law on Consumer Protection*, Official Gazette of Croatia No. 41/14.

The EU adopts a specific approach towards the enlargement process of the Western Balkans, through the conclusion with each of these states and territories of a Stabilization and Association Agreement (SAA). For consumer protection, the SAAs are relevant as they formalize and reaffirm the obligation of these countries, already envisaged by Copenhagen criteria, to align their national legal systems completely with EU law. In all the SAAs, requirements of consumer protection are underlined.

In an effort to align their national consumer law with EU consumer law and to develop a functional and efficient system of consumer protection, each of the Western Balkan countries has adopted several pieces of consumer protection legislation over the last two decades. This has led to a 'hyperinflation' of consumer laws. It has appeared so far difficult or even impossible to design a functional system for consumer protection. In these countries, the acceptance of the EU model of consumer law is seen as a mandatory prerequisite for further progress in the European integration process rather than as an opportunity to introduce a highly advanced regulatory regime of consumer protection in their national legal systems.[37]

The capacity of domestic legal systems to absorb EU consumer rules has generally not been satisfactory, and there is a chronic lack of enthusiasm by competent policy-makers to ensure the application of these rules in practice. One of the biggest shortcomings of consumer protection in these countries is a weak and underdeveloped consumer movement that lacks capacity, knowledge, and support; put simply, consumers do not know what rights they should have. This is why despite the fact that they follow the EU model, national consumer laws of the Western Balkan countries are characterized by 'mistransposition, slow or non-existent uptake, insufficient enforcement, and various sources of institutional non-or malfunctioning'.[38]

In the last couple of years, however, progress is noticeable. In the annual progress reports, the European Commission pointed out that development of consumer protection is noticeable in the majority of Western Balkan countries, but that there is still a need to strengthen institutional and non-governmental capacities for enforcement of consumer protection.

5. *EEA–EFTA States*

The powerful effect of EU consumer law on the legal system of non-EU Member States may also be observed in the case of three countries which are parties to the European Economic Area (EEA) Agreement. The EEA is an association between the twenty-eight Member States of the European Union and three members of the European Free Trade Association (EFTA), Iceland, Norway, and Lichtenstein.[39] Switzerland is the only EFTA member which is not a member of the EEA, although it has its own system of bilateral relations with the EU.

[37] Durovic *supra* note 16.
[38] Svetiev, 'How Consumer Law Travels', 36 *Journal of Consumer Policy* (2013) 209, at 228.
[39] Agreement on the European Economic Area (EEA), OJ 1994 L 1/3.

EFTA countries have a close relationship with the EU, in particular in the commercial field. However, for varying reasons they do not want to become members of the EU. The EEA Agreement, which entered into force on 1 January 1994, has tightened the relationship of the EU with Norway, Iceland, and Liechtenstein. The EEA provides inter alia, for free movement of goods, without constituting a customs union.[40] It emphasizes the requirements of consumer protection. Under the homogeneity principle, the EEA–EFTA states have to transpose EU consumer law into their national legal systems completely. Annex XIX on consumer protection is regularly updated and it provides for a list of all consumer protection Acts adopted at the European level. In addition to this, consumer protection was identified as one of the areas where further efforts on strengthening of the cooperation among the parties to the EEA Agreement are required.[41]

The EEA Agreement thus enables an immediate and automatic influence of EU consumer law in the EEA–EFTA countries, since these countries have to implement the measures adopted by the EU without participating as such in the legislative process. Representatives of EEA–EFTA countries may, however, participate in the drafting process of EU consumer legislation without having voting rights. Some time ago a need was identified for more involvement of EEA–EFTA countries in the area of consumer protection but there have been no results so far.[42]

As a consequence of being a party to the EEA Agreement, consumer laws of these countries have been significantly affected by EU consumer law.[43] In this, the EFTA court, with its seat in Luxembourg, has also played an important role. For instance, in *EFTA Surveillance Authority v. Iceland*,[44] the EFTA court found that by failing within the time limit prescribed to adopt the measures necessary to implement into its national legislation the Act referred to at point 7b of Annex XIX to the EEA Agreement (i.e. Directive 2008/122/EC on timeshare)[45] as adapted to the EEA Agreement by way of Protocol 1, Iceland has failed to fulfil its obligations pursuant to the EEA.

E. Consumer Law in the Countries that are Party to the European Neighbourhood Policy

1. *The European Neighbourhood Policy and Consumer Protection*

The second category of countries consists of EU neighbours to its east and south, the countries of Eastern Europe, Southern Caucasus, the Middle East, and North

[40] See J. Stuyck and A. Looijestijn-Clearie (eds), *The European Economic Area EC-EFTA—Institutional Aspects and Financial Services* (1994).

[41] Art. 78 of the EEA Agreement, OJ 1994 L 1/3.

[42] Joint Parliamentary Committee, 'Report on Consumer Issues in the EEA' (1999), M/20/R/019-PE 230.222, at 9.

[43] Arnason, 'The European Union Seen from the Top—The View of an Inside-Outsider', in J. Nergelius (ed.), *Nordic and Other European Constitutional Traditions* (2006) 39.

[44] EFTA Court Case E-16/13, *EFTA Surveillance Authority v. Iceland*, judgment of 6 December 2013.

[45] Directive 2008/122/EC on the protection of consumers in respect of certain aspects of timeshare, long-term holiday product, resale and exchange products, OJ 2009 L 33/10.

Africa, all of which comprise part of the common European Neighbourhood Policy (ENP). None of these countries is officially part of the enlargement process, although some have demonstrated their intention to become part of it (Moldova, Georgia, and recently Ukraine).

Despite the impossible or uncertain EU future of these countries, the European Union intends to establish a 'closer political association and progressive economic integration into the EU Internal Market' with them.[46] The ENP emerged in 2003, shortly before the accession of ten new Member States in 2004. The ENP is described as 'a very sophisticated policy which is promoting the use of a wide range of instruments for the realization of a large array of objectives'.[47] One of its main objectives is to share the benefits of EU enlargement, including those regarding consumer protection standards, with countries that are geographically close to the EU by cooperating with them with a 'significant measure of economic and political integration'.[48] Moreover, these countries have been offered the opportunity to take part in key aspects of EU policies and programmes.[49]

Consumer protection is considered to represent one of the 'core aspects' of the ENP policy.[50] In 2011, while revising its ENP policy objectives, the European Commission pointed out that enhanced cooperation with these countries shall take place for all aspects of the internal market, and expressly mentioned the issue of consumer protection.[51] Accordingly, EU consumer law and policy has materially affected and influenced the national legal systems and polices of the countries covered by the ENP policy.[52]

As a condition for 'enhanced political stability, security, sustainable economic development, shared prosperity, and more liberalized trade regimes, and resultant improved access to the European market, offered by the European Neighbourhood Policy', the EU expects these countries to harmonize their national legal regimes with EU consumer law.[53] This tendency is confirmed in the action plans signed between the EU and each of the ENP countries. Moreover, acting under the umbrella of the ENP and primarily through the provision of institutional and financial aid, the Commission supports the alignment of ENP countries' consumer laws with EU law.

[46] European Commission and High Representative of the European Union for Foreign Affairs and Security Policy, 'Joint Communication: A New Response to a Changing Neighbourhood: A Review of European Neighbourhood Policy', COM (2011) 303 final, at 2.

[47] M. Cremona and G. Meloni, 'The European Neighbourhood Policy: A Framework for Modernization?', EUI Working Paper LAW 2007/21, at 1.

[48] European Commission, 'Communication from the Commission—European Neighbourhood Policy—Strategy Paper', COM (2004) 373 final, at 5.

[49] Ibid., at 8.

[50] Tovias and Magen, 'Reflections from the New Near Outside: An Israeli Perspective on the Economic and Legal Impact of EU Enlargement', 10 *European Foreign Affairs Review* (2005) 399.

[51] European Commission and High Representative of the European Union, *supra* note 48, at 9–10.

[52] See R. Petrov and P. Van Elsuwege (eds), *Legislative Approximation and Application of EU Law in the Eastern Neighbourhood of the European Union: Towards a Common Regulatory Space?* (2014).

[53] Harpaz, 'When East Meets West: Approximation of laws in the EU–Mediterranean Context. EU–Mediterranean Policy', 43 *Common Market Law Review* (2006) 993.

The EU's financial, technical, and institutional assistance has been managed through the European Neighbourhood and Partnership Instrument (ENPI), replaced in 2014 by the European Neighbourhood Instrument (ENI). Particularly important are the 'twinning projects' provided by the EU to countries seeking to align their national legislation with EU law. Twinning projects are tools for cooperation between public administrations of EU Member States and the equivalent institution in a country covered by the ENP (or a candidate or potential candidate country). One of the main goals of the twinning projects is drafting laws according to EU law models.

Some of the projects deal with consumer legislation. This is the case, for instance, with the QUALEB Programme in Lebanon on the reform of Lebanese consumer legislation, or the twinning projects which took place in Moldova and Armenia. In Egypt, a twinning project between Egypt and three EU Member States—Germany, Spain, and France—was initiated in 2012. Accordingly, these three countries were expected to transfer their knowledge and experience in the field of consumer protection and to support the alignment of Egyptian consumer legislation with EU consumer law.[54]

2. *Eastern Partnership and Consumer Protection*

On its eastern borders, the EU completed negotiations with Georgia, Armenia, and Moldova on Deep and Comprehensive Free Trade Agreements (DCFTA) in 2013. This initiative represents a fundamentally important part of the SAAs with these countries. Eventually, on 27 June 2014, Moldova and Georgia, as well as Ukraine, signed SAAs including DCFTAs with the EU.[55]

In order to start negotiations with the EU on the DCFTA, Georgia had to undertake substantial reforms of key regulatory areas. It has been required to work on aligning its consumer legislation with EU law. In this regulatory reform process, the EU has helped via the ENPI and the Comprehensive Institution Building Programme. Individual Member States also helped; for example, the German development agency GIZ worked on the alignment of Georgian consumer legislation with EU consumer law.[56]

These new association agreements are aimed at strengthening political, economic, and trade relations between these countries and the EU. Accordingly, the necessity for further work on core consumer protection reforms is reaffirmed. Prior to the association agreements, partnership and cooperation agreements between the EU and Georgia, Moldova, and Ukraine also included a separate article on consumer

[54] See *Strengthening the Structures of Consumer Protection in Egypt and Reinforcing the Capacities of the Egyptian Consumer Protection Agency*, EG 10/ENP-AP/HE/15, available at <http://www.ee-aa.org.eg/EEAA/Gallery/List.aspx?Main=Gallery > (last accessed 22 August 2015).

[55] European Commission, *The EU's Association Agreements with Georgia, the Republic of Moldova and Ukraine*, MEMO/14/430 of 23 June 2014, available at <http://europa.eu/rapid/press-release_MEMO-14-430_en.htm?locale=en> (last accessed 22 August 2015).

[56] Information available at <https://www.giz.de/en/worldwide/20324.html> (last accessed 22 August 2015).

protection, providing for the alignment of the partner country's consumer protection law with EU law as well as the exchange of information in this area.[57]

The 2014 SAAs with Georgia, Moldova, and Ukraine pay particular attention to consumer protection. First, it is provided that 'the Parties shall cooperate in order to ensure a high level of consumer protection and to achieve compatibility between their systems of consumer protection'.[58] In order to achieve these objectives, the SAA provides that the cooperation may comprise, when appropriate: (a) the approximation of consumer legislation, while avoiding barriers to trade; (b) promoting exchange of information on consumer protection systems; (c) promoting training activities for administration officials and other consumer interest representatives; and (d) encouraging the development of independent consumer associations, and contacts between consumer representatives, as well as collaboration between authorities and non-governmental organizations (NGOs) in the field of consumer protection.[59]

3. *Partnership with Southern Mediterranean Countries and Consumer Protection*

There is also a marked intention of the European Union to conclude DCFTAs establishing an advanced stage of mutual commercial relations with its southern neighbouring countries. In that respect, the EU has commenced the negotiations with Morocco and it has given a mandate to the European Commission to start talks with Tunisia, Egypt, and Jordan. Alignment of consumer legislation of these countries with the EU's will represent an important element of the agreements to be concluded.

The existing Euro–Mediterranean Association Agreements already provide for cooperation in this field geared to making consumer protection schemes in the EU and the partner countries compatible, in order to eliminate barriers to trade, the establishment and development of systems of mutual information on dangerous food and industrial products and interconnecting these (rapid alert systems), exchanges of information and experts, and the organization of training schemes and supplying technical assistance.[60]

4. *Consumer Protection in the Action Plans*

The action plans with countries that are party to the ENP contain important consumer protection requirements for these countries. However, these requirements

[57] Art. 72 of Partnership and Cooperation Agreement with Moldova, OJ 1998 L 181.

[58] Art. 345 of the Association Agreement with Georgia, OJ 2014 L 261; Art. 38 of the Association Agreement with Moldova, OJ 2014 L 260; Art. 415 of the Association Agreement with Ukraine, OJ 2014 L161/3.

[59] Art. 346 of the Association Agreement with Georgia, OJ 2014 L 261; Art. 39 of the Association Agreement with Moldova, OJ 2014 L 260; Art. 416 of the Association Agreement with Ukraine, OJ 2014 L161/3.

[60] Art. 61 of Euro–Mediterranean Association Agreement with Egypt, OJ 2004 L 304/39.

differ per country. In the European Union–Palestinian Authority Action Plan, the requirements of consumer protection are identified as among 'other key areas'. Accordingly, this action plan refers to the need to improve the compatibility of consumer legislation in order to remove obstacles to trade, but also to maintain a high level of consumer protection, promotion of exchange of information among relevant stakeholders, and to encourage the development of independent consumer associations.[61]

The Action Plans in place between the EU and Morocco, Tunisia, and Jordan contain similar provisions, with some variations.[62] By contrast, the Action Plan with Israel only refers to promotion of cooperation in the field of consumer protection.[63]

F. EU Consumer Law in Third Countries

1. *Disparities in Consumer Protection Legislation as Non-Tariff Barriers to Trade*

For countries that remain outside both the enlargement process and the ENP, the impact of EU consumer law on domestic legal systems varies considerably. Overall, the effects are the most significant in the area of consumer safety. Two reasons may explain this. First, safety requirements are obstacles to trade and their removal is part of the CCP for which the Union has an express exclusive competence.[64] Second, the EU is particularly concerned that products originating from third countries meet European safety standards. The increased concern on the part of European policy-makers with respect to safety of consumers is in part a consequence of the crisis related to bovine spongiform encephalopathy (BSE) in the last decade of the twentieth century when the public accused the Commission of not reacting adequately.[65]

In addition, relevant regulatory requirements including consumer protection are among the biggest obstacles to the implementation of trade agreements and the facilitation of trade.[66] International trade agreements concluded by the EU also usually address and institutionalize a number of issues in addition to trade in the strict sense, including consumer protection. Through these agreements, the EU is also disseminating its values and the influence of its regulatory regimes.

The presence of differences in regulatory regimes of consumer protection may represent one of the biggest obstacles in negotiations of preferential trade agreements. Non-tariff barriers to trade (NTBs) include the requirements of consumer

[61] Action Plan with Palestinian Authority, OJ 2013 L 125/23.

[62] Action Plan with Morocco, OJ 2005 L 285/17; Action Plan with Tunisia, OJ 2005 C 327/29; Action Plan with Lebanon, at 28, Action Plan with Jordan, OJ 2005 L 228/29.

[63] Action Plan with Israel, OJ 2005 L 233/11.

[64] Art. 207 TFEU.

[65] Quintillan, 'Free Trade, Public Health Protection and Consumer Information in the European and WTO Context', 33 *Journal of World Trade* (1999) 147, at 150.

[66] Grainger, 'Trade Facilitation: A Conceptual Review', 45 *Journal of World Trade* (2011) 39, at 53–54.

protection and one of the goals of free trade agreements is to eliminate these obstacles. For instance, currently the removal of non-tariff barriers by Japan is an important element of EU–Japan negotiations on a free trade agreement.[67]

Dealing with the negative trade impacts of divergent regulatory cultures, and putting in place mechanisms to minimize and resolve trade disputes stemming from regulatory divergences, were identified as an increasingly important trade policy issue for the twenty-first century.[68] An example is Canada: the existence of significant differences between regulatory regimes of consumer protection caused significant burdens in negotiations of the free trade agreement, the Comprehensive Economic Trade Agreement (CETA), which was eventually agreed in 2013.[69] However, the CETA does not require alignment of regulatory frameworks of consumer protection between the EU and Canada. It has only established the possibility for the introduction of reciprocal information exchange in relation to the safety of consumer products and related preventive, restrictive, and corrective measures that have been taken.[70]

2. *EU Consumer Law as the Most Advanced Regulatory Regime of Consumer Protection*

The EU has supported the work on improvement of consumer protection legislation as part of its support of the economic development of some of the world's most underdeveloped and developing countries. These projects on economic development are based on the European model which puts an emphasis on policy objectives such as consumer protection and environmental protection. For instance, the EU led a project on strengthening consumer protection in Fiji, one of the countries which is the farthest from its borders.[71] Similarly, in Uganda, GIZ, representing Germany as one of EU Member States, worked on improving consumer protection particularly in the area of financial services.[72]

3. *Free Trade Agreement with South Korea*

KOREU (the EU–South Korea Free Trade Agreement) entered into force on 1 July 2011 and contains some provisions relevant to consumer protection.[73]

[67] European Commission, *First Round of EU-Japan Trade Talks a Success*, MEMO/13/348 of 19 April 2013.

[68] Hussey and Kenyon, 'Regulatory Divergence: A Barrier to Trade and a Potential Source of Trade Disputes', 65 *Australian Journal of International Affairs* (2011) 381, at 382.

[69] See Krstic, 'Regulatory Cooperation to Remove Non-tariff Barriers to Trade in Products: Key Challenges and Opportunities for the Canada–EU Comprehensive Trade Agreement', 39 *Legal Issues of Economic Integration* (2012) 3.

[70] Art. X7 of the CETA.

[71] See EU project 'Strengthening Consumer Rights in Fiji through Advocacy and Enforcement of Consumer Protection Laws', information available at <http://www.consumersfiji.org/donor-funded/european-union-funded-project> (last accessed 22 August 2015).

[72] See GIZ project 'Financial System Development', information available at <http://www.giz.de/en/worldwide/19361.html> (last accessed 22 August 2015).

[73] Free Trade Agreement between the European Union and South Korea, OJ 2011 L 127/6.

In particular, what has been envisaged is the protection of consumers against certain forms of misleading commercial practices in the context of geographical origin of a product.[74] In addition to this, the KOREU has established a basis for regulatory dialogue in relation to consumer protection in e-commerce and transparency in relation to consumer protection standards.[75]

4. *Consumer Protection in the Free Trade Agreement with the US*

Intense negotiations between the EU and the US on a free trade agreement continue, and consumer protection represents one of the most sensitive topics. What seems to be particularly notable is the fear expressed by consumer groups that the conclusion of the free trade agreement will eventually lead to a decrease in the general level of consumer protection in Europe.

On 23 October 2012, the European Parliament adopted a non-legislative resolution in which it called for the start of negotiations on a free trade agreement between the EU and USA, but it pressed the promotion of the interests of the EU in these negotiations in particular areas, including consumer protection.[76] Negotiations between the EU and the US on the Transatlantic Trade and Investment Partnership (TTIP) started in July 2013. Reducing non-tariff regulatory barriers is described as 'the key part of trans-Atlantic trade liberalization'.[77]

Concerns about the potential negative impact on the regulatory regime of consumer protection in Europe have reached the highest political level. During the round of negotiations which took place in March 2014, President Obama pointed out: 'I have fought my entire political career and as president to strengthen consumer protections. I have no intention of signing legislation that would weaken those protections.'[78]

It remains to be seen how the final text of the agreement between the US and EU will affect the systems of consumer protection of both sides as each adopts a very different approach towards this matter. American legal scholarship can show a rather critical attitude vis-à-vis EU consumer law and its basic concepts. The four main regulatory techniques of EU consumer law (the binding character of its provisions, the imposition of a duty to inform, the consumer's right of withdrawal, and the rules relating to consumer contracts) are sometimes described as 'ineffective, and perhaps worse—inefficient and harmful to consumers'.[79]

[74] Art. 10.21 of the Free Trade Agreement between the European Union and South Korea, OJ 2011 L 127/6.

[75] Art. 7.49(1)(d) and Art. 7.22(1) of the Free Trade Agreement between the European Union and South Korea, OJ 2011 L127/6.

[76] European Parliament, *Resolution of 23 October 2012 on Trade and Economic Relations with the United States*, 2012/2149(INI).

[77] European Commission, *Independent Study Outlines Benefits of EU–US Trade Agreement*, MEMO/13/211 of 12 March 2013.

[78] Speech of US President Obama, available at <http://uk.reuters.com/article/2014/03/26/usa-eu-summit-trade-idUKL5N0MN35T20140326> (last accessed 22 August 2015).

[79] Bar-Gill and Ben-Shahar, 'Regulatory Techniques in Consumer Protection: A critique of European Consumer Contract Law', 50 *Common Market Law Review* (2013) 109, at 124.

5. Consumer Protection and the EU Relationship with China

In the EU relationship with China, consumer protection requirements are very important, in particular when it comes to consumer safety. The German State Development Agency, GIZ, was involved in China on a project of product safety and consumer legislation and trained many stakeholders.[80] The goal was to improve the general framework of consumer protection in China, which adopted its first law on protection of consumer's rights and interests in 1993 and EU consumer law was taken as a model.[81]

6. The Trade Agreements with South East Asian (ASEAN) Countries

In the case of ASEAN countries, negotiations of trade agreements continue with Thailand, Vietnam, and Malaysia. Irrespective of the progress in negotiation, some countries of the region based their consumer laws on those of the EU. This is, for example, the case with Vietnam where the recently adopted consumer protection law was substantially inspired by the EU consumer *acquis* and where one of the co-financers of the drafting of the 2010 Law on Consumer Protection was the EU–Vietnam Multilateral Trade Assistance Project (EU–Vietnam MUTRAP).[82]

7. Free Trade Agreements with South American Countries

The Association Agreement with Chile was concluded in 2002 and it entered into force in February 2003.[83] The agreement has established tight regulatory cooperation between the EU and Chile.[84] It emphasizes the need to make consumer regimes compatible, it provides for the establishment of an early warning system and the exchange of information, various training activities, and technical assistance.[85]

The trade agreement between the EU, on the one side, and Colombia and Peru, on the other, was concluded in June 2012.[86] It is focused on protection of consumers in the area of cross-border e-commerce against all kinds of unfair commercial practices of traders in the cross-border context, as well as on cooperation between enforcement authorities.[87] The agreement also contains provisions that aim at

[80] GIZ, *Consumer Protection and Product Safety Programme*, available at <http://www.giz.de/en/worldwide/15567.html> (last accessed 22 August 2015).

[81] Shigang and Guangyan, 'The Problems of China's Consumer Protection Law in the Legal Practice', 14 *International Journal of Business and Social Science* (2012) 65, at 70.

[82] See European Trade Policy and Investment Support Project (MUTRAP), information available at <http://mutrap.org.vn> (last accessed 22 August 2015).

[83] Association Agreement between EU and Chile, OJ 2002 L 352/3.

[84] See Steger, 'Institutions for Regulatory Cooperation in "New Generation" Economic and Trade Agreements', 39 *Legal Issues of Economic Integration* (2012) 109.

[85] Art. 29 of the Association Agreement with Chile, OJ 2002 L 352/3.

[86] Trade Agreement between the European Union and Colombia and Peru, OJ 2012 L 354/3.

[87] Arts 163(1)(d), 166, and 210(1)(b) of the Trade Agreement between the European Union and Colombia and Peru, OJ 2012 L 354/3.

limiting information requirements on labels, thus avoiding burdensome obligations on traders to disclose information which is not relevant to consumers.[88] Moreover, it urges cooperation in public awareness of consumers.[89]

4. Conclusion

This chapter analysed the external action of the EU in the field of consumer protection, especially the way the Union exports consumer law and policy outside its borders. A particularly powerful tool for the dissemination of EU consumer law is the conclusion of international agreements by the Union with other countries as part of the process of strengthening mutual economic, political, and social relations. These agreements differ depending on the nature of the relationship of the Union with the country concerned, but very often they contain provisions that are related to consumer protection. Particularly important in this respect are the provisions contained in some of these agreements that impose the requirement of alignment of consumer legislation of the country concerned with that of the Union.

It is obvious that differences in the regulatory regimes of consumer protection represent a significant form of non-tariff barrier for cross-border trade. Alignment of consumer legislation through an international agreement may help to remove obstacles to trade between the EU and its trade partner. The EU has built a very advanced system of consumer protection. It expects its close partners, especially those who benefit from an accession process, an association, or another form of advanced cooperation with the Union, to adapt their consumer legislation to that of the EU. As a consequence, citizens of these countries may also benefit from the high level of consumer protection of the European regulatory regime. In that context, a similarity is noticeable between these two major consequences of extending EU consumer law beyond EU borders and the two main objectives of European consumer policy: strengthening the internal market through the removal of barriers, and the achievement of a high level of consumer protection.[90]

[88] European Commission, 'Highlights of the Trade Agreement between Colombia, Peru and the European Union', MEMO/12/487 of 26 June 2012.

[89] Art. 256(2)(d) and (e) of the Trade Agreement between the European Union and Colombia and Peru, OJ 2012 L 354/3.

[90] See in that regard: Art. 1 of Directive 2005/29/EC on unfair commercial practices, OJ 2005 L 149/22; Art. 1 of Directive 2011/83/EU on consumer rights, OJ 2011 L 304/64.

11

EU Regulatory Private Law in the Energy Community

The Synergy between the CEER and the ECRB in Facilitating Customer Protection

*Anna-Alexandra Marhold**

1. Introduction

European regulatory private law in the energy sector has not yet been studied in depth, arguably even less so from the perspective of EU external relations law.[1] To fill part of this gap and to show that this topic offers a rich seam for analysis, this chapter will discuss one area where these two fields of law intersect. It will focus on a case study involving the Energy Community Treaty (EnCT), and two relevant regulatory bodies: the Energy Community Regulatory Board (ECRB) and the Council of European Energy Regulators (CEER).[2] It will discuss their role in the facilitation of customer protection in the EnCT region.[3]

We use the term 'synergy' in the title of the chapter to describe the cooperation of the CEER and the Energy Community Regulatory Board, because the term's meaning can be defined as '*the interaction or cooperation of two or more*

* I am grateful to Professor Marise Cremona, Professor Hans Micklitz, Barend van Leeuwen, Federico della Negra, Cristiano Artizzu, and Lucila de Almeida, without whose valuable advice I would not have been able to write this chapter. Many thanks also to Vasyl Chornyi for his ever-useful comments.

[1] Hans Micklitz explains the concept of European regulatory private law as: 'the space where regulatory law intersects with private economic activity. This understanding of private law includes the directives and regulations the EU has adopted horizontally with regard to particular groups of citizens: workers, migrants, consumers, women; or vertically with regard to particular sectors: telecommunications, postal services, energy (electricity and gas), transport, financial services or product safety.' See for more details: Micklitz, 'The Visible Hand of European Private Law', 28 *Yearbook of European Law* (2009) 3.

[2] The Council of European Energy Regulators (CEER), information available at <http://www.ceer.eu> (last accessed 9 April 2015), and the Energy Community Regulatory Board (ECRB), established pursuant to Art. 58 of the Treaty Establishing the Energy Community (signed 15 October 2015, entered into force 1 July 2006), OJ 2006 L 198/18 (EnCT).

[3] Ibid.

organizations, substances, or other agents to produce a combined effect greater than the sum of their separate effects'.[4] This seems an appropriate way to label the interaction between the two platforms. Both bodies coordinate with other regional and international regulatory platforms in energy and the outcome in turn affects private law relationships in the national jurisdictions of the Energy Community members.[5] As result, the sum is greater than their separate effects: attempting to strengthen the impact of EU regulatory private law in the Energy Community. This is especially visible in the promotion of customer protection in the Energy Community by means of the ECRB.

The chapter is structured as follows: after setting out the fundamental elements of the EU Internal Energy Market (IEM), section 1 discusses the function of the CEER, a non-for-profit platform where EU energy regulators can coordinate best practices. Apart from being active on the EU level, the CEER additionally has an international strategy and is actively involved beyond the borders of the EU.

Section 2 will then turn to the EnCT and its regulatory board. The ECRB serves as the coordinating platform for exchange of knowledge and development of best practices for gas and electricity markets and customer protection in the Energy Community. The section will put two and two together and demonstrate how, through the synergy between the CEER and the ECRB, EU private regulatory law in the area of customer protection is strengthened in the region of the Energy Community. Two studies the ECRB has conducted will be at the centre of this assessment: 1) The Treatment of Vulnerable Customers in the Energy Community and 2) the Status Review of Customer Contracts in the Energy Community.[6] The conclusion will recap the findings of this chapter.

In essence, what the chapter intends to show is that the EnCT goes beyond the mere export of the EU Internal Energy Market model abroad. In fact, it functions also as a vehicle for extending the reach of EU regulatory private law in EnCT contracting parties' jurisdictions.

2. The EU's Engagement in Energy Regulation at Union Level and Beyond: The Case of The Council of European Energy Regulators

A. Inside the IEM: The fundamentals

The EU Internal Energy Market for Gas and Electricity as we know it today has its roots in the European regional integration and single market idea of the

[4] See Oxford English Dictionary, available at <http://www.oxforddictionaries.com> (last accessed 9 April 2015).

[5] For instance with the Energy Regulators Regional Association (ERRA) and the International Confederation of Energy Regulators (ICER).

[6] ECRB, *Treatment of the Vulnerable Customer in the Energy Community* (2014) and ECRB, *Status Review of Customer Contracts in the Energy Community* (2013); both reports are available through the Energy Community website at <http://www.energy-community.org> (last accessed 9 April 2015).

1950s.[7] It is a de facto realization, amelioration, and completion of the European single market in several phases, extending from the free movement of goods and persons to the free movement of services, including network services. Network services cover energy services such as electricity and gas transmission. The larger goals of the IEM are the fulfilment of the EU's energy policy objective of an affordable, sustainable, and secure supply of energy for Europe.[8] To pursue this aim, the IEM seeks to transform and integrate the national energy markets of the EU Member States into a single European market for energy.[9] Instruments for its realization are the opening up of gas and electricity markets across Europe by means of cross-sector standardization, separating operation activities, and fostering competition in the field. The IEM implies that electricity and gas can be freely traded in the whole area of the EU and the European Free Trade Association (EFTA) states.[10]

During the first phase of implementing the IEM in the late 1980s and early 1990s, transit opened up for electricity and gas through the main European networks, which meant that Member States could no longer oppose flows of electricity and gas from other Member States through their territory.[11] In what was called the Second Package in the mid-1990s, the market was further liberalized through the Electricity and Gas Directive (96/92/EC and 98/30/EC respectively), which established common rules for activity in the two industries. The rules prescribed by the directives were subsequently transposed into the national legislation of most Member States.

Additionally, the Second Energy Package prescribed the 'unbundling' of networks, starting with the milder forms of 'accounting unbundling' in the 1990s, to 'legal unbundling' imposed in 2003. The term 'unbundling' in the IEM generally refers to the breaking up and separation of energy sales and transmission activities of energy companies.[12] 'Accounting unbundling' refers to separation 'on paper' between transmission and sales of energy. 'Legal unbundling' implies that

[7] The idea of a common market for goods and free circulation of goods and capital for the European Union was first coined by French Foreign Minister Schuman in the 1950 Schuman Declaration, proposing the creation of a European Coal and Steel Community, available at <http://europa.eu/about-eu/basic-information/symbols/europe-day/schuman-declaration/index_en.htm> (last accessed 9 April 2015). The principles were first laid down in the Treaty Establishing the European Economic Community 1957 (Treaty of Rome), 298 UNTS 3; see Florence School of Regulation (FSR) Encyclopedia, 'EU Internal Energy Market for Gas and Electricity', available at <http://fsr-encyclopedia.eui.eu> (last accessed 9 April 2015).

[8] See European Commission (DG Energy), *Single Market for Gas & Electricity—What Do We Want to Achieve?*, available at <http://ec.europa.eu/energy/gas_electricity/index_en.htm> (last accessed 9 April 2015).

[9] Ibid. [10] FSR Encyclopedia, *supra* note 7.

[11] Directives 90/547 (for electricity), OJ 1990 L 313, and 91/296 (for gas), OJ 1991 L 147, opened transits through the main European networks. Also generally see T. Daintith and L. Hancher, *Energy Strategy in Europe—The Legal Framework* (1986); Gramlich, 'Regulating Energy Supranationally: EU Energy Policy', 3 *European Yearbook of International Economic Law* (2012) 371 and K. Talus, *EU Energy Law and Policy: A Critical Account* (2013).

[12] 'Accounting unbundling' refers to separation *on paper* between transmission and sales of energy; see for instance the Note of DG Energy & Transport on Directives 2003/54 and 2003/55 on the Internal Market in Electricity and Natural Gas of 16 January 2004.

the transmission activities of the gas and electricity network have to be established as separate companies next to the sale of energy, even if they remain part of a bigger energy consortium.[13]

The same Electricity Directive (2003/54/EC) and Gas Directive (2003/55/EC) also incorporated rules on customer protection in the IEM. Article 3 of the directives is devoted to public service obligations and customer protection. Transparency regarding contractual terms and conditions is required by Article 3(3) of the Electricity Directive and Article 3(5) of the Gas Directive.[14] Protection of household customers shall include the measures explicitly mentioned in Annex I of both directives.

Nevertheless, in the EU's view, the market for electricity and gas transmission remained ineffective and not competitive enough. When the European Commission issued yet another set of rules in 2007 with the adoption of a Third Energy Package, the IEM entered a new stage. The new Electricity and Gas Directives from the Third Energy Package (2009/72/EC and 2009/73/EC respectively) prescribed the most rigorous forms of unbundling, so-called full ownership unbundling.[15] Ownership unbundling prescribes the complete separation of companies' energy generation and sales from their transmission network activities, requiring them to be operated by two completely independent entities, pursuant to Article 9 of Directive 2009/72/EC.[16]

The rationale for full ownership unbundling is in essence to uncouple the true natural monopoly elements of the energy sector from the elements where

[13] FSR Encyclopedia, *supra* note 7. Note: Two types of entities are essential when it comes to unbundling activities and transmission and distribution in electricity and gas, the transmission system operator (TSO) and the distribution system operator (DSO). TSOs and DSOs are both endowed with transporting energy form one point to another, but while the TSO transmits energy (electricity or gas) from the power plants where it is generated and transports it over the main grid, the DSO takes over the energy from this larger grid at what is called a regional or local distribution transformer point, and delivers it to individual consumers. Second Energy Package unbundling legislation thus resulted in national energy companies having to split off their previously vertically integrated transmission and distribution activities functionally, for accounting purposes, and legally. In turn, the detached TSOs and DSOs which emerged as a result of this unbundling had to allow access to the network without discrimination in order to promote competition.

[14] Art. 3(3) and 3(5) of Directives 2003/54 and 2003/55, OJ 2003 L 176.

[15] The Electricity and Gas Directives of the Third Energy Package are Directive 2009/72 concerning common rules for the internal market in electricity and repealing Directive 2003/54/EC (text with EEA relevance), OJ 2009 L 211/69, and Directive 2009/73 concerning common rules for the internal market in natural gas and repealing Directive 2003/55, OJ 2009 L 211/94, both dated 14 July 2009.

[16] TSOs had to accordingly be entirely separated from the larger energy consortium, accompanied by an increased regulatory scrutiny of their activities. The reason for this is that the TSO usually is a natural monopoly due to the investment in infrastructure necessary for its functioning, not to mention the public utility nature of the service it provides (namely the distribution of energy). In economics, a natural monopoly refers to an industry, in which is most efficient (involving the lowest long-run average cost) for production to be permanently concentrated in a single firm rather than contested competitively. The natural monopoly scenario is often utilized when regulating public utilities; see generally S. Berg and J. Tschirhart, *Natural Monopoly Regulation: Principles and Practices* (1988). The European Commission generally refers to gas transmission services as 'services of general economic interest' and subjects them to specific public service obligations; see Art. 10 ('Designation and Certification of Transmission System Operators') of Directive 2009/72, *supra* note 15. Note that while for TSOs there now is full 'OU', DSOs are still allowed to resort to legal unbundling *only*. For

competition is possible.[17] While this remains the ultimate objective, the reality is that more often than not, vertically integrated energy consortia still dominate the national energy markets of many Member States. Because these consortia are difficult and time-consuming to break up, less demanding versions of unbundling are tolerated under the 2009 directives to date. Member States can thus pick and choose what milder form of unbundling best fits their national electricity and gas sectors, as long as Third Energy Package objectives are met.[18]

Three formal EU level bodies have to briefly be touched upon in connection with the IEM and streamlining of the unbundling process: the Agency for the Cooperation of European Regulators (ACER) and the two European Networks for Transmission System Operators (ENTSOs).

ACER is a formal EU agency with legal personality established by Regulation 713/2009/EC, whose aim it is to fill the regulatory gaps.[19] Its mission is to complement and coordinate the activities of national energy regulators (NRAs) at EU level and work towards the completion of the single EU energy market for electricity and natural gas.[20] It does so by uniting senior representatives of all Member States' NRAs in a Board of Regulators, which consequently cooperate on developing EU-wide rules to enhance competition. Additionally, ACER monitors both of the ENTSOs' practices (see below) at EU level, and last but not least, it observes the functioning of the energy market in general. ACER pursues these objectives by designing framework guidelines and network codes, apart from issuing recommendations for national regulators and the EU.[21]

The ENTSO for electricity (ENTSO-E) and for gas (ENTSOG) are sector-specific platforms, mandated directly by the EU's Third Energy Package. ENTSO-E is a network of 41 electricity transmission system operators, which promotes closer cooperation among them to foster the implementation of the EU energy

instance, a TSO has to be certified by its national regulatory authority (NRA), see A. Johnston and G. Block, *EU Energy Law* (2012) 37 and 60.

[17] Johnston and Block, *supra* note 16, at 36.

[18] Note in this respect the ISO and ITO scenario: while 'full ownership unbundling' remains the basic model and target, vertically integrated energy companies can resort to two other alternatives: the independent system operator (ISO) and independent transmission operator (ITO) model. Under the former model, the transmission network can remain in the ownership of the energy company. Nevertheless, the transmission network itself has to be managed by an ISO, which has to perform all day-to-day network operator functions and must be completely separate from the energy company. In the ITO scenario, the transmission networks can also remain under the ownership of an energy consortium, but the transmission subsidiaries would be set up as independent joint stock companies carrying their own brand name and subject to stringent regulatory control. Most EU Member States whose transmission systems are controlled by vertically integrated undertakings prefer this last scheme of unbundling to comply with the Third Energy Package.

[19] Regulation 713/2009 of 14 August 2009 establishing an Agency for the Cooperation of Energy Regulators (ACER) (known as the ACER Regulation), OJ 2009 L 211/1.

[20] Ibid., para. 6.

[21] Network codes are a set of rules drafted by the ENTSO, with guidance from ACER, to facilitate the harmonization, integration, and efficiency of the European electricity market. Each network code is an integral part of the drive towards completion of the internal energy market, and achieving the EU's energy objectives; see the Official EU Network Codes website, available at <http://networkcodes.entsoe.eu> (last accessed 9 April 2015).

policy.[22] The two main pillars of ENTSO-E are the integration of renewable energy sources into the power system and the completion of the IEM. ENTSO-E uses a combination of drafting of network codes and the development of a pan-European coordination network.

ENTSOG focuses on the same task as ENTSO-E of drafting network codes and development plans tailored to the gas sector.[23] It brings together the transmission system operators for gas of each of the Members States. ENTSOG is currently composed of 44 TSO members and three associated partners from 26 European countries.[24] The main task of ENTSOG is to contribute to the optimal management of the internal gas market by developing network codes on thematic issues such as capacity allocation, network connection, and operational security. Furthermore, ENTSOG is in charge of a network development plan, mapping out European gas infrastructure and taking into account various development scenarios. In addition, it monitors annual winter and summer gas supply outlooks.

With regard to the development of network codes, guidelines, and development plans, ACER first adopts a framework guideline on the basis of the work programme of the Commission.[25] Subsequently, ACER sets out principles for the development of network codes, which are then 'outsourced' to the ENTSOs. Both ENTSOs work in close coordination with ACER: each of the ENTSOs proceeds to draft the actual network codes in line with the ACER framework guidelines. When ready, the guidelines are subject to review by ACER and approved by the Commission.[26] During the final stage, the draft code is adopted accordingly through the comitology process and becomes a stand-alone EU regulation in the form of a legally binding European-wide network code.[27]

B. The Council of European Energy Regulators

We will now turn our attention to the Council of European Energy Regulators (CEER). This regulatory body presents the clearest example where EU regulatory private law in the energy sector comes together both with regard to the content of the rules (customer protection) and in their making (on Union level and beyond). This section will first discuss the function of the CEER. Then, it will describe how the body engages in rule making and how its efforts may translate into EU law. Subsequently, the section will discuss how the CEER is involved beyond EU borders and active in these international frameworks, namely the Energy Regulators Regional Association (ERRA) and the International Confederation of Energy Regulators (ICER).[28]

[22] ENTSO-E was established by Regulation 714/2009 of 14 July 2009, OJ 2009 L 211/15.

[23] ENTSOG was established by Regulation 715/2009 14 July 2009, OJ 2009 211/36.

[24] See Members on ENTSOG website, available at <http://www.entsog.eu/members> (last accessed 9 April 2015).

[25] Johnston and Block, *supra* note 16, at 148.

[26] Ibid., at 148–149.

[27] On the comitology process see Arts 290 and 291 Consolidated Version of the Treaty on the Functioning of the European Union (TFEU), OJ 2008 C 115/47.

[28] Energy Regulators Regional Association (ERRA), information available at <http://www.erranet.org>, and the International Confederation of Energy Regulators (ICER), information available at

While ACER is a formal EU agency, the CEER is its 'informal' counterpart, describing itself as 'the voice of Europe's National Regulatory Authorities of electricity and gas at the EU and international level'.[29] Because the CEER is not-for-profit, it lies outside the tight regulatory framework of EU law that brings together regulators and stakeholders in the formal EU setting.[30] It was established in 2000, and while it also comprised Member State NRA representatives, it connects them in a more casual way. The CEER's work is complementary to that of the ACER, ensuring that there is no overlap, and focuses on thematic working groups for each sector. For instance, it remains the main interface for the development of strategies and recommendations on customer-related issues.[31]

Its Customer and Retail Markets Working Group has three task forces working on: 1) customer empowerment regarding billing, complaint handling, alternative dispute resolution, price comparison tools, and protecting vulnerable energy customers; 2) retail market functioning, such as smart metering, monitoring, and market design for both electricity and gas markets, and; 3) strategy and communication, which works on the development and implementation for a 2020 Vision for Europe's Energy Customers. Additionally, the CEER offers a platform for cooperation and exchange of information and best practices amongst NRAs to facilitate the creation of a single and competitive IEM for gas and electricity in the EU.

Apart from that, in contrast to ACER and the ENTSOs, the CEER has a mandate to engage actively at the international level by coordinating with regulatory organizations around the world, and this will be elaborated upon further below.[32] In the global context, the CEER exchanges best practices within the framework of ICER, the International Confederation of Energy Regulators. At the regional level, the CEER interacts with bodies such as the Central and Eastern European Energy Regulators Regional Association. Last but not least, the CEER conducts joint activities with the regulatory board of the Energy Community Treaty, which will be discussed in section 2.

C. CEER Rule-Making and Convergence into EU Law

It is undisputed that regulation by platforms such as the CEER contributes substantially to the formation of law. However, since the processes are soft in nature, they are not always easy to discern. Nevertheless, although the coordination efforts are non-binding, they can, and ideally should, harden over time.[33] This process,

<http://www.icer-regulators.net/portal/page/portal/ICER_HOME> (both websites last accessed 9 April 2015).

[29] See description of its mission on the website of CEER, *supra* note 2.

[30] Micklitz, 'Regulatory Strategies on Services Contracts', in F. Cafaggi and H. Muir Watt (eds), *The Regulatory Function of European Private Law* (2009) 35.

[31] See the CEER Customers and Retail Markets Working Group, information available at <http://www.ceer.eu> (last accessed 9 April 2015).

[32] See *CEER's International Activities: Core Strategies and Objectives*, Ref: C12-ISG-25-03, 26 February 2013.

[33] Micklitz, *supra* note 30, at 48.

known as 'convergence through soft coordination', can lead to standardization. It mainly comes to fruition when guidelines and recommendations actually contribute to shaping contract rules and EU regulation.[34] Confirmation of hardening of a soft rule can inter alia happen when the judiciary refers to private regulation.[35] But how does this convergence work?

As Cafaggi puts it, self-regulation, through bodies such as the CEER, can function as an agent of harmonization and complements European legislation through standard setting.[36] By producing soft law instruments, self-regulation, in concrete terms, can: 1) complement legislative functions by, for instance, making suggestions on the definition of contract terms; 2) contribute to regulation by defining sector-specific guidelines, and/or; 3) fulfil a monitoring function with regard to correct implementation at EU level.[37] In its functioning, it can either supplement or even substitute harmonization in a sector-specific way.[38] Cafaggi further distils four essential modes in which the private and public interact: 1) hybridization, where there is a transnational cross-fertilization taking place between the public and private sectors; 2) collaborative rule making, when both private and public actors are involved in the process of drafting rules; 3) coordination, where drafting and standardization happens independently but both processes are mutually influenced, and, finally; 4) competition, occurring when private actors raise the standards so high that the public actor loses legitimacy.[39] It is safe to assume that with respect to a platform such as the CEER and the way it interacts with the formal EU regulator, mainly the first three occur.

It is difficult to find explicit evidence to prove that certain standard-setting activities directly influence EU law making at a higher level, although examples do exist. Those which come closest are instances where the Commission affirms that a certain recommendation by a private regulatory platform will be taken into account when drafting legislation. Alternatively, confirmation of hardening of a soft rule can happen when the judiciary refers to private regulation.[40] The existence and activities of more informal bodies such as the CEER reveal that there is a two-way dynamic. In the completion of the single market, we witness both top-down and bottom-up cross-fertilization.[41] First, top-down legislation coming from the EU (e.g. single market acquis, the IEM, the Third Energy Package, etc.) trickles down to the private law sphere to private actors (e.g. in the form of businesses,

[34] Van Leeuwen, 'Free Movement of Services, European Standardisation and Private Law' in H. Micklitz, Y. Svetiev, and G. Comparato (eds), 'European Regulatory Private Law—The Paradigms Tested', EUI Working Paper LAW 2014/04, 27, at 29. Walter van Gerven has written on this bottom-up convergence through soft coordination; see for example van Gerven, 'Private Law in a Federal Perspective', in R. Brownsword *et al.* (eds), *The Foundations of European Private Law* (2011) 337.

[35] Cafaggi and Janczuk, 'Private Regulation and Legal Integration: The European Example', 12 *Business and Politics* (2010) 1, at 25.

[36] F. Cafaggi, 'Self-Regulation in European Contract Law', EUI Working Paper LAW 2006/43, at 3.

[37] Ibid. [38] Ibid. [39] Ibid.

[40] Cafaggi and Janczuk, *supra* note 35, at 25.

[41] Cafaggi, 'New Foundations of Transnational Private Regulation', 38 *Journal of Law and Society* (2011) 20, at 44.

consumer organizations, etc.) who subsequently have to take action to implement the changes mandated from above.[42] Consequently, bottom-up, national energy regulators are formed which then unite in private regulatory platforms on EU level, such as the CEER. They coordinate best practices, standards, and draft recommendations, which are subsequently (hopefully) taken into account by the formal EU regulator.

Because of the way the CEER operates, how its activities influence EU law can be somewhat opaque at first sight. Nevertheless, there are several areas of regulation where the results of the CEER's efforts are clearly distinguishable. What immediately catches the eye, for example, is that the CEER is often mentioned for its positive contributions to the completion of the single energy market through consultations with the European Commission. In the following excerpt, taken from an EU Communication from the Commission to the Council and the European Parliament, the CEER (together with the Florence and Madrid fora) is credited with developing a voluntary agreement on conditions for access to gas storage, called 'Guidelines for Good TPA Practice for Storage System Operators':[43]

> the European regulatory fora for electricity and gas . . . have done excellent work *on developing innovative solutions on key issues, for instance recently a voluntary agreement on conditions for access to gas storage.* In this way the CEER, the European Regulators Group and the Florence and Madrid Forums have made significant contributions to the development of the internal market, in line with Commission policy to promote co-regulation and better regulation.[44]

This observation fits in the hybridization dynamic of self-regulation discussed above.[45] However, the CEER goes beyond mere development of voluntary agreements. It takes an active coordination role with regard to European rule-making in the field of energy. These efforts in fact border on collaborative rule making (this and coordination are two other modes of private–public interaction discussed by Cafaggi).[46] The CEER is particularly effective in the areas of energy efficiency and consumer protection in the context of the EU's energy policy. When it comes to energy efficiency, the Commission, in cooperation with the CEER, has for instance developed guidelines on good regulatory practices to reduce transmission and distribution losses:

> The Commission will develop by 2008, *and agree thereafter guidelines in co-operation with the Council of European Energy Regulators (CEER)* on good regulatory practices to reduce transmission and distribution losses, developed in collaboration with the European

[42] On this phenomenon see, for example, Leczykiewicz and Weatherill, 'Private Law Relationships and EU Law; in D. Leczykiewicz and S. Weatherill (eds), *Involvement of EU Law in Private Law Relationships* (2013) 1.

[43] See ERGEG 'Guidelines for Good TPA Practice for Storage System Operators' of 23 March 2005, available at <https://www.e-control.at/documents/20903/-/-/d07be6a0-5aaa-432f-89d4-d5d7c7073f36> (last accessed 9 April 2015).

[44] See European Commission, *Report on Progress Creating the Internal Gas and Electricity Market (Communication)*, COM (2005) 568 final, at 13 (emphasis added).

[45] See Cafaggi, *supra* note 36.

[46] Ibid.

Regulators' Group for Electricity and Gas (ERGEG), considering inter alia, charges, incentives, locational signals and cross-border incentive differences.[47]

The Commission furthermore cooperated on a memorandum of understanding (MoU) with the CEER under the auspices of the Directive on Energy End-Use Efficiency and Energy Services (2006/32/EC).[48] This directive was put in place to provide a framework for EU cooperation on energy efficiency linked to the EU-wide White Certification Scheme. In the field of consumer protection, the CEER's responsibility extends to technical assistance and the exchange of best practices at the request of the EU:

The Commission, with support from CEER, will facilitate Member States' exchange of best practices on key consumer-related issues, including price comparison tools, transparent pricing and billing, and elaborating the concept of vulnerable consumers.[49]

The Commission also tends to refer to the CEER in response to energy regulation questions it receives from the European Parliament. According to the Commission, CEER figures as the authoritative information body for consumer protection standards in the energy sector across the EU regarding, inter alia, matters concerning energy affordability.[50]

In 2013, the CEER furthermore launched a legal task force under the Implementation, Benchmarking and Policy Working Group, which follows the developments and implementation of the Third Energy Package.[51] The task force provides advice on legal and institutional issues in relation to the implementation of the package and specific queries from NRAs.

It becomes clear that the CEER mainly affects EU rule making when it works together with the Commission in drafting best practices and developing guidelines. It is difficult to present explicit evidence of how the CEER recommendations translate into hard EU legislation, but the examples given point in the direction of transformation from soft coordination into binding rules. The CEER's consultation efforts can undoubtedly solidify into formal EU regulation in the energy field eventually. Its interaction with the formal regulator thus lies somewhere between

[47] See 'Treatment of Losses by Network Operators', ERGEG Position Paper for Public Consultation, Ref: E08-ENM-04-03, 15 July 2008; European Commission, 'Action Plan for Energy Efficiency—Realising the potential analysis of the action plan for energy efficiency' (Communication), COM (2006) 545 final, at 11 (emphasis added).

[48] Ibid., at 20.

[49] European Commission, *Making the Internal Energy Market Work (Communication)*, COM (2012) 663 final, at 8.

[50] Written questions by Members of the European Parliament and their answers given by a European Union institution of 4 December 2014, OJ 2013 C 354E/01, answer given by the Commissioner for Energy: 'The Commission is currently conducting compliance checks to verify the completeness and quality of the transposition of the legislation. The Status Review of Customer and Retail Market Provisions 2012 prepared by the Council of European Energy Regulators (CEER) details social protection instruments in each Member State with respect to energy affordability'; see CEER, *Status Review of Customer and Retail Market Provisions form the Third Package as of 1 January 2012*, Ref: C12-CEM-55-04, 7 November 2012.

[51] See CEER, Implementation, Benchmarking and Monitoring Working Group, information available at <http://www.ceer.eu/portal/page/portal/EER_HOME/EER_ACTIVITIES/IBM_WG> (last accessed 9 April 2015).

the collaborative rule making, and coordination modes of self-regulation.[52] It is in this way that the CEER, slowly but surely, is making its contribution to the completion of the IEM, albeit in the shadow of more traditional regulators (ACER and the ENTSOs) in the field.

D. CEER's Involvement on the International Level: A Regulatory Triangle

There are several international energy platforms and initiatives which operate in the area of regulatory private law and where the EU is either directly or involved in standards and agenda setting. The CEER is a good example of where the EU is indirectly involved in energy regulation at the international level. It is worth noting as an aside that self-regulation in the field of energy on the international level is not as elaborate as in, for instance, banking and finance (e.g. think the Basel Committee).[53]

While the CEER arguably operates somewhat in the shadow of ACER and the ENTSOs when it comes to energy regulation within the boundaries of the Union, the opposite is true regarding the CEER's activities at the international level. ACER and the ENTSOs are designed to function (almost) exclusively on the EU level, but the CEER has the explicit mandate to go beyond Europe's borders and engage in international standard setting in energy. It houses an international strategy group, dedicated to working with third countries and exchanging best practices and experiences with fellow regulators and authorities and to provide assistance to them where possible.[54] It also has ties with the International Energy Agency and several other regulatory associations worldwide.[55]

We will briefly look at the platforms that are of importance for the countries of the Energy Community: the Energy Regulators Regional Association (ERRA) and the International Confederation of Energy Regulators (ICER). The interaction of the CEER with ERRA and the ICER reveals a regulatory triangle in the energy field at the EU, regional, and international levels. All of these platforms are interlinked and they cooperate on setting standards in different ways. Through ERRA and the ICER, CEER, and thus indirectly the EU, can influence standard setting beyond its boundaries. One place where this regulatory triangle comes to fruition is in the activities of the Energy Community Regulatory Board.

1. The Energy Regulators Regional Association

The ERRA is a voluntary organization comprising independent energy regulatory bodies primarily from the Central European and Eurasian region (including all EnCT members).[56] Regulators from Africa, Asia, the Middle East, and the US are also affiliated.[57] It was established in 2000. Its purpose is to: 1) improve

[52] See Cafaggi, *supra* note 36. [53] See Chapter 8 of this book.

[54] See *CEER's International Activities, supra* note 32, at 3. [55] Ibid.

[56] Information available at <http://www.erranet.org> under History (last accessed 9 April 2015).

[57] ERRA at present has 24 full members, five associate members, and seven affiliate members.

national energy regulation in member countries (including enhancing regulatory methods and practices); 2) foster development of stable energy regulatory bodies with autonomy and authority (separate legal entities), and; 3) improve regulatory cooperation.[58] The EU is not a member of ERRA, but it is present through the membership of its Eastern EU Member States, which cooperate on a number of sub-regional initiatives within the ERRA, such as the Baltics Working Group, Southeast Europe Initiatives, and the Danube Region Strategy.[59] The CEER does not have an official 'seat' in ERRA either, but functions as a 'partner organization'.[60] In this capacity, the CEER organizes courses and training programmes with the regulators of non EU countries, which are ERRA members.[61] They cover areas such as acquiring economic and legal skills that are needed to design and manage successful regulatory systems for the electric power industry.

2. *The International Confederation of Energy Regulators*

Lord Mogg, the Chair of ICER, dubbed this confederation the 'New Kid on the Bloc' as it came into being only in 2009.[62] As with ERRA, ICER is a voluntary framework for cooperation and is the standard setting body in energy, but in the global rather than the regional context. It unites energy regulators and regulatory associations from around the world and includes over two hundred regulatory authorities, spanning six continents. Not surprisingly, it houses the CEER and ERRA among its member organizations (the CEER chairs the organization at present). The ICER thus provides an additional platform where the EU through the CEER indirectly coordinates energy at the extra-EU level.

ICER undertakes joint analyses of a variety of regulatory topics and promotes exchanges on training and education practices. It focuses its work on four key areas: 1) reliability and security of supply; 2) the role of regulators in responding to climate change; 3) competitiveness and affordability, and; 4) the independence, powers, responsibilities, best practices, and training of regulators. These activities often occur with the cooperation of the ERRA and the CEER. For instance, the ICER together with the CEER organized a workshop on renewable energy strategy in 2012, which resulted in a report on renewable energy and distributed generation including international case studies on technical and economic considerations.[63] Additionally, ICER also hosts the World Energy Forum, the leading conference

[58] See ERRA, *Founding Principles—The Energy Regulatory Organization for Central/Eastern Europa and Eurasia*, available through the ERRA official website, *supra* note 56.

[59] See ERRA, 'Other Activities—Sub regional', available at <http://www.erranet.org/OtherActivities/Subregional> (last accessed 9 April 2015).

[60] See ERRA 'Other Activities—CEER', available at <http://www.erranet.org/OtherActivities/CEER> (last accessed 9 April 2015) and the *CEER's International Activities, supra* note 32, at 4.

[61] Ibid.

[62] As he mentioned in a 2013 online interview for the Florence School of Regulation, accessible through<http://fsr.eui.eu/Publications/VIDEO/MonthlyInterview/2013/JANUARY2013-LordMogg.aspx> (last accessed 9 April 2015).

[63] See the CEER–ICER Workshop on Renewable Energy Strategy, held in Brussels on 20 June 2012, information available at <http://www.icer-regulators.net/portal/page/portal/ICER_HOME/

on energy regulation worldwide, bringing together stakeholders in the field every three years.[64]

3. The Synergy between the CEER and the ECRB in Facilitating Customer Protection in the Energy Community

A. Exporting the IEM Model to the European Neighbourhood: The Energy Community Treaty

Energy is rarely an isolated matter, confined to national or even regional borders. On the contrary: it is perhaps one of the most globalized sectors worldwide. It therefore comes as no surprise that the EU internal energy market is not a hermetically sealed undertaking. The pursuit of the IEM to create a well-functioning internal market for energy for the EU would be simply unthinkable without energy connections and supply from abroad. The European market is connected through fixed grids, most of which have been in place for decades. They extend far beyond the borders of the EU into Russia and Kazakhstan, North Africa, and Turkey.[65] Whether directly or indirectly through platforms as the CEER, the EU is actively engaged in energy regulation beyond its borders: 'energy security' is one of the key concepts of the EU's energy policy. This section will briefly discuss one element of the EU's efforts in exporting the IEM abroad, by means of the Energy Community Treaty framework. We discuss this to demonstrate how the EnCT in essence functions as a vehicle to extend the reach of European regulatory private law beyond Europe's boundaries.

From the 2007 Lisbon Treaty onwards, the EU's external legal competences have developed through Article 216 TFEU which states that the EU may conclude agreements with one or more non-Member States and international organizations.[66] This capability to enter into agreements is legitimized if it is 'necessary in order to achieve, within the framework of the Union's policies, one of the objectives referred to in the Treaties'.[67] With regard to the energy sector, these objectives are set out in Article 194 TFEU, stipulating the rules of pursuing a coherent EU energy policy.[68] Although this particular part of the TFEU deals with

activities/ICER_Events/ICER_CEER_Workshop_on_RES> (last accessed 9 April 2015) and the resulting report, ICER, *Report on Renewable Energy and Distributed Generation: International Case Studies on Technical and Economic Considerations*, Ref: I12-CC-17-03, 21 February 2012.

[64] See, for example, the 2015 World Energy Forum website <http://www.wfer2015.org> (last accessed 9 April 2015).

[65] For a good overview, see for instance S. S. Haghighi, *Energy Security—The External Legal Relations of the European Union with Major Oil and Gas Supplying Countries* (2007).

[66] Art. 216 TFEU provides that '[t]he Union may conclude an agreement with one or more third countries or international organisations where the Treaties so provide or where the conclusion of an agreement is necessary in order to achieve, within the framework of the Union's policies, one of the objectives referred to in the Treaties, or is provided for in a legally binding Union act or is likely to affect common rules or alter their scope.'

[67] Ibid.

[68] Art. 194 TFEU (Part Three: Union Policies and Internal Actions—Title XXI Energy).

Union policies and *internal* actions, several paragraphs of the article implicitly refer to the extra-EU dimensions of this policy. First of all, Article 194, paragraph 1(b), emphasizes the need to ensure the security of supply of the EU.[69] Moreover, paragraph 1(d) promotes the interconnections of energy networks.[70] In view of this, the EU has concluded several agreements with third parties relevant for the energy sector, most notably the Energy Community Treaty.

The EnCT was concluded in 2006. It came into being before the entry into force of the Lisbon Treaty and its introduction of Article 194 TFEU, on a multiple set of legal bases, largely internal market (implied external powers) and trade (express external power).[71] The EnCT was originally targeted at the south-east European countries of Bosnia and Herzegovina, Serbia (and later Kosovo), Montenegro, former Yugoslav Republic of Macedonia, and Albania exclusively. The underlying idea was to create a win–win situation where the EU would strengthen its security of supply while the Balkans would benefit from a coherent approach in mending their disintegrated energy markets.[72] Consequently, the EnCT rests on three main pillars: 1) achieving greater energy security for the EU; 2) attracting investments and fostering economic and social stability in the geographical area on the EnCT; by 3) exporting EU single energy market acquis abroad.[73] Hence, though concluded prior to the entry into force of the Lisbon Treaty, it is clear that the EnCT fits into the objectives of EU's energy policy pursuant to Article 194 1(b) and (d) TFEU on security of supply and interconnection of energy networks.[74]

In short, the EnCT is a way for the EU to expand the geographical area of the IEM to third countries in the immediate European neighbourhood, pursuant to Article 2 of the EnCT.[75] Van Vooren and Wessel call this 'externalizing the acquis', that is, the application of EU law to market participants from outside of the EU.[76]

[69] Art. 194(1)(b) TFEU states that '[i]n the context of the establishment and functioning of the internal market and with regard for the need to preserve and improve the environment, Union policy on energy shall aim, in a spirit of solidarity between Member States, to: (b) ensure security of energy supply in the Union.'

[70] Art. 194(1)(d) TFEU: '*promote the interconnection of energy networks*'. In 2010, these legal obligations were met with the realization that the EU should have a coherent external energy strategy as well, followed by the development and publication of the EU Energy Strategy for 2020, promulgating the broader guidelines and future ambitions of the Union, see European Commission, 'Energy 2020, A Strategy for Competitive, Sustainable and Secure Energy' (Communication), COM (2010) 639 final; See also 'A Legal History of Fragmentation and Coherence in EU External Action' in B. Van Vooren, *EU External Relations Law and the European Neighbourhood Policy—A Paradigm for Coherence* (2012) 24.

[71] Art. 194 TFEU.

[72] Cameron, 'The EU and Energy Security: A Critical Review of the Legal Issues' in A. Antoniadis, R. Schütze, and E. Spaventa, *The European Union and Global Emergencies* (2011) 125, at 137. Also see the official website of the Energy Community Treaty, at <http://www.energy-community.org> (last accessed 9 April 2015).

[73] European Commission, *Report from the Commission to the Council to the European Parliament and the Council under Article 7 of Decision 2006/500/EC (Energy Community Treaty)*, COM (2011) 105 final, at 2.

[74] Kaderjak, 'The January 2009 Gas Crisis in Central and Eastern Europe', 5 *European Energy Law and Policy Yearbook* (2012) 121.

[75] Art. 2 EnCT; Talus, *supra* note 11, at 244.

[76] B. Van Vooren and R.A. Wessel, *EU External Relations Law—Text, Cases and Materials* (2014) 454.

The goal of the EnCT is liberalization, completion of the energy markets of the contracting parties to the Community Treaty, and connection of these markets to the IEM. After the Ukrainian–Russian gas disruptions in 2009, the EnCT's membership expanded as Moldova and Ukraine acceded to the Treaty in 2010 and 2011 respectively.[77]

The EnCT seeks to create a single market for *network* energy (i.e. electricity and gas) spanning the area of the EU and the parties to the EnCt. The means to achieve this are originally based on the Second Energy Package Directives 2003/54/EC and 2003/55/EC (Article 2 paragraph 2 EnCT).[78] EnCT members subsequently had to enact Third Energy Package legislation by January 2015. It goes without saying that EnCT contracting parties cannot implement directives directly as they are targeted at EU Members States. Article 3 states that contracting parties have to implement 'the acquis communautaire on energy, environment, competition and renewables... *adapted to both the institutional framework of the Energy Community and the specific situation of each of the Contracting Parties*'.[79]

The mechanism used in the EnCT is what the Treaty calls the 'extension of the acquis communautaire on energy'. It is taken up in Title II of the Treaty.[80] The meaning of 'extension of the acquis' in this instance is limited to comprising the acts (EU directives and regulations) listed in Annex I to the Treaty (Article 10 EnCT).[81] It obliges contracting parties to implement the content of the directives listed in this annex (for instance, the Second Energy Package directives of 2003) as if they were intended for them directly and by the timeline set out in Annex II.[82]

The Energy Community Treaty goes beyond merely extending the EU IEM acquis, however. The formal IEM model and the EnCT 'package' includes rules and regulations that fall broadly within the scope of regulatory private law, both in the way the rules come into being and concerning their effect on private law relations in the field of energy in EnCT contracting parties' jurisdiction.

To what extent regulatory private law extends its reach into the energy sector depends on the different aspects of energy law, each with distinct objectives. In the context of liberalizing the EU electricity and gas markets, ownership unbundling, rules on third party access to transmission, the position of independent regulatory authorities, pan-European stakeholder networks, and, last but not least, rules on customer protection and public service obligations come to mind. For instance, the EnCT obliges contracting parties to take over the EU acquis on the environment (Chapter III), competition (Chapter IV) and renewables (Chapter V).[83] More importantly, as mentioned in section 1 earlier in this chapter, the Second Energy Package Directives that are part of the Energy Community framework include articles on customer protection: Article 3 of the Directives is devoted to public service obligations and customer protection. Transparency regarding contractual

[77] See Energy Community website, *supra* note 72, under Members.

[78] See Directive 2003/54, OJ 2003 L 176/37, and Directive 2003/54, OJ 2003 L 176/57; see also Gramlich, *supra* note 11, at 371 *et seq*.

[79] Art. 3 EnCT (emphasis added).

[80] Title II of the EnCT.

[81] Annex I 'List of Acts Included in the "Acquis Communitaire on Energy"' EnCT.

[82] Ibid.

[83] EnCT Chapters III, IV, and V.

terms and conditions is required by Article 3(3) of the Electricity Directive and Article 3(5) of the Gas Directive.[84] Protection of household customers includes the measures explicitly mentioned in Annex I of both directives. It is here that the ECRB comes into play.

On the administrative level, the EnCT has its own institutions, mirroring the decision-making structures of the EU: a Ministerial Council comprising a representative of each contracting party (the EU has two), a rotating presidency, and a secretariat in charge of monitoring energy markets.[85] Last but not least, and a focal point in this chapter, the EnCT houses the Energy Community Regulatory Board (ECRB) pursuant to Article 58 ECT, which serves as the coordination platform for exchange of knowledge and development of best practices for gas and electricity markets and customer protection in the Energy Community.[86] The ECRB is the independent regional body of energy regulators in the Energy Community and beyond. Its activities build on three pillars: providing coordinated regulatory positions to energy policy debates, harmonizing regulatory rules across borders, and sharing regulatory knowledge and experience. The Regulatory Board additionally advises other Energy Community institutions on statutory, technical, and regulatory rules.

The ECRB is composed of representatives from NRAs of EnCT contracting parties, observers and participants.[87] One regulator of each Energy Community participant and a representative of ACER assist the EU in fulfilling its coordinating role as vice-president in the board.[88] This is interesting because ACER in principle is not responsible for international tasks reaching beyond the EU; the Council of European Energy Regulators is.[89] However, this perhaps goes to show how the EU views the Energy Community as an extension of the internal model of the IEM. It automatically extends ACER's involvement beyond its intended EU mandate to pursue an active role in the ECRB. As will become clear in this chapter, the CEER is also actively involved in the board, though interestingly enough, this is not explicitly reflected in Chapter III of the EnCT legal framework.[90]

The board further issues recommendations on cross-border disputes involving two or more regulators upon their request. It has the competence to initiate a dispute settlement procedure in case a party fails to comply with Energy Community Treaty obligations. Thus far, such disputes mainly consisted of the EU admonishing EnCT members to make sure they comply with the timely implementation of the treaty.[91] In this respect it should be mentioned that what sounds straightforward in Energy Community 'theory' does not always translate effortlessly into practice: the actual timely implementation of the treaty seems the most challenging part. Making the shift from political commitment to ensuring that EnCT

[84] See Art. 3(3) of the Electricity Directive and Art. 3(5) of the Gas Directive, *supra* note 12.
[85] See Energy Community website, *supra* note 72, under 'Who we are' and Belyi, 'The EU's External Energy Policy' in M. M. Roggenkamp *et al.* (eds), *Energy Law in Europe* (2007) 195, at 210.
[86] Art. 58 EnCT.
[87] See Art. 59 EnCT.
[88] Ibid.
[89] See *CEER's International Activities, supra* note 32.
[90] See Art. 58 and Chapter III EnCT.
[91] Ibid.

Contracting Parties apply and enforce the rules is a difficult task, demanding time and patience, as noted by a Commission report on the Energy Community Treaty in 2011.[92]

B. The Synergy Between the CEER and the ECRB in Facilitating Customer Protection: Introducing the Regulatory Triangle

One of the pillars of the ECRB is to facilitate customer protection in the region of the Energy Community. It does so under the heading of Customers and Retail Market.[93] We have already mentioned that while the ACER has an 'official spot' in assisting the EU in the Energy Community Regulatory Board (ECRB) by means of Article 59 EnCT, the CEER has not.[94] However, even though CEER does not sit in an official capacity on the ECRB, it is connected to the regulatory board in several ways. It is also worth bearing in mind that the ACER and the CEER cooperate closely with each other, often apparently speaking with one voice in the context of the Energy Community Treaty and the ECRB.

As a reminder, to prevent overlap with the ACER's work, the CEER primarily focuses on international issues and small consumers.[95] In this capacity, the CEER's customer and retail markets working group focuses on: 1) customer empowerment regarding billing, complaint handling, alternative dispute resolution, price comparison tools, and protecting vulnerable energy customers; 2) retail market functioning, such as smart metering, monitoring, and market design for both electricity and gas markets, and; 3) strategy and communication.[96] This mandate is extremely relevant for the ECRB's work on customers and the retail market in the Energy Community. If one puts two and two together, it reveals CEER's activities in the context of the EnCT: the CEER cooperates with the ECRB as a partner or as its counterpart, and its international strategy consists of developing joint projects with geographical neighbours with a view to contributing to the harmonization of regulatory practices across EU borders.[97] In its international strategy, the CEER notes that: '[i]n addition to welcoming regulators from EU candidate countries as observers, CEER notably looks forward to continuing joint activities and to deepening working relations with the Energy Community Regulatory Board (ECRB) in areas of cooperation beyond those linked to ACER tasks and duties.'[98] In one instance, the work that was first initiated by the CEER in south-eastern Europe was subsequently taken over and

[92] Ibid. Also, for example, see Talus, *supra* note 11, 'The International Dimension of EU Energy Law and Policy'.

[93] See the ECRB Customer and Retail Market Section on the Energy Community website, *supra* note 72.

[94] Art. 59 EnCT.

[95] Bernard, 'Unbundling in Practice—Networks in the Internal Energy Market', 5 *European Energy Law and Policy Yearbook* (2012) 55.

[96] CEER Customers and Retail Markets Working Group, *supra* note 31.

[97] See Annual Report on the Activities of the Energy Community 2014, at 5 and *CEER's International Activities, supra* note 32, at 4.

[98] *CEER's International Activities, supra* note 32, at 4.

continued by the ECRB.[99] Through the ECRB, the CEER normally provides experience and assistance on energy regulation that fall within its purview, notably on costumer-related issues, to the Member States of the Energy Community. It is here that the role of the CEER and the ECRB with respect to introducing EU regulatory private law in the field of costumer protection in the Energy Community is most visible.

The scope of the CEER's activities includes the exchange of knowledge between national regulators of the Energy Community and the EU on topics of common interest, in particular related to customer involvement and retail market liberalization. For example, the CEER focuses on coordination concerning smart meters, consumer awareness, and collective switching with EnCT Member States.[100] EnCT contracting party regulators and regulatory associations approach the CEER to obtain specific advice, which is carried out through EU-funded assistance projects such as the Technical Assistance and Information Exchange (also known as TAIEX; an EU scheme providing advice and training to help partner countries near the EU to apply and enforce EU law, and monitor their progress in doing so) and twinning projects. In addition, it holds annual workshops together with EnCT countries, themed around subjects such as strengthening the role of household customers.[101] These workshops take place in the context of the ECRB customer and retail markets working group, which provides a joint ECRB/CEER Workshop on Customer Issues.[102]

Moreover, under the guidance of the regulatory board, the CEER cooperates with the Energy Community members in developing guidelines and good practices, most notably on the quality of electricity supply. The CEER issued its extensive Benchmarking Report on Quality of Electricity Supply in 2011, examining electricity quality in EU Member States. More importantly, the report contains an annex devoted entirely to EnCT Member States.[103] It assesses continuity of supply, voltage quality, and commercial quality of electricity in the countries concerned. What is more, the 2011 Benchmarking Report led to the development of CEER/ERCB Guidelines of Good Practice on the Implementation and Use of Voltage Quality Monitoring Systems for Regulatory Purposes.[104] This set of highly technical guidelines recommends ways in which countries measure the voltage quality of electricity, both inside the EU and in the Energy Community.[105] These are some

[99] See Art. 14.2 of the ECRB Internal Rules of Procedure, stating that: '[t]o the extent possible, the work agreed and done with the Council of European Energy Regulators South East Europe Working Group shall be continued by the Energy Community Regulatory Board.'

[100] See Artizzu, 'International Cooperation and Consumer Protection in Retail Energy Markets', 1 *Opinio Juris in Comparatione—Studies in Comparative and National Law* (2013) 111, at 127–128.

[101] Held in Vienna, see the CEER Annual Report 2013, at 17, available at <http://www.ceer.eu> (last accessed 9 April 2015).

[102] Ibid.

[103] See Fifth CEER Benchmarking Report on the Quality of Electricity Supply (2011), available through the CEER website <http://www.ceer.eu>.

[104] See CEER–ECRB, *Guidelines of Good Practice on the Implementation and Use of Voltage Quality Monitoring Systems for Regulatory Purposes*, Ref: C12-EQS-51-03, 3 December 2012, available through the Energy Community website, *supra* note 72.

[105] Ibid., at 5.

examples where the cooperation between the CEER and the ECRB contributes to facilitate implementation of customer protection in the national jurisdictions of EnCT Member States.

However, as the title of the chapter suggests, there is more to the cooperation between the CEER and the ERCB. In the authors' view, one can speak of a synergy between the two bodies working together on customer-related issues in the context of the Energy Community Treaty. The reason for this is that, as the previous section demonstrated, CEER also coordinates its best practices at regional level (with the ERRA) and at the international level (with the ICER). This means that in its activities with the ECRB, the CEER disseminates what it has coordinated on regional and international levels to the Energy Community, albeit indirectly, embodying a regulatory triangle comprising the CEER, the ERRA, and the ICER.

The ECRB thus becomes a platform where EU, regional, and international standards and best practices come together to the benefit of the entire Energy Community. A good example of the ECRB as a regulatory platform for EU (through CEER) and regional standards (through ERRA) is some of the combined activities that have taken place, such as the joint Energy Community–CEER and ERRA Consumer Workshop dealing with retail markets, price comparison tools, and consumer engagement and involvement.[106] The result of this coordination creates a sum that is bigger than its separate parts, especially in the area of customer protection.

What should be noted in this respect is that the manner in which these regulatory platforms are intertwined may be less of coincidence than one may initially think, because one person heads them all.[107] Lord Mogg is the Chairman of ACER, the President of CEER, *and* the Chairman of ICER. Only ERRA seems not be presided over by Lord Mogg, perhaps because it is the only platform with a strong focus on Eastern Europe and Central Asia. This might explain the strong connection between the ACER and the CEER, and the European involvement in the ICER through the CEER (CEER presides the ICER).

C. The ECRB and EU Regulatory Private Law in the Energy Community: Outcomes for the Treatment of Vulnerable Customers and Customer Contracts

How then does this EU, regional, and international coordination within the Energy Community Regulatory Board affect customer contracts directly in the national jurisdictions of the Energy Community Member States? While it is clear that the activities in sharing best practices of the CEER–ERRA–ICER regulatory triangle do contribute to facilitating customer protection, it might be more

[106] See the joint Energy Community–CEER–ERRA Consumer Workshop held on 9 October 2013 in Vienna; information available at <https://www.energy-community.org/portal/page/portal/ENC_HOME/CALENDAR/Other_Meetings/2013/9_Oct> (last accessed 9 April 2015).

[107] For the background of Lord Mogg KCMG (John Mogg), see the website of the UK Parliament, at <http://www.parliament.uk/biographies/lords/lord-mogg/3855> (last accessed 9 April 2015).

difficult to produce concrete evidence regarding how this coordination affects customer contracts in the Energy Community directly.

Nevertheless, the ECRB does conduct very useful status reviews on how the acquis communitaire on consumer protection laws that are part of the Energy and Gas Directives are implemented in the Energy Community. The body has conducted two important studies on the influence of EU customer protection on national legislation in the EnCT region: 1) the Treatment of the Vulnerable Customer in the Energy Community (first prepared in 2011, and subsequently updated in 2012 and 2013) and 2) the Status Review of Customer Contracts in the Energy Community (April 2014).[108] Both reports collected data through questionnaires to regulatory authorities of all the EnCT contracting parties.

As mentioned earlier in section 1, Article 3 of the Electricity Directive 2003/54/EC and Gas Directive 2003/55/EC covers public service obligations and customer protection.[109] Transparency regarding contractual terms and conditions is required by Article 3(3) of the Electricity Directive and Article 3(5) of the Gas Directive. Energy Community Member States are urged to ensure a high level of customer protection regarding transparency in contractual terms and conditions, general information, and dispute-settlement mechanisms. Additionally, household customers should be able to choose their suppliers and enter into contracts with them.[110] The directives also mention special protection for vulnerable customers, by stating that contracting parties 'shall in particular ensure that there are adequate safeguards to protect vulnerable customers, including appropriate measures to help them avoid disconnection'.[111] A precise definition of this term is not given in EU law, nevertheless, in the context of the EnCT framework, the directives require that members formulate a definition of vulnerable customers and take appropriate measures providing social security benefits and guaranteed energy supply to them.[112]

The first ECRB report on vulnerable customers looked at household consumers.[113] Moreover, it looked at national regulatory law (energy-related laws and social protection schemes) with respect to customers in the energy sector, rather than at private contracts.[114]

The report analysed the whole spectrum of EnCT Member States to see to what extent they have defined what constitutes a 'vulnerable customer' and what kind of support schemes are in place for this category of consumer. It concludes that there has been some progress in defining and protecting vulnerable customers in the

[108] See ECRB, *supra* note 6.

[109] Art. 3 of the Electricity and Gas Directives, *supra* note 15.

[110] ECRB, *Status Review of Customer Contracts in the Energy Community, supra* note 6, at 5.

[111] ECRB, *Treatment of the Vulnerable Customer in the Energy Community, supra* note 6, at 1; Recital 2 and 24 and Art. 3(5) of the Electricity Directive; Recital 2 and Art. 3 (3) of the Gas Directive.

[112] See paras 45 and 53, Art. 3(7) and (8) of the Directive 2009/72 of the European Parliament and Council of 13 July 2009 concerning common rules for the internal market in electricity and repealing Directive 2003/54, OJ 2009 L 211. For the gas market, see paras 33, 44, 50, and Art. 3(3) and (4) of the Directive 2009/73 of the European Parliament and Council of 13 July 2009 concerning common rules for the internal market in natural gas and repealing Directive 2003/55, OJ 2009 L 211.

[113] *See* ECRB, *Treatment of the Vulnerable Customer in the Energy Community, supra* note 6.

[114] Ibid., at 20.

Energy Community, although several EnCT Member States lack such a definition (such as Albania, Macedonia, Moldova, and Ukraine).[115] Despite the fact that they do not explicitly use the term 'vulnerable customer', most EnCT countries nevertheless have support schemes for these people in place in one way or another.[116]

Across the EnCT region, there is great variety with regard to what categories of vulnerable customers are entitled to qualify for governmental support, but poor health and disability seem to be the common denominator. The report also concluded that the implementation of economic support schemes is preferred over non-economic measures. In the majority of cases, the costs of providing economic support to vulnerable customers are covered through governmental budgets, but cross-subsidies appear sometimes as well (for instance in Ukraine).[117] However, to the ECRB's discontent, almost none of the EnCT countries was able to provide figures on the market share of the households receiving support.[118]

The second ECRB report, the Status Review of Customer Contracts, is especially interesting for customer protection in contracts. It clearly shows how EU regulatory private law is exported and how it influences private law in the Energy Community.[119] The report assesses customer contracts across the whole EnCT region to determine to what extent the acquis communitaire with respect to customer protection has been implemented in EnCT contracting parties, and how it has affected energy supply contracts. The report examines gas and electricity supply contracts for household customers in the Community. This means it focuses on rules related to the conclusion, termination, and amendment of the contract, the content of the contract, the rights and obligations of contract parties, etc. Again, EnCT contracting parties' regulatory authorities provided the data in preparing the report.[120] The definition of a 'supply contract' used in the report is: 'a contract for supply of electricity or gas is an agreement concluded between a supplier and the customer involving the supply and purchase of electricity/gas under conditions agreed by the parties in concordance with regulations'.[121]

Contracts for the supply of electricity and gas generally build on national rules for civil contracts on sale and purchase. Due to the fact that they deal with energy supply, which is traditionally a heavily regulated sector, they are usually subject to special legal regulation. However, cross-references between contract law, general law on consumer protection, and specific energy sector regulations are applicable in the jurisdictions of EnCT contracting parties.

Just as in the case of the definition of a 'vulnerable customer', the report reveals that not all EnCT members maintain a specific definition of what a supply contract for electricity and gas entails.[122] For instance, Macedonia, Moldova, and

[115] Ibid., at 5 (Table 2) and 20. [116] Ibid., at 21.

[117] Ibid., at 13 and 20. [118] Ibid.

[119] ECRB, *Status Review of Customer Contracts in the Energy Community, supra* note 6.

[120] Ibid., at 7: The NRAs of the Energy Community Members first and foremost assured that the customer-related provisions of the Electricity and Gas Directives are transposed into their national legislations, and they also provided the relevant legal references.

[121] Ibid.

[122] Ibid. Albania, Bosnia and Herzegovina (for electricity), Kosovo, Serbia, and Ukraine do have definitions for this.

Montenegro have not formulated such a definition; they instead apply the general definition for sales contracts provided in national civil and/or commercial law.[123] Nevertheless, whether defined or not, general rules of sales contracts apply across the board in EnCT countries.

An important finding in the report with respect to implementation of customer protection in energy supply contracts in the Energy Community is that although all CPs have transposed customer-related provisions into their national legislations, there is still room for improvement.[124] This is especially true with regard to transparency in relation to contracts. Customers' rights could, for instance, be strengthened by improving information provisions and other contractual terms in order to facilitate switching, so customers can make better informed choices with regard to their supplier. For example, with respect to Ukraine, the ECRB notes that: '[t]he Electricity Law does not provide a framework for customer protection compliant with the acquis due to the lack of requirements for provision of information, contractual arrangements and quality of service.'[125]

While most household customers within the EnCT jurisdiction only conclude one contract with a gas/electricity supplier, there are several countries (Albania, Bosnia and Herzegovina) where customers need to enter into two contracts, one for the supply of energy and one for the distribution, and this may impede transparency if a customer wishes to switch companies.[126] Across the whole EnCT region, there seems to be a universal practice that supply contracts are measured from the metering point of a house.[127] An element which has not been implemented in the great majority of EnCT contracting parties is the opportunity to offer customers combined contracts for the supply of a broader group of services, such as the supply of electricity combined with TV and the Internet.[128]

Furthermore, there is a legal obligation for suppliers to enter into a supply contract in all EnCT contracting parties. The duration of contracts is usually regulated by law (such as in Kosovo and Ukraine).[129] In case the period is undetermined, the supplier determines a standard duration and the customer has the right to negotiate. Also, in all EnCT contracting parties, the suppliers are obliged to inform the customer of the contract conditions prior to the conclusion of the contract.[130] This is in line with the Electricity and Gas Directive requiring that conditions of contracts shall be fair and that suppliers shall ensure that the conditions are well known in advance by their customers.[131]

[123] Ibid., at 7. [124] Ibid., at 60.

[125] See Energy Community website, *supra* note 72, under Areas of Work—Ukraine Electricity.

[126] ECRB, *Status Review of Customer Contracts in the Energy Community, supra* note 6, at 60.

[127] Ibid. Note: The supply contract is also related also to another issue: in case a customer owns several facilities with different addresses, he/she may have one or more contracts. In the investigated Energy Community, contracting parties' and other markets' supply contracts are always signed separately for each facility of the same owner. Regarding the number and types of contracts household customers may conclude, the regulators explained in which cases a customer may enter into contracts with different suppliers. For example, in Bosnia and Herzegovina and Serbia, under certain circumstances, customers may have several suppliers for one metering point. However seven out of thirteen regulators stated that having more than one supplier is not possible at all.

[128] Ibid. [129] Ibid., at 61. [130] Ibid. [131] Ibid.

What further flows from the report is that in the vast majority of EnCT contracting parties, the regulator possesses competences related to contracting. The implication thus is that in order to protect customers against unfair contractual terms, regulators can use private law regulatory tools, such as standardized contract terms. In Kosovo and Macedonia, this means that the regulator uses a standard contract form or template. In Ukraine, it implies that the government approves a standard contract on electricity usage and natural gas supply for households. It is the regulator who monitors the execution of these standard contracts.[132] For Moldova, it means the regulator has pre-contractual competences and can issue decisions that oblige the supplier to conclude a contract with the customer, while in Bosnia and Herzegovina suppliers are obliged to submit standard contract forms to the entity regulator before offering it to the customer. The majority of EnCT countries make use of standardized contracts; Bosnia and Herzegovina and Moldova are the only EnCT members where the supply contract is negotiable.

The report concludes that most of the required provisions listed in Annex 1 of the Electricity and Gas Directives are included in the electricity and gas supply contracts for households in the contracting parties to the Energy Community.[133] For instance, contracts generally include clear conditions for their renewal and termination. Additionally, as required in Annex I of the directives, customers have to be given adequate notice of any intention to modify contractual conditions and need to be informed about their right of withdrawal when notice is given, an obligation which has been implemented in all countries of the Energy Community.[134] In some countries, elements such as the time for initial connection, the type of maintenance service offered, or compensation and refund arrangements in case of lower service quality levels, are missing, however.[135]

It becomes clear that the ECRB does what it can with regard to monitoring the implementation and influence of the IEM acquis in the Energy Community. Since the Electricity and Gas Directives deal with customer protection clauses that influence energy supply contract in the EnCT region directly, this proves that the EnCT goes beyond the mere exportation of the EU energy acquis. In fact, it provides a very pure form of regulatory private law beyond the borders of the EU, but the ECRB manages to do so in cooperation with the CEER and the regulatory triangle that comes with it, creating a synergy in the facilitation of customer protection in the Energy Community contracting parties.

[132] Ibid.

[133] Annex 1 of the Gas and Electricity Directives, *supra* note 15, and ECRB, *Status Review of Customer Contracts in the Energy Community, supra* note 6, at 61.

[134] Note, however, that the prescribed timelines for this earlier notification differ among countries. It is, for example, 30 days in Albania and 15 days in Serbia.

[135] ECRB, *Status Review of Customer Contracts in the Energy Community, supra* note 6, at 61.

4. Conclusion

This chapter sought to show that the interplay between CEER rule-making and coordination with the Energy Community Regulatory Board fulfils an important role in exporting EU regulatory private law beyond Europe's borders. In the field of customer protection, the aim is to strengthen the implementation of the IEM energy acquis in the Energy Community. The chapter started out by explaining the basic functioning of the IEM. It then turned to discussing the role of the Council of European energy regulators. The example of the CEER showed how informal rules in energy can be coordinated on the EU level and provided a study of how the EU indirectly coordinates energy regulation at the regional and international levels.

The chapter then discussed the Energy Community Treaty and its regulatory board. As the coordination platform for exchange of knowledge and development of best practices for, amongst others, customer protection in the Energy Community region, the board serves as a platform for disseminating customer protection to the contracting parties. Through the cooperation between the CEER and the ECRB, a synergy emerges as the CEER is also actively involved with the regional platform, the ERRA, and the international platform, ICER. Since the ECRB has joint activities with the CEER and with all these platforms, the sum is greater than its parts, resulting in stronger customer protection in the national jurisdictions of the Energy Community through dissemination of EU regulatory private law.

12

Non-Measurable Negotiations

The EU between Transnational Regulation of Pharmaceuticals and Private Law

Marco Rizzi

1. Transnational Regulation and Private Law: Two Stems Apart

The aims of this chapter are to look at the role of the EU in regulating pharmaceutical safety in the internal market, and to contrast that role with the EU's peculiar capacity of co-regulator in the transnational space of pharmaceutical safety and efficacy governance. The intent of the analysis proposed here is to highlight a dichotomy between the internal and external roles of the EU in pharmaceutical rule-making. Whereas throughout the second half of the 20th century the EU has gained an ever more prominent and centralized role in the regulation of medicines within its borders, culminating with the adoption of Directive 2001/83/EC[1] on the Community code relating to medicinal products for human use (and subsequent amendments and addenda), externally the situation is one of significant complexity. The intricacies of the transnational institutional framework of pharmaceutical regulation need to be addressed and described in order to understand the EU's regulatory role for the traditional private law dimension. What is contended here is that while a form of regulatory private law has been developing at a transnational level with intrinsic limits (what will be referred to as 'non-measurable negotiations'), traditional forms of private law have the potential to vindicate a significant role for the EU as a negotiator in transnational regulatory private law-making.

2. The Framework and the Argument

Ever since the International Conference of Drug Regulatory Authorities (ICDRA) held by the World Health Organization (WHO) in 1989, regulators from the US,

[1] Council Directive 2001/83/EC on the Community Code relating to medicinal products for human use, OJ 2001 L 311/67.

EU, and Japan have underlined the necessity for transnational common ground in the making and implementation of regulatory standards leading to marketing approval of new pharmaceutical products. The reasons for this push are associated with the global nature of the pharmaceutical market and the multinational dimension of the major industries involved, strongly advocating for simplified procedures allowing speedier global marketing of new products. With the institution of the International Conference on Harmonization of Technical Requirements for Registration of Pharmaceuticals for Human Use (ICH) in 1990,[2] the regulators of the US, EU, and Japan created an informal forum where regulators and regional representatives of the pharmaceutical industry could negotiate guidelines touching on major regulatory aspects ranging from safety to efficacy, with the declared purpose of facilitating new products' access to global markets, avoiding duplication of procedures caused by regulatory diversity.[3]

Within this informal transnational regulatory network, the EU, represented by both the European Medicines Agency (EMA) and the Commission, participates as a co-regulator (or more appropriately as a negotiator), exercising one vote within the Steering Committee (the executive body of the ICH), alongside the US and Japan governments and representatives of industry from those three regions (a total of six voting members). This chapter analyses the mechanisms of adoption of ICH guidelines contrasted with the internal mechanisms of the EU, inspired by the concept of deliberative democracy.

Next, this chapter focuses on the procedural mechanisms of the ICH to suggest a second dichotomy, between the formal and substantial role of the EU representatives within the Steering Committee. A close look at ICH structure suggests the existence of a hardly regulatable power play among the prime actors of the network. In particular, the completely informal nature of the forum's practice makes it difficult to introduce rigorous procedural checks and balances and 'deliberative standards'. Therefore the actual weight of each actor *within* the ICH is a rather complicated element to measure. The extraordinary impact of its guidelines in the transnational regulation of medicines makes it crucial to open the issue to debate.

To uncover these issues the chapter will refer to the adoption of key harmonizing guidelines as 'pilots' for a general discussion on the forum:

- ICH guideline E6 on good clinical practice (GCP)—the key document allowing acceptance of global clinical trials results.
- ICH guideline E9 on statistical principles for clinical trials (SPCT)—providing a set of general principles on the applicable standards for global trials (highly deferential to the interest of maintaining a plurality of approaches to the use of placebos in the conduct of trials on humans).

[2] See *infra* section 4 on the birth and development of ICH; see also ICH, *History*, available at <http://www.ich.org/about/history.html> (last accessed March 2015); and Berman, 'The Role of Domestic Administrative Law in the Accountability of IN-LAW: The Case of the ICH', in J. Pauwelyn, R. Wessel, and J. Wouters (eds), *Informal International Lawmaking: Mapping the Action and Testing Concepts of Accountability and Effectiveness* (2012).

[3] See ICH, *Vision*, available at <http://www.ich.org/about/vision.html> (last accessed March 2015).

After analysing this double dichotomy, the chapter will switch focus to the consequences (actual or potential) of the evolution of the regulatory arena on a consolidated pillar of private law: products liability. Starting from the premise that complementarity between products liability and regulation is essential for the successful achievement of both sets of rules' endgame (product safety and consumer protection), the chapter argues that a changing landscape in regulation calls for a reconsideration of product liability's role: a 'new role' for old rules. The focus is on the concepts of complementarity and regulatory compliance. A seemingly consolidated judicial formalistic and deferential approach (to regulatory decisions) could (and possibly should) evolve into a more substance-oriented test.

The chapter will therefore be structured as follows. Section 3 will give a brief account of the evolving development of the EMA (describing how the EU has internally overcome the issue of transnational regulatory practices), while section 4 will move to a similar description of the ICH, focusing on its controversial structure. This should uncover the first dichotomy between the strong internal EU regulatory design and its 'lighter' external position. Section 5 will critically analyse the mechanisms of adoption of essential ICH guidelines, highlighting the second dichotomy between the formal and substantial role of the EU as a transnational 'regulatory negotiator'. Section 6 describes the structural difficulties that ensue from the attempt to systematize a regulatory framework that has the ICH at its top through theoretical constructions very much dependent on the EU internal architecture (and therefore ill-suited to address its *external* role). The tentative conclusion here is that the ability of the EU to expand the scope of its policies and vision in the field of pharmaceutical regulation is highly dependent on its strength as a negotiator, hardly measurable in the absence of clear transparency guarantees. Section 7 will finally explore the other side of the pharmaceutical safety and efficacy coin. In the unsettled regulatory environment described throughout the chapter, old rules of torts can claim a renewed role in adequately complementing pharmaceutical regulation.

3. EU Internal Regulatory Framework

The EU regulatory system for medicinal products is arguably the most complex and extensive system it possesses, comprising a 'very substantial body of Community legislation and case law'.[4] It has been amended regularly since the first directive was introduced in 1965 as a response to the Thalidomide tragedy[5] (at which time only a few countries already had regulatory systems in place).[6] In parallel to EU

[4] Jacobs, 'Foreword', in R. Goldberg and J. Lonbay (eds), *Pharmaceutical Medicine, Biotechnology and European Law* (2001) xiii; C. Hodges, *European Regulation of Consumer Product Safety* (2005) 38.

[5] H. Teff and C. R. Munro, *Thalidomide: The Legal Aftermath* (1976); Griffin and Shah, 'The Development of the Control of Human Medicines in Europe from Classical Times to the Year 2000', in J. P. Griffin and J. O'Grady (eds), *The Textbook of Pharmaceutical Medicine* (44th edn, 2002) 58; J. Abraham and G. Lewis, *Regulating Medicines in Europe* (2000).

[6] See, for example, the US Food Drugs and Cosmetics Act (FDCA) 1938.

regulations, *Thalidomide* was also the trigger for the adoption of the stringent mechanisms devised by the German law of pharmaceutical products (the 1976 *Arzneimittlengesetz*).[7] This legislation will be further discussed below in the analysis of the EU Product Liability Directive[8] and its relationship to special national regimes of liability for specific product categories. As suggested above, exploring the potential for an approach based on complementarity between regulation and liability requires first an analysis of the regulatory environment. It is, however, significant to notice at this preliminary stage that both the birth of regulatory requirements for marketing authorization and the embryo of the debate that will lead to the adoption of the Product Liability Directive share a common root.[9]

The full historical account of the evolution that occurred between the 1960s and today is beyond the scope of this chapter, but it is worth keeping in mind some key developments in regulatory evolution.[10] To promote collaboration between the Member States and the EU Commission, in 1977 the Committee for Proprietary Medicinal Products (CPMP)[11] began its mandate. As an independent networking scientific committee, its function was to foster harmonization of assessment standards and facilitate cooperation between national agencies and the EU Commission. The result of this initiative was to provide 'the first EU-level forum for MSs representatives, from which grew networks of contacts'[12] among scientific experts coming from their authorities of origin in the Member States.[13] Alongside the legislation provided by the directives, the CPMP started to produce detailed scientific guidelines on drug testing, creating a body of supplementary technical 'soft law'.[14]

During the 1980s, a significant trend started at a European level, combining and complementing harmonization with mechanisms of mutual recognition of national rules and standards where they complied with EU minimum requirements.[15] The reasoning behind this was that even in the presence of full harmonization of the rules, final decisions on marketing authorizations would always have to

[7] *Gesetz über den Verkehr mit Arzneimitteln (Arzneimittelgesetz—AMG)*, of 24 August 1976.

[8] Council Directive 85/374/EEC on the approximation of the laws and administrative provisions of the Member States concerning liability for defective products, OJ 1985 L 210.

[9] R. Goldberg, *Causation and Risk in the Law of Torts: Scientific Evidence and Medicinal Products Liability* (1999).

[10] This reconstruction owes very much to the works of Cuviller, 'The Role of the European Medicines Evaluation Agency in the Harmonisation of Pharmaceutical Regulation', in R. Goldberg and J. Lonbay (eds), *supra* note 4, at 137; and Sauer, 'New Drugs in the Global Economy: Risk Assessment and Risk Management in the EU and Co-Operation with the US' (lecture held at the University of Pittsburgh, 13 November 2000).

[11] Council Directive 78/420/EEC amending Second Directive 75/319/EEC on the approximation of provisions laid down by law, regulation or administrative action relating to proprietary medicinal products, OJ 1978 L 123/26.

[12] Sauer, *supra* note 10.

[13] See also Wahlroos, 'Control of Medicines in the European Union and Drug Information', in J. L. Valverde and P. Weissenberg (eds), *The Challenges of the New EU Pharmaceutical Legislation, Volume 6: Pharmaceutical Policy and the Law* (2005).

[14] See Cuviller, *supra* note 10; and Hodges, *supra* note 4.

[15] Sauer, *supra* note 10, and Cuviller, *supra* note 10; on the 'trend' see R. Rhodes, *Understanding Governance: Policy Networks, Governance, Reflexivity and Accountability* (1997).

be made on a case-by-case risk/benefit assessment by Member State authorities.[16] In the absence of unified decision-making procedures[17] there would always be the potential for divergent assessments. In response to the intricacies of conflicting regulatory outputs, the decision taken was to rely temporarily on mutual recognition of Member States' authorities' decisions.

These preliminary stages led to the Member States and the Commission proceeding with a natural step forward, entailing a shift 'from harmonisation of rules to harmonisation of decision-taking'.[18] The key move in this direction was the creation of a properly European marketing authorization system with Council Regulation 2309/93/EEC, reinforced by the establishment of the EMEA (now EMA)[19] as an advisory body for the Commission. In agreeing to create the EMA, Member States began to renounce, if only partially, their sovereignty over the authorization of medicines.[20] Alongside the inauguration of the EMA, the regulation introduced the marketing authorization architecture that is still in place with two alternative procedural mechanisms, centralized and decentralized.[21]

The centralized procedure was initially compulsory for pharmaceutical products derived from biotechnology only, and optional for other innovative products.[22] Since 2004,[23] the scope of the compulsory application of the centralized procedure has been expanded and specified: a marketing authorization application (MAA) must be made directly to the EMA for evaluation by the CPMP (renamed CHMP, Committee for Medicinal Products for Human Use, since 2001). The actual marketing authorization is then issued by the Commission on the basis of the EMA's advice.[24] A centralized marketing authorization is valid throughout the whole EU. The post-marketing surveillance is now disciplined by the recently adopted Directive 2012/26/EU,[25] whereby the EMA avails itself of the network of national Member States' authorities to undertake effective pharmacovigilance.

[16] Sauer, *supra* note 10, and Cuviller, *supra* note 10.

[17] See Cuviller, *supra* note 10, at 140, and among others Feldschreiber, 'Marketing Authorisation', in P. Feldschreiber (ed.), *The Law and Regulation of Medicine* (2008) 103, at 103–111.

[18] Sauer, *supra* note 10; see also Alder, 'Roles and responsibilities of the Regulator', in Feldschreiber (ed.), *supra* note 17, at 73–1013; on the move towards transnational decision-making see R. Dehousse and C. Joerges (eds), *Good Governance in Europe's Integrated Market* (2002); C. Joerges and G. Teubner, *Transnational Governance* (2004); Scott, 'Regulating Constitutions', in C. Parker *et al.* (eds), *Regulating Law* (2004) 226.

[19] Council Regulation 2309/93/EEC laying down Community procedures for the authorisation and supervision of medicinal products for human and veterinary use, and establishing a European Agency for the Evaluation of Medicinal Products, OJ 1993 L 214.

[20] See below on the progressive move towards the centralization of regulatory procedures.

[21] A third route exists for purely national marketing authorization where the product is marketed in one MS only.

[22] See Annex to Council Regulation 2309/93/EEC, OJ 1993 L 214/1.

[23] Council Regulation 726/2004/EC laying down Community procedures for the authorization and supervision of medicinal products for human and veterinary use and establishing a European Medicines Agency, OJ 2004 L 136/1.

[24] Note that the Commission never departs from EMA's opinions.

[25] Directive 2012/26/EU of the European Parliament and of the Council of 25 October 2012 amending Directive 2001/83/EC as regards pharmacovigilance (Text with EEA relevance), OJ 2012 L 299/1.

The decentralized procedure is based on the principle of mutual recognition of national authorizations between Member States as elaborated in the 1980s. While originally widely adopted for the majority of non-biotech new medicines,[26] its use for innovative products is progressively diminishing. The procedure allows for a national marketing authorization holder to extend the validity of his authorization to one or more selected Member States' markets. The EMA functions as an arbitrator in case a Member State refuses to recognize the validity of an applicant's authorization. The main committee involved is the Coordination Group for Mutual Recognition and Decentralised Procedure–Human (CMDh)[27] created in 2005 to mediate disagreements between Member States. If conciliatory attempts fail, the matter is referred to the CHMP for arbitration (subsequently enforced by the Commission).[28]

The history of the creation of the EMA is therefore eminently supranational. At the time the first EU legislation was adopted in the field, almost no Member State had in place an autonomous legal framework for the regulation of medicines. The parallel development of national authorities and EU legislation was a key factor in facilitating harmonization of both rules and decision-making.[29] The progressively stronger move towards centralization of procedures suggests that today the EU can be considered a highly integrated market in the pharmaceutical field, and that its legislation is de facto domestic in nature.

The regulatory system for pharmaceutical products was extensively revisited in 2001 (and regularly amended ever since) with a significant codification initiative.[30] The reform did not substantially modify the peculiar coexistence of two procedures.[31] As suggested above though, there has been a trend towards greater reliance on the centralized procedure, reshaping the EU regulatory model in a centralized fashion,[32] and reinforcing the decision-making power of the CHMP. Although the

[26] Sauer, *supra* note 10.

[27] See EMA, *Coordination Group for Mutual Recognition and Decentralised Procedures—Human (CMDh)*, available at <http://www.ema.europa.eu/ema/> under 'Committees' (last accessed 1 March 2015).

[28] Both mechanisms are now disciplined by Council Directive 2001/83/EC on the Community code relating to medicinal products for human use, OJ 2001 L 311/67.

[29] Feldschreiber, 'The Structure and Function of Medicines Regulation in Europe', in Feldschreiber (ed.), *supra* note 18, at 3.

[30] Council Directive 2001/83/EC, *supra* note 25; Council Directive 2004/27/EC, OJ 2004, L 136/34; Council Regulation 726/2004/EC, *supra* note 23.

[31] See Rizzi, 'Regulating Risks in Pharmaceutical Law: the Need of an Optimal Interplay between Product Safety and Product Liability', 1 *Opinio Juris in Comparatione* (2011) 25, at 6 note 17. The first Directive 65/65/EEC called for the introduction of national authorization systems, and reforms to the mutual recognition procedures have slowly but gradually been introduced since then, for example under Directive 87/22/EEC. The centralized procedure introduced by Regulation 2309/93/EEC was effectively established on a trial basis, restricted to certain categories of products, which have been significantly expanded over time. Whereas some authors suggest that the decentralized system is outdated and should be abandoned altogether, see Hodges, *supra* note 4, at 40, others suggest that it could be taken as a model for an international marketing approval procedure: see Purnhagen, 'The Challenge of Globalisation in Pharmaceutical Law: Is an International Drug Approval System Modeled after the European System Worth Considering?', 63 *Food and Drug Law Journal* (2008) 623, at 644–645.

[32] Since the creation of the EMA, the mandatory scope of application of the centralized procedure has been regularly expanded. It is now regulated by the Annex to Council Regulation 726/2004/EC,

committee's function is formally purely advisory, its decisions are in fact always conclusive as there has been no case where the Commission has departed from the agency's advice.

Several factors contributed to the suggested centralization of regulatory procedures: first, the greater coherence of such a model in the context of a European single market and, second, the fact that the operational history of the mutual recognition system has been less than satisfactory as it has led to inefficiencies and anomalies in the delivery of safety.[33] The major factor introducing an element of uncertainty is the definition of risk as provided by Article 28 of Directive 2001/83/EC, according to which risks related to the use of medicinal products are: 'any risk relating to the quality, safety or efficacy of the medicinal product as regards the patients' health or public health; any risk or undesirable effects on the environment'. The subsequent Article 28a describes the risk/benefit balance as: 'an evaluation of the positive therapeutic effects of the medicinal product in relation to the risks as defined in point 28'. A risk is, therefore, 'any risk'.[34] A study conducted in 2010 among EMA regulators has shown that there is no clear understanding of what a 'risk' is under the current regulatory framework for the EU pharmaceutical market.[35] Here is a strong argument *contra* the decentralized procedure: with conceptions of risk varying considerably within a single regulatory authority, the degree of variation is consistently increased by involving multiple regulatory authorities.

The EMA was born as a networking agency with explicit centralized powers only for a limited number of cases. However, because of the operational failure of the decentralized model, it has acquired an increasingly centralized role, thus creating a strong domestic framework (the EU). This framework, however, appears to be vulnerable when permeated from the outside, for the very reasons that promoted a shift from decentralized to centralized procedures *within* the EU.

4. An International Conference or a Pure Negotiating Platform?

Whereas the European regulation for pharmaceutical approval is situated within a precise legal framework, at an international level the situation appears to be very much dependent on negotiating processes rather than clear legal regulations,

supra note 23. The procedure is optional for other products, but progressively preferred for the reasons explained below.

[33] The need for a more consistent use of the centralized procedure has been stressed by many as the decentralized procedure has not achieved its functional scope of facilitating pharmaceutical distribution in the EU market, and has created some confusion, see Feldschreiber, *supra* note 17, at 103–111.

[34] The lack of clarity on the concept of 'risk' in the regulatory framework for marketing approval suggests that the CHMP's de facto decision-making power is rather a policy-making power, as the legislative vagueness leaves room for substantial discretion for the decision-makers.

[35] Phillips, 'EMA Risk-Benefit Project' (presentation at the British Institute of International and Comparative Law, 29 September 2010), showing that among EMA regulators, 51 different definitions of 'risk' were collected.

despite the growing transnational breadth of production and testing: EU aggregate figures give a clear picture of the phenomenon. Reports published by the EMA in December 2013 provide revealing overviews of the distribution and numbers of patients, investigator sites and pivotal clinical trials included in Marketing Authorization Applications (MAA) submitted to the EMA between January 2005 and December 2011.[36] Data show that 62 per cent of the overall patient population in pivotal clinical trials submitted to the EMA were from non-EU countries, comprising 37.3 per cent from the ROW region (Rest of the World, comprising Africa, Middle East/Asia/Pacific, Australia/New Zealand, Central/South America, CIS, Eastern Europe non-EU), and 31.5 per cent from North America (US and Canada).[37] The number of patients recruited in the EEA is progressively decreasing, and the major contributors are Finland, Germany, and Poland.[38] In contrast, the number of patients recruited in the ROW area, primarily in middle- and low-income countries, is proportionally growing, with China, Costa Rica, Philippines, Japan, Brazil, Russia, Thailand, and South Africa as major contributors (with a range of 120 to over 200 patients recruited per pivotal clinical trial per country in MAAs submitted to the EMA).[39] The overall trend as regards clinical trial sites increases in ROW low- and middle-income countries is substantially proportionate to that of patients.[40] A further element of interest is the number of patients per site registered in submitted clinical trials reports to the EMA for MAAs. While the EU/EEA/EFTA registers 13 patients per site,[41] and North America 10, the ROW averages 17 (the peak being Africa with 23, followed by Central/South America with 19).[42] These rates are particularly significant because of structural difficulties in quality control by investigators in developing country sites.[43]

We suggested above the existence of a dichotomy between the domestically designed EU regulatory framework and the role of the EU in the transnational dimension of regulatory processes. Since 1989, regulators and the pharmaceutical industry found a common interest in attempting to eliminate unnecessary delays in the global development and distribution of new treatments through the harmonization of requirements for drug approval at a transnational level, an initiative consistent with the global nature of the pharmaceutical market. The mission

[36] The data are partial as not all products for the relevant period are included, and secondly, most trials are excluded as not published and/or not registered. For the full report, see EMA, *Clinical Trials Submitted in Marketing Authorization to Applications to EMA: Overview of Patients recruitment and the Geographical Location of Investigator Site*, Doc. Ref. EMA/INS/GCP/676319/2012, 11 December 2013, available at <http://www.ema.europa.eu/docs/en_GB/document_library/Other/2009/12/WC500016819.pdf> (last accessed 1 March 2015).

[37] Ibid., at 9, Table 2. [38] Ibid., at 22, Figure 12. [39] Ibid., at 23, Figure 13.

[40] Altavilla, 'Ethical Standards for Clinical Trials Conducted in Third Countries: The New Strategy of the European Medicines Agency', 18 *European Journal of Health Law* (2011) 65, at 65–67.

[41] The number is inflated by the higher average number of patients per site in eastern European countries (16 per site) compared to older western European countries.

[42] EMA, *supra* note 36, at 21, Figure 11.

[43] Major concerns comprise (1) structural deficiencies in data control quality, (2) divergences in therapeutic culture, (3) ethical misconduct with scientific implications, and (4) issues related to patient recruitment, treatment-naivety, and genetic aspects of treatment success or failure.

of the ICH is accordingly to make recommendations towards achieving greater harmonization in the interpretation and application of technical guidelines and requirements for pharmaceutical product registration.[44]

The ICH is organized as a hybrid public/private transnational regulatory network; its Steering Committee is the main body issuing legally non-binding guidelines for its members.[45] Decision-making is structured as a negotiation process among the members of the committee, the composition of which is worth recalling: EMA (together with a representative from the Commission), the United States Food and Drug Administration (FDA), the Japanese Ministry of Health, the European Federation of Pharmaceutical Industries and Associations (EFPIA), the Japan Pharmaceutical Manufacturers Association (JPMA), and the Pharmaceutical Research and Manufacturers of America (PhRMA).[46]

The harmonization activity of the ICH can take four different shapes: the development of a new guideline (formal ICH procedure), the creation of questions and answers to assist the implementation of a new guideline (the Q&A procedure), the revision or modification of existing guidelines (the revision procedure), and the addition of standards to existing guidelines and recommendations (the maintenance procedure).[47] The output of ICH work is normally translated into domestic regulatory frameworks through policy documents.[48]

In 2000, after a decade of existence, the ICH announced that it has been 'successful in achieving harmonisation, initially of technical guidelines and more recently on format and content of registration applications'.[49] Topics discussed by the forum have ranged over the entire terrain of drug testing, from pharmacokinetics to packaging requirements. After 20 years, ICH celebrated the achievement of significant steps forward in the achievement of common procedures and harmonized marketing application forms.[50] Overall, activity in the second decade has been less frenetic and is slowing down, and only a few guidelines and standards are at

[44] See ICH, *Vision*, available at <http://www.ich.org/about/vision.html> (last accessed 1 October 2014).

[45] It has been argued that ICH guidelines possess a de facto binding effect, the major example being the E6 ICH guidelines on GCP largely drawn upon in the draft of Directive 2001/20/EC on GCP, as noted by S. Kraphol, *Risk Regulation in the Single Market* (2008), at 84 and Purnhagen, *supra* note 31, at 638. However, *how* these guidelines are implemented, not only in the EU but in all ICH constituents, can be problematic, as suggested below.

[46] These are associations representing major R&D pharmaceutical industry engaged in the development of new drugs, excluding, for example, manufacturer of generics.

[47] On the harmonization procedures see <http://www.ich.org/about/process-of-harmonisation.html> (last accessed 1 March 2015): for a full and detailed account of the ICH organization see Purnhagen, *supra* note 31, at 637–640.

[48] See *infra*, section 4.

[49] ICH SC, *The Future of ICH—Revised 2000* (Statement on the occasion of the Fifth International Conference on Harmonisation, 9 November 2000), available at <http://www.ich.org/fileadmin/Public_Web_Site/ABOUT_ICH/Vision/The_Future_of_ICH_-_Revised_2000.pdf> (last accessed 1 March 2015).

[50] ICH, *The Value and Benefits of ICH to Drug Regulatory Authorities—Advancing Harmonization for Better Health*, available at <http://www.ich.org/fileadmin/Public_Web_Site/News_room/C_Publications/ICH_20_anniversary_Value_Benefits_of_ICH_for_Regulators.pdf> (last accessed 1 March 2015).

various stages of the ICH process at this time.[51] Whereas consensus was reached quickly in many non-controversial areas,[52] others are proving much more difficult to harmonize, which allows for some critical observations.

First, the composition of the decision-making body raises an immediate problem in terms of legitimacy: the negotiation process excludes representatives of patients while ensuring an inclusion of representatives of the industry. It has been observed that 'the pharmaceutical industry is involved in the harmonization process right from the beginning and is able to influence the ICH directly from its heart as a member of its main working unit'.[53]

When ICH negotiations are successful in finding consensus for the adoption of guidelines, local implementation shows varying degrees of success, bringing into question the effectiveness of their harmonizing potential. For example, the GCP guidelines outlined by ICH[54] have been fully implemented in the EU,[55] including the parallel Good Manufacturing Practice (GMP) guidelines, whereas the two issues are considered separate and are independently regulated in the US.[56] The GCP guidelines, however, were intended to integrate the two aspects, as 'the authors of this clinical guideline had an excellent appreciation for the ramifications of inadequate manufacturing or packaging on the clinical program'.[57]

In a global environment in which harmonization of regulatory procedure is struggling to overcome resistance of competing regulatory styles, a transnational regulatory practice is well underway. The ability of the EU to have an impact on the negotiations leading to the adoption of guidelines has implications for the quality of its internal regulatory framework, beyond the major focus of this part of the book—whether informal negotiating processes give the EU more leeway to transnationally expand the scope of its own policies.

[51] Currently one is undergoing a process of open consultation, and four are under Q&A procedure, see <http://www.ich.org/products/open-consultation.html> (last accessed 1 March 2015).

[52] Such as basic guidelines on drug quality standards, necessary toxicity tests, and expectations for good clinical practice. See <http://www.ich.org/products/guidelines.html> (last accessed 1 March 2015).

[53] Purnhagen, *supra* note 31, at 638–639.

[54] ICH, *Tripartite Harmonized Guidelines—Guideline for Good Clinical Practice E6* (1996), available at <http://www.ich.org/products/guidelines/efficacy/article/efficacy-guidelines.html> (last accessed 1 October 2014).

[55] Directive 2001/20/EC on the approximation of the laws, regulations, and administrative provisions of the Member States relating to the implementation of good clinical practice in the conduct of clinical trials on medicinal products for human use, OJ 2001 L 121/34.

[56] See the FDA's guide to regulations on GCPs, available at <http://www.fda.gov/downloads/Drugs/.../Guidances/ucm073122.pdf>; and separately its guide to regulations on GMPs, available at <http://www.fda.gov/Food/GuidanceComplianceRegulatoryInformation/CurrentGoodManufacturingPracticesCGMPs/ucm110877.htm> (both last accessed 1 March 2015).

[57] Simmons and Bernstein, 'Navigating Differences between FDA and EMA for Regulatory Compliance During Drug Development', *BioPharm International* (2006) 2; see also ICH, *supra* at note 44, section 5.14.

5. The Transnational Way: Negotiation over Deliberation

The focus now turns to the ICH mechanisms of guidelines adoption and the role of its agents. Two excerpts from essential ICH guidelines subsequently implemented by its state members constitute our starting point.

ICH guidelines E6 on GCP:

Clinical trials should be conducted in accordance with the ethical principles that have their origin in the Declaration of Helsinki, and that are consistent with GCP and the applicable regulatory requirement(s) . . . A trial should be conducted in compliance with the protocol that has received prior institutional review board (IRB).[58]

ICH guideline E9 on Statistical Principles for Clinical Trials (SPCT):[59]

The focus of this guidance is on statistical principles. It does not address the use of specific statistical procedures or methods. Specific procedural steps to ensure that principles are implemented properly are the responsibility of the sponsor. Integration of data across clinical trials is discussed, but is not a primary focus of this guidance.[60]

While both are very complex documents, technically and procedurally specific, they do not seem to provide firm guidance on the interpretation of data and risk/benefit parameters.[61] On the substance of data interpretation, the terrain where experience, funding, and therapeutic cultures play crucial roles, investigators enjoy very wide autonomy. It is interesting here to focus on the mechanisms of production of guidelines such as the ICH E6 and E9. We contend that far from being a simple set of minimum technical standards, these rules are rather the clear expression of trade-oriented choices, upholding rapid access to market and free flow of products with health protection as a somewhat subsidiary goal, notwithstanding strong commitments in the founding ICH documents.[62] The key question for observers is then: 'who makes these fundamental value choices?'

We have outlined above the structure of the ICH and its steering committee,[63] the heart of the negotiating process. In addition to the six original members, four

[58] ICH, *supra* note 54, at 9.

[59] ICH, *Tripartite Harmonized Guidelines—Statistical Principles for Clinical Trials* (1998), available at <http://www.ich.org/fileadmin/Public_Web_Site/ICH_Products/Guidelines/Efficacy/E9/Step4/E9_Guideline.pdf> (last accessed 1 October 2014), at 2.

[60] Selected principles on data gathering and monitoring are spelled out in other guidelines, but they tend to be extremely sector-specific, and not quite oriented at providing general principles of good conduct.

[61] The guidelines are deferential to the autonomy of investigators in this matter. In other fields, the idea of risk assessment is narrowly defined instead of broadly suggested, as in the case of nuclear and radioactive materials, where the risk/benefit assessment is defined by a precise equation, Council Directive 2013/59/EURATOM laying down basic safety standards for protection against the dangers arising from exposure to ionising radiation, OJ 2014 L13/1, at 137 et seq.

[62] See ICH, *Vision*, available at http://www.ich.org/about/vision.html (last accessed 1 October 2014).

[63] See also ICH, *Organisation of the ICH*, available at <http://www.ich.org/about/organisation-of-ich.html> (last accessed 1 October 2014).

'observers' participate in the ICH.[64] The role of this group of non-voting members is to foster communication between countries that are not ICH members and those that are. The current observers are the WHO (which plays a strong role in connecting ICH and non-ICH countries for the purpose of ensuring comparable minimum standards, circulating ICH guideline drafts around non-ICH countries for comment and criticism), the Swiss pharmaceutical regulatory agency (Swissmedic), and Health Canada.

The steering committee is supported by ICH Coordinators and the ICH Secretariat. It not only determines procedures and policies for the ICH and selects topics for harmonization, but also monitors the progress of all harmonization activities. The steering committee consists of 15 members (the six voting members—each having double representatives—plus the observers described above), with an additional seat provided for a non-voting member of the International Federation of Pharmaceutical Manufacturers and Associations (IFPMA). The steering committee operates directly from the IFPMA office in Geneva.

In developing harmonized guidelines (the formal ICH procedure), the ICH follows a five-step consultative mechanism.[65] The process is triggered by one of the members or non-voting observers, which presents a 'concept paper' on a specific issue to the steering committee.[66] Once the steering committee has endorsed the concept paper, an expert working group (EWG) drafts a preliminary guideline based on the concept paper's desired goals. After the preliminary guideline has been approved by the steering committee, it undergoes regulatory consultation processes in the three ICH regions. The key actors at this stage become the regional agencies. The EMA in particular follows its procedure for guidelines and triggers a public consultation mechanism.[67] Comments can also be submitted directly to the ICH, and the WHO circulates the draft guidelines among its members for comments and observations. Commenting is therefore open to anyone from any country interested in taking part in the discussion. The results of the consultations are sent back to the ICH EWG, which elaborates an amended draft guideline to be adopted by the steering committee as a harmonized ICH guideline. While the commenting procedure is conceived as open and inclusive, the internal deliberative mechanisms are exclusive and scarcely transparent, as the proceedings of the steering committee and the negotiation processes are not published. Actual

[64] Ibid.; ICH, *Steering Committee*, available at <http://www.ich.org/about/organisation-of-ich/steering.html> (last accessed 1 October 2014).

[65] All decisions, both in the steering committee and in the subordinate working groups, are taken by way of consensus. The five steps of the formal ICH procedure are: 1) consensus building—technical document; 2) a. six-party consensus on technical document; b. Draft guideline adopted by ICH regulators; 3) regional regulatory consultation and discussion; 4) adoption of ICH-harmonized tripartite guideline; 5) implementation.

[66] Full description available at <http://www.ich.org/about/process-of-harmonisation/formalproc.html> (last accessed 1 March 2015).

[67] EMA, *Procedure for European Union Guidelines and Related Documents within the Pharmaceutical Legislative Framework* (2009), Doc. Ref. EMEA/P/24143/2004, available at <http://www.ema.europa.eu/docs/en_GB/document_library/Scientific_guideline/2009/10/WC500004011.pdf> (last accessed 1 October 2014).

decision-making is left to the internal mechanisms within the steering committee. It is important to note that the lack of access to the steering committee's internal proceedings does not allow for a full appreciation or evaluation of the fate of regional consulting results.

The implementation stage of the five-step formal ICH procedure is entrusted to the agencies, which adopt ICH guidelines for the conduct of internal marketing approval procedures (*within* the legal framework governing the margins of autonomy of agencies for their rule-making activity, but *outside* the rule-making mechanisms domestically in place).[68] While ICH guidelines are formally legally non-binding, they can arguably be considered de facto binding[69] due to the nature and extent of their use at a domestic level.[70] The de facto binding role of ICH guidelines is strikingly suggested by the heavy reliance on these guidelines by national law-makers designing domestic and regional legislation.

The majority of ICH guidelines do not actually end up being adopted as formal acts of law: they instead remain in the domestic legal frameworks as policy documents (e.g. administrative updates of the existing regulatory system) or instruments of 'governance' (which are not strictly speaking legal)[71] used to interpret and implement national pharmaceutical law and procedures. The domestic impact of such guidelines can therefore be dramatic in light of the dimensions of the global clinical trials phenomenon briefly suggested in the previous section.

To summarize, industry and regulators have found their interests converging over the last two decades, with a mutual desire to reduce the use of 'human, animal and material resources' as they work to 'eliminate unnecessary delay in the global development and registration of new drugs'.[72] The opportunity to cut costs and draw from large pools of potential patients is a potent driver for globalizing pre-marketing procedures. As the length of EMA approval procedures has been a constant object of criticism,[73] the opportunity to formalize market pressures into a set of regulatory guidelines represents a way for Western agencies to lessen their

[68] In the example of the GCP, the guideline was adopted by the FDA and published in the Federal Register, 9 May 1997, Vol. 62, No. 90, p. 25691-25709; and by the EMA in July 1996, issued as CPMP/ICH/135/95/Step 5, subsequently translated (as a consolidated administrative practice) into Directive 2005/28/EC laying down principles and detailed guidelines for good clinical practice as regards investigational medicinal products for human use, as well as the requirements for authorization of the manufacturing or importation of such products, OJ 2005 L 91/13. While the preliminary guideline underwent the comment consultation procedures, the final outcome is the result of a further negotiation at ICH level the proceedings of which are exclusive and not accessible.

[69] See Purnhagen, 'Competition of Agencies in European Pharmaceutical Law—Does It Exist, Is It Desirable and How to Handle It?', 1 *European Journal of Risk Regulation* (2010) 227.

[70] See Purnhagen, *supra* note 31; S. Kraphol, *supra* note 45, at 86 et seq.

[71] See Berman, 'Informal International Law Making in Medical Products Regulation', in A. Berman *et al.* (eds), *Informal International Law Making: Case-Studies* (2012) 353; and on the questionable legitimacy of these practices see Ehnert, 'The Legitimacy of New Risk Governance—A Critical View in Light of the EU's Approach to Nanotechnologies in Food', 21 *European Law Journal* (2015) 44.

[72] Purnhagen, *supra* note 31, quoting Hoff, 'The Regulatory Environment for the New Millennium', 34 *Drug Information Journal* (2000) 659.

[73] Andersson, 'The Drug Lag Issue: The Debate Seen from an International Perspective', 22 *International Journal of Health Services* (1998) 53.

regulatory burden, and for the industry to cut costs and delays in new products approvals substantially.[74] The protection of health and safety appears to be a subsidiary focus, both in the structure and in the stated goals of the venture.[75] The answer to the question 'who makes the fundamental value choices?' finds its answer in a negotiation process between industry and regulators acting within broad legislative frameworks, originally conceived for internal mechanisms and therefore scarcely equipped for transnational permutations.

6. What Kind of Governance and What Role for the EU?[76]

Describing which type of governance model (among those suggested and analysed in a quite florid literature)[77] is in place in the pharmaceutical system is a rather difficult endeavour. This section proposes an interpretation that underlines the dangers of the dichotomies referred to in the introduction.

Section 3 of this chapter briefly showed how advisory committees have, over time, gained power going far beyond simple consultancy and becoming real policy-makers. A comprehensive account of the evolution of administrative law in this sense has been developed by Karl-Heinz Ladeur who describes this process of attraction of power by administrators as an inherent trait of administrative law.[78] This process, the argument goes, is natural and finds a legitimating balance through experience, as administrative law is more the result of administrative

[74] A goal clearly stated by the ICH itself: 'Regulatory harmonisation offers many direct benefits to both regulatory authorities and the pharmaceutical industry with beneficial impact for the protection of public health. Key benefits include: preventing duplication of clinical trials in humans and minimising the use of animal testing without compromising safety and effectiveness; streamlining the regulatory assessment process for new drug applications; and reducing the development times and resources for drug development': ICH, *Vision*, available at <http://www.ich.org/about/vision.html> (last accessed 1 October 2014).

[75] As confirmed by the marginal role played by stakeholders outside the restricted 'regulator–industry' sphere.

[76] Reaching clear conclusions on the actual role and power exercised by each agent in informal international bodies such as the ICH is a rather laborious and potentially frustrating task. Depending on one's standpoint, the outcome of the analysis can take very different directions. See, for example, in this book Chapters 8 and 9. Whereas Wouters and Odermatt (Chapter 8) conclude that there is indeed a greater role for Europe to be played in the financial regulatory arena (see 'Conclusions'), Marcacci points out that in the same area, Europe has not lived up to its international ambitions (see Chapter 9, section 2). While Marcacci's conclusion is arguably prospective whereas Wouters and Odermatt are being descriptive, a measure of uncertainty casts a shadow over the exact *modus operandi* of transnational informal regulatory bodies.

[77] See among many others, Kingsbury, Krisch, and Stewart (special eds), 'The Emergence of Global Administrative Law', 68(3) and (4) *Law and Contemporary Problems* (2005) 15; Sabel and Zeitlin, 'Learning from Difference: The New Architecture of Experimentalist Governance in the EU', 14 *European Law Journal* (2008) 271; Dehousse and Joerges, *supra* note 18; Scott and Trubek, 'Mind the Gap: Law and New Approaches to Governance in the European Union', 8 *European Law Journal* (2002) 1; Walker and de Burca, 'Reconceiving Law and New Governance', 13 *Columbia Journal of European Law* (2007) 519.

[78] K.-H. Ladeur, 'The Emergence of Global Administrative Law and the Evolution of General Administrative Law', Osgoode CLPE Research Paper No 16/2011.

'experimentation' (and subsequent 'judicialization') than the output of a legislative mechanism. Considering administrative law as a self-generating endeavour, stabilized *ex-post* by courts or legislators, allows for an analysis focused on societal dynamics leading the evolutionary process of norm self-generation.[79] Ladeur describes these dynamics starting from the 'society of individuals' intimately linked with a form of administrative law based upon individual decisions, a stage that coincides in the language of statecraft with the age of the 'state-nation'.[80] The following stage runs parallel with the move to the 'nation-state', and is defined as the 'society of organizations', where individual decisions give way to collective concerns such as planning laws and forms of welfare state. Subsequently, as the state has moved to its most recent evolution, the 'market state', dynamics have evolved to the current 'network society', which requires new administrative forms and procedures for decision-making.[81] The core idea of Ladeur's theory is that 'the globalization process does not invade a stable domestic administrative... legal system from outside, but [is] also a consequence of an evolutionary process that disrupts the legal system from within'.[82]

In this reconstruction the move from domestic to transnational is a natural process consistent with national experiences, a consequence of societal dynamics that led to the kind of global networking of which the ICH is a perfect example. A general objection can, however, be raised to this conception of administrative law, specifically focusing on our field of interest. If it is true that regulators and regulated have always discussed the terms of the rules, the transnational dimension introduces a rather new and different phenomenon. Regulators and industry are participating *as peers* in the elaboration of ICH guidelines, which themselves contribute to the shaping and implementation of national or regional norms as discussed above. This seems hardly comparable to general administrative law as traditionally conceived in Western democratic nation-states.[83] Exclusively describing the contemporary state of administrative law as reflecting the natural course of societal dynamics runs the risk, from a legal standpoint, of underestimating the profoundly different context in which the 'networks' are operating (uncharted transnational territories)[84] as opposed to the 'organizations' (previously operating in domestic constitutionally and legally defined domains). Bringing the focus back to the question 'what role for the EU?', the risk is to misread the nature of the shift: if transnational negotiation is the natural evolution of

[79] Ibid., at 5 et seq.

[80] We use here the evolution of statecraft as described by Bobbitt, moving from the 'state-nation' that provided for the recognition and protection of individual rights and liberties, to the 'nation-state' that focused on collective goals through the provision of welfare, to the current 'market-state' where the state is taking a less pervasive and more permissive role in maximizing economic opportunities. See P. Bobbitt, *The Shield of Achilles* (2003), Book I, Parts II and III.

[81] Ladeur, *supra* note 78, at 24 *et seq*.

[82] Ibid., at 6.

[83] On Western administrative regulation, see above all A. Ogus, *Regulation: Legal Form and Economic Theory* (2004).

[84] Consider the example of the ICH: no administrative agency in the EU could be constructed in a way that a) involves only one-sided stakeholders together with the regulators; and b) lacks clear procedural rules on transparency, participation, and access to documents. However, its informal nature,

administrative law, the role of single agents gets diluted in the concept of 'administrative experimentalism'.

A different line of thinking has elaborated the idea of 'experimentalist new governance'.[85] This theory grounds the legitimacy of regulatory models in processes alternative to traditional representative democratic circuits, through the concept of 'deliberation'. A deliberative process is a 'soft process', including all major stakeholders of a given field, where governance is achieved in *functional* rather than traditional *structural* or *institutional* terms.[86] This soft process of consultation is accredited as legitimate by standards of 'alternative deliberative democracy'.[87] Typically, this process is an informal one, as the socialization of the stakeholders involved (something referred to as 'epistemic communities', e.g. the comitology mechanisms of the EU) does not necessarily descend directly from legislative acts.[88] It is also 'multi-level', as it involves actors ranging from national administrations to supranational bodies without establishing a real hierarchy, blurring the distinction between centralized and decentralized decision-making and favouring instead networks of diverse decision-makers.[89] Moreover, to overcome the most immediate criticism identifiable in the departure from representative democracy's classic forms of accountability and legitimacy, the deliberative process is essentially inspired by principles of transparency, access, and participation.[90]

EU pharmaceutical regulation arguably falls within the scope of 'experimentalist new governance' because the EMA includes major stakeholders involved in the pharmaceutical market, promoting a central role for scientific committees assisted by various actors, such as representatives of patients, physicians, and governments.[91] Decisions within the agency bodies are taken by way of consensus through deliberation (when possible, voting being the last resort option). As intriguing as this suggestion may be, it falls short of addressing the issue of transparency properly, which per se undermines the conclusion. If the potential for EU domestic regulatory mechanisms to fall within the scope of an experimentalist mode of governance can be argued, such a hypothesis does not fully confront the transnational dimension and its implications. The above description of the ICH mechanisms, and of the substantial impact of its guidelines, point emphatically to the necessity of moving the reflection to a transnational level. The rule-making mechanism here

and the context in which it operates (the uncharted transnational territories) allow for greater flexibility. Arguably, the ICH exists *because* at a transnational level negotiations can escape scrutiny.

[85] See the essential contribution of Sabel and Zeitlin, *supra* note 77, at 271–327.

[86] Ibid., at 274. [87] Ibid., at 273.

[88] See Neyer, 'Explaining the Unexpected: Efficiency and Effectiveness in European Decision-Making', 11 *Journal of European Public Policy* (2011) 19.

[89] See Sabel and Zeitlin, *supra* note 77, at 273; see also contributions by M. Egeberg (ed.), *Multilevel Union Administration: The Transformation of Executive Politics in Europe* (2006) and H. C. H Hofman and A. H. Türk, *EU Administrative Governance* (2006).

[90] A recent, interesting, and comprehensive discussion can be found in Ehnert, *supra* note 71.

[91] The Management Board of the EMA comprises two representatives of the Commission, two from the Parliament, and one per each Member State. As of 2004 with Regulation 726/2004/EC, representatives from organizations of patients and doctors were also given seats on the board alongside scientific experts.

is structurally non-inclusive, and modelled around goals set by a restricted number of stakeholders. The basic value choice is very much trade-oriented, and no real counterpart is involved in the negotiation process. The fundamental guidelines on GCP and SPCT are good examples of procedural regulations, leaving a wide margin of appreciation in the substance of the standards, which have been incorporated by agencies supposed to ensure deliberative processes.[92] The mechanisms of production and adoption of ICH guidelines raise a question about the fate of the numerous procedural standards conceived at the domestic level to balance the disproportionate discretion that new governance agents benefit from, vis-à-vis traditional rule-makers in representative democratic circuits. The scenario described in this chapter suggests that there is a tendency to 'hollow out' procedural standards when the scene is set at the transnational ICH level.[93] Strong domestic procedural mechanisms, accepted as legitimate, legitimating, and effective in principle, are here circumvented.

This discussion on the model of governance characterizing pharmaceutical regulation suggests uneasy answers. While designed and described as an example of 'new governance' domestically, at a transnational level it resembles more a reversed version of the transnational private law theory elaborated by Calliess and Zumbasen in *Rough Consensus and Running Code*.[94] While the theory proposes an understanding of bottom-up societal regulation of transnational private law, the pharmaceutical system seems to be organized in a very top-down fashion, whereby the consensus and the running code are reached and infused in the regulatory mechanisms by selected stakeholders and interests. Confronting such a closed pyramidal system makes it difficult to give an account of the role that each agent involved is actually able to perform.

The tentative conclusion[95] is therefore that the EU is an active participant in the transnational regulatory arena in the field of pharmaceutical products, primarily through its voting membership within the ICH. The impossibility of analysing case-specific processes of guidelines adoption, however, invites the following remark. The role of the EU (as of any other ICH agent) is highly dependent on its bargaining power. Such power being intrinsically variable and dependent on political and economic strength (variable both in time and across the spectrum of negotiated topics), two separate but equally relevant points ought to be raised. First, because of the informal nature of the network, subject only to its own

[92] There is no real access to information about what participation has been guaranteed in the adoption process of the GCP and SPCT guidelines: the internal ICH documents are not accessible, only the final guidelines literally transplanted into domestic regulatory frameworks.

[93] The issue is raised by Mendes, 'EU Law and Global Regulatory Regimes: Hollowing Out Procedural Standards?', 10 *International Journal of Constitutional Law* (2012) 988.

[94] G. P. Calliess and P. Zumbansen, *Rough Consensus and Running Code—A Theory of Transnational Private Law* (2010). The theory is based on the idea that a *rough consensus* among stakeholders in a given field becomes a *running code* through a *pilot phase* in which the content of the consensus acts as a proposed standard, followed by a *recognition phase* in which the standard becomes recommended, and eventually a *binding phase* where the standard is adopted. The process, being inclusive and non-hierarchical, is eminently bottom-up.

[95] Bearing in mind the caveats suggested *supra* at note 76.

internal rules, it is difficult to imagine an internal system of checks and balances presenting strong procedural guarantees. Consequently, depending on the topic at stake, the EU is either a strong agent, in which case it has the potential to expand the scope of EU policies and vision to a transnational level, or a weak one, which can cause internal policies and legal standards to be lowered to a potentially weaker negotiated level. We suggest in conclusion that an essential contribution of the EU to the current ICH system could take the form of procedural negotiation, pushing for publication of internal proceedings, at least as regards the fate of the regional consultation processes, thereby progressing from 'hollowing out' to 'exporting' procedural standards of transparency.

7. Transnational Regulation and Product Liability: Prospective Thoughts

This chapter (as others in this book)[96] is primarily focused on that special kind of private law identified by Hans-W. Micklitz as 'regulatory private law'.[97] It is, however, necessary to keep in mind that the output of this regulatory private law (standards, guidelines, and other 'soft law' instruments) does not exist in a vacuum. One must resist the temptation to relegate phenomena such as the one described here in the somewhat mystical realm of '*hic est governance*', and ask instead what are the legal implications of a transnational 'soft law' shift in regulation. Therefore, we now adjusts our focus and consider a branch of traditional and very European private law:[98] product liability. These brief thoughts on product liability rotate around two main concepts, the nature of which is either in the process of, or has the potential to, undergo significant adjustments: complementarity and regulatory compliance. These will be considered in turn to conclude with a suggestion on the relationship between the external dimension of regulatory private law and the internal potentials of traditional private law.[99]

The first concept to be addressed is 'complementarity'.[100] This is essentially a rather simple idea, based on the premise that regulation alone is unfit to achieve

[96] See again Chapters 8 and 9, this book.

[97] See Chapter 1, this book; and H.-W. Micklitz, Y. Svetiev, and G. Comparato (eds), 'European Regulatory Private Law—The Paradigms Tested', EUI Working Paper LAW 2014/04.

[98] Or tentatively so as divergences persist on key issues such as the notion of defectiveness, see Fairgrieve and Howells, 'Rethinking Product Liability: A Missing Element in the European Commission's Third Review of the European Product Liability Directive', 70 *Modern Law Review* (2007) 962. Product-specific regimes are also in place in the field of pharmaceuticals (for instance in Germany and Spain). Yet, product liability remains one of the first attempts to create a unified regime within a pillar of private law such as the law of torts.

[99] A fully fledged analysis of such an intricate issue is way beyond the scope of this chapter. These are, as the section's title suggests, 'prospective thoughts'. They should be read accordingly. As for the current state of pharmaceutical product liability, a fantastic descriptive account can found in R. Goldberg, *Medicinal Product Liability and Regulation* (2013).

[100] F. Cafaggi, *Institutional Framework of European Private Law* (2006) 191. The theory of functional complementarity a) on a positive level shows the reciprocal influences of the two techniques, and b) on a normative level calls for a high degree of coordination.

the goals of product safety and efficacy for a variety of factors ranging from risks of 'capture',[101] to the limited resources available to regulatory agencies[102] for the enforcement or monitoring of the correct implementation of regulatory requirements. Generally, highly technical fields tend to develop at an unmanageable rate for regulators.[103] This opens room for manoeuvre to be left to external actors to complement the efforts of regulators in achieving legislative endgames of pharmaceutical safety and efficacy.[104] The suggested factors are of general relevance; they apply to regulatory schemes regardless to whether these are domestic or transnational. The idea of complementarity is not an exclusive feature of transnational phenomena as it attempts to address structural deficiencies of regulation. This argument was restated by the US Supreme Court in 2009,[105] in the case *Wyeth v. Levine*,[106] where the Court struck down the unorthodox application of the doctrine of preemption introduced in pharmaceutical litigation by the FDA three years earlier.[107] Specifically, the Court rejected Wyeth's argument that tort claims 'interfere with Congress purpose to entrust an expert agency to make drug labelling decisions that strike a balance between competing objectives',[108] stating that such an argument relies on an 'untenable interpretation' of congressional intent and an 'overbroad view' of agency's power to pre-empt state law.[109] The conclusive argument being that traditionally, in the US legal system, regulation and product liability form two sides of a mechanism of checks and balances where the latter corrects failures of the former.[110] The presence of collective redress mechanisms, specifically in the form of class actions, has been the essential tool for the practical achievement of these checks and balances.[111]

[101] For a general definition see A. Ogus, *Regulation: Legal Form and Economic Theory* (2004) 57: 'the ineffectiveness of regulatory agencies in meeting the public interest goals assigned to them could most plausibly be explained by assuming that they had been subverted by pressure, influence, and "bribery" to protect the interests of those who were the subjects of the regulation'. In the context of transnational pharmaceutical regulation the risk lies in the ICH structure where industry representatives negotiate guidelines with regulators as peers.

[102] See EMA, *supra* note 36, at 24–27, the rate of inspections of clinical trials sites is extremely low as only 357 sites have been inspected out of 70.291, primarily due to lack of resources.

[103] The literature on this topic is extremely abundant, see as a reference S. Jasanoff, *Designs on Nature: Science and Democracy in Europe and the United States* (2007).

[104] As laid down in Council Directive 2001/83/EC on the Community Code relating to medicinal products for human use, OJ 2001 L 311/67. Note that paras (2) and (3) of the preamble discuss the complex relationship between the safeguard of public health and development of the pharmaceutical industry.

[105] In this section, the US scenario is mentioned several times. The reasons are manifold, ranging from a genuine comparative interest to the observation that the EMA and the FDA cooperate closely in regulatory processes leading to marketing approval of new pharmaceutical products (both bilaterally and at the ICH level). There is a further motive shortly suggested *infra* note 135—the possible adoption of the TTIP agreement.

[106] US Supreme Court *Wyeth v. Levine*, 555 U.S. 555, 129 S. Ct. 1187, 173 L. Ed. 2d 51 (2009).

[107] FDA, Requirements on Content and Format of Labelling for Human Prescription Drug and Biological Products, 71 Fed. Reg. 3922, 3934 (2006).

[108] *Wyeth v. Levine, supra* note 106, at 1199. [109] Ibid. [110] Ibid.

[111] A striking example of a dichotomy between the two sides of the Atlantic from the past decade is the case of *Vioxx*. While in the US the prospect of collective litigation led to an out-of-court settlement little short of US$5 billion, there is little evidence of litigation in the EU despite a wide diffusion of the product in the internal market. For an interesting perspective suggesting that out-of-court

The EU has, however, traditionally maintained a different approach to compensation regulatory correctives, relying heavily on indemnification schemes based on insurance and social security systems rather than on tort litigation.[112] Arguably, this has created a form of de facto preemption of product liability claims. The aggregate statistics on product liability litigation in the EEA over twenty years, collected by the Commission in periodic five-yearly reports from 1995 to 2011,[113] confirm that European product liability has faced structural obstacles in establishing its role in victims' compensation. An in-depth analysis of the vast range of reasons leading to this observation is beyond the scope of this chapter, but it is possible to identify few essential factors. In 2003, Mathias Reimann offered five explanations[114] for product liability being a major feature of the US legal system while lagging behind in Europe. These explanations have to do with institutions (US courts being traditionally more activist than European ones, and relying on specific features ranging from the role of juries to the exponentially higher damage awards),[115] procedures (the much higher availability of aggregate litigation in the US, coupled with stronger discovery rules, makes it significantly easier for plaintiffs to prove the existence of both defect and causation),[116] the legal profession (European lawyers have a much lesser tendency to specialize than their US colleagues),[117] the role of insurance (first party insurance is still the European prime method of victims' compensation, through public, semi-public, or private insurance, and/or no-fault compensation schemes),[118] and the broader social environment (the level of publicity that product liability receives in the EU, from media attention to the political debate, are incomparable to the US scenario).[119] A common assumption underlying this divergence between the two sides of the Atlantic is that the EU is politically committed to achieving product safety through public (or publicly administered) regulatory requirements whereas the US rely more substantially on private litigation.[120]

settlements of that magnitude favour closure of the settlement over consent of the plaintiffs (resulting in reduced compensation) see Erichson and Zipursky, 'Consent versus Closure', 96 *Cornell Law Review* (2011) 256.

[112] As thoroughly explained in an analysis that remains substantially valid more than ten years later in Reimann, 'Liability for Defective Products at the Beginning of the Twenty-First Century: Emergence of a Worldwide Standard?', 51 *American Journal of Comparative Law* (2003) 751. See also a brief discussion below.

[113] European Commission, 'First report on the application of Directive 85/374/EEC concerning liability for defective products', COM (1995) 617 final; European Commission, 'Second report on the application of Directive 85/374/EEC concerning liability for defective products', COM (2000) 893 final; European Commission, 'Third report on the application of Directive 85/374/EEC concerning liability for defective products', COM(2006) 496 final; European Commission, 'Fourth report on the application of Directive 85/374/EEC concerning liability for defective products', COM(2011) 547 final. The reports show a low impact of PL litigation in the EEA, with a tendency to increase over the years.

[114] Reimann, *supra* note 112. [115] Ibid. at 807 and 812–816.

[116] Ibid. at 816–822. [117] Ibid. at 816–822.

[118] Ibid., at 822–832. See also Commission Reports, *supra* note 113.

[119] Reimann, *supra* note 112, at 832–835.

[120] Ibid. at 810; see also C. Hodges, *supra* note 4; Howells, 'The Relationship between Product Liability and Product Safety—Understanding a Necessary Element in European Product Liability Through a Comparison with the US Position', 39 *Washburn Law Journal* (2000) 305.

However, a closer look at the recalled Commission Reports on the application of the Product Liability Directive in the European Economic Area shows a progressive increase in the volume of litigation and out of court settlements.[121] The reasons identified are an increase in 'consumer awareness, better organization of consumer groups or improved means of accessing information'.[122] While these explanations certainly play a significant role, there is more. Recent cases have put into question the reliability of the well-established European regulatory architecture for pharmaceuticals.[123] Aggressive litigation in France on the widely diffused medicine *Mediator*[124] has led to a withdrawal of the product from the market, signifying the existence of renewed scope for a complementary approach. A strong signal in this direction comes from the recent CJEU decision in the *Novo Nordisk Pharma* case.[125] The court has held that national product-specific legislations imposing stricter liability mechanisms than the one provided by the Product Liability Directive are not affected by the directive's regime under Article 13.[126] While this was always the goal of the provision, the novelty is that amendments posterior to the adoption of the directive's regime are protected, not only the legislation existing at the time the directive was notified. This was crucial in the case at hand where the provision placed under scrutiny of the Court was a 2002 amendment to the *Arzneimittelgesetz* introducing paragraphs 84(2) and 84a.[127] Specifically, paragraph 84(2) creates a presumption that, when the medicine under judicial scrutiny is generally capable of causing harm, the damage in the specific case is caused by the product. Paragraph 84a introduced a consumer right to 'require the manufacturer of a medicinal product to provide him with information on the adverse effects of that product'[128] when the facts of the case suggest that the product has caused damage. The court recognizes that the German legislation does not 'undermine the effectiveness of the system of liability provided for under Directive 85/374',[129] but rather intends to eliminate or reduce the asymmetry of information between the manufacturer and the consumer, helping the latter to prove defectiveness and causation.[130] The combination of these two elements represents a powerful means of

[121] Commission Reports, *supra* note 113; see also Lovells, *Product Liability in the European Union: A Report for the European Commission* (2003), MARKT/2001/11/D, at 39 discussing the progressive increase of out of court settlements.

[122] European Commission, 'Fourth report', *supra* note 113, at 4.

[123] See the brief description *supra* section 2 of this chapter.

[124] See the latest judgment of a prolonged saga: Tribunal Administratif de Paris, n. 1312345/6 (2014). Civil litigation involving the producer *Laboratoire Servier* is still pending.

[125] Case 310/13, *Novo Nordisk Pharma GMbH v. S.*, jugdment of of 20 November 2014.

[126] Council Directive 85/374/EEC on the approximation of the laws and administrative provisions of the Member States concerning liability for defective products, OJ 1985 L 210, Art. 13: 'This Directive shall not affect any rights which an injured person may have according to the rules of the law of contractual or non-contractual liability or a special liability system existing at the moment when this Directive is notified.'

[127] *Arzneimittelgesetz—AMG, supra* note 7, the presumption of a causal link referred to in para. 84(2) of the AMG and the right to information under para. 84a of the AMG were inserted in the AMG by the law amending the legislation on compensation for damage (*Zweites Schadensersatzrechtsänderungsgesetz*) of 19 July 2002 (BGBl, 2002, p. 2674).

[128] Case 310/13, *supra* note 125, para. 29.

[129] Ibid., para. 30. [130] Ibid., para. 32.

both consumer protection and judicial monitoring. Thus, while national courts are being increasingly solicited as recognized by the Commission's reports, the CJEU, in sanctioning the strong German legislation, is endorsing a complementary approach, questioning the EU's traditional quasi-exclusive reliance on non-litigious mechanisms.

The argument can be further developed. In the presence of problematic transnational elements suggested above, the scope for complementarity widens as the 'non-measurable negotiations' introduce exogenous elements into regulatory schemes designed within and for the EU:[131] if complementarity is first conceived domestically, it is called for *a fortiori* transnationally. On this premise, it is possible to make a suggestion on 'regulatory compliance', and conclude with a remark on the interactions between 'regulatory' and 'traditional' private law.

In product liability, regulatory compliance is a complex issue the intricacies of which cannot be debated here. Suffice it to say that it is not per se a defence for manufacturers: the only defence explicitly mentioning regulatory requirements is provided by Article 7(d) of the Product Liability Directive[132] shielding a producer from liability where 'the defect is due to compliance of the product with mandatory regulations issued by public authorities'. Short of that, regulatory compliance is not an automatic defence. It provides 'strong evidence' that the product is not defective without freeing a producer from liability.[133] The correct observance of a given standard, in product liability litigation, is therefore strong but not conclusive evidence of a product's safety, as confirmed by the wording of Article 25 of Directive 2001/83/EC, whereby a marketing authorization 'shall not affect the civil and criminal liability of the manufacturer and, where applicable, of the marketing authorization holder'.[134]

It is in this area that courts can exercise a meaningful form of complementarity, questioning the actual value of compliance to standards the adoption of which is now beyond the haven of EU's procedural safeguards.[135] While the

[131] See again the discussion *supra* section 2, describing the EU regulatory architecture as strongly EU-centred (with an ever-growing move from decentralized to centralized procedures).

[132] Council Directive 85/374/EEC on the approximation of the laws and administrative provisions of the Member States concerning liability for defective products, OJ 1985 L 210.

[133] Regulatory compliance in pharmaceutical product liability litigation has been recently discussed by R. Goldberg, *Medicinal Product Liability and Regulation* (2013) 136–161.

[134] Council Directive 2001/83/EC on the Community Code relating to medicinal products for human use, OJ 2001 L 311/67, Art. 25.

[135] See Mendes, *supra* note 93. Moreover the chapter is willingly staying clear of the debate surrounding the possible future adoption of a Transatlantic Trade and Investment Partnership (TTIP) between the US and the EU. For now, with limited information available on the contents of the treaty to be, a sensible observation to make is that, in the event of an adoption, the EU should cautiously get ready for a stronger role of litigation in complementing regulation. We have discussed how this is common practice in the US, and Europe may need to adapt to that system of checks and balances. This is because the nature of TTIP as a 'living agreement', whereby regulators' reciprocal commitments can become legally binding through sectoral annexes, has the potential to result in regulatory processes progressively detaching from the previously agreed policy choices as sharply suggested by Alberto Alemanno, *A Reality Check of TTIP—Beyond Popular Account* (2014), available at <http://www.euractiv.com/sections/trade-industry/reality-check-ttip-beyond-popular-account-301443> (last accessed March 2015). See for an in-depth discussion Alemanno, 'The Transatlantic Trade and

general tendency in medicines litigation is to rely heavily on regulatory decisions (the deferential approach),[136] the product liability legislation allows for courts to take a 'hard look'[137] into the regulatory process leading to marketing approval. The goal is to question whether *formal* compliance can be considered *substantially* satisfactory in light of the legislative goals of safety and efficacy. If not, an adverse judgment would question the validity and legitimacy of requirements considered inadequate by European courts.

8. Conclusion

A concluding remark calls for the observation of two separate but possibly mutually influential elements. Externally, the 'regulatory private law' through which the EU negotiates safety and efficacy standards seems to be hollowing out EU's procedural mechanisms, the phenomenon we refer to as 'non-measurable negotiations'. As suggested above, the EU could perform an important role in 'exporting' its internal procedural standards into ICH for the sake of greater transparency and accountability. On the other hand, internal 'traditional' fields of private law can perform a review of transnational standards by allowing courts to foster complementarity and make substantial checks on satisfactory compliance to fundamental legislative goals. Concluding with the example used in this chapter, the internal dimension of traditional European product liability could gain an external regulatory function by putting the EU as a transnational negotiator in the position to press for the adoption or review of judicially scrutinized standards.

Investment Partnership (TTIP) and Parliamentary Regulatory Cooperation', European Parliament Policy Report (April 2014). Complementarity on the one hand, and a substance-based approach to regulatory compliance on the other may prove *a fortiori* necessary was the TTIP to be adopted.

[136] The tendency that we call deferential is one that makes courts 'reluctant to criticize' regulatory decision, especially on technical matters such as marketing authorization of pharmaceutical products. A good overview of the phenomenon is provided by Goldberg, *supra* note 133, at 135–140.

[137] The conceptual distinction between the deferential approach and the 'hard look' doctrine is drawn by S. Jasanoff, *Science at the Bar—Law Science and Technology in America* (1997). The interesting suggestion she makes, for the purposes of this piece, is that a thorough judicial review of administrative decisions on risk regulation can have a pedagogical effect on regulators; a different way to suggest the similar conclusion drawn here.

Index

References to footnotes will be followed by the letter 'n'